Political obligation in its historical context

Essays in political theory

JOHN DUNN

*Fellow of King's College and Reader in Politics in
the University of Cambridge*

CAMBRIDGE UNIVERSITY PRESS

Cambridge
London   New York   New Rochelle
Melbourne   Sydney

Published by the Press Syndicate of the University of Cambridge
The Pitt Building, Trumpington Street, Cambridge CB2 1RP
32 East 57th Street, New York, NY 10022, USA
296 Beaconsfield Parade, Middle Park, Melbourne 3206, Australia

First published 1980

Printed in Great Britain at the University Press, Cambridge

British Library Cataloguing in Publication Data
Dunn, John
Political obligation in its historical context.
1. Allegiance — Addresses, essays, lectures
I. Title
323.6'5'08   JC328   80-40037
ISBN 0 521 22890 5

FOR MY MOTHER

Contents

vii

Preface

Those essays in this collection which have been published previously are in most cases reprinted here with only a few minor amendments of style. I have, however, restored cuts which were made in the original printing on grounds of space or economy, wherever these in my view affected the meaning of what I wished to convey. The lists of personal acknowledgements in the reprinted essays are omitted since, when taken together, they became tiresomely repetitive. It is a sobering experience to see how lengthy is the list of those on whose generous aid my work has depended heavily at one point or another in the last seventeen years. Gratitude keeps its shape better than many other feelings; and I remain extremely grateful for all the help which I have been given. I am especially grateful, too, on this occasion to Patricia Williams for once again giving me the chance to make my thoughts public and for her extraordinary kindness and patience in the course of helping me to do so.

The essays were first published as follows:
Chapter 2 in *Philosophy*, XLIII, April 1968 (the journal of the Royal Institute of Philosophy)
Chapter 3 in *The Historical Journal*, X, 2, 1967
Chapter 4 in John W. Yolton (ed.), *John Locke: Problems and Perspectives*, Cambridge University Press 1969
Chapter 5 in Christopher Hookway & Philip Pettit (eds.), *Action and Interpretation: Studies in the Philosophy of the Social Sciences*, Cambridge University Press 1978
Chapter 6 in Dennis Austin & Robin Luckham (eds.), *Politicians and Soldiers in Ghana 1966–1972*, Frank Cass, London 1975
Chapter 7 in a special issue of the *Ceylon Journal of Historical and Social Studies* in 1980, edited by Dennis Austin, Kingsley de Silva & A. Jeyaratnam Wilson
Chapter 8 in *The British Journal of Political Science*, IV, 4, October 1974
Chapter 9 in Seweryn Bialer & Sophia Sluzar (eds.), *Strategies and Impact of Contemporary Radicalism* (Volume 3 of a 3 volume study on *Radical-*

ism in the Contemporary Age by the Columbia University Research Institute on International Change), Westview Press, Boulder, Colorado 1977

I am grateful to the editors and publishers of these volumes or journals for the opportunity to reprint my essays in the present collection.

The introduction identifies the theoretical problem to which the book as a whole is addressed and indicates how the individual essays bear on this problem. The conclusion states a view of the nature of this problem and a consequent judgement on the sense in which, and the degree to which, it is soluble in principle. The intervening essays are divided into two sets. The first of these, focused on the history of political theory, stresses the historical and theoretical intricacy and heterogeneity of the questions to which political theory has been addressed. The second set attempts to display the grounds for this variety and complexity not simply in the history of abstract thought but in addition in the diversity of human material and cultural existence.

Cambridge
September 1979

1
Introduction

This book is concerned with a mildly eccentric venture, an attempt to re-capture intellectually a sense of the shape and character of one of the central theoretical problems in human existence. This problem — roughly, how far human beings have good reason to see and feel themselves as morally con-strained by political organisations (villages, parties, armies, states) and morally committed to sustain these in the face of hazard — has never been easy to confront directly. But very drastic historical pressures, both intellectual and social, have made it extravagantly more difficult for us to confront it than it was for the great European thinkers of the seventeenth and eighteenth centuries to do so. In response to these pressures, all too intelligibly, the problem has been shrunk, truncated or trivialised; and purported solutions to it have come to rest more and more blatantly upon parochial cultural pieties or insti-tutionally routinised intellectual habits. Since no one today appears to be in a position to offer (and since it may even be true that no one today *could* be in a position to offer) a clear and decisive universal solution to this problem, there are evident attractions to the view that both academic modesty and political delicacy dictate that we should leave its full theoretical enormity discreetly unmentioned. Modesty and delicacy are fine values; but in this instance their sway is not without peril. The world is not becoming politically any easier to understand. The ritual reassertion of parochial political tra-ditions in resolute mutual incomprehension can hardly be expected to pro-vide a sound basis for enhancing our political understanding, while the view that a deepening political incomprehension of what is happening in the world will furnish us with the soundest guidance on how to act upon it puts a dis-maying level of trust in the dexterity of providence. Our own credulities have their charms; but the same can scarcely be said by anyone for the credulities of *all* their fellow human beings.

This book records a protracted and, it must be admitted, an as yet some-what faltering effort to recapture a measure of intellectual control over this problem. Its strategy depends for whatever effect it can secure on the cogency of the conception of the *nature* of the issue which is set out in the final chapter. The arguments of this last chapter in effect repudiate the idea

1

that a theory of political obligation could in principle offer valid universal *solutions* to this problem of practical reason. But they do so in a manner which does not obviously license (and which certainly does not depend upon affirming) the presumption that rational value for human beings is a function either of socially imposed dogmatisms or of individual whim. At least at the level of intellectual intention, they reject both cognitively painless styles of relativism (which are readily interpreted and perhaps correctly interpreted as nihilist) and cognitively arbitrary styles of moral absolutism (which fail to acknowledge — and which are indeed incompatible with a recognition of — the profound historicity of the human condition). They presume that ethical appraisal is in part a fully cognitive activity, that it is irretrievably a part of the human condition to be exposed to the vicissitudes of politics and that what it is rational for human beings to do in relation to the political domain depends both upon ethical understanding and upon practical judgement of social and political causality.

The remainder of the chapters in the volume explore the grounds for and the implications of these presumptions from a variety of different angles. Being written over nearly a decade and a half, they naturally show some variation in intellectual judgement and considerable shifts in intellectual taste. One group, a set of exercises in and reflections upon the history of political theory, develops some of the implications of Collingwood's observation that 'the history of political theory is not the history of different answers to the same question, but the history of a problem more or less constantly changing, whose solution was changing with it'.[1] The problem whose history of continuity in difference I here seek to isolate is usually titled the problem of political obligation. A valid theory of political obligation can only be a theory of the nature of the conceptual space which constitutes the continuity of the problem. But in recognising the immense degree of historical individuation of the problem as a problem of practical reason, it precludes the discovery of universal *solutions* to this. In exploring the historicity of even the profoundest reflection on this question in the past, these chapters may help to show why cognitively more strenuous versions of relativism, so far from implying an ethical and epistemic nihilism, may be a condition of establishing the rational authority of value in human existence.

The second group of exercises is academically more heterogeneous but perhaps also more distinctive. While the first group investigated the contextual rationality of political thinking, the second considers from a variety of standpoints the contextual rationality of political action and the roots of this rationality in the nature of man and of human society. Some of the standpoints are geographically and historically very particular indeed. Others are, at least in affectation, considerably loftier and less determinately located. But all of them seek to hold in mutual relation ethical appraisal and causal understanding. The view that these two modes of thought have been permitted to drift decidedly too far apart is now becoming in some circles an intellectual commonplace, though in other — and still perhaps wider — circles it remains a matter of firm conviction that one or other of these modes is, in relation to human existence, cognitively the only available option. But the attempt to pursue, academically speaking, in broad daylight *both* modes of thought at once remains relatively unusual; and the measure of intellectual recklessness (or insensitivity) which their joint pursuit demands makes it easy to see why this should still be the case. The intellectual costs of such prudence may be relatively slight in some zones of academic inquiry; but in relation to politics they are, have always been, and will always remain prohibitively high.

'The identity of the history of ideas' takes as a starting point a dissatisfaction with the range of genres prevalent in the mid 1960s in the historical study of human thinking, stressing the bifurcation of analytical energy and interest then apparent between philosophers and historians and arguing for the view that this separation had had and was continuing to have a decidedly malign effect on the intellectual quality of the products of both. Since 1968 the implications of the line of thought behind it have been patiently explored and very greatly clarified and extended in the work, in particular, of Quentin Skinner.[2] In the historiography of political theory at least, some parts of the arguments which it contains have now become relatively commonplace[3] — more especially the stress on the categorical impropriety of anachronism and the need for and difficulty of distinguishing the intellectual autobiography of the historian from the intellectual biography of past thinkers. The stress on the historian's obligation to maintain this distinction as clearly as she or he can manage plainly implies a more crudely realist conception of the status of the past than is offered by such an influential hermeneutic thinker as Gadamer.[4]

In the present context these methodological injunctions to practising historians are of less importance than two other aspects of the arguments which it advances. The first of these, somewhat hastily set out in this instance and exceptionally difficult to develop with precision at greater length, is the stress on the exceedingly delicate and complex relations between the historical site in which an elaborate piece of reasoning is worked out and the precise content of that piece of reasoning. The directions in which epistemology has developed in American and English philosophy since the early and mid 1960s have underlined very sharply the importance of the claim that: 'To abstract an argument from the context of truth-criteria which it is devised to meet is to convert it into a different argument.'[5] But this development has not, unfortunately, provided uncontentious guidance on how to formulate considerations of this character in a clearer and more decisive manner. It may well, however, be thought by now to have provided rather powerful epistemological grounds for doubting the felicity of the preponderant development of political philosophy, over roughly the same time span, as the very abstract analysis of a small number of supposedly timeless ethical concepts.

These developments in epistemology (the work in particular of Quine, Feyerabend, Kuhn, Rorty, and even in some ways of Putnam and Davidson[6]) have undoubtedly brought distinctively historicist and distinctively rationalist perspectives on human cognition into much more urgent and dynamic relations. Strikingly relativist styles of theory have been sustained by aggressively rationalist forms of argument, while more realist positions have been defended by increasingly cunning and historically particular analysis of instances of theoretical argument. The view that 'historical specificity and philosophical delicacy are more likely to be attained if they are pursued together, than if one is deserted for the other at an early stage of the investigation'[7] no longer appears as resolutely intellectually philistine as it perhaps did in 1968. Indeed, the prospect of establishing firmer intellectual control over the somewhat tumultuous heritage of recent epistemology appears now to depend largely on the more strenuous pursuit of this particular wager. Finally (and at a less intellectually demanding level) it seems worth underlining a single more pragmatic consideration, perhaps predominantly aesthetic in implication but arising out of the attempt to see historical and philosophical constraint and potentiality in relation to one another. To write the history of ideas as the history of an *activity*, thinking, which is intrinsically both difficult and exciting is certainly no closer to a common intellectual intention amongst historians of ideas today than it was in the late 1960s. There remain good reasons for at least attempting to write rather more of it in such terms, partly simply because history so written would be more interesting and humanly more alive, but partly also because history so written would be truer to its ostensible subject matter, more adequate to the real thinking men and women on whose lives it is parasitic,[8] and, by virtue of being truer to its subject matter, decidedly more revealing about such profound issues of social understanding as the nature of ideology and the character and limits of intellectual freedom.

'Consent in the political theory of John Locke' considers a far narrower range of issues. Negatively, it seeks to establish that the interpretation of the place of consent within Locke's political theory has been severely distorted by scholars who have failed to heed Collingwood's cautions and have as a result been led by their anachronistic preconceptions into reading even the text of the *Two Treatises of Government* itself in an inattentive fashion.[9] More positively, it attempts to use a considerably wider range of evidence about Locke's beliefs to identify the theoretical problems which the place of consent in the argument of the *Two Treatises* posed for him and, in part at least, to explain why he adopted the solutions which he did adopt to these problems or why he failed to perceive the weakness of some of the arguments which he advanced in the effort to solve them.[10] The main historical conclusion which it advances is that Locke's understanding of the problematic rationality of political obligation was drastically more intricate than commentators have for the most part presumed. Perhaps more importantly (and certainly more controversially) it also gives grounds for judging Locke's understanding of this issue as, within his own terms, considerably more adequate to the intrinsic *theoretical* complexity of the issue than that of the great majority of thinkers, past or present, who have addressed it.

'The politics of Locke in England and America in the eighteenth century' develops two widely distinct themes. The first of these is negative and historiographical. After providing a somewhat brusque résumé of a considerable amount of research on the intellectual reputation of (and responses to) Locke's *Two Treatises of Government* in the eighteenth century, it deploys this as a critique of the essentially mythological conception of the character of political thinking in England and America during this period which was widely prevalent at the time of writing in 1964. This exercise in demythologising has won something less than universal assent. But little, if any, intellectually cogent criticism has been offered of the validity of the precise claims which the essay in fact asserts, though there have naturally been a number of useful subsequent extensions and minor amendments of what was at best a preliminary and somewhat summary attempt to sketch an extremely complex set of processes;[11] and in numerous respects, and quite independently, myth has been supplanted by impressively concrete historical understanding.[12] The most important lacuna in the essay's treatment of its titular subject matter I now consider to be the failure to separate out more clearly the historical vicissitudes of Locke's analysis of property from those of his general theory of political legitimacy and the right of resistance, and more particularly the failure to emphasise the continuing and rather narrowly institutionalised tradition of theoretical commentary on the standing of his theory of property to be found in the writers on natural jurisprudence, stemming from his correspondent, the editor and French translator of Pufendorf and Grotius, Jean Barbeyrac, both in continental Europe and in Scotland. Some traces of this sequence can be identified at various points in the annotation; but its skimpy treatment in the outline of the text as a whole represents a simple error of intellectual judgement.[13]

It is, however, the more positive theme of the essay which is of greater importance in the context of the present volume. What it attempts is to show, admittedly very sketchily, the extremely specific set of intellectual and political goals to which Locke addressed himself in writing his book, the profound impact which these goals exerted upon the character and content of the book itself and the striking degree to which those who did in fact read it (and even think seriously about its implications) in the century and a quarter succeeding its publication failed to grasp what Locke had in fact argued in it, let alone why he had argued as he did. As a historical study the essay attempts, however cursorily, to identify both the situational and biographical rationality of the work's original identity and the subsequent contextual rationality of the responses of its readers over roughly a century, of what it meant to them and why for the most part they understood it so poorly. This genre of historical study of a work's odyssey from inside the mind of its creator out into the necessarily plural and largely uncomprehending world of history is not attempted as often as it might be. It is certainly a dismayingly labour-intensive type of study if it is to be pursued in a more systematic fashion than it is in this instance. But it is also a type of study which, if it were to be pursued more systematically, would offer an extremely rich promise of illuminating the historical modulations of ideology; and it is at least possible that its more proficient pursuit might also help to focus more clearly the intrinsic historicity of both the questions and the answers which constitute the theoretical problem of political obligation.

To insist on the intrinsic historicity of these questions may perhaps be simply to insist flatly on a fact about the history of ideas and to wager more or less intrepidly that the human future will at least in this respect resemble the past. But to insist on the intrinsic historicity of the answers is philosophically more committing. The second group of essays considers at length two main grounds for undertaking such a commitment, the presumption that at least some component of the historical heterogeneity of the values which men espouse represents a constitutive characteristic of human nature and the judgement that power and causality are central terms of political theory. The first of these views, taken on its own, is of course readily compatible with the most cognitively effortless varieties of relativism. The second, taken on its own, is equally readily compatible with (and has indeed been frequently conjoined with) a comprehensively non-cognitive conception of the epistemic status of human values. But if the two views are taken firmly together, they may perhaps serve to establish a meaning for the claim that it is not an obstacle to, but rather a precondition for, the validity of answers to the theoretical problem of political obligation that they should be intrinsically historical. The concluding essay sets out this conception as clearly as I am as yet able. The second group of essays considers from a variety of viewpoints one or other of the two views on which it is jointly based.

'Practising history and social science on "realist" assumptions' considers the question of what sorts of knowledge of human beings individually or collectively are in principle possible. Focussing on the relations between language and consciousness, it distinguishes two quite different types of knowledge about our species which may be open to us, one which registers a range of distinctively human properties broadly as human beings conceive these and a second which identifies aspects of the human present and attempts to assess aspects of the human future in a theoretical medium from which it has carefully laundered out all, as Charles Taylor has termed them, 'anthropocentric properties'. The history of western epistemology since the scientific revolution of the seventeenth century has lent enormous intellectual impetus to this latter cognitive approach and has on occasion cast considerable doubt on the claims of the former to possess any epistemic status at all. It has been argued recently from a variety of standpoints that such conclusions are both morally offensive and epistemologically absurd.[14] 'Practising history' fully endorses this conclusion; but it also seeks to show that the conclusion does not in any way militate against systematic inquiry into social causality (though it has, of course, many implications as to how such inquiry is appropriately to be conceived). In relation to human beings the successful analysis of social causality always may (and is often likely to) involve the explicit recognition, within the causal theory, of anthropocentric properties. At least above the level of neurophysiology, it is a theoretical error about the nature of man to regard human belief as a causally inert dependent variable. But it is also a theoretical error about the nature of human society to consider human action as though this could occur outside a context of social causality which sets many of the limits of what it is or is not open to a human being to bring about.

At least equally importantly, the grounds for rejecting the moral and epistemological sufficiency of a non-anthropocentric model of man are also grounds for doubting the validity of any ahistorical moral absolutism. A creature which was validly conceived simply as a pleasure-maximising and pain-minimising mechanism could very plausibly be supposed a creature for which the rational content of value was theoretically determined outside history — for example, as the maximising of pleasure and the minimising of pain.* But once the theoretical complexity of language, its centrality in human existence, and its key role in determining the character of human consciousness are fully recognised, such an ahistorical conception of the rational content of human value seems merely the imposition of an arbitrary theoretical whim. As speaker of a language and as holder of beliefs, man is a type of creature in relation to which the fact that it both interprets many of its own properties and shapes some of these as a result of its own interpretations is not merely an externally related matter of fact, but a constitutive characteristic. As a theory of what is rationally of value for such a creature, utilitarianism seems more a decisive exercise in denial than an attempt to take into full theoretical account all the relevant considerations.[15] For such a creature valid answers to all but the most artificially causally insulated problems of practical reason will necessarily be intrinsically historical.

The remainder of this second group of essays consider at varying levels of historical and geographical specificity the implications, in relation to this intrinsic historicity of human understanding, of the concepts of power and causality. They begin with political impotence. 'From democracy to representation' analyses a single parliamentary election in a rural constituency in Ghana, seeking to explain its outcome in terms of the beliefs and sentiments of the relevant actors and to explain these beliefs and sentiments in their turn in terms of the social, economic and political context of this area as the

---

* The application of what was theoretically determined would always, of course, take place firmly within history.

7

twentieth century has shaped this. It emphasises the absurdity of the weight-less cosmopolitan presumptions which lie behind the official constitutional and theoretical categories that define this electoral episode at a national or international level. In the place of such blithe and conscious exercises of free will by a sovereign people, it sets out the dimensions of a single political choice as history has made this available. An evanescent constitutional form (there have been three wholly unconstitutional violent changes of regime in the succeeding decade) and an economy which has been progressively dis-membered ever since, together underline with some brutality the political impotence of the denizens of Ahafo Asunafo. It is a fair test for a theory of rational political obligation that it should be able at least to *address* the predicament of the myriads of people in the world today (as at every stage throughout the earlier political history of the human species) whose pros-pective leverage on the historical process is as slight as that of the Ahafos in the summer of 1969. But to address such a predicament is certainly not necessarily in any sense to discern a rose in the cross of what was then its present.

The focus of 'Hoc signo victor eris' is somewhat wider. It sketches a com-parison between the bases of effective political allegiance for the electoral politics of Ghana and of the island of Sri Lanka, seeking to explain these in terms of the beliefs, sentiments and practical situations of the inhabitants of these countries. It also considers the very different external limits on the scope of electoral politics in the two countries which have been set by the unconstitutional intervention of the armed forces or by popular revolt. In conclusion it counterposes the political ends which the beliefs of their inhabitants give them good reason to value, with the claims of the incumbent state powers in each society, underlining the gross discrepancy between the types of action which the former give their citizens good reason to perform and the types of action which the latter presume them to be obliged to per-form. Whatever else might be true, it argues, the citizens of these countries cannot, at least, plausibly be supposed to have as rational obligations the set of political obligations which their rulers presume them to have. Yet it is also little, if any, more plausible to presume that the obligations in relation to politics which they do rationally possess can be identified convincingly without fully recognising the presence of the social and economic structure and the cultural substance of each society both within the internal scheme of belief which furnishes each of them with good reasons for doing anything and within the external causal context which restricts narrowly for them (as it does for all men) what it is within their power to bring about.

'Democracy unretrieved' discusses the relation between ethical theory and the causal constraints of social and political reality from a very different perspective. It considers the cogency of Professor C.B. Macpherson's influ-ential theoretical analysis of liberal democracy, not as a historical account of the origins and development of liberal ideology but in its more ambitious guise as an assessment of the practical prospects of liberal democracy as a form of state. In this respect the analysis which Macpherson advances is at least as inadequate as his purely historical account of the development of liberal thought is inept. Moreover, the inadequacy of his analysis in this respect is of considerably greater importance than its purely historical deficiencies. By isolating a theoretical characterization of society which articulates rather few of its causal properties and by evaluating these properties as though they constituted an adequate *summary* of the properties of such societies as a whole, Macpherson gravely misjudges both their ethical merits and demerits and their practical strengths and weaknesses. What he has to offer on his own account, in consequence, is simply a relaxed ideology in lieu of a serious political theory. Such a failure is distinctively more surprising (and correspondingly more instructive) in the case of a theorist whose analysis starts out from a conception of social causation than it would be in the case of theorists whose thinking concentrates narrowly on the abstract analysis of a small number of ethical categories. It serves here to underline the central importance in political theory at all times of an explicit and convincing analysis of what precisely is causally and evaluatively at stake in politics. The key weaknesses of Macpherson's thinking lie in his quest for an epistemically (and thus morally) improper degree and style of theoretical simplicity in political theory. To be valid a political theory can (and indeed must) be both rigorous and conceptually elaborate. What it cannot be is at the same time theoretically simple and decisive in its practical implications.

'The success and failure of modern revolutions' considers the most interesting and intellectually puzzling aspect of the relation between theory and practice in modern politics. In a number of contexts in twentieth-century history it is apparent that the beliefs of revolutionaries have had a decisive practical effect. It does not seem likely in the great majority of cases that these effects were, even very broadly, what was intended by the agents themselves. Those who devote their lives to the practice of revolution, professional revolutionaries, have what are plainly epistemically the most ambitious theories of political obligation (of what exactly is politically to be done and why) which are extant today. Such theories stand at the opposite extreme of ambition, both intellectually and politically, from those which incumbent political authorities everywhere in the world seek to inculcate in their subjects or which the majority of the latter seem inclined to credit of their own accord (however large the discrepancies between these two may be in particular instances). When the explicit or implicit causal component of such revolutionary theories is considered systematically, it is difficult (at least without opting for a cognitively effortless relativism which destroys the epistemic status of all theories) to absolve them of the charge of epistemic presumption. In itself this verdict remains both valid and important. But two considerations, both underemphasised in the essay itself, need to be added to it, if its implications for the theory of political obligation are to be assessed correctly. The first is simply that it is essential to recognise the part which such beliefs play within political causality — to grasp the degree to which, by being believed, they change the world and make history. The second, equally ambivalently, is that it is a merit of such theories as theories of political obligation that they should include, as they do, an explicit causal theory of what can or cannot be caused politically to occur, even if it is a more specific and a practically more important demerit that, as they are actually espoused, these theories are in most instances to such a large degree false.

'Political obligations and political possibilities' attempts to draw the moral of these thoughts. Whether men (as they at the time historically are) do have rational political obligations, it argues, depends on four types of consideration: on what they do value and believe; on what they have good reason to value and believe; on how the social and political world then is; and on how it then could be *caused* to become (where 'could' implies *historical* causal possibility and not merely logical possibility). Only if all of these considerations are seen in relation to one another can the issue of the rationality and character of political obligations be adequately investigated. To see why this is the case is to see how to restore the concept of political obligation (though not necessarily, of course, of the obligations of their subjects to obey incumbent state powers) to the centre of political philosophy. It is also to see how it can be conceived in a manner which is neither (in conceptual terms) culturally parochial nor ethically nihilist.

The historicity of the question

2

The identity of the history of ideas

Two types of criticism are frequently levelled at the history of ideas in general* and the history of political theory in particular. The first is very much that of historians practising in other fields; that it is written as a saga in which all the great deeds are done by entities which could not, in principle, *do* anything. In it, Science is always wrestling with Theology, Empiricism with Rationalism, monism with dualism, evolution with the Great Chain of Being, artifice with nature, Politik with political moralism. Its protagonists are never humans, but only reified abstractions — or, if humans by inadvertence, humans only as the loci of these abstractions. The other charge, one more frequently levelled by philosophers, is that it is insensitive to the distinctive features of ideas, unconcerned with, or more often ineffectual in its concern with, truth and falsehood, its products more like intellectual seed catalogues than adequate studies of thought. In short it is characterised by a persistent tension between the threats of falsity in its history and incompetence in its philosophy.[1]

At first sight both these charges seem plausible. One might well suppose that the status of propositions about the history of thought would be at issue both in the accuracy of their location of a particular event in the past and in the adequacy of their understanding of the nature of the event so located. Statements about a type of event in the past, statements that event *X* took place at time *P*, may be mistaken in their claims that 'the event that took place at time *P*' was an event of *X*-type or that 'an event of *X*-type' *did* take place at time *P*. Concentration on the identification of some types of event (e.g. in the history of ideas, the subtler sorts of analysis of classics of philosophy) may well lead to greater concern for analytical complexity and force than for mere historicity,[2] and concentration on mere historicity may

* I mean this term to be used as widely as its use in common speech would suggest, its subject-matter as, in principle, all past thoughts, not just the rather individual meaning given to it by Professor Lovejoy and his pupils. The argument of the piece is that the histories of particular intellectual practices, of science, history, political theory, economics, theology, etc., are special instances of this single unitary category and that whatever autonomy they enjoy within it is simply a matter of literary convenience. In other words it is denied that a coherent account can be given of any of them which lends to them any sort of epistemological discreteness.

13

well lead to a shabby sort of level of understanding of what it was that did exist in the past. In this way the two types of criticism can readily be seen as the advocacy of different forms of inquiry within the common subject-matter. This would make the issue between them not one of truth or falsity but merely of the tactical choice between competing simplifications. The cartographic metaphor is clearly apt here. It is not convenient to attempt to represent all conceivably replicable features of a geographical environment on any single map. But this tells us nothing of the ontological limitations of cartography. Maps are maps, not regrettably ineffectual surrogates for physical environments. And if such a choice between competing evils is necessary, it must be equally legitimate to represent it as a choice between competing goods. This painless resolution is in fact that which most practitioners adopt (in so far, that is, as they see any need for resolution; this is, at worst, for them a matter of discounting risks; not, of course, a matter of making statements which are deliberately false, historically or philosophically). After one has chosen the aspect of a subject-matter which most concerns one, the criticisms of those whose interest in it is very different are discounted. If choice is necessary and some sort of failure certain, then one *should* plainly choose to discount the costs of the type of failure one has chosen. Such axioms about the necessary limitations of human skills are nothing but the most ordinary common sense.

What I wish principally to argue in this paper is that the costs of such self-abnegation are much higher than is normally recognised; that the connection between an adequate philosophical account of the notions held by an individual in the past and an accurate historical account of these notions is an intimate one; that both historical specificity and philosophical delicacy are more likely to be attained if they are pursued together, than if one is deserted for the other at an early stage of the investigation. In other words, I wish to claim that the disagreements over the appropriate subject-matter and form of explanation for the history of ideas, though they are indeed persuasions to choose to examine one form of description of intellectual acts in the past rather than another, are also something more. What is in question is not merely a choice between true (or false) stories but a problem intrinsic to the attempt to tell stories about this type of data. More precisely, I wish to claim: 1, that the completion of both types of investigation is a necessary preliminary to the construction of an indefeasible explanation of either type; 2, that a sensitive exercise of both types of explanation and a realisation of the sort of problems which an audience would have in following the story will tend to produce a convergence of tactic in this pursuit; that a rational explanation of a past philosophical dilemma, a causal explanation of a past philosopher's enterprise and an account of either of these rendered intelligible to an ignorant layman will display a considerable symmetry of form and that most of the unsatisfactory features of the history of ideas as written comes from its notable lack of resemblance to any such form. I hope to

14

make these somewhat cloudy notions clearer in the final sections of this paper.

There is nothing very obscure about the notion that much of the history of ideas as written displays a certain philosophical crassness, whether or not this is true. But what exactly are we to make of the complaint mentioned above about the 'bloodlessness' of the history of ideas? I shall attempt to dramatise this charge in what follows, in order to make its appeal more obvious.* The point, in essence, is simple enough. Apart from odd examples in the history of religious development or scientific discovery, few branches of the history of ideas have been written as the history of an *activity*. Complicated structures of ideas, arranged in a manner approximating as closely as may be (frequently closer than the evidence permits) to deductive systems have been examined at different points in time or their morphology traced over the centuries. Reified reconstructions of a great man's more accessible notions have been compared with those of other great men; hence the weird tendency of much writing, in the history of political thought more especially, to be made up of what propositions in what great books remind the author of what propositions in what other great books. Key principles of the explanatory thought-systems of social groups, of communities, and of whole countries have been pursued through the centuries. As a make-weight to this type of analysis, we have biographies of great thinkers which identify the central arguments of their more important works, sketch in their social background in some detail and expatiate upon their merits or moral relevance to the present day. Finally we have formal philosophical analyses of the works of great philosophers or scientists which tell us what Hobbes's theory of obligation or Plato's theory of justice or Galileo's theory of motion is and how far we should accept it.† All of these enterprises are recognised, and properly recognised, as forming part of a pursuit which can be labelled as the 'history of ideas'. Yet none of them is necessarily bound to (and few ever in fact do) provide any sort of historical account of an activity which we would recognise, in common sense terms, as 'thinking'. The history of thought as it is characteristically written is not a history of men battling to achieve a coherent ordering of their experience. It is, rather, a history of fictions — of rationalist constructs out of the thought processes of individuals, not of plausible abridgments of these thought processes. It consists not of representations, but in the most literal sense, of reconstructions, not of plausible accounts of how men thought, but of more or less painful attempts to elaborate their ideas to a degree of formal intellectual articulation which there is no evidence that they ever attained.

* In practice, it does not always seem relevant in particular instances. The sense in which it *is* true is I hope made clear by the end of the paper.

† This list is, of course, a caricature and intended as such. It is not even adequate as a preliminary typology of the sort of books there are. Notably it does not begin to give an account of the best or the worst of the books that are written. In the latter case this is hardly a vice. But it is important to emphasise, in order to avoid misunderstanding, the very remarkable quality of much of the work which has been done in these subjects by Cassirer, Koyré, Kemp Smith, Lovejoy and many others.

Because of these features, it is often extremely unclear whether the history of ideas is the history of anything which ever did actually exist in the past, whether it is not habitually conducted in a manner in which the relationship of evidence to conclusion is so tenuous that it provides no grounds at all for assent. For there are certain banal truths which the customary approaches appear to neglect; that thinking is an effortful activity on the part of human beings, not simply a unitary performance; that incompleteness, incoherence, instability and the effort to overcome these are its persistent characteristics; that it is not an activity which takes its meaning from a set of finished performances which have been set up in type and preserved in libraries, but an activity which is conducted more or less incompetently for most of their waking life by a substantial proportion of the human race, which generates conflicts and which is used to resolve these, which is directed towards problem-solving and not towards the construction of closed formal games; that the works in which at a single point in time a set of problems issue in an attempt at a coherent rational ordering of the relevant experience are in some sense unintelligible except in terms of this context; that language is not, as the seventeenth-century savants mocked, a repository of formal truths donated by God to Adam but simply the tool which human beings use in their struggle to make sense of their experiences. Once talking and thinking are considered seriously as social activities, it will be apparent that intellectual discussions will only be fully understood if they are seen as complicated instances of these social activities.

All of this is, of course, to beg the question at issue; but it has its glib plausibility. Whether it has anything else is what I shall try to show. May the charge perhaps amount to nothing more interesting than a pun on the word 'understanding'? The notions of understanding and explaining historical events have recently received a considerable amount of philosophical attention.[3] Complicated issues of epistemology and of the logical forms of explanations have been extensively explored and the practice of historians somewhat clarified. But the extent of the disagreement which remains is still considerable and its precise character frequently elusive.

Consider the following plausible historians' assignments. 1, Explain why Plato wrote the *Republic*. 2, Explain why Plato's ideal state had an authoritarian political structure. 3, Explain why Plato criticises Thrasymachus's account of justice in the *Republic*. 4, Explain why the Roman empire in the west collapsed. 5, Explain why there was a French Revolution between 1750 and 1820. 6, Explain why there was a French Revolution in 1789. 7, Explain why there was not an English Revolution in 1831.

Some of these seem to be problems about states of consciousness of agents; others do not. Some seem to demand an account of the set of premises which make a given argument or set of arguments seem cogent. Some seem to be answerable by a detailed narrative of a period of time in the past. Others do not seem to be susceptible of narrative treatment at all.

16

That is to say, a story of the periods in point seems to leave the question raised quite unanswered. What story could possibly explain why there was a French Revolution between 1750 and 1820? It would need a most remarkable story of 1789 to seem an appropriate answer to that question. Why should one wish to assimilate one set of these questions to another, still less reduce them all to one sort? Or, to put the issue differently, why should one suppose that the venerable dispute between idealist and positivist philosophers of history, or its more recent avatar, that between the exponents of causal and those of 'rational' or narrative explanations, between the notions of history as applied general sociology or as stories which happen to be true, is a real dispute at all? Is it not rather an attempt to legislate for the type of historical explanations which should ideally be given, a lengthy exercise in the persuasive definition of the adjective 'historical'? What conceivable set of causal laws could 3 be subsumed beneath, or what narrative or set of reasons constitute an answer to 4 or 5? Giving reasons for why an argument seemed cogent to an individual in the past, or why an act seemed appropriate is not an instance of subsuming anything under a causal law, though there are certainly causes for the appearance of cogency in the argument or appropriateness in the act. No explanation of the persistence and change of a complex social system over time can be adequately provided by a story. But both of these last two enterprises, whether or not they have ever been carried out in a definitively satisfactory manner, represent intelligible and characteristic *explanatory*** enterprises of historians and the attempt to reduce them to the same type of enterprise is absurd. But to insist that there is a correct model for historical explanation implies that one or other of these, causal or rational, must be merely provisional, preliminaries to the construction of an explanation of the approved form. In any case, does either of them provide an appropriate form of explanation for the history of ideas (surely an ideal example for those with a strong distaste for the more scientistic aspirations of historians)?

What *is* the subject-matter of the history of ideas; past thinking, philosophy, ideas, ideologies? And what indeed is its form; a set of narratives, a set of subsumptions of individual instances under covering laws, a set of reconstructed rationalia for specific philosophical performances? Most urgently, how far does causality intrude into this sensitive intellectualist inquiry and

---

* Most historical writing for better or worse does not consist largely of explanations. This lends an adventitious force to the position of the critics of 'causal' explanation. But if the stories are still to be true, some sort of concern for causality seems to be inexpugnable. The most elegant literary constructs in history do come to grief on aesthetically trivial facts. Pragmatically the dispute is really over what to do with the data, once gathered. The solution must surely be that a historian may organise them in any way which he can show to be conceptually coherent. In the particular instance which I am discussing in this paper the difficulty has been that the conceptual organisation chosen has often deformed the data. Different historians do (and there can be no reason why they should not) design their work as attempts at applied general sociology or at 'stories which happen to be true'. Professional disputes may, causally, arise over this difference of taste but they are conducted, by professional etiquette, as disputes over the *truth* of propositions about the data. In this, at least, professional etiquette seems unassailable.

how far are its permitted intrusions a matter of intellectual taste on the part of the historian and how far a matter of professional obligation; how far in short is the meaning of any set of ideas irreducibly infected by the conditions of its birth?

One might want to say that any statement made by any individual at any time could only be said to be *fully* understood if one knew the conditioning-history and the set of present stimulus conditions which elicited it. And yet human beings do to some extent understand each other and by the time they reach the age of speech the very notion of such a history of their conditioning seems to elude our pictures of them. (No one has ever been able to provide such a specification; and indeed, who would seriously claim to be able to imagine what it would be like to know such a story and then confront the individual whose story it was, what the logical relations between such a story and our own descriptions of actions would be like?)* Clearly, if this were a necessary condition for understanding a statement we could not have acquired the very notion of understanding statements. Indeed, one might say that to suppose anything so implausible is simply to confuse psychology with epistemology, to mistake the genetics of a statement for its logical status, a tired error. But the initial proposition was not that one could not understand statements *at all* but that one could not *fully* understand them; that any understanding was in principle liable to be exposed as including a specific misunderstanding of some feature of what it is claimed to understand. But what sort of feature? For any explanation of a given linguistic act in terms of its history can only give at best the necessary and sufficient conditions of its occurrence. It cannot give any full account of its *truth* status.† This does not mean that such an explanation cannot include an account of why X thought it to be true (in so far as he did do so) – plainly this must be included – nor even an account of why X thought it was true though many with the same values as X and greater specific skills would have been able to show conclusively why it was false. What the explanation cannot give in purely historical terms is an account of why it *is* true or false. To put the point most simply, in the history of science, the full set of statements about the sufficient conditions of Aristarchus of Samos's heliocentrism does not serve to tell us the senses in which his theory was true or false.*

---

* This does not, of course, mean that such a novel form of comprehension could never come our way, just that it would *be* novel, i.e. we cannot know what it would be like until we know what it is like. See very helpfully Charles Taylor, *The Explanation of Behaviour* (London 1964), pp. 45–8 esp.

† This claim is ambiguous. It does not hold for those propositions the truth or falsity of which depends solely upon the speaker's sincerity in asserting them; reports of intentions, more dubiously promises. For a superb account of the problems raised by these see J.L. Austin, *How to do things with words* (Oxford 1962). Issues of sincerity do affect the truth status of propositions in works of the highest intellectual complexity (indeed, this insight has been made the key to an entire method of interpretation by Professor Leo Strauss and his distinguished group of pupils from the University of Chicago), but it is clear that the truth status of any proposition of any descriptive complexity cannot rest purely on the sincerity of its proponent.

* There is an important conventional sense in which one can understand what anyone says without knowing whether it is true or false. But consider, for example, the project of writing a history of

If this assertion is correct, important conclusions follow. In the history of philosophy, for example, the only account of a past philosophical performance which could be said to be complete at any one time must comprise the complete Skinnerian story of its genesis* *and* the best available assessment of its truth status. Furthermore it implies that every complete account in the history of philosophy is implicitly dated. (Not, of course, every statement in the history of philosophy; as, for example, 'Plato wrote the *Republic*'; 'the following words occur in the *Republic* in the following order'; even, 'Locke's *Essay* contains criticisms of a doctrine that there are innately known truths'.) For its truth is contingent on the adequacy of this philosophical assessment; and the criteria for the adequacy of the assessment change over time. Perhaps, though, the point is trivial. So, after all, do the criteria for truth claims in psychology; say, from Aquinas to Descartes, to Bain, to Skinner. In the nineteenth century the idea of a complete physics did not seem fatuous and hence a complete psychology at least in principle conceivable. Today, where the idea of an indefeasible physical truth is so puzzling, the idea of an indefeasible psychology seems grotesque. Perhaps it is grotesque. In which case the claim collapses into the banality that all explanations are implicitly dated. One could also perhaps argue for a necessary time-specificity in the philosophical account on lines parallel to those which Danto uses[4] to distinguish between contemporary- and future-specific descriptions of events, as in the Yeats poem on Leda and the Swan: 'A shudder in the loins engenders there/ The broken wall, the burning roof and tower/And Agamemnon dead.' But it seems equally plausible today to argue for a time-specificity in the causal story. It's not simply what true statements there are to make about the past (the contemporary- or future-specific descriptions of the past) which alters; but what one knows the past to have been like. In the same way changes in physical or chemical knowledge may have effects in geology which alter the geological story, while the history of the human race as such at most alters the labels attached to different areas of the geological subject-matter.

Even at this level of abstraction the argument clearly implies that there are two necessary components to the *identification* of every past performance of philosophical importance, two descriptions of the act which require very different verificatory procedures. A major argument of this paper is that much of the incoherence and implausibility in the history of ideas stems from the

science without beliefs as to the truth or falsity of any scientific propositions. Conversely, if Aristarchus thought that the earth moved around the sun, we can understand the notion, as expressed in these terms, without much difficulty. But we do not thereby know, or at least may not know (i.e. do not *know*) what Aristarchus meant unless we know the ontological and physical contexts at the very least which gave definition to his claim. Rudely, what we know is that Aristarchus anticipated one of our more firmly established beliefs. But this is self-celebratory gibberish, not history. It is a poor attempt at understanding Aristarchus.

* Here, as elsewhere, this phrase is used for exemplary purposes. I have no wish to foreclose on any form of attained causal explanations of behaviour, but I do not wish, particularly in the face of Charles Taylor's *The Explanation of Behaviour* (London 1964), to assert that the explanations must be ultimately reducible to statements in a 'physical-object' data language — whether a peripheralist analysis of behaviour or a centralist analysis in terms of neuro-physiology or bio-chemistry.

failure to separate these adequately and that most abstract methodological arguments in the subject depend upon an effort to make one of the two descriptions of the act all-important and the other trivial. They err in proffering one description as the overriding, the *correct*, description of the performance in place of the other. It seems clear that both descriptions are in principle correct, that they constitute answers to different questions about the nature of the act. What is much less clear (perhaps, even, not always true in practice) is the claim that they cannot be brought off perfectly well separately. The causal story is clearly a very intricate piece of historical explanation but the philosophical analysis may well seem simpler. May we not follow a suggestion of Alan Ryan's[5] in leaving to the historian the question of 'what Locke intended' and confining our attention to 'what Locke said'? The question then is simply how we may know 'what Locke said'. Perhaps, if we examine the history of political theory we shall contrive to discover such a temporally inviolate entity.

What is it that the history of political thought is the history of? Two things, at least: the set of argued propositions in the past which discuss how the political world is and ought to be and what should constitute the criteria for proper action within it; the set of activities in which men were engaged when they enunciated these propositions. The precise degree of abstraction which places a given proposition inside or outside the category is obviously pretty arbitrary. But the identification of the continuum on which this break occurs is simple enough — roughly from the *Republic* or *Social Choice and Individual Values* to the single expletive 'Fascist'. To the two types of history there correspond two sorts of integral explanation, 'rational' and causal.* Between the two, and punningly encompassing both, there lies a third, narrative, which is 'rational' without the humility and causal without the criteria of achievement. The first looks like a history of political arguments; the second a history of political arguing. One develops the coherence which a set of political propositions seems to have held for its proponents and comments on the status of this coherence (places it within criteria of rationality and irrationality to which we accede today); it maps the logic of arguments and sets these out against its own prescriptive logic, so that their structure can be grasped clearly. All the statements contained in it are statements about the relationships of propositions to propositions. Men, breathing, excreting, hating, mocking, never step inside it. Their role is merely to

---

* This again is a wild over-simplification. I have deliberately begged the most intractable question about psychological explanation (what the form of an adequate causal explanation of a piece of human behaviour would be) by talking of the more behavioural 'activity' rather than the more intellectualist 'act'. I quite accept that understanding an act is never just a matter of subsuming a piece of behaviour under a set of causal laws, but I should certainly want to claim that part of doing so is frequently just such an operation. But cf. Alasdair Macintyre, 'A Mistake about Causality in Social Science' in Peter Laslett and W.G. Runciman, *Philosophy, Politics and Society* (2nd Series) (Oxford 1962), and convergent arguments in Anthony Kenny, *Action, Emotion and Will* (London 1963); Charles Taylor, *The Explanation of Behaviour* (London 1964). Also Peter Winch, *The Idea of a Social Science* (London 1958).

label a particular set of propositions with the name which they bear themselves. Their names appear in this story but never their selves. It is a tale to be told by clever and subtle men, and it signifies much but in it there is neither sound nor fury. But history, surely, is about the world and not about propositions. Where, in the world, do these propositions have their place? In what does their historicity consist? The answer plainly is that they are not merely propositions, logical structures; they are also statements. Men have said (or at least written) them. So the men appear again in the story, appear as speakers. It is in the role of the speaker that this disembodiment of the proposition begins to be threatened.

For there are three ways in commonsense terms that one may misunderstand what it is that a man has said. The meaning one attributes to his words may not be a meaning that can properly be attributed to them in his public language (in which case the only way the interpretation could be correct would be if he characteristically misused his language in this particular way). The meaning which one attributes to them may not have been that which he intended them to bear.* The meaning which one attributes to his act in saying them may be mistaken. One's identification of the speech act may fail in its grasp of the lexical possibilities, of the historical actuality of the proposition which he intended to enunciate (usually one of the lexical possibilities),† or of what he was doing in saying it. The failure to grasp a set of propositions correctly may be due to what is necessarily a mistranslation (an error about language), in fact a misinterpretation of what someone has said (an error about a propositional enterprise of a human being) or a misinterpretation of his behaviour in saying it (an error about the nature of a complex action).

If the historicity of the history of philosophy or political theory consists

---

* I.e. it may not have been what he *meant*, cf. p. 18, n. † and p. 303, n. 5. What a man meant to say may differ from what he succeeded in saying in numerous ways. He may, for instance, as in many of the cases considered by Sigmund Freud in the *Psychopathology of Everyday Life*, speak a word different from the word which he intended to speak; or he may speak a word in a foreign language thinking that it has a meaning which is other than the meaning which it does have, a common occurrence; or he may use a word in his own language persistently while misunderstanding its meaning (whether by mistaking it for another with a similar sound, a malapropism; or by simple misidentification). All of these seem peripheral. It is hard to imagine a man who never said what he meant to say (not, of course, one who never said what he meant (where meant = felt like saying)). There is nothing conceptually difficult in the notion of a consistent hypocrite. Indeed, if by chance one were confronted by someone who never said what they meant to say, one could only interpret their behaviour as the result of severe and peculiar brain damage. There are, of course, numerous instances where men say things which are not consistent with other things which they say or feel and one could, under some circumstances, describe these states of affairs as instances of men not meaning what they say. But this is a very derivative usage and surely cannot be construed as meaning that they did not intend to convey what they did convey but rather that they did not realise the implications of what they, intentionally, said and would not have said it if they had realised these. The suggestion in note 5 (p. 303) depends upon there being a general distinction between what men succeed in saying and what they intend to say. The distinction which *does* exist between these two scarcely seems of the right type. If one is interested in trying to understand an argument, the least one would normally attempt to do is to establish what the protagonist meant.

† It is more common for someone from an alien culture to misunderstand what a person has said than it is for people in any culture not to say what they mean.

21

in the fact that the statements *were* made at a particular date by a particular person, then it seems that the enterprise of identification can be confined to the avoidance of the first two types of misunderstanding. Surely, one might say, it matters what Socrates *said*, not just what words he used but what he was saying in using them — what he meant. But it does not matter, as far as the history of philosophy is concerned, what he was *doing* in saying them. Philosophy as the manipulation of faeces, as the denunciation of a sibling, as the placation of a God or a Party, as a cry of pain, as a mode of self-gratification, may be an apt enough description of the historical activities of philosophers, but it has nothing to do with the history of philosophy. No description of the psychological state of the philosopher can infect the truth or falsity of what he maintains. Philosophy is about truth not about action. It may be a profound sociological truth (well, it *might*, anyway) that social-ism is a cry of pain.[6] But this tells us nothing of the truth status of such propositions and arguments as constitute Socialism. In logical terms, one can yelp truth as readily as speak it.*

The problem, however, is more pressing than this. There are occasions on which one cannot know what a man means unless one knows what he is doing. Suppose a person were to give a parody of the sort of argument nor-mally produced in favour of a position which he particularly detests — say, in an argument about the justification for punishing homosexual acts as such, to describe an alleged causal relationship between changes in the sexual mores of the Roman aristocracy and the military collapse of the Roman empire in the West. If, at the end of the impassioned and sneering recital, a listener were to be asked what the speaker in question had said, it might be possible for him to provide a full record of the words used and in the correct order and with perfect understanding of the rules for the use of each particu-lar word and yet still not have *understood* what was said. Of course, such a misapprehension could readily be described as a failure to grasp what the speaker was doing in saying those words; and this is clearly an apt description. But it does seem at least equally natural to describe it as not understanding 'what he was saying'. 'Doing things with words' *is* saying things, just as saying things is doing things with words.[7] Parody or even irony are not just acts which hold the world at a respectful distance. They are ways of saying things about the world. It would surely be impossible to write a coherent account of Plato's ideas in the *Gorgias* or Hume's in the *Dialogues concerning Natural Religion* without taking note of the fact that some of the prop-ositions which they contain are highly ironical in character. On the other hand a coherent account of the arguments in these works clearly does not necessarily itself contain lots of ironical propositions. The point that needs

---

* I.e. say it yelpingly; not yelps *are* propositions. Just that the truth-status (whatever that may be) of the proposition 'God is Love' is no different when it is gasped out by the dying martyr in the blood-stained arena from when it is enunciated with the plummy self-assurance of a well-fed agnostic in a role which is religious only as an inconvenient historical hangover.

22

emphasis is only that the identification of what Plato or Hume's arguments are is contingent on understanding what they were doing in enunciating certain propositions at particular points in their works. But the sort of specific and primitive failure of identification here in question is hardly the most frequent danger. Must it not in any case be possible to elicit the correct identification of the meaning from the text itself? For, it would be most embarrassing if it *is* the case that we need some accurate emotional and cognitive chart of Plato's experiences while writing the work, or some sort of abridged story of his intellectual career beforehand, in order to grasp it fully, since we manifestly know almost nothing about these except from the pages of the dialogues.[8] But, to take a vulgar example from the causal story as we have had it told, just what sort of light does it shed on the arguments of the *Republic*, supposing that it were in some sense true, to say that it is an instance of the ideology of the declining Athenian political élite?

Clearly it does not tell us whether any particular argument in the work is true or false. But if the claim about the causal story can be sustained, it must to some degree improve our identification of the arguments as arguments. At first sight this seems implausible. For, what sort of acts can we adequately identify in terms of their social causation? Crudely, one can provide an account of the social causation of acts which can be specified as the performance of socially defined roles (this is circular). These can be widely differentiated and may not look as though they have any social component at all; attacking the government, defending (or affirming the rationality of) the social structure, loving one's wife, praising God, philosophising. The sole necessary condition is that the act must appear only as an instance of the role (cf. 'loving one's wife' with 'how one loves one's wife'), and the role must be specified in the description of the general social order. The only particulars which appear in the account must appear as instances of universals. No description of a social structure, taken by itself and without the addition of a huge number of dated statements about the individual, could enable one to deduce the complete life story of the individual. This is quite irrelevant to the issue of whether one can in principle predict all human behaviour; merely a logical feature of any explanation of individual acts in terms of a social structure. This manifestly does not mean that one cannot improve one's understanding of an individual act by improving the social description of it (cf. Why is he kneeling in discomfort in the gloom consuming that tasteless food and ill-flavoured wine? Answer, he is partaking of the Body and Blood of Christ. But compare the complexity today of the demand: 'Describe just what he is doing in "worshipping God" in that way'). But what would it mean if it were true, ignoring the vulgarity of the chosen phrasing, that the *Republic* was ideology for the declining Athenian political élite, as it were, an acceptable substitute for being Critias? It clearly would not mean that any description of the social role of the declining Athenian political élite would have written the *Republic* for you. It is a very abstract

23

description of the book and what we are interested in, if we are interested in the history of philosophy or political theory, is a very concrete description. What could be said to be socially caused about the *Republic* is at most certain features of it.* The authoritarian political structure of Plato's Utopia is not the *Republic*, is not why it appears in the history of political thought, let alone philosophy.[9]

But here again we have clearly rejected too much. For those features of the *Republic* for which we might attempt to sketch causal explanations in terms of the social history of Athens can certainly tell us something about the arguments of the book as such. It is when we come to look for the unstated premises of Plato's arguments or attempt to understand why the stated premises seemed to him to need no further extrinsic justification, that we see their relevance. All arguments have to start somewhere. Different sorts of explanations of the plausibility of a premise to an individual provide different sorts of blocking-off points to the account which can be given of his argument. The constant threat of anachronism, the wholly spurious transparency which sometimes characterises what men have said in the past, makes the correct identification of the premises of arguments, and the explanation of these, the basic precondition for an adequate account, whether historical or philosophical. If we are to understand the criteria of truth or falsehood implicit in a complex intellectual architectonic, we have to understand the structures of biographical or social experience which made these criteria seem self-evident. To abstract an argument from the context of truth-criteria which it was devised to meet is to convert it into a different argument. If, in our insistent urge to learn from the arguments of the past, we assume that its consequently enhanced intelligibility will teach us more, we merely guarantee that what it teaches us must be something different from what it says and furthermore that what it teaches us must be much closer to what we already know. If the effort to learn from philosophers of the past is a plausible philosophical heuristic, it would be most odd if it can be best carried out *in general* by failing to grasp their actual arguments. As John Passmore put it recently: 'Too often, indeed, such polemical writings consist in telling men of straw that they have no brains.'[10]

If we wish to exploit the causal story, the history of philosophising, for such a purpose, and if we are never granted access to the very special causal stories previously suggested as paradigms for explanation, from what sort of stories can we benefit? Motive-explanations and ideological explanations can

* This does not mean that the ideas of stupid people can be explained causally while the ideas of those who share our own incomparable advantages elude such crude determination — though there is a faint and horrible grain of truth in an extreme version of such a view. Cf. Karl Popper's famous argument (set out in brief in the preface to *The Poverty of Historicism*, pp. ix–xi and refs. there (London 1960, 2nd ed.)). But the Popper argument does not apply to making causal statements about past ideas — it is the logical oddity of predicting *new* ideas on which it insists. It is a purely contingent (though highly intractable) fact that in the case of the *Republic* the sort of data which survive go no distance whatever towards providing an account of the sufficient conditions for the writing of the book.

both be made causal in form (the former with some difficulty) and both could under some circumstances lend greater intelligibility to a complex structure of ideas; but they certainly raise problems. Even a sociological theory like functionalism is wildly evasive when given consistent causal interpretation[11] and there have been psychological experiments about emotions designed to establish empirically what are necessary logical truths.[12] Even if they are to function as blocks to further rational explanation they must be rationally-connected motives or ideologies or no explanation can be provided of the specific intellectual explicandum, just a description of it which suppresses its intellectual specificity. Clearly the sort of jejune retrospective sociology of knowledge or random biographical information which we have at our disposal before, say, the nineteenth century are not going to help very much. But even if this is very much a counsel of perfection, or despair, it is not one which we can honourably avoid. There must be a point in any argument at which a man stops being able to give reasons — and at that point the organism has to give them for the man. Some, very general, seem almost biological data; like the demand to give general reasons for the practice of self-preservation. Such a request, while it is intelligible enough to some (and could even be said to have a whole modern philosophy devised as an attempted answer), must simply seem a category mistake to most people. A few such teleological laws are widely credited as axioms. In describing a philosophical project coherently some of the premises must be authenticated in this way, extra-intellectually. Any deductive system must have some axioms and there are some claims for anyone which are simply axioms, where a request for a reason for the statement will only be met by a causal explanation of its axiomatic status, that it is one of the stipulations of man's history. 'I just *do* think eating people is wrong.' Such causal explanations may be hard indeed to find in the past. Even if our explanatory accounts come to include explicit fictions as explanatory terms (and after all most historical accounts contain more or less discreet fictions), at least this will enable others to attempt to test their truth or falsity. Only if we learn to make our fictions explicit are we ever likely to escape from our present conceptual morass, from the persisting problem of never knowing just what we are talking about.*

Having in this disheartened way evaded the question of what sort of stories to look for in the history of philosophising, there remains the question of what to look for the stories of. The history of philosophy, that Platonic activity which has been extricated belatedly from causality, deodorised, anaesthetised, pure, *that* history must necessarily be written in terms of current philosophical interests. This does not mean that it has to be falsified in terms of our current philosophical tastes, because the causal story, in so

---

* There are, of course, dangers in learning to talk precisely about fictions instead of trying to talk about the confusions of the world. Cf. in another area C. Wright Mills, *The Sociological Imagination* (New York 1959). But it is still important in all innocence to advocate the attempt to combine both.

far as we can still discover it, has always to be elaborated first. Its historicity is its sufficient and its sole legitimate immunity from our philosophical prejudices. To call these arbitrary is vacuous. A man for whom the philosophical articulations of a society, thinned out in the tortuous distillations of rationality from 'the fury and the mire of human veins', appear arbitrary is a man whose inadvertence takes in both the philosophical and the causal stories, a man for whom everything must be arbitrary. And in the insight that every human interest is arbitrary (as with the story that all human experience is a dream) we do not gain a truth, we merely lose a word. If we did not write it in terms of these current philosophical interests there would be no interests in terms of which to define it. A philosophical analysis of the *Republic* seems apt, where one of the *Iliad* or the *Gortyn Code* does not, and this scarcely raises a problem. Epics and law codes in primitive societies simply are not philosophical — even though one might be a little embarrassed by being pressed on the status of — say — Blake, or Milton, or Dante; and even though Peter Winch writes as though any sociological analysis of the *Gortyn Code* was necessarily 'philosophical'.[13]

No doubt there are true claims to be made in these areas by somewhat stretching the meaning of the word 'philosophical'. But the central point remains that epics and law codes are conceptually set in well-defined areas of activity, whatever one can learn *from* them about the history of philosophy,[14] and appeal explicitly or implicitly for their standing to many criteria altogether discrete from the nature of truth.* The history of philosophy, like the history of science, must needs be Whig as to subject-matter, just as, like all history, it must be Tory as to truth. This does not mean that one should *necessarily* study Kant rather than Christian Wolff; only that one should select philosophically interesting philosophy, after one has identified what philosophy there is to study.† The criteria for selecting this, as indeed in a broader sense the criteria of what in the identified past is philosophy at all, are provided by philosophy today. But the criteria provided by philosophy today need never be merely those of philosophy yesterday. The criterion of future philosophical interest is the achievement of the investigator, not the tradition of the Schools. What we can learn from the past is always what we can succeed in learning; and the educative past can change — as if some disused Mendip lead-working were one day to disclose a new and precious sort of uranium.

But this hardly provides any very helpful direction. To bring together the threads of Utopian persuasion, we must return to the contexts of the utterances which men produce. If a statement is considered in a fully open con-

---

* Not that one would not employ philosophical notions at any point in the attempt to explain and assess them; only, that most of the operation of understanding them (even after the story of how they come to be there is told completely) has nothing to do with philosophy.

† *Mutatis mutandis*, this would apply to the history of any specialised form of reflection. Each such special extrapolation is derived from an unitary matrix, the causal story of past human thought, the set of necessary and sufficient conditions for the set of past human thoughts.

text, its meaning may be any lexically possible set of colligations of the uttered propositions. A man might mean by it anything that a man might mean by it. The problem of interpretation is always the problem of closing the context. What closes the context in actuality is the intention (and, much more broadly, the experiences) of the speaker. Locke, in talking, talks about what he talks about. The problem of the historian is always that *his* experience also drastically closes the context of utterance; indeed all too readily turns a fact about the past into a fact about the intellectual biography of the historian. If in the seventeenth century Locke and Hobbes are the two English political theorists whom we all read and if, had we been writing Locke's major work, we should surely have wished to address ourselves mainly to the works of Hobbes, it is a very simple ellipse to suppose that Locke must surely have been addressing himself to Hobbes. Indeed it is so simple that men will go to the most extraordinarily intricate theoretical lengths to rescue this somewhat subjective 'appearance'.[15] The solution to the historian's problem is formally simple, to substitute the closure of context provided by the biography of the speaker for that provided by the biography of the historian. But such a project is not merely, in a trivial sense and *pace* Collingwood, logically impossible. It is also in a more pragmatic sense overwhelmingly difficult. But the difficulty is not one which we can consciously agree to evade. Communicating what Locke said and understanding what Locke said both involve making comprehensible the utterance of *Locke*. It is here that the symmetry between understanding, explaining and giving an account of a philosophical claim becomes strongest. For any of these activities must necessarily include what are in effect abridgments of the other two activities and any of them which fails to do so may be in principle corrigible by either of the other two. The problem of communicating, for instance, the meaning of Plato's *Republic* to an audience, the sort of problem which the dim privacy of our writing in the history of ideas so notably fails to solve, is the prototypical problem for the historian of ideas. For it demands not the sort of flashing of professional credit cards, the Great Chain of Being, associationism, Vico, which serve well enough inside the profession when we all feel tired, that rigid and dead reaction to recognised points which as Professor Wisdom complained of aesthetics is 'sometimes found in dog fanciers and characteristic of the pharisees',[16] but grasping the point of the original intellectual enterprise. In the reconstitution of this enterprise, the identification of the problem, the identification, again *pace* Collingwood, of why it was a problem for its proponent (and why many things which would be for us were not for him — firmly a part of the causal story), and in the critical judgement of the solution, we turn a theorem about an intellectual enterprise in the past into an intellectual enterprise in the present. All the premises in our own understanding and representation are inserted firmly into the past as hypotheses for historical adjudication. When the audience can think of no more questions to ask and when we can think of no new questions to ask and can get no more answers to our old questions from the evidence, such an investigation is completed; until the next investigation follows in due course. What I wish to emphasise is that such an investigation, if at any time it were carried to a conclusion, would be the only sort of explanation which would necessarily meet both those types of criticism of the history of ideas in general or the history of philosophy or political theory in particular which I began by noting. All this indeed is whistling to keep our courage up and in no immediate danger of instantiation. But unless we have a picture of the possible shape of success, it will be hard to see why we do it all so badly.

3

Consent in the political theory of John Locke

It is widely agreed that the notion of consent plays a central role in the political theory which Locke sets out in the *Two Treatises of Government*. Professor Plamenatz, Mr Gough, Professor Kendall and Professor Waldmann all discuss the notion as though it were the fulcrum of that theory. It is also widely assumed that the *Two Treatises of Government* is a simple abstract of Locke's formal political reflexion and that it must contain in a readily ascertainable form all the basic premises of his political reasoning. More pointedly (since that is the character which works of political theory are supposed properly to display) it is presumed that it contains both a theory of political obligation and a theory of how political life both is and should be conducted, a normative and descriptive theory of the polity. These assumptions do not appear at first sight very misleading — it might seem that, if true, they would designate clearly the area to be analysed and, if false, they can readily be seen to be so. But paradigms for the conduct of investigations can do much to determine the perceived results of the investigations.[1] The point of this paper is to discuss a typical misunderstanding which seems to me to derive from an improper paradigm.

The place of consent within the theory of the *Two Treatises* is simple, if frequently misunderstood. But government by consent is too much of a contemporary shibboleth and Locke a historical figure of too much eminence for the theory to have been left intact in its seventeenth-century context. 'Consent', so the reasoning seems to go, is a necessary condition for political legitimacy in the *Two Treatises*. Government by consent is the proper mode of government.[2] Locke was a great liberal philosopher. Hence the *Two Treatises of Government* must needs advocate government by consent, that is, must contain a theory of consent as the proper guarantee for governmental legitimacy. 'The argument of the *Treatise* is that government is not legitimate unless it is carried on with the consent of the governed. But the *Treatise* says little indeed about how government should be organised in order to have the consent of the governed.'* Government by consent means

---

* John Plamenatz, *Man and Society* (London 1963), 1, 209. See also pp. 211, 227; but cf. p. 210, 'Locke's *Treatise* is not concerned to justify any form of government; it is concerned rather to

29

that the proper conduct of government is predicated on the psychological state of the governed. Hence Locke's account of consent is to be criticised for setting up inadequate criteria for judging the continuing psychological relationship between governors and governed. But this is not what Locke's theory of consent is about. It is a theory of how individuals become subject to political obligations and how legitimate political societies can arise. It is not in any sense whatsoever a theory of how government should be organised.

This paper is intended to give an account of the place of consent in the *Two Treatises*.* To do this convincingly, I attempt to do three things.† Firstly I claim that what would have been, if he had formally elaborated them, Locke's theory of political obligation and his theory of the state are not set out in the *Two Treatises*, and that his theory of political obligation, in so far as it can be discerned in his other writings, differs sharply from that assumed by most criticisms of the *Two Treatises*; that what this book does in fact contain is an exposition of certain necessary limitations upon political obligation; and that we make both a historical and a philosophical mistake when we suppose that that theory is incompatible with the general theory indicated elsewhere in his writings. Secondly, I set out a brief outline of the argument of the *Two Treatises*. Thirdly, I examine the precise implications of the notion of consent used in this work.

Any general theory of political obligation must derive it, at least in part, from descriptive features of the human social situation. Even a purely theological theory must include statements which designate in the descriptive language of the society concerned the person or persons to whom obedience is owed. But the general account of the basis of political duty to which Locke appears to have held throughout his life as a writer has much more than such a minimal reference to the society for which it was devised. It was

---

assert the right of the people to resist their rulers when they are misruled by them.' The implications of this are hardly grasped in the rest of the account given. Plamenatz's treatment in *Man and Society*, 1, 209—41, and its development of his criticisms in his *Consent, Freedom, and Political Obligation* (Oxford 1938), esp. pp. 7—8 is (with the exception of some parts of Kendall's book cited in note 2 (p. 304) the most careful and penetrating analysis of Locke's position on consent yet produced (but see also p. 52, n. †). Were it not for the misunderstanding of what Locke's theory of consent was about, it would be most impressive. For other accounts, which share the misunderstanding, see M. Waldmann, 'A Note on John Locke's Theory of Consent', *Ethics*, LXVIII (i); J.W. Gough, *John Locke's Political Philosophy* (Oxford 1956), ch. III, pp. 46—71; C.B. Macpherson, *The Political Theory of Possessive Individualism* (Oxford 1962), pp. 194—262 and for a more incidental example C.W. Cassinelli, *The Politics of Freedom* (Seattle 1961), pp. 86—101, 177. An extremely helpful brief treatment is Raymond Polin, *La Politique Morale de John Locke* (Paris 1960), pp. 209—12.

* For a brief general account of the political context to which the *Two Treatises of Government* was addressed see, below, ch. 4, pp. 54—57.

† The conviction such summary presentation could induce is necessarily qualified. The interpretation sketched here is developed at greater length in J. Dunn, *The Political Thought of John Locke*, Cambridge 1969. The account of consent given here stands by itself. The rest of the argument is designed to encourage the abandonment of certain forms of commentary on such an account, by questioning the paradigms on which such commentary is based. (I hope, that is, by showing an element of Locke's thought developing in the context of his own intellectual preoccupations, to emphasise how hard it is to grasp this, if we continue to pay close attention to our own preoccupations in the same area). It is presented here informally and schematically.

indeed, as any such general theory must be, a compound of sociological banality and ethical truism. But more importantly, since his ethical theory was at all times set out in theological terms, political duty was always discussed as a duty to God. From the *Treatises on the Civil Magistrate*,[3] the *Essays on the Law of Nature*[4] to the *Two Treatises* itself,[5] to incidental observations on the basis of property rights in his notebooks[6] and even to the *Reasonableness of Christianity*,* all political obligations are set in a single dominating context. They are as they are because of the nature of fallen man, capable of reason but liable to sin, because of the character of the natural world, and because both of these are the work of God. Perhaps the simplest and clearest expression of this construction of political duty out of human rationality and the human biological situation comes in a note written in his journal for 15 July 1679 on the law of nature.[7] 'If he finds that god has made him & all other men in a state wherein they cannot subsist without society & has given them judgement to discern what is capable of preserving & maintaining that society can he but conclude that he is obliged & that god requires him to follow those rules which conduce to the preserving of society.' Political obligation is a conclusion of reason based on the necessary features of specifically human biological existence, an elementary theorem of the human condition.

It is a mistake to suppose that if Locke had at any point in his literary life been asked the simple moral question, 'Why should men obey legitimate authority in a legitimate political society?', he would have replied that they had consented to do so. Consent may explain the origins of political legitimacy. It may indicate how it is that a particular individual at some specific time becomes liable to particular political obligations. But it is simply not the reason why Locke thought most men were obliged to obey the legitimate exercise of political authority. The notion of consent is deployed in the *Two Treatises* in order to expound certain limits on the possible extent of political obligation. Plainly it could not have achieved this exposition plausibly if it were incompatible with his general notions of political obligation. But the general ground of political obligation is not what Locke was attempting to discuss in the *Two Treatises* and to suppose that he would have written the same book if it had been what he was attempting to discuss is jejune. More precisely, consent denotes the occasion of incurring political obligations. To suppose that it must therefore constitute the ground of these obligations is to make the error of confusing the occasion of incurring an obligation with the general ground of the duty of honouring it. It is not that the obligation incurred on the specific occasion is different in *kind* from the general obligation; rather that the nature of the occasion is defined by the context of

---

* John Locke, *The Reasonableness of Christianity*. Cited from *The Works of John Locke* (7th ed.) (London 1768), III, 1–99. (Cited hereafter as *Reasonableness. Works.* vol. etc.) In this work Locke does not discuss political duties specifically; but the argument that the acceptance of the Christian revelation renders conveniently otiose the full deduction of the law of nature has the effect of reducing complex ethical calculations to the moral truisms of an existing Christian social morality.

potential obligations. In other words, if we are to understand what Locke meant by consent it is vain to attempt to extrapolate it solely from the *subjective* characteristics of the occasion on which consent is given. Consent cannot simply be understood as a subjective fact, a fact about the psychology of the individual. It has to be understood primarily as a legal fact about the divine order of nature.

The argument of the *Two Treatises* is very simple in outline. 'Men being all the Workmanship of one Omnipotent, and infinitely wise Maker; All the Servants of one Sovereign Master, sent into the World by his order and about his business, they are his Property, whose Workmanship they are, made to last during his, not one anothers Pleasure.'[8] They belong to God and hence they have no right to destroy themselves.[9] All their duties and responsibilities are owed in the first place to God and the *duty* of self-preservation is perhaps the most fundamental of these. It is natural to describe it as a right held against other human beings but it must be understood primarily as a duty towards God. A man can only transfer to others a right which he himself possesses.[10] The possession of rights is a jural not an empirical matter. It can most easily be elucidated by examining the ethical rules which hold between men who confront each other outside any framework of positive law.* The degree of biological differentiation is not so great as to justify the inference that any human being has been created for the benefit of another,[11] and the identity of status implied by their common relationship with God precludes the possibility of such a doctrine. Hence it is only as a result of their own voluntary actions that men can confer legitimate authority upon other men (though not all political duties are instances of the rights of authorities to demand obedience; where a political authority has broken its trust and an individual is threatened, he may be obliged not to resist the authority, even though the latter has no *rights* over him, if the effect upon his fellow men makes such resistance intolerably costly).† Voluntary action does not, of

---

* This relationship, the state of nature, is a convenient abstraction which has numerous empirical instances; but it is not specified at all in terms of empirical criteria of social simplicity or complexity. That it *can* have instances is dialectically important to Locke since it excludes most of Filmer's arguments; but the argument itself would remain intact if there had never been a single instance of an unequivocal state of nature in human history. It is an error to suppose that it has somehow been vitiated by the researches of Sir Henry Maine and his successors. It is a theological not a sociological argument. That it was ideologically important, given the legalistic and obsessively historical conventions of English political dispute at the time and given the level of intellectual competence likely to be displayed by admirers of Sir Robert Filmer, is obvious enough but in no way affects the status of the argument itself.

† John Locke, *Two Treatises of Government*, ed. Peter Laslett (Cambridge 1964), 2nd Treatise, para. 176, ll. 34—40 (p. 404). 'He that troubles his Neighbour without a Cause, is punished for it by the Justice of the Court he appeals to. And he that *appeals to Heaven*, must be sure that he has Right on his side; and a Right too that is worth the Trouble and Cost of the Appeal, as he will answer at a Tribunal, that cannot be deceived, and will be sure to retribute to every one according to the Mischiefs he hath created to his Fellow-Subjects; that is, any part of Mankind.' But cf. para. 108 (p. 422) and para. 225 (p. 433) where it is merely stated that private individuals will not in fact exercise such a right when their grievance is not widely shared; not that it would be wrong of them to do so. What is in question here is simply the point that a right is defeasible by other conflicting rights; cf. Laslett (ed.), op. cit. 1st Treatise, para. 42 (p. 188) for the possible conflict between

course, imply the absence of motive, even of overwhelmingly powerful motive. Nor does it imply a formal verbal commitment. All that it implies is the absence of coercion. Consent in this fairly clear, though not behaviourally very precise, sense is a necessary condition for the legitimate authority of one man over another. But it is not a sufficient condition. Men's psychological reach exceeds their juristic grasp. As biological organisms, their capacity to assent is not confined to those cases in which the law of nature legally empowers them to do so. Legitimate authority is not co-extensive either with the totality of legally permissible moral commitments or with the totality of actual psychological assents. Certain sorts of injustice must always destroy the legitimacy of political authority, even if those who suffer them are physically coerced or ideologically befuddled into submitting to them. Locke's theory does not make consent equivalent to either efficient physical control or successful conditioning. Its most essential element remains a sort of formal rationality which no contingent truths of psychology could impugn.

The sole source of legitimate authority (though, as said above, not the sole basis of political duty) is, then, the rational consent of individuals. What they can rationally consent to is limited by their own rights. One major limitation on their own rights to dispose of themselves, the suicide taboo, is the basis of the account of necessary limitations on political authority given in the *Two Treatises*.[12] Because men cannot kill themselves, they cannot give to others a right to kill them — though they can make it possible for others to punish them, if they break the law of nature, since this involves no transfer of rights* and is merely a prudential calculation. Hence any act of a legitimate or illegitimate political authority which unjustly threatens the life of an individual subject voids the political rights of the authority.† In this way the *Two Treatises* extrapolates the right of resistance to unjust power from the suicide taboo. This structure of argument is the context in which Locke's discussion of consent in the *Two Treatises* is set.

Besides employing the term 'consent' elaborately in the *Two Treatises*, there are numerous other pieces of writing, published and unpublished, in which Locke makes use of it in an analytically important way. It would be possible to examine the various contexts in chronological order; indeed to do so would have substantial analytical advantages. But any such advantages would be drastically offset by the inordinate repetition and huge length that

rights based on 'Justice' and those based on 'Charity'. See also J. Dunn, 'Justice and the Interpretation of Locke's Political Theory', *Political Studies*, XVI, 1, Feb 1968, 68–87.

* When men break the law of nature, their jural status collapses and they become liable to the executive power of the law of nature in the hands of those upon whom they have legally made war. The basis upon which sovereign authorities exercise political power is this executive power of the law of nature ceded to them by their subjects. (See Laslett (ed.), op. cit. 2nd Treatise, paras 7–11 etc.)

† It doesn't, of course, as emphasised in n. † (p. 32 above), void all the social duties of the subject — his right of resistance in the circumstances is contingent on a reasonably low cost to others of its exercise. But in so far as his duty to obey the sovereign could previously be expressed as a right of the sovereign to exact obedience, it can no longer be so expressed. Men's duties to God — and hence to their fellow-men — are more demanding than their duties towards those set in authority over them.

such a method of presentation would demand. Hence, at this point, the words are merely listed and subsequently they are referred to only in order to cast light on the role which the notion has in the *Two Treatises* itself.* It will be convenient to begin with an interpretation of Plamenatz's: that Locke took consent to mean 'a voluntary act intended by the doer of it to give other people a right they would otherwise not have'.[13] This strong sense of the notion may well be necessary for the execution of the enterprise which Plamenatz attributed to Locke in writing the *Two Treatises*. But is it what Locke himself meant? He seems, rather, and in his other writings as much as in the *Two Treatises* to use the term consent, like assent, for the uncoerced acceptance in whatever disposition, of a practice, sentiment, or opinion.†

---

* The texts in question are (in chronological order, except that works published in Locke's lifetime are given at the date of publication, rather than at the conjectural date of composition): (1) English and Latin *Tracts on Government*. See p. 304, n. 3. Cited as Abrams (ed.), op. cit. (2) Latin *Essays on the Law of Nature*. See p. 304, n. 4. Cited as Von Leyden (ed.), op. cit. (3) English *An Essay concerning Toleration* (1667), printed in H.R. Fox Bourne, *The Life of John Locke* (London 1876), I, 174—94. Cited hereafter as *Toleration* Fox Bourne, op. cit. (4) Notes (n.d. ? 1669—70) on Samuel Parker's *A Discourse of Ecclesiastical Politie* (1669), MSS. Locke, c. 29, fos. 7—9. Printed in Maurice Cranston, *John Locke: A Biography* (London 1957), pp. 131—3. Cited by MSS. ref. (5) Draft of Locke's Essay, *An Early Draft of Locke's Essay* (ed. R.I. Aaron and J. Gibb) (Oxford 1936) — the draft of 1671. Cited as Aaron and Gibb (ed.), op. cit. (6) Draft B of Locke's *Essay* (also 1671), *An Essay concerning the Understanding, Knowledge, Opinion, and Assent* (ed. B. Rand) (Cambridge, Mass. 1931). Cited hereafter as Rand (ed.), op. cit. (7) The notes 'Excommuni-caçõn' (1673/4), MSS. Locke c. 27, fos. 29, *a, b* (printed in Peter, Lord King, *The Life of John Locke* (London 1830), II, 108—19. Cited as King, op. cit. (8) The note 'Toleratio' (1679) in MSS. Locke d. I, fo. 125. Cited by MSS. ref. (9) Locke and James Tyrrell's manuscript treatise in criticism of Edward Stillingfleet's *The Mischief of Separation* (1680) and *The Unreasonableness of Separation* (1681), MSS. Locke, c. 34. Cited as Stillingfleet and MSS. ref. There are problems about the status of the manuscript which is in the hands of Tyrrell, Locke, and Locke's amanuensis, Sylvester Brownover. It is evident that it was quite literally a joint composition and it seems clear from the manuscript and from Tyrrell's correspondence (see esp. MSS. Locke, c. 22, fos. 55, 57) that it must largely have represented Locke's own ideas. (10) *An Essay concerning Human Understanding* (ed. J.W. Yolton, London 1961). Cited as *Hum Und.* (11) *A Letter concerning Toleration*, English and Latin texts ed. M. Montuori (The Hague 1963). Cited as *Let Tol.* (12) Notes on William Sherlock's *The Case of the Allegiance due to Sovereign Powers Stated and Resolved . . .* (London 1691), MSS. Locke, c. 28, fos. 83—96. Cited as Sherlock notes and MSS. ref.

† For an early typology see John Locke, *Essays on the Law of Nature*, ed. W. Von Leyden, p. 160. 'Consensus autem hominum diversimode considerari potest; primo enim divide potest in consensum positivum et naturalem; positivum eum vocamus qui ex pacto fit, vel tacito, . . . vel expresso . . . ' See p. 161 n. 1, for the continuity of Locke's usage from Latin into English and p. 164, 'Secundo consensus naturalis, in quem scilicet homines feruntur, instinctu quodam naturae sine alicujus foederis interventu, triplex esse potest: Primo morum sive actionum, ea scilicet convenientia quae in hominum moribus et communis vitae usu reperitur. Secundo opinionum, quibus homines varium praebent assensum, aliis firmum et constantem aliis tenuem et instabilem. Tertio principiorum, quae hujusmodi plane sunt ut facilem a quovis homine mentis suae compote extorqueant assensum, nec quivis unquam sanus repertus est qui de eorum veritate intellectis terminis dubitare possit.' Clearly consent in the sense critical to the argument of the *Two Treatises* must be an example of *consensus positivus*. But, as such, most of the critical instances can be assimilated only by something close to a legal fiction. It is easier to understand Locke's readiness to employ such a fiction if attention is paid not just to the objective moral features of the situations in which men live (the central importance of which I have stressed previously) but also to the degree to which the social psychology of legitimate political communities was seen by Locke as a series of *consensus naturales*. Since he saw the dominant characteristic of most men's actual life as an unreflecting acquiescence, there seemed nothing very strenuous, morally speaking, in reading the thoughtless acceptance of the benefits of a practice as an acquiescence in the practice itself. His total lack of respect for the cognitive activities of most men in all social ranks made it simple to ignore the actual ambivalence of many of their attitudes, still more the rationality of such an ambivalence.

Clearly in behaving in such a manner men need not at all be *intending* to proclaim their recognition of a set of duties, still less to create a set of duties for themselves *ex nihilo*. What is suggested is clearly not that in doing *X*, men are intending to do *Y*; but rather that doing *X* may be construed as doing *Y*. What enables one to construe an example of one category of actions as an example of another category of actions in such a case must necessarily be a feature of the context in which the action is performed, not some peculiarly subtle feature of the state of mind of the agent at the time of decision. Plamenatz criticises Locke for making duties which are essentially contextual contingent purely on the psychological states of individuals, and then in prudent concern at the anarchic implications of so doing, promptly rendering this psychological criterion nugatory.[14] I shall attempt to argue, in contrast, that there are no duties in Locke's philosophy (except the duty to worship God) which are not largely contextual in their specification; that consent is crudely behavioural in its form and that no very complex features of the mind of the agent are relevant in its identification. There are complicated philosophical problems which arise over questions of the sense in which one may be said to intend the consequences of one's actions* and it might be supposed that these arise even more critically over the issue of how one could construe consenting to some state of affairs as consenting to some other state of affairs. But Locke deliberately uses the notion in such an unspecific manner and for such a limited purpose that this line of approach seems wholly to miss the point.

In the *Two Treatises* men are said to consent to many different states of affairs and to do so in many different ways. Consent is said to be present at the inception of legitimate polities. It occurs on every occasion at which an individual by explicit or implicit choice becomes a member of a legitimate political community. It appears whenever a community chooses its representatives in the manner to which it has previously consented and whenever these representatives vote. It is responsible for the rise of a money economy and it is an attribute of every subsequent monetary transaction. It is also displayed by those who deliberately (though not necessarily enthusiastically) participate in the unjust practices of their rulers. Rather fewer circumstances present any reliable indication of the absence of consent. Simple coercion is perhaps the clearest. Submission is just *not* the same as consent. Absolute monarchies also to some extent lack its sanction or at least, more unequivocally, such of them as are of any scale or degree of social sophistication and complexity. Most revealingly of all, those who do not specifically participate in the immoral actions of their rulers cannot be said to have consented to the actions. Clearly here an axiom of interpretation is being invoked, rather than a bet about the states of mind of the population. The criteria needed before one can be presumed to have done wrong are much more searching than those needed to establish that one has done right.

* See, for example, G.E.M. Anscombe, *Intention* (Ithaca, N.Y. 1963), esp. pp. 37–49.

The *Two Treatises of Government* was written not as a set of instructions in how to institute legitimate political societies *ab initio*, but as an abridgement of a particular tradition of constitutionalist thought. It was intended to draw out the implications of one conception of an existing political community. It aimed to restore a previous political health; not to initiate but to revert.[15] Hence it is easier to understand the force and bearing of its conceptions in the context of concrete behaviour which they are designed to explicate. Consent inside settled political societies appears overtly at three points, at the occasion on which an individual becomes a member of the political community and at the points at which the community chooses its representatives or these chosen representatives make laws. There are two sorts of membership in a political community, temporary and permanent, and two corresponding ways of incurring it, tacit and explicit (or express) consent. Some form of consent is necessary because of the 'State all Men are naturally in . . . that is, a *State of perfect Freedom* to order their Actions, and dispose of their Possessions, and Persons as they think fit, within the bounds of the Law of Nature, without asking leave, or depending upon the Will of any other Man.'[16] Men can only consent for themselves; they cannot, for instance, do so for their children,[17] any more than they can sin for their children.[18] But to stress, in this way, the irreducible necessity of individual consent for the legitimacy of political authority raises obvious problems.[19] For when does any such consent take place? And how is it given? It is, Locke thought, the type of occasion on which it *is* normally given which leads people to ask such questions or, more simply, to assume erroneously that they are naturally subjects.[20] This is hardly surprising since it is not a necessary condition for the giving of consent that there should be *any* 'Expressions of it at all'.[21] If a government is legitimate almost any adult behaviour within the boundaries of the country — that is, all behaviour except emigration — constitutes consent. Why should this be so? There are two possible reasons. It might be the case that all persons who live in a certain geographical area do in fact share a certain attitude of mind towards the political authorities of such an area. But Locke plainly does not believe anything so odd. The only other possibility is that such a situation in itself implies certain *prima facie* duties; that the duties are derived from the context and can, at most, be voided by considerations about the state of mind of the subject.

The circumstances in which a man cannot be said to have consented are confined to those in which he has been coerced. Anyone who voluntarily derives benefits from an existing political society incurs political obligations towards it.[22] This is because the setting up of a political society is the creation of a jural space, as well as of a physical protection; both of which are designed to secure the enjoyment of the participating individuals and both of which, at the level of social development reached in seventeenth-century England, as in many places, are necessary conditions for the existence of any such security. In such societies the lives, liberties and properties of the citizens are guaranteed by the legal system as rights and protected by the political system as goods. It is as recognised rights, that is to say, in Locke's terminology, as 'regulated by the laws', that they are in fact protected; and this legal protection of real goods in such societies is empirically necessary for their real protection. The mixture of empirical and ethical considerations is subtle and its exposition is more than a little muddled by Locke's need, in setting out his notion of the 'state of nature', to defend it against the vulgar and polemically effective Filmerian critique of man's natural freedom.[23] To make the situation somewhat clearer it is convenient to consider in relation to this account two recent critical analyses of succession to property; those of Plamenatz and Macpherson.[24] Plamenatz is struck by the contradiction between Locke's claim that inheritance of property implies consent to the political authority of the society in which the property is situated and his inclusion of the natural right of bequest within the natural right of property. This hiatus is certainly the fault of Locke; but it is a flaw in his presentation of his argument, the inadvertency of his phrasing, rather than a flaw in the argument itself. The misunderstanding arises in two areas: in the failure to take account of the fact that Locke's natural rights are not unitary in their specification, and in the misapprehension of just how Locke defines the political relationship.

The situation is as follows: (1) A man institutes a government to protect his property. (2) The government passes laws which regulate the status of the property at all subsequent stages. (3) What the property *now* is is what the legal rules specify.[25] (For Locke, as for any other observer, seventeenth-century English property rights were a highly complex and artificial phenomenon, specified by the law. This did not mean that they were unnatural, in the sense of morally improper — though Locke himself certainly thought that some exercises of property rights which were legally impeccable were morally wrong — but they certainly were not natural in his eyes in any restricted, biologically-given, sense. That is just not the sort of notion which his notorious 'natural right to property' advances.) (4) Hence no man can possess the property without becoming liable to (namely, in Locke's terminology, 'consenting to') the rules. (5) Hence, to accept property implies accepting the rules which regulate it as legally valid, accepting the legitimacy of the legal sovereign, implies in fact political obligation. Plamenatz fails to take account of just what is implied in joining a political society. A member of a political society accepts *all* rules made by the society.* What a man's

---

* This is an exaggeration. There are various exceptions. Rules which command actions to which the individual does not have the legal authority to consent (under the law of nature); rules which are not properly arrived at under the constitution of the country; rules which order the performance of actions which are intrinsically wicked do not oblige subjects. All statements made in this section of the text are only true *ceteris paribus*. The exceptions listed in this note must always be kept in mind. Political obligation in Locke never involves *per se* consent to actions which are in principle wrong.

property is in the state of nature is what he has legitimately accumulated. What his property is in the polity is what the laws say it is. (This does not mean that *any* law which specifies what his property is (e.g. a law for the expropriation of Jews) is necessarily binding. But it does mean that nothing which is not so specified according to the legal rules *is* his property unless the specifying rule as such is illegitimate.) Property right is a legal right in form like any other right. This does not sound much like the Locke whom we all know. Indeed if it were all that Locke said about property, then clearly the Locke whom we all know would be a figment of the historical imagination (an exaggeration). But, of course, it is not. No express limits are implied logically in the conception of laws which the sovereign may pass to regulate property. But all such laws are subject to invalidation by the higher principle of the law of nature. A law which had the effect of removing a man's property without his consent* would be in breach of the law of nature. But such a law could in general only be produced without a man's consent if it did not meet the criteria for positive legality in the society. For what a man consents to in joining a society is precisely the positive law-making system.†

However, there are more exacting practical implications to the law of nature than this suggests.[26] There may be no internal legal grounds which make invalid the (formally legal) arbitrary and malicious confiscation of property;* but higher law considerations provide no support for such unjust enactments and it is not clear that the victims would be in any but the (positive) legal sense obliged to comply.† To suppose that there are (positive) legal reasons why a formally valid law can be voided for moral impropriety

---

* This has a rather technical (i.e. evasive) meaning in Locke which will be examined later.

† More precisely, what a man consents to is a continuing decision-procedure. This is what *constitutes* a political society (see Laslett (ed.), op. cit. 2nd Treatise, para. 95, ll. 4—14 (pp. 348—9); para. 96, ll. 1—17 (pp. 349—50); para. 97, ll. 1—14 (p. 350); para. 98, ll. 1—18 (pp. 350—1); para. 99, ll. 1—11 (p. 351); para. 134, ll. 11—21 (p. 374); para. 141, ll. 1—16 (pp. 380—1); para. 198, ll. 1—11 (pp. 415—16); para. 212, ll. 16—22 (pp. 425—6) and ll. 29—32 (p. 426); para. 216, ll. 1—7 (p. 427); para. 227, ll. 4—18 (p. 434); para. 89, ll. 1—19 (p. 343). In view of the oddly vehement and largely irrelevant literature on Locke's attitudes to the rule of the majority, (see esp. W. Kendall, *John Locke and the Doctrine of Majority-Rule* (Urbana, Ill. 1959)), it is worth emphasising here that, apart from its role as a piece of political clap-trap in the sections on non-parliamentary taxation, majority consent only appears in Locke as the minimum form of decision-procedure constitutive of a political society. It is an error, furthermore, to suppose that majority-consent is the only form of decision-procedure which is acceptable in Locke's eyes (see p. 38, n. 26), or even, in effect, one which he would ever have much favoured in any political society (see n. * below). Even the will of one man could be acceptable in some circumstances. See Laslett (ed.), op. cit. †nd Treatise, para. 111, ll. 1—9 (pp. 360—1).

* It would be an even more egregious error to suppose that he imagined that such a procedure would guarantee the rightness of the decisions. Since compatibility with the law of nature is not a criterion of *legal* validity, but is a necessary condition for the full obligatory force of a legally valid law, it is peculiarly absurd to interpret Locke's position as theory of positive rights and duties deriving solely from the moral authority of any human decision-procedure.

† Note that this might equally well hold even if the enactment was one to which the sufferers had 'consented' through their representatives. Locke claims that nothing of the sort would happen in politics with elective representative governments. He did not claim that if it did, it would thereby become legitimate. See Laslett (ed.), op. cit. 2nd Treatise, para. 138, ll. 14—41 and para. 142, ll. 10—15 (pp. 379, 381).

is a logical error. To suppose that all formally valid laws are morally obligatory is a moral error. Neither error is made by Locke. Legally correct rules
which arbitrarily deprive anyone of his property are at best dubiously binding. Every man has a *prima facie* right to inherit property bequeathed to him
and an arbitrary legal interference with such a right would not be morally
binding on the injured party. But such *prima facie* rights in no way exempt
an inheritor from holding the property on precisely the terms on which its
previous owner held it. The property which the inheritor has a natural right
to inherit *is* what the rules specify, a set of rights with contingent duties.
The rights can to some extent be voided by the wrong actions of the inheritor
and in the same way the duties can to some extent be voided by the
iniquities of the authority to which they are owed. But after the initial
express consent which establishes the political community has been given,
there no longer exists a set of rights unencumbered with contingent duties.
It seems that here too it is a failure to take full account of the context in
which Locke's arguments are set which leads Plamenatz to misunderstand
their bearing and to mistake their success.

If it is the question of the express consent which initiates political society
that, in this way, misleads Plamenatz, it seems to be a misconception of the
express consent which makes an individual a full member of a society which
misleads Macpherson. He wishes to show that Locke made the propertyless
into subjects of his class state but excluded them from full membership in
it.[27] It was, in his opinion, in order to carry out this unattractive project
that Locke developed the distinction between a tacit and an express consent.
The first category is employed because of the impossibility of demonstrating
in any other way that the propertyless are subject to the laws of political
society. With careful skill, it assimilates the situation of the propertyless in
their own society, their rights and duties, to those of resident aliens.[28] But
does Locke's concept in fact do this? Macpherson's claim rests squarely on
the proposition that 'the only men who are assumed to incorporate themselves in any commonwealth by express compact are those who have some
property, or the expectation of some property in land'.[29] But the only evidence which he cites[30] for this interpretation will not bear the weight put
upon it. In the passage cited Locke states that any man who makes himself a
subject of political society in order to protect his property submits this to be
regulated by the laws of the society. It is true that he takes land as the
example of property with which to continue the exposition of the point at
issue, and it seems likely that it was both empirically the case that he
thought of land as paradigmatic for other forms of real property and dialectically the case that land fits his argument here more neatly than movable
property (most of all, money). But by any canons of interpretation the fact
that he takes land as his example cannot in itself be taken to imply that he
thought there were no other examples. The paragraph in question was not
intended to give an exhaustive statement of the motives that might lead men

to join a political society; it was designed to emphasise that property inside political societies can only be held subject to the rules of those societies.

Furthermore, even if Macpherson's inference was a permissible interpretation of the paragraph itself, it would still not have had the implications he suggests. For the paragraph considers only the inception of political society and not the circumstances under which men may wish to incorporate themselves in the existing political societies in which their families have lived for centuries. To suppose that Locke would have considered the actual nature of their motivations under such vastly different circumstances as identical is absurd. To take the relationship about which Macpherson himself has been most emphatic; the fact that at the inception of political society there would have been no adult who did not own land (or, at least, could not do so if he wished), and hence no non-land-holding adult would have had reasons to incorporate himself into a political society,* does not imply that in the maturity of political societies when there are many men born into their society without any property in land or the probability of acquiring it, such men could have no reason for incorporating themselves into their society. Thus, once it is noted, as it is by Macpherson himself,[31] that 'Not every proprietor of land is necessarily a full member of the society — foreigners and even natives who have not actually incorporated themselves in the society may possess land there', there ceases to be any reason to accept his conclusion that 'every full member is assumed to be a proprietor of land'. The problem then returns to where it is in the text of Locke himself — how it is in fact that men *do* incorporate themselves in society; just what sort of a performance *is* an 'express' or 'explicit' consent?

There is no very clear answer to this question and it is a damaging lacuna in Locke's theory that there should be none. At this point, at best, an account can be given of the sort of considerations which make his statements intelligible; no account of how the statements as they stand are consistent is possible because as they stand they do not make adequate sense. Macpherson's attempt to resolve this problem is ingenious but unconvincing, both in the detail examined above and in the general interpretation of Locke's position which it involves.† The problem remains that Locke gives no instances of

* This argument involves taking the sociological fantasy which Locke is here constructing as seriously as Macpherson does and accepting the assumption (which, as said above, I do not) that one can extrapolate from Locke's phrasing the precise limits of his intentions. What I wish to emphasise is that, even if one accepts Macpherson's methodological assumptions, his argument cannot carry out the work which he assigns to it.

† See generally the article by Ryan cited on p. 37, n. 24 and Jacob Viner, 'Possessive Individualism as Original Sin', *Canadian Journal of Economics and Political Science*, XXIX, no. 4 (1963), 548–59; Macpherson's reply, ibid. pp. 559–62; and rejoinder by Viner, ibid. pp. 562–6; also, Laslett, 'Market Society and Political Theory', *The Historical Journal*, VII, no. 1 (1964), 150–4. The central error of Macpherson's interpretation, not perhaps brought out very clearly in these critiques, seems to arise over his analysis of class differentials in rationality in Locke's theory. Locke's entire theory is based upon the potential rationality of all adult human beings and, although he clearly thought that there were substantive differentials in rationality, it is equally clear that he did not think these ran along class lines. In all practical matters, Locke's notion of rationality was behavioural, 'living according to the law of reason', rather than intellectualist.

what he means by an express consent except that of a landowner previously in a state of nature who joins himself to a commonwealth. Can Locke really have meant that the only political societies in which all adult (male) inhabitants were members of the 'Body Politick' were ones which had only just been established and that the only members of the English 'Body Politick' in 1680 were naturalised property-holders? It is hard to believe this. It is hardly likely to be an accident that the example which Locke does give of men who were, over a period of time, 'subject to the laws' of a commonwealth, is of resident aliens.* It might be conceivable that he regarded those without property in England as enjoying a status identical to that of resident aliens; but it is scarcely credible that he should have extended this status to himself or to his patron, the great political magnate, the first Earl of Shaftesbury. Yet when had these two latter given a 'positive engagement, and express Promise and Compact'[32] to incorporate themselves into the realm of England? There are a number of occasions on which certain groups of people in seventeenth-century England were required to perform actions which could reasonably be described as giving positive engagements or making express promises or compacts *as* members of the society. The most notable of these was the requirement to take the oath of allegiance and supremacy.[33] Such oaths, for the most part, seem only to have been imposed upon public office-holders but it is clear that any member of the community was in principle liable to have them administered to him, if disaffection was prevalent and if a magistrate had any reason for doubting his loyalty.[34] Conceivably, by extension, the oath that a parish constable was required to take at his inception might have been regarded as a similar positive engagement. However this does not get us much further. For these oaths are always taken as such by men who are already in any common sense understanding 'members of the society'.

To return to the passage quoted above (footnote below), resident aliens are said not to be 'Subjects or Members' of the commonwealth in which they live; though 'subject to' the laws of England, they are not English 'Subjects'. But could it be true that Locke thought the huge mass of propertyless labourers were not English subjects? Or are there three categories involved — Members, Subjects, and those 'subject to the laws'? What would best make sense of these murky statements and is it likely that Locke believed what would best make sense of them? The simplest assumption, perhaps, would be that he thought of all natural-born Englishmen (who did not expressly decide, at some point close to the time at which they came of age, to emigrate) as members of the society; and that he thought of their express consent as a hypothetical event, like the express consent of the

---

* Laslett (ed.), op. cit. 2nd Treatise, para. 122, ll. 1—20; esp. ll. 12—16 (p. 367): 'thus we see, that *Foreigners*, by living all their Lives under another Government, and enjoying the Priviledges and Protection of it, though they are bound, even in Conscience, to submit to its Administration, as far forth as any Denison; yet do not thereby come to be *Subjects or Members of that Commonwealth*'.

propertied, as the answer they would give if asked the question, 'Are you an Englishman, a subject of the King of England?'[35] For even if the large property-owner was more likely to proclaim his membership of the political society in a definite public act, through holding a public office like a justice-ship of the peace or a lieutenancy of the militia, any adult male Englishman was just as much liable to have an oath administered to him, if his conduct gave reasons for suspicion.[36] To suppose that a suspected supporter of the Fifth Monarchist Venner who agreed to take the oath of allegiance would have thereby become a member of English society, while a rich landowner who had never held public office had not, is inconceivable. For all Locke's insistence on the explicitness of an express consent, it seems that what must be important is the disposition manifested by behaviour, rather than any specific occasion. Men must be supposed expressly to consent to their nationality, their membership in a given society, by their settled disposition to identify themselves as such (those who are not immigrants are, after all, seldom in doubt about their nationality). All this seems rather weak; but, I fear, the weakness is Locke's own and cannot readily be amended by sub-stituting an extrinsic strength.

A further problem arises over the nature of an express consent. Those who are not full members of a society are stated to have a natural right of emi-gration, though not of taking their property with them when they emigrate.* But this natural right to emigrate does not apply to the members of the political society.[37] In other words, at the point at which a man becomes a perfect member of a society he loses the right which he previously enjoyed to leave it at will. Locke gives no reason for this position — it is a consequence of the definition which he gives of membership in political society — and it seems not to have any function in the structure of the theory. There is no particular reason why he would have thought it right to prevent those emi-grating who wished to do so, even if the political society which they wished to leave was in itself fully legitimate.† What the position implies is simply that no one who accepts voluntarily his membership in a political society can subsequently claim any *right* to leave it at will, if the political authorities of the society object to his doing so.

Once a man is inside political society the issue of consent arises again only over the taxation of property. Locke's discussion of property is designed precisely to remove the right to it from the historically inconceivable

---

* Laslett (ed.), op. cit. 2nd Treatise, para. 120, ll. 1—21 (p. 366); para. 121, ll. 1—9 (p. 367). Though Locke's phrasing is even vaguer than usual over this issue, it seems (esp. para. 120) to be his property in *land* which he cannot take with him — for obvious reasons — and not property in money or goods. He can sell the land (para. 121, l. 8) which would presumably only make sense if he could take the money with him. That is, a man may inherit property without political obligation but whilst he is actually exploiting it (and hence deriving benefits from the government of the country within which it is located) he is obliged to obey the laws of that country. Cf. also para. 118, ll. 1—25 (pp. 364—5).

† If the society in question were the France of Louis XIV and the intending refugees were persecuted Huguenots, of course, he regarded their right of emigration as beyond question.

42

'express Compact of all the Commoners'[38] so successfully demolished by Filmer.[39] But, if the origin of property is independent of consent, its transfer can only be made by consent. Indeed, the definition of property is simply that *'without a Man's own consent* it *cannot be taken from him.'*[40] This does not mean, as has been emphasised above, that a man can hold property in an actual political community without thereby incurring duties. A man has a right to his own property and he has a *'Right,* before any other Man, to *inherit,* with his Brethren, his Fathers Goods'.[41] But the exercise of this right, if a parent has been a member of a political society, is contingent on accepting the rules of the society. This is not because there is something imperfect about his right of inheritance; he *does* have a right of inheritance before all other men — it is because this right (like all other rights in Locke except that of self-preservation, a right which is also a duty) is a conditional and not an absolute right.[42] How is this right of the political society to regulate and articulate the property rights of individuals compatible with their right to do with it whatever they wish; how, for instance, is this compatible with the right of the state to raise taxes? Locke's answer again seems dimly inconsequential. The state as such has *no* right to raise taxes.[43] No tax can ever legitimately be demanded as a right by any sovereign; all taxes can only be specific gifts from particular subjects.

But, naturally, such a position is totally incredible. The puzzle is to be solved by invoking the constitutional notion of representation.* Men choose deputies, representatives, to give their consent for them; if the legal structure of the society is such that there are no facilities for their choosing their representatives, or if the appointed machinery for choosing their representatives is interfered with,[44] no tax can have any legitimacy except that conferred upon it by the individual voluntary acquiescence of the taxed. The duty to support the expenses of government in due proportion to the benefits received from it is a duty which can be enforced only when it is explicitly recognised as such by the man who owes it.† An air of massive bad faith hangs over this whole area of the argument. For what is necessary, finally, is not the (inconceivable) consent of each individual but the consent of the majority given by their representatives (see footnote † below), as conveniently alleged to exist in the proper practice of the English constitution and as undeniably ritualised in English political rhetoric for decades. But

---

* This is not a genetic account of how Locke came to use the idea. He used it because it applied to the particular constitution about which he was writing and because it was intrinsic to the specific tradition of political language which he employed. I am only here indicating what function it serves in the theory as presented.

† Laslett (ed.), op. cit. 2nd Treatise, para. 140, ll. 1–11 (p. 380). 'Tis true, Governments cannot be supported without great Charge, and 'tis fit every one who enjoys his share of the Protection, should pay out of his Estate his proportion for the maintenance of it. But still it must be with his own Consent, i.e. the Consent of the Majority, giving it either by themselves, or their Representatives chosen by them. For if any one shall claim *Power to lay* and levy *Taxes* on the People, by his own Authority, and without such consent of the People, he thereby invades the *Fundamental Law of Property*, and subverts the end of Government. For what property have I in that which another may by right take, when he pleases to himself?'

why should the consent of the majority suffice? The obvious suggestion, that this is the minimum decision-procedure constitutive of political society,[45] that it is what a man consents to in becoming a member of a political society at all, will hardly suffice. For, if a *past* consent is adequate to ensure obligation, an absolute monarchy created by the consent of its members would have arbitrary power over the property of its subjects.* It seems unlikely that Locke meant this. It cannot be because it does constitute *in fact* the agreement of all individuals that Locke takes the consent of the majority as its equivalent. There *is* an extraordinary elision between the consent of each property-holder and the consent of the majority† of the representatives of the majority of the property-holders, as chosen according to the English franchise in the late seventeenth century. It seems implausible that Locke was altogether unaware of any such elision. Why should he have made it and how can it make sense?

Firstly, it must again be emphasised that the *Two Treatises of Government* is a very specifically directed book. Causally, the reason why Locke does not consider the possibility of the oppression of a minority by a majority, and hence does not denounce it, is simply that it is not relevant to the issue about which he *is* writing. What he is attacking is the exploitation of a huge majority by a small minority. Had there been operative French representative institutions, he would not have regarded the confiscation of the property of the Huguenots on account of their religious beliefs as being in any way less arbitrary because it was carried out as a result of the votes of the Estates, representing the enthusiastic consent of the majority of the French population. He uses the cant of English constitutionalism in this insouciant (not to say careless) manner, not because it guarantees an administration of spotless purity but because he considers one particular theory of the English constitution as likely to provide better administration than others. What is in question is not Utopia but the most desirable political arrangements that Shaftesbury or William III might reasonably aspire to bring about. To attempt to extrapolate the Lockean Utopia from such unpromising materials is a sterile exercise and the results, by necessity, faintly ludicrous.

But why should the 'consent of the majority' have this favoured pragmatic status? At the formal level no suggestions are even offered — it seems an uneasy amalgam of the arguments for majority-consent as a minimum decision-procedure and of the *a priori* equality in moral rectitude or turpitude of all men, a simple axiom, *ceteris paribus*, more rather than less. This

* Or, if it did not have 'arbitrary' power, then neither would a majority of the members of a community have 'arbitrary' power over the property of the minority (see below). Majority-consent is a minimum necessary condition for being in a political society at all, whereas absolute monarchy based on consent is a particular form of a political society. But if what is in question is the threat to property, one's presumed reason for entering political society at all, it is obscure why this should make any difference.

† *Sic.* Taxes were voted in Parliament. Cf. Laslett (ed.), op. cit. 2nd Treatise, para. 96, ll. 12–17 (p. 350).

seems unexceptionable and useless — but then it is not how it is used. It is where it *is* used that its plausibility and its pragmatic quality are most readily seen. For it is not *any* set of representatives or deputies which can be trusted in this way to further the interests of those whom they represent.[46] Most governmental bodies are always liable to think of themselves as having distinct interests and to behave accordingly. They are all too frequently disposed to make inroads on the property of the subjects for their own benefit and without any justification.[47] However, 'This is not much to be fear'd in Governments where the *Legislative* consists, wholly or in part, in Assemblies which are variable, whose Members upon the Dissolution of the Assembly, are Subjects under the common Laws of their Country, equally with the rest.'[48] Men remain sinful. Government remains imperfect. In governments with elective assemblies like the English, arbitrary expropriation of property is less to be feared than it is in other governments which lack this incomparable advantage. Absolute power may normally be an acceptable form of political authority, if it is in practice confined to the requirements of military defence or within social structures as simple as the patriarchal family. But the appropriation of property, unlike military leadership, needs more persistent referenda, if it is to be prevented from being arbitrarily exercised. It is the combination of temptation with opportunity which makes a sovereign's right to tax without the 'consent' of his subjects into such a dangerous threat. A particular institution generates the dangers; these are best alleviated by another institution. In an absolute monarchy any tax ever levied derives whatever legitimacy it has solely from the individual psychological attitude of each taxed subject at the particular point in time at which he is taxed. In a Parliamentary government like England's there is a definite decision-procedure which if it is operated without chicanery guarantees the consent of the majority of the taxed.* We do not know whether Locke thought that this was the best conceivable political system. What we do know is that he thought of it as merely a human institution and not a generator of autonomous moral values. In the last resort the criterion for the just exercise of *its* powers, too, is the axiom: 'the power of the Society, or Legislative constituted by them, can never be suppos'd to extend farther than the common good; but is oblig'd to secure every ones Property'.[49] The moral authority of *all* institutions is restricted by the maxim of rational choice.[50]

Consent, then, inside political societies is both the mode in which individuals acquire their political obligations and the institutional precondition for each man to feel a reasonable security in his own possessions. But it is also what creates political society in the first place and this may well seem more peculiar. It is not very remarkable to base a political theory on the fact

---

* Or, perhaps more precisely, the consent of those who pay the larger part of the tax. (Laslett (ed.), op. cit. 2nd Treatise, para. 158, ll. 4–9, p. 391. *N.B.* it is taxation for which the Parliamentary safeguard is considered desirable. The responsibility for the interests of those who are too poor to pay taxes might rest more directly on the autonomous executive than on a Parliament elected by a property-based franchise.)

that men do to some extent recognise the legitimacy of the societies in which they live. It is harder to see how such a recognition could precede in time the social matrix from which it derives. Here, surely, we have not only historical fantasy but logical error. But do we? Consent is an axiomatic precondition for the legitimacy of any political authority because men are naturally equal in their status as the property of God.[51] But the crucial term here is legitimacy, not precondition. For it is a precondition not for the existence of any society whatsoever but for the existence of a society with an authority which has a *right* to the obedience of its members. Locke shows a great, and a justified, impatience with the question of the historical authentication of consent as the basis of primitive government, not because he did not know more than Filmer about primitive government* but because his argument is in no way contingent on the historical questions of how primitive governments did begin. All that is necessary for his argument, except in so far as its efficacy simply as propaganda is concerned,[52] is that there should be *some* instances of men confronting each other in 'a state of nature', that is, outside any shared structure of positive law. (Strictly speaking not even this degree of evidence is necessary to the argument; but its expository cogency is undoubtedly much strengthened by it.) To establish this, the Swiss and Indian in the woods of America[53] are quite sufficient. The perfunctory pre-history of government which is from time to time invoked adds nothing to the theory and lends to it a degree of historical contingency which it clearly did not have in Locke's mind. The whole account is correspondingly obscure. There seem to be two historically substantial stages, an authentically primitive one and an advanced constitutional one; and the confusion seems to derive from the attempt to conflate the two. The first stage, patriarchal monarchy and military leadership in war time, is discussed as an example of political authority based upon consent; while at the same time it is clearly recognised to be devoid of 'known standing laws'.[54] Advanced political societies, like England, are (when their constitutional proprieties are not being infringed by the iniquities of their governors) characterised by 'known settled laws' and by a legislative process which is at least to a significant extent controlled by elected 'deputies' of

---

* He was in fact one of the best informed students in the Europe of his time of variations in the moral, social, political, and religious practices of non-European countries; a fact which has led Laslett to observe that he 'may be said to have done more than anyone else to found the study of comparative anthropology' (Laslett (ed.), op. cit. p. 98 n.). Certainly he played a major role in the planning and assembling of material for the fine collection produced by his publisher John Churchill, in four folio volumes, in 1704 (*A Collection of Voyages & Travels in 4 Volumes* London, 1704). For the extent of his interests see: G. Bonno, 'Les Relations Intellectuelles de Locke avec la France', *University of California Publications in Modern Philology*, XXXVIII, no. 2 (Berkeley 1955), 37—264 (especially on Thévenot and Bernier); *John Locke's Travels in France 1675—9*, ed. John Lough (Cambridge 1953); Correspondence in the Bodleian; Notebooks in the Bodleian; Journals in the Bodleian and British Museum (Add. MSS. 15642); Notes to *Essays on the Law of Nature*, ed. Von Leyden; *Essay concerning Human Understanding*, etc. For the works contained in his library see John Harrison and Peter Laslett, *The Library of John Locke* (Oxford 1965). The total bulk is extremely impressive. I emphasise its existence to show how extended is the context in which Locke elaborates his 'political rationalism'.

'the People'. If government normally begins as monarchy,[55] and if to change the legislative is to set up a new government, there must have been some occasion in the past at which each advanced society acquired its governmental form. One may conjecture that this occasion normally resulted from previous injustice, either on the part of an incumbent monarch[56] or on the part of an alien conqueror.[57] In either case there must have been some definite occasion on which the people, either in person or acting through elected representatives,* voluntarily recognised the legitimacy of their government.[58]

It is clear what sort of occasion in English constitutional mythology is being invoked here, though whether Locke thought of it as a specific historical occasion or the authentic 'Ancient Constitution' itself,[59] is obscure. It is equally clear what sort of circumstances could not be considered as instances of the institution of governments by consent. Conquest was one of the favoured accounts for the origins of the English constitution (favoured, for obvious reasons, only by those who wished to give an absolutist interpretation of that constitution). Though, in its historiographical form, the Norman Yoke, it hardly enters the purview of Locke's argument as this survives, in the less historically contingent form of unrecorded past usurpation it is a frequent theme of Filmer's (as of Hobbes's and most other absolutist theorists of the period). Indeed it played the role of an absolutist historico-legal fiction in a manner closely analogous to the Whig historico-legal fiction of the contract. The rejection of conquest as a basis for political legitimacy, and the distinction between consent and submission by which this rejection is carried out, are the most unequivocal indications of what sort of purchase his notion of consent was intended to have upon concrete social situations. It is thus far from surprising that the only piece of writing after the publication of the *Two Treatises* itself which indicates a renewal of Locke's interests in the problem of the grounds of political duties should focus upon the issue of the legitimacy of a usurping regime. In the notes which he wrote out on William Sherlock's *Case of Allegiance* he confronted a theory even more crudely Panglossian than that of Filmer.[60]

Sherlock maintained that all social events of any complexity are a dispensation of divine providence, their causation a result of the subtle deflections by the deity of men's corrupt motives. To Locke, this seemed abject superstition in general and morally corrupt in particular. To assert, as Sherlock did,[61] that 'The Revolutions of Governments are not the Subjects Duty, but God's Prerogative' was simply grotesque. Furthermore, it made

---

* How their representatives would have to be chosen to be considered as authentically representing them (that is, the nature of the franchise which would be necessary) is not a subject that Locke ever discusses at all clearly. In an existing political society, the problem is avoided by the consideration that the franchise is a part of the constitution (i.e. in itself something which the people have consented to) (Laslett (ed.), op. cit. 2nd Treatise, para. 158, ll. 3—16, and 35—9 (pp. 391—2). A maxim of fairness is necessarily involved (ll. 36—7) but what would constitute fairness is almost wholly obscure, outside a settled political society (except that, for purposes of assessing taxation, representation according to potential tax burden appears to be recommended (ibid. 7—9)).

right a simple function of power. It meant that majorities, even rebellious majorities, must axiomatically be in the right.[62] Above all it destroyed the very notion of legitimacy and reduced to nullity any tolerable definition of the political relationship.[63] It assimilated submission wholly to consent. But a general submission is not the same as a general consent.[64] It may often serve as an indicator of such a consent; but in itself it does not constitute consent at all. Neither particular verbal performance nor coerced behavioural acquiescence suffice. What is necessary is *choice*.[65] The Greek Christians, hence, have a continuing right of resistance to their Turkish masters. They have never chosen the framework of government under which they live; and they are treated by their rulers in a manner which could only be permissible if they were 'slaves under the force of war', a situation which cannot even in principle last beyond a single generation.[66] What makes the critical difference is the absence of compulsion and the existence of choice.[67] Of these two, it is the absence of compulsion which comes closest to being a simple behavioural criterion. Choice is not seen as a particular historical event in the mind of the subject. Rather, the absence of compulsion is a necessary condition for the existence of choice. Certain behaviour in a particular context implies choice.* But if the behaviour is caused by external force, then it does not imply choice. This is certainly not a trivial criterion — it is because the 'noise of War . . . makes so great a part of the History of Mankind' that men have made the error of mistaking the force of arms for the consent of the People.[68] It is precisely the hideous preponderance of force in human history, and the sycophantic ideologies which this has generated, which it is the purpose of Locke's political theory to confront and to expose.

But the confrontation is not achieved by turning the entire weight of the legitimate social order upon the shifting consciousness of individuals at arbitrarily selected points in time. Such a conception would indeed be democratic, not to say anarchic; and, if Locke were to predicate such a claim of the English political community in his day, he could have done so only in the most radical bad faith. The legitimacy of the polity could no more be solely a construct out of such psychological contingency than the moral order itself. The exaggeratedly individualist and voluntarist character of such a theory would deprive every existing polity of its legitimacy. To follow why Locke did not see it as having this result, it is necessary to understand the structure of ideas within which it is to be interpreted. To see why it is that Locke should have adopted so early and held with such little strain the queasy historical fiction that governments have originated from the consent of the people,[69] it is necessary to take note of the assumed sociology which underlies his argument and the criteria for rational choice and legal authority which are embedded in it. The most central assumption of his political theory, the irrelevance of history, was not an easy theme to bring to bear on

---

* This is plainly not a philosophical analysis of what it is to choose; simply a substantive moral rule about what may be counted by others as a choice.

48

the relentless legalism of English political discourse in the seventeenth century. Indeed, it was such a difficult task to do so that much of our own critical literature on Locke has significantly failed to grasp it. The strenuous attempt by Professor Richard Cox, for instance, to decode the true meaning of the Lockean doctrine from the 'real' empirical character of the 'state of nature' is only the most single-minded of such enterprises.* To a greater or lesser extent this misunderstanding seems still to colour most of our interpretations. In the remainder of this paper, I shall argue that it is the continuity of reason and the general human propensity to accept even minimally legitimate hierarchies of authority which best define Locke's theory and which lead him to his characteristic insouciance before the contingencies of history. Finally, I shall attempt a brief and somewhat more formal summary of the nature of his conception of consent.

The role of reason in the definition of the contours of consent alters to some extent from one stage of social development to another. Initially, whatever a man 'actually consents to' is licit,[70] unless it is in itself something which he does not have the authority to consent to — i.e. it is in itself an action which it could never be licit for him to perform.[71] Thereafter, whatever a man has acted in such a way as to make himself responsible for, he may be said to have consented to, and reason enters the relationship only as the criterion of what sort of action constitutes making himself responsible for what other sort of action. Reason implies, for instance, that the legitimate exercise of any authority must be limited to the pursuit of the ends which the authority may be held to serve. These ends are known by a process of rational inquiry (in principle), by knowledge of the law of nature.[72] A more specific instance of this position is that the authority derived by a political society from the consent of its subjects is limited to acts which it is in the general interest of the subjects to empower.[73] Still more restrictively, where the actions of the political authorities, even in a perfectly legitimate policy, are in themselves vicious, the subjects cannot be held responsible for them unless they have directly expedited them.[74] On the other hand, particular exercises of authority to which the people have not yet specifically consented or which are in direct conflict with the structure of rules to which the people have consented may be considered to carry the consent of the people where they clearly further the ends for which the rules were originally established.[75] All these examples have one feature in common. They are all

* Richard H. Cox, *Locke on War and Peace* (Oxford 1960), chs. I and II esp. For an example of the odd forms of argument employed, see pp. 42–4 on Palantus and the foundation of Tarentum (cf. Laslett (ed.), op. cit. 2nd Treatise, para. 103, ll. 1–4 (p. 353), where Locke claims that the foundation of Tarentum by Spartan exiles constitutes an example of men setting up a political authority over themselves by their own consent, and after they had previously been independent of one another (i.e. in a 'state of nature'; loc. cit. ll. 5–6)). Cox's own description makes clear that the Spartans were voluntary emigrants from a political society to an area in which the authority of that society did not hold. Hence they were *independent one of another* (loc. cit. l. 3), that is to say none had any *prima facie* right of authority over another except as a result of the voluntary consent of the other. This is a simple paradigm case of Locke's argument about the derivation of authority. Cox's energetic manoeuvres around the passage are completely beside the point.

instances of rational interpretations of the nature of consents given by a people within a legitimate society. The question of the rational criteria for originating a legitimate political society is never faced very firmly; but the position implied is clear enough. What constitutes the legitimacy of a political society is precisely its recognition as legitimate by its subjects.[76] The issue of just what such a recognition would be like as an event in the world is not discussed because it had happened long enough ago in England for its precise historical character to be irrelevant. But the formal nature of the claim is clear — it is the recognition of legitimacy which creates the legitimacy of the sovereign.* It would seem more natural, perhaps, today to put this as the recognition *constituting* rather than creating the legitimacy; but, when taken with Locke's account of revolutionary right, his analysis of legitimacy seems markedly similar to that recently favoured by Professor Hare.[77] Of course, in context and intention it is radically different; I emphasise the resemblance in detail merely to make the exposition a little more intelligible.

Locke's expectations about the viability of social authority are nowhere systematically expressed. To complicate the matter further, the point at which they are voiced most explicitly in the *Two Treatises* is one at which he might well be suspected of disingenuousness. Even if, as I think probable, the position there stated is wholly sincere (however great the change may seem from his anxieties of 1660 and the *Tracts on Government*), what it asserts is more the behavioural inertness of the people than its normative acceptance of the legitimacy of authority.[78] This sense of voluntary moral acquiescence is less spelled out; but it is often invoked. In the discussions of prerogative and of the patriarchal origins of political authority[79] as in the incidental assumptions about the efficacy of social order,[80] it is a continuing theme. The phrase which perhaps best summarises the notion is 'voluntary assent and acquiescence'. There is nothing very creative about such a response. Where authority is legitimate, it is both a simple duty and a natural inclination to acquiesce in it.

There is an illuminating analogy between the way in which Locke talks of consenting to authority in this way and his conception of assenting to the truth of beliefs about the world.[81] Occasionally he even uses consent and assent interchangeably. The notion of a truth is not contingent on whether individuals *do* assent to it† — but the only way in which it can be known to

---

* More abstractly, for those who are members of a particular political society (the vagueness is present in Locke; but does it damage the argument?) there is a primary sense in which to predicate legitimacy of its authorities has a crucial illocutionary force which is more than simply descriptive. See J.L. Austin, *How to do things with Words* (Oxford 1962).

† In this respect it is plainly stricter than its political analogue. Consent is a necessary condition for a legitimate political society. No human psychological state can be a necessary condition for a notion being true. However it seems very likely that Locke would have held that men living in a non-political context in a complex society had a duty to confer political legitimacy upon that society by their consents. Plainly such a notion is quite irrelevant to the theme of the *Two Treatises* itself; but it was far from irrelevant to its subsequent polemical career. Some such assumption seems to make

be true is in such an assent. Men have a responsibility to 'regulate' their assent; they have cognitive duties[82] and they have a duty not to assent to false ideas. There is an order of potentially recognised legitimacy and potentially apprehended truth; the order of nature. There are also orders of authorised legitimate governments and systematically apprehended truths: the orders of political society and of Science. These latter are frailer and more contingent in appearance; and because Locke is concerned so sharply with epistemology, it seems often in his writing as if they are all there is. But this is to take a methodological empiricism and voluntarism for an ontological one. It is their reluctance to admit the degree of intellectual disorder which he displays here that has misled commentators into wishing a more elegant theory upon him.

What, then, is the role of consent in the theory of the *Two Treatises*? And what are the criteria for its existence in the world? For one to be said to have consented to a practice there are the following necessary conditions: (1) The occasion on which one is said to have consented must have been one on which one was acting voluntarily — that is to say that the claim that an act displays consent is defeasible by the demonstration that it was directly coerced; consent is not the same as submission. But to act voluntarily does not imply to act without powerful motivations[83] — it is precisely because there are such compelling economic reasons for any man to remain in his country of birth that he is so clearly obliged to consent to its government, if legitimate. (2) Nor does it mean to choose explicitly and self-consciously to accept the practice — this is 'express' or 'explicit' consent. (And even 'express' consent does not depend upon having any reasonable future grasp of the probable consequences of accepting the practice.)[84] What the occasion must be is one which indicates a *prima facie* disposition to take (normally, presumably indefinite) advantage of the practice. (3) The practice must be legitimate in itself.* This latter is the most complex criterion. It is also probably the most important. It explains why the fact that the Greek Christians do not emigrate (and the fact that they presumably use such roads and other utilities and administrative facilities as the Turkish regime provides) in no way enhances the legitimacy of the Turkish regime. In these

---

better sense of the embarrassing situation in which Locke was placed by his friend William Molyneux's invocation of his authority in defence of the English ascendancy in Ireland in the latter's *The Case of Ireland's being Bound by Acts of Parliament in England* (Dublin 1698) and the extensive debate which this evoked.

* I.e. it must itself have been formally legitimate in the past (where a populace in a state of nature fails to set up a political authority by its consent, all individual members of it might be said to be morally at fault but no existing locus of power would necessarily acquire any authority over them because of this). This is the most equivocal issue (and the only one about which an inquiry like W. Kendall's makes sense). The most essential premise, as said above, is the ideological viability of hierarchy. The problem as Locke sees it is not that men are *not* prone to accept legitimate hierarchies, but that they are all too prone to accept illegitimate ones. But their acceptance and sanctioning of such hierarchies cannot be construed to their disadvantage in particular cases except when it is specific to those cases. The only act which can be *construed* to one's disadvantage is the voluntary exploitation of a practice — and that only when one has broken the rules which define the practice.

terms most governments in the world of his day must have seemed to Locke of highly dubious legitimacy. It explains why not deserting the territory of a monarch who starts an unjust war does not make one guilty of waging unjust war oneself. In other words, to summarise, where a practice is legitimate and a role involves participation in the practice, consent to doing so and hence consent to its responsibilities is axiomatic — all potential doubts are resolved in favour of the practice. But when it is illegitimate the doubts are resolved in favour of the agent. In the last resort the judge of the legitimacy of a practice can only be God. The terrestrial consequences may not reveal his judgement of the act; but the eternal ones will do so, just as they will reveal his judgement of every other human act.

Locke has sometimes been accused of propounding a sort of political solipsism. It is easy to see how a theory which bases political obligation upon consent might be open to such a charge.* But no such hubris does in fact dominate Locke's vision of politics. The shells which men have built for their shelter in the conduct of their social life are frail and impermanent; the responsibilities which they bear are heavy and the dangers which threaten them incessant. All the best and all the worst which they represent is a product of the shifting struggle in every human conscience of reason and passion, good and evil. In this unedifying drama the consent of men, as I have tried to show, is merely the mode in which political authority acquires such legitimacy as it has. But legitimacy is no final and irrevocable achievement. Human life is always a broken-backed affair, whose sole sufficient rationale must remain in another world than this. Such a theory provides a bizarre starting point indeed for the investigation of any topic in contemporary political theory. Can either be much illuminated by so odd a tactic?

---

* Since the completion of this article Hanna Pitkin has treated Locke's theory of consent in an article, 'Obligation and Consent', *American Political Science Review*, LIX, no. 4 (Dec. 1965), 990–9 and LX, no. 1 (March 1966), 39–52. See esp. pp. 994–7. While I do not at all agree with the general argument of the article and consider the framework within which Locke's concept is analysed as importantly misleading, the account of the structure of the concept seems to me unusually lucid, perceptive, and just.

4

The politics of Locke in England and America in the eighteenth century

The Boston Gazette, 1 March 1773 (advertisement of first American edition of *Second Treatise*):

This Essay alone, well studied and attended to, will give to every intelligent Reader a better View of the Rights of Men and of Englishmen, and a clearer Insight into the Principles of the British Constitution, than all the Discourses on Government — The Essays in Politicks and Books of Law in our Language. — It should be early and carefully explained by every Father to his Son, by every Preceptor in our public and private Schools to his Pupils, and by every Mother to her Daughter.

Rev. William Jones, in *A Letter to the Church of England*, 1798 (cited in W. Stevens, *Life of The Author, The Theological, Philosophical and Miscellaneous Works of the Rev. William Jones . . .* , London, 1801, 1, 1):

while the age abounds with affected declamations against human authority, there never was a time when men so meanly submitted their understandings to be led away by one another. It is an honour to submit our faculties to God who gave them, but it is base and servile to submit to the usurpations of man in things pertaining to God. And he asks, whether the doctrines of Mr. Locke, whom the world is gone after, will prepare any young man for preaching the gospel of Jesus Christ, when he was the oracle to those who began and conducted the American Rebellion, which led to the French Revolution; which will lead (unless God in his mercy interfere) to the total overthrow of Religion and Government in this kingdom, perhaps in the whole Christian World; the prime favourite and grand instrument with that mischievous infidel Voltaire, who knew what he was about when he came forward to destroy Christianity as he had threatened, with Mr. Locke in his hand.

Leigh Hunt, *The Examiner*, 10 June 1810 (*Leigh Hunt's Political and Occasional Essays*, ed. L.H. and C.W. Houtchens, New York, 1962, p. 108):

it was Locke, and such men as himself, who, in teaching us to give up our mental liberty to no man, taught us to give up our personal liberty to no man; but to prefer even the consciousness of independence to a slavery however worshipful — To such a man as Locke, therefore, every Englishman owes love and reverence, and not even Nelson himself, though he died on the waves bequeathing triumph to his countrymen, deserves a more glorious acknowledgement of their gratitude, than he who, dying in solitude and in silence, with no glories about him but the anticipation of heaven and the meek sublimity of departing virtue, bequeathed to his countrymen the love of what is rational.

It is one of the enduring clichés of American historiography that much of the political theory of the founding fathers of the United States can be identified in a work by an English philosopher of the seventeenth century, 'the Great Mr. Locke'.[1] This particular cliché, like so many others in American historiography, has been subjected to some damaging criticism in recent years. It is widely regarded today as deriving from a somewhat naïve view of the history of ideas[2] and a more than somewhat pernicious view of the nature of the American Revolution.[3] It is not here intended to pass judgement on the conceptual or empirical issue of how far it makes sense to say that Locke's *Two Treatises of Government* were a cause of the American revolution. This diffidence is a product of rational decision as well as simple ignorance. It is not at all clear what the dispute between Professor Boorstin and his critics is about, or precisely what it means to question whether men's political and social ideas derive from their reading or their social experience. In literate communities they necessarily derive in different senses from both, and the language which we have for discussing such an issue at the moment and the psychological theories we have for analysing it are insufficiently sensitive to make the crude antithesis at all enlightening. This essay then is not concerned with any topic as central and unmanageable as the causation of the American Revolution. What is attempted is an outline history of the ways in which a single book was sensed to be relevant in England and America in the eighteenth century, a brief sketch of the sort of work that Locke's book is, an account of the types of intellectual response which it evoked in England and America in the eighteenth century, and some degree of explanation of why these responses should have been as they were, of what made it seem trivial or significant, relevant or boring, attractive or insufferable.

To understand the book itself, as much as the ambiguities which its readers managed to elicit from it, it is necessary to recall a little about the political situation to which it was addressed and the persistent intellectual preoccupations of Locke's life from which it emerged. At the time at which the bulk of the *Two Treatises* was written, John Locke was living largely in London as the confidant, friend, political aide and personal physician to one of the most prominent political figures of the day, Anthony Ashley Cooper, Earl of Shaftesbury. During this period Shaftesbury was directing a campaign to exclude from the throne the prospective heir, the brother of Charles II, the Catholic James, Duke of York. Shaftesbury's power was based upon an impressive political organisation, centred on London and backed by the dissenters, a large proportion of the mercantile interests, a formidable group of country gentry, and the London mob.[4] It was a grouping which carried offensive and immediate historical overtones to much of the community and to no one more than the king himself. Few enduring emotional loyalties can be discerned among the fitful and disenchanted manœuvres of Charles's life, but his family retained for him a certain appeal which men like Clarendon who had given their entire lives to his service seldom exerted. For two full years the patronage resources of the crown, the acquiescent judiciary, the full range of prerogative powers and the private financial assistance of the French monarch were manipulated to crush Shaftesbury and to preserve the succession for James. In Parliament and in the corporations of London and the great cities, in the courts of law, in the counties and in the London streets, the struggle was fought out. It was not just a struggle to exert political power which the protagonists already had at their disposal. It did not end with the manipulation of existing resources of patronage and coercion, but branched out into efforts to create and mobilise new types of political power. It was a struggle to win control of men's minds, an exercise in persuasion, and in consequence it was a struggle waged by necessity in books and pamphlets as much as it was within the normal institutions of English political life.[5] In short it was — and to a degree that threatened the stability of the entire political system — an ideological struggle.

Shaftesbury's tactical aim in the struggle was to extend his political control from the cities into the rural areas, among the gentry. Here he met a difficult ideological target. The major emotive focus of his propaganda, the popish scare, exercised as compulsive a fascination over the Anglican gentry as it did over their dissenting neighbours. But in their case, unlike that of the dissenters, there was no convenient intellectual link between this atavistic and xenophobic theological disquiet and their publicly affirmed theory of politics. Anti-popery, both as an ideology and as a latent form of mass hysteria, had a power over the seventeenth- and eighteenth-century English imagination comparable in its destructive potential to that of the *pactes de famine* which with their most profound convulsion sent the lewd peasant mobs howling through the chateaux of France early in 1789 and turned the manœuvrings of a Frondeur nobility into the first great social revolution of modern history. But although, as Defoe said, 'there be many who cry out against popery who know not whether it be a man or a horse', although it formed as central a part of the English political consensus as anti-communism forms in America today, it could only provide in this context reasons why political change was desirable. It could not in itself empower men to take political initiatives which would otherwise have been illicit for them. And in the crisis of 1679—81 this was just the dynamic change which Shaftesbury needed to effect. For the official political doctrine of the Anglican church, as enunciated in almost all its weighty theological treatises from 1600 onwards, as expressed in the canons of the convocation of 1606, as taught to children in the catechism books, and above all as preached to the congregations year after year in the parish churches in what were the largest public gatherings many men attended in their entire lives, was chillingly simple. It was that men's political duties were exhaustively determined by their terrestrial superiors, that though under grave conscientious scruples they might rightly decline to carry out those decrees of authority which were in direct breach of divine law, they could under no circumstances have the right to resist such authority.

Of course, the image of the English political system was by now sufficiently complex in the minds of many men to make for considerable and convenient ambiguity as to the precise location of this authority. But for Anglicans after 1660, however large the segment of the political system within which the authority was held to reside, this ambiguity did not readily extend to the notion that there could be sufficient external reserves of authority to over-balance that of the king. And if one fact was unambiguous about the political situation in these years it was that Charles opposed the exclusion of his brother from the succession to the throne. Thus any attempt to prevent the succession of a Catholic to the throne of England meant explicit and self-conscious resistance to the sovereign. It implied action which within the law of England was hard, if not impossible, to distinguish from high treason. The resulting choice facing the Anglican gentry was impossible to decide within the incoherent ordering of their own most elemental social values. It was a choice between a levelling republican assault, redolent with the acrid over-tones of 1649, upon the entire structure of social authority, and the accept-ance of a royal policy which outraged their deepest religious prejudices and stimulated their most obscure emotional anxieties. The practical choice which faced them was naturally very different, and to the cool manipulative vision of Shaftesbury or Halifax, Sunderland or indeed Locke, it doubtless appeared very different. But the choice which the country gentry made was primarily the choice which they felt themselves to make. To exert influence upon that choice it was above all necessary to present a more coherent order-ing of their values, to show that the political tradition within which the dis-senters saw their conduct was not necessarily either empirically absurd or socially subversive. The gentry had to be persuaded that there could be reasons for rebellion which could make it neither blasphemous nor suicidal.

The most elaborate, and perhaps at the relevant social level the most influential, exposition of the political ideology of the country gentry was to be found in the writings of an obscure Kentish squire called Robert Filmer. These demonstrated, with a wealth of scriptural reference and a certain amount of sustained attention to the currently respectable political theory, that men are by biological and theological necessity born into a state of help-less physical and legal impotence, that they live their entire lives under the dominion of a sovereign power and are indeed his property, to be disposed of, exploited, maimed or murdered as he wished and without even the right to object, that this authority had been conferred on Adam, the first father and hence the first king, directly by God, and that all subsequent fathers had enjoyed such an authority over their sons and all kings such an authority over their subjects.[6] The sole constraint which operated upon the monarch within this theory was the other-worldly sanction of divine reward and punishment. The only fully political actor, the only player with a creative role, was the ruler himself. In the domain of politics, men's duties derived from their place in a hierarchical order, an order directed in its activities by a king in lonely confrontation with his God. His subjects had no responsibility or religious duty to take initiatives. Their duty was simply to respond. They were meshed from their birth into a web of authority in family as in kingdom, and their sole commitment was not to struggle. To reject this interpretation of political duty in favour of the claim that governments derive their legitimacy from the consent of individuals was thus regarded as a rejection of the revealed will of God in his bequest of authority to Adam. It was also a rejection of the authority of the sole reputable source for early human history, the book of Genesis, and the most elementary biological fact about the human condition, that all men are necessarily born in a state of helpless physical dependence within the authoritarian institution of the family. It is thus vicious, blasphemous, and intellectually absurd to deny the universal political duty of passive obedience. To answer these charges Locke needed to rescue the contractarian account of political obligation from the criticisms of impiety and absurdity. Only in this way could he restore to the Anglican gentry a coherent basis for moral autonomy or practical initiative in the field of politics.

The precise ideological purchase and explicit political intent of Locke's work can be adequately understood from this outline, but the conceptual dimensions of the book require further elucidation.[7] He needed, it is clear, a theory which rescued the contractarian account of political obligation from the damaging charges levelled against it by Filmer. He needed a theory which outlined a set of possible limitations on political obligation without thereby impairing the legitimacy of the existing social and political order. In short he needed a charter for political revolution which would be in no way socially subversive. In many circumstances such an aim could have been simply enough realised by a pragmatic argument. But the deep moral inhibitions felt by the Anglican gentry necessitated a more theoretical and complete form of therapy. The resulting theory cannot be taken as an adequate summary of Locke's ideas about politics. But there is no good reason to suppose that it contains any important structural ideas which Locke would in any sense have wished to repudiate. The doctrine has two very different aspects to it, one naturalistic and the other theological. It is the latter which forms the basis of Locke's argument for the necessary limitations upon political obligation; and it is the fact that the latter, the theology, was readily mistaken for the former, the psychology, which explains most of the criticism the work has received from 1690 to the present day. The core of Locke's intellectual development from the first of his writings which we have, written at Oxford early in the 1660s, to the expositions of St Paul's epistles upon which he was working at his death resides in a tension between religious conviction and insistent epistemological doubt. All through his life, so far as we know, Locke believed that there was a God, that there were determinate moral rules and that men could in principle have true knowledge of these rules. Yet all through his life he worried over the nature of the criteria for having attained true knowledge. And when at the end of his life he had reduced faith in God to a belief that certain historical propositions were true, and moral excellence to the skilled calculation of extra-terrestrial self-interest, this intellectual contrivance was not a sign that he lacked religious affections or deep moral feelings but only that he had understood that psychological certitude and emotional authenticity are no guarantee of true knowledge. The philosophy which embodied these beliefs is nowhere systematically developed in Locke's works. The subjects of his writings were a set of precise discrete issues. There is nothing which remotely resembles a Lockean *Summa* or even a Lockean *Treatise of Human Nature* — just specific works on coinage or epistemology or the limits of political obligation or education or toleration.

It is possible, nevertheless, to discern in these works at least the outlines of an intellectual system. It is a system of radical individualism, an individualism as radical in social terms as that of Hobbes and in its potential social implications considerably more subversive. It was not devised as a description of society or of individual human psychology and hence can scarcely be criticised as an inadequate description of these. Indeed there are many reasons to suppose that Locke's assumed sociology and psychology were considerably more realistic than those of his recently resuscitated patriarchalist opponents,[8] that he accepted the reality and efficacy of social conditioning so effortlessly that he did not even feel the need by 1680 to discuss it in a work about political obligation. The key image of his philosophy was not that of Hobbes, a set of discrete, irreducible, purposive organisms in ceaseless conflict. He believed as implicitly as Hobbes and indeed as most of the contemporary orthodox that men are naturally sinners — in the understanding of the day this was no more than an empirical observation. But he had a much profounder grasp than Hobbes of the majority of men's lack of any sort of psychological autonomy. He feared the arbitrary compulsive reflex destructiveness of the hungry peasantry or unemployed artisans. But he understood his society well enough to know that the threat of anarchy came not from their determined and indomitable wilfulness but from the disruption of the elementary securities of their joyless lives.[9] What really threatened the fabric of seventeenth-century English society was not the exuberant self-will of the consciously exploited but the sheer panic of the starving and helpless. To Locke, men in the world were for the most part heteronomous to the last degree. They drew their religious, their moral, even their scientific views of the world from the blind and unthinking imitation of their fellows. His individualism was not an individualism of psychological, of emotional autonomy. It was, rather, an epistemological individualism. The primary category of human experience was cognition. It was in knowing that a man became properly human, even transcended human experience, and it was as knower that he was necessarily an individual. To be saved a man needed to attain not emotional prostration before a hidden God but a knowledge of the truth of religious propositions. Emotions might well be induced by external manipulation, and a belief in the truth of statements could be instilled in the same way; but knowledge could not. For knowledge by definition was active, a performance. No man could know for another man. Even the incidence of divine grace was to be determined not by emotional conviction but by the purely naturalistic process of believing statements to be true. A terrifying burden was to be placed upon the intellects of all men, and the burden was the more terrifying because it was precisely identical for all men. In the critical experiences of their lives men were henceforth equal, and equal in a thoroughly terrestrial way. Gone were the assumptions that religious discriminations and moral consciousness were a privileged attribute of the higher orders, that the equality of man was at worst a fact about the next world, in which the secret and ambivalent motions of a man's heart were to be the criterion of his salvation and about which one could blithely proclaim that to God all hearts were open, precisely because they were impervious to any more immediate inspection. Instead men's moral performance was to be judged in terms of their understanding, their reasoning, an activity in which the criteria for skill and success had an implacable tendency towards publicity. The privileged privacy of the royal conscience was desecrated for ever. Soul-searching must concede to argument its status as the primary mode for the elucidation of right governmental action.

All this is cast at a suspiciously abstract level and may well appear somewhat evasive, but it should eventually go some way towards explaining that peculiar ambiguity of Locke's doctrine, which made it at the same time democratic in long-term implication to an extent that no society in human history has ever been and yet for seventy years sufficiently conservative for most of the English aristocracy and intellectuals to accept it with heedless complacency as a satisfactory ideology for the closed caste-society of eighteenth-century England.

Locke argued in the *Two Treatises* that no man was born into a condition in which another man had a right to dispose of him at pleasure. No human being was born with rights over another human being. The legitimacy of the legal order which exists among men is derived solely from their acceptance of it. Most men come to accept more or less unthinkingly their membership in a highly articulated social order, and obligations are thus incurred by a combination of psychological assent and utilitarian benefit. But men do not have the legal right to incur whatever obligations they may feel psychologically compelled to incur — they can only transfer to rulers an extent of authority which they themselves already possess. And they do not, for instance, possess authority over their own lives. They do not have the right to commit suicide and hence they cannot confer upon the ruler the right to take their life at his will. This has some very odd implications. It means that the psychological acceptance of absolute power is morally more or less equivalent to suicide, is indeed a sin of some enormity; and hence that no degree of psychological passivity on the part of his subjects can confer legitimacy upon the power of an absolute monarch. Only fully legal authority exercised for the general good can be binding upon the conscience of the subject, and each single individual in the community had an irreducible right to judge the legitimacy of the act or the authenticity of the intention, if it impinged upon him in a sufficiently threatening fashion. And it was logically necessary that each individual should be left in this position as judge, both because of his persistent duty, as long as he remained a fully moral agent, to preserve his own life and because to judge was an act of the intellect and no human being could be excluded from the possibility of correct intellection by the judgement of another human being.

I have deliberately pointed up all the most anarchistic implications of Locke's political doctrine in this way in order to show its connection with his religious and philosophical ideas. The specific political doctrine which emerged from the work in 1679—81 and which made its publication such a natural gesture in 1690 was merely the dignifying of the legal order of the English polity. The right of political initiative was to be restored to the English ruling class by the demonstration that the hierarchy of social authority could be granted moral rationality without it being necessary to believe in the impossibility of just opposition to the crown. They were to be taught indeed that all the good reasons for obeying the king at other times implied that when he acted illegally and against the public interest he ought to be resisted. This was the doctrine which the great Whig lords like Somers embraced so readily, and it was the doctrine which gave the work its pre-eminent place as the official ideological defence of the revolution of 1688 during the succeeding seventy years.

That it was this doctrine which emerged is not surprising. Not only was it the doctrine in which men wished to believe; it was also the doctrine which Locke intended to advocate. The image which he held of the society in which he lived combined a very acerbic moral vision with a considerable degree of acceptance of the conventional social pieties. It is no accident that when he talks of the deepest religious sin, he talks of it as rebellion against God. It is not by accident that in the course of the *Two Treatises* he attempts to demonstrate that if a king acts tyrannically it is the king who is properly guilty of rebellion and not his subjects who resist him. Locke's emotional involvement with the maintenance of social stability was at all times acute and his understanding of the contemporary social order was firmly hierarchical.[10] He clearly felt instinctively a lot of the aristocratic overtones in the contemporary value system and both expected and accepted the continued psychological dependence of the majority of the population upon clergy, gentry and aristocracy. The degree of moral responsibility incurred by the individual who initiated a rebellion was huge and alarming. It was not a responsibility which Locke could have imagined any but the members of the aristocracy carrying with success. The right to destroy the legal order of society because of the threat of unjust power was a right that each man held; but it was a right which by the necessities of social structure few could exercise with responsibility, and its validity as a right depended logically upon the responsibility with which it was used. But there remained for Locke a persistent tension between an acceptance of this conventional fabric of values and the prescriptions implied by his philosophical views. It remained after all true that he *had* justified rebellion, and the terminological quibble over just who was really guilty of rebellion reflected moral outrage at the Filmerian notions as well as embarrassment at the breach of a taboo.

Many of the assumptions about the relative value of different social groups which were made explicit in Filmer's works Locke found deeply revolting. The notion that children were at the disposal of their fathers, were almost created to be at their disposal, that subjects were created for the benefit of monarchs, seemed to him blasphemous. The primary category of his religious thought, the equality of men as liable to sin and as capable of the knowledge of religious truth, disrupted these subliminal convictions of seventeenth-century social values. In such a perspective it was not just irrational, it was emotionally impossible to believe that the majority of mankind were delivered over into the hands of the rich, like the animals, to be enjoyed at their pleasure. Psychological dependence and compulsive acquiescence might justify themselves morally by their utility, but moral paternalism can no longer be prescriptive, a matter of right. Social configurations which serve the happiness of mankind remain morally secure, but the criterion is no longer trifling. The manipulative control of one man over another is no longer necessarily an embodiment of divine providence. Providence is torn up out of the social world which men have created by their actions, and each part of this world is made subject to challenge and scrutiny. Henceforth men confronted each other in a social world created by the intricate patterns of their own compulsions, and they confronted each other alone. No longer were they braced against or enveloped within institutions which embodied the indefeasible provision of their God. Their sufferings in the world were demythologised, ceased to wear the protective vestment of divine punishment, and became natural events to be guarded against to the best of their active abilities. The world was to be given back to men to make what they could of it, free from the inhibitions born of centuries of misunderstood theology. Even that almost automatic psychological acquiescence on which Locke was so justified in relying in the stable society of seventeenth-century England as the formal basis of the state's legitimacy bore its own dialectical implications. If the complex of seventeenth-century social duties is incurred through unthinking acquiescence, there is placed upon every dissentient member of the society, from the beginning of his adult life, the duty of making vocal and active the dissent which he feels. If thoughtless servility brings down upon the individual such a crushing moral burden, there is a moral as well as a psychological incentive to make explicit a dignified but total dissent.

The potential activism contained in this complex of notions can be well understood in a contrast between Locke and Hobbes. It is Locke's superior insight into social psychology, his deeper sense of the empirical cohesiveness of society, which made it possible for him to combine a purely ethical individualism and a broader social basis for permitted political action with an assurance that society would not thus collapse. Hobbes's crushing sense of elemental human hostility combined with his epistemological individualism led him to restrict the possibility of correct and autonomous individual action to the immediate biological drive of avoiding death and to extrude the very possibility of it from the field of politics. In this perspective his political doctrine is simply a secularised version of the prevalent Anglican or Filmerian theory, but without the latter's equivocations. Locke's theory too is based upon the necessity of individual epistemological autonomy. But his epistemological doctrines were much less sceptical than those of Hobbes. They emerged largely out of reflexion upon the notions of ethical and religious knowledge. Hobbes's epistemological individualism was not of this immediate political relevance. It was of no importance that the ignorant and the stupid, who seemed to him just as to Locke to make up the huge mass of the population, necessarily had to garner their knowledge for themselves. The necessary privacy of cognition of the stupid was a matter of no social purchase. But even the stupid have souls and hence cannot escape from their responsibility for the cognition of their elementary duties, both religious and political. 'The candle that is set up in us shines bright enough for all our purposes'.[11] The metaphor is not a careless one. The central truths and duties of human experience are accessible to all through their intellects. In the relationship with God in which, through the mediation of grace, they come to know the truths of religion, all men are equal. It is the possibility of this perception which confers an irreducible autonomy on every human individual. In the field of politics it is this religiously guaranteed autonomy which ensures that men can only incur their political duties through their own actions and that they can never be deprived of the right to claim that these duties had been abrogated. Their claim, when made, was in Locke's words 'an appeal to heaven'.[12] The words were meant literally. It was a fact about the public world and not merely about each man's soul that he had such a right of appeal.

The work which emerged anonymously from the presses in the aftermath of the revolution of 1688 enjoyed no great immediate éclat. Only three Englishmen who were not personal acquaintances or correspondents of Locke are known even to have mentioned it with approval in the fourteen years before its author's death,[13] and at no time do we know him to have made explicit written admission of his authorship. In the various obituaries which appeared in the two years after his death, it nowhere features very prominently.[14] All through the eighteenth century its reputation trailed that of his major philosophical work, *An Essay concerning Human Understanding*. In France, where it was not published under Locke's name until 1749,[15] it was almost unknown as a work of his throughout the first half of the century. In England its status as the outstanding exposition of the principles of 1688 derived more from the enormous esteem in which the *Essay* was held than from any close reading of the book itself. That the greatest of modern European philosophers should have written a work in defence of the revolution was a sufficient recommendation. It was felt to contain principles of the most indubitable and parochial political orthodoxy and its intellectual quality was guaranteed by the identity of its author. It seemed above all to be an unexacting exposition of those features of the English way of conducting politics which made it so clearly superior to that of any other community. It was this slackly ideological reading of the book which represented the characteristic English understanding of it for most of the eighteenth century. Indeed it persisted with considerable tenacity even after a time at which the implications of the book for practical politics had become violently contested.* At this point what was contested was normally not its theoretical truth but its substantive relevance.

It seems to have retained this tensionless ideological comfort for both radicals and conservatives, for William Molyneux and Walter Moyle, Richard Price, Richard Watson, and James Burgh as much as for the more conventional John Cary and Simon Clement, Chesterfield and Blackstone, Sir John Hawkins and Thomas Elrington.[16] It was a work much recommended to the young and seldom read with any care by the adult.

There are very simply literary reasons for this career, a number of plain facts about the character of the book which although obscured in recent years by the progress of the history of political science make the vagaries of public interest in it and of its reputation easy to explain. It was a work which expounded a single argument and which expounded it in a dogged and less than elegant manner. Locke's intellectual tactics in this as in most of his other works are perhaps best described in the jargon of a very different activity, as a sort of saturation bombing. They owe more than he himself would have cared to admit to the scholastic procedures of the educational institution in which he spent his early maturity, procedures which he afterwards rejected with such scorn. In most of his works these tendencies were to some degree checked by the constructive intellectual urge to expound his own notions in an unambiguous fashion. But in the *Two Treatises* he was in fact released from the need to do this. The intention of the book was twofold, to destroy the current Anglican theory of politics so completely that it

---

* At times the implications of this conception of theoretical truth were reduced to an inscrutable minimum. Cf. Sir John Hawkins, *The Life of Samuel Johnson, LL.D.* (London 1787), p. 503, 'Nor has any of those who deny the right of a mother-country to tax its colonies, attempted to prove an exemption, by any other arguments than are to be found in Mr. Locke's Essay on Government, a discourse of general import, and which applies to no existing constitution on earth.'

ceased to exercise any influence upon the wills of his political audience, and to persuade these latter to take the political initiative and resist the crown. For emotional and conceptual reasons the first was a very difficult assignment, but the alarm generated by anti-popery made the second a matter of no difficulty whatsoever once theoretical inhibitions of patriarchal passive obedience had been shattered. Hence the almost perfunctory fashion in which Locke treats the question of the justification of specific revolutionary action and the endless length at which Filmer's ideas are savaged from one end of the book to the other. What the Tory gentry in the full tide of their xenophobia needed was not to be persuaded that this if ever was the time to resist the monarch, but rather to be persuaded that it could ever under any circumstances be legitimate for them to resist the monarch. What they needed was to be persuaded that their existing political inclinations were legitimate, to be told the reasons why what they wanted to do but feared that they should not do was the *right* thing to do.

It was this very specific role, the justification of political resistance by the ruling class to the logically and psychologically linked threat of idolatry and arbitrary power, which created the vulgar meaning of the book. Whether their taste was for conservative or for radical action, provided it was within the currently permitted dimensions of the English political system men could devise a painless historical and political sanction for their political intentions. It was at most a symbol for an entire tradition in the conduct of politics, an ambiguous tradition as all such traditions are, and of those who did read the book most read it as men read the Declaration of Independence today, as an affirmation of faith in the viability of the tradition, not as an exercise in the critical assessment of contemporary political achievement. It remained in all the pejorative overtones of the phrase a theoretical work, pre-eminently a work which one would recommend to one's nephew to read at university as Chatham[17] did, or to one's pupil as Richard Watson did.[18]

The circumstances in which it was likely to be read carefully were restricted. Philosophers and academic writers on political theory, worried reactionary clerics or political revolutionaries, might have reason to take it seriously, and at different times members of all these categories did do so. But for the most part it was no more than a name in a litany, even if intellectually the most distinguished name. For those of radical proclivities the litany would contain many names, Sydney, Milton, and Somers, later Hoadly, Trenchard and Gordon, and it would portray the events of 1688 as a less lurid re-enactment of 1649. For those of a more conservative disposition it would probably refer to fewer names, frequently only to Locke and the immortal Hooker, and 1688 would appear as a re-enactment of 1558, not of 1649. In neither case would the ritual incantation exert any more discernible operational impact on their political conduct than would, say, that of Abraham Lincoln in the politics of contemporary America. It was not that Locke meant nothing to those who favoured the different litanies; merely that there is no

64

reason to suppose that anything Locke ever wrote caused the least deflection of their political behaviour from the paths it would otherwise have followed. The use of his name was more a feature of their affective life than a guarantee of any energetic conceptual exploration. It belonged to the rhetoric not to the analysis of politics. It may seem surprising that the name and the book it stood for should have exerted such a persistent and effortless appeal, but societies frequently exhibit over long periods of time a level of incoherence in their ideology which outrages the *a priori* certainties of many sociologists. It was only a recurrence of the circumstances for which the work had first been written, the need for justifying revolution in the future in conditions of extreme danger instead of the flaccid rationalisation of a past *coup d'état*, which brought the two interpretations into dramatic confrontation.

Yet the dispute for the soul of Locke which split the airy Whig consensus over the last thirty-five years of the eighteenth century did not exhaust the range of critical responses which the book evoked. There are two separate traditions of its rejection which go back to the early years of the century, a self-consciously philosophical, and a more uninhibitedly conservative one. The philosophical can be traced through the writings of Shaftesbury and Bolingbroke, Hume, Paley and Bentham to its incarceration in the flatter platitudes of nineteenth-century political science.[19] The more conservative, which remained throughout the century the dominant teaching of the Anglican church and by far the most widely believed theory of political obligation in the population at large, was first outlined at length as an explicit attack on Locke's political thought by the non-juror Charles Leslie in 1703.[20] It can be traced in this form by explicit acknowledgement through the writings of George Horne, Bishop of Norwich, and William Jones, Jonathan Boucher and John Whitaker of Manchester.[21] But in a slightly less full-blooded but equally conservative persuasion it represented throughout the eighteenth century the official Anglican theory of 1688 as embodied in the writings of William Sherlock and Offspring Blackall, Bishop Berkeley, Samuel Johnson and Dean Tucker.[22] As they stand these categories are somewhat misleading — Tucker for instance and even Berkeley give lengthy philosophical reasons for their dissent, and Hume, among the unambiguously philosophical critics, is clearly motivated by a conservative political intention. The conceptual core of their criticisms of Locke is for the most part simply a rejection of the historical plausibility and analytic relevance of the notion of the state of nature. The great bulk of this criticism is totally irrelevant to anything Locke said but since it shares this irrelevance with much contemporary academic comment on the text this is hardly surprising. What is interesting about the various objections is not their more or less sophisticated presentation of a limited number of arguments but the structures of feeling within which the unacceptable features of the Lockean doctrine are located. In the purely academic tradition of discussing political obligation, the work is seldom even noticed in the first half of the century in

Britain, and only once, in an annotated Latin edition of 1724 by a Scottish professor called Carmichael of Pufendorf's standard text, the *De Officio Hominis et Civis*, was the Lockean doctrine adopted in its entirety and the *Two Treatises* recognised as the relevant academic authority.[23] Elsewhere, as in Hutcheson, a similar doctrine is adopted directly from Locke's continental sources or as with Hume, Paley or Bentham the theories appear only for perfunctory dismissal.[24] It was only in the second half of the century when Locke's vast philosophical eminence conferred an intellectual stature on the work despite its previous low reputation, and when its practical implications became so hotly contested, that there was any great pressure to treat it with full intellectual seriousness. With the possible exception of Hume's initial attack in the *Treatise of Human Nature*,[25] the only politically disinterested philosophical attack on Locke's political doctrines before the 1760s was that of his pupil and friend the Third Earl of Shaftesbury, and Shaftesbury's careless and ill-conceived rejection was directed more by his violent hostility towards Locke's epistemological rejection of ethical naturalism than by any understanding of the meaning of the *Two Treatises*.[26] Except for their shared and not very relevant conviction that the state of nature was empirically a dubious notion and a certain dim sense that it might have subversive implications, there is little of interest in the self-consciously philosophical critiques.

It is with the more uninhibited attacks of the Tory divines from Leslie to Boucher, Whitaker and the author of the *Divine Institutes*, that more interesting responses can be found. There were many facets to their rejection of Locke and there were shifts of emphasis over the century — scriptural history for instance tended to play a diminishing role in the argument — but the main structure of their ideas remained stable. Since it represents in many ways a less hysterical and better-judged response to the political theory of the Enlightenment than the lurid and much praised bludgeonings of De Maistre, it is worth a brief and sympathetic treatment. In the hands of its first protagonist, the non-juror Charles Leslie, the criticism achieved its most invigorating and perhaps its most thorough exposition. The destructive criticisms levelled against the book may have owed a heavy debt to Filmer; but in Leslie's writings the patriarchalist hypothesis had found, as even Hoadly grudgingly admitted, its ablest exponent to that date.[27] The attacks on the historical plausibility of the contract theory, while not for the most part criticisms of the precise theory which Locke had enunciated, undoubtedly devastated the entire conventional Whig political theory of the succeeding century. And the image of the social order which they advanced to refute Locke was undoubtedly the image held as an item of religious faith and moral belief by the majority of their contemporaries. For them the texture of the social world which confronted men was at all points homogeneous. From the womb to the grave men were at every moment powerless. The vast articulated order of social authority protected them throughout

66

their lives, taught them all their duties and repressed all their anarchic impulses. It confronted them at every point as a visible embodiment of the providence of God. Its ethical legitimacy was no more defeasible by the will of an individual than was the law of gravity. That this was a matter of literal truth, not of metaphor, in Leslie's eyes can be seen from a very surprising claim which he makes in an attack on Hoadly.

The Sum of the Matter betwixt Mr. *Hoadly* and Me is this, I think it most Natural that *Authority* shou'd *Descend*, that is, be *Derived* from a *Superiour* to an *Inferiour*, from *God* to *Fathers* and *Kings*, and from *Kings* and *Fathers* to *Sons* and *Servants*: But Mr. *Hoadly* wou'd have it *Ascend*, from *Sons* to *Fathers*, and from *Subjects* to *Sovereigns*; Nay to *God* Himself, whose *Kingship* the men of the *Rights* say, is *Derived* to *Him* from the *People*! And the *Argument* does Naturally Carry it all that Way. For if *Authority* does *Ascend*, it must *Ascend* to the *Height*.[28]

For men to claim credit for the creation of the miraculous edifice of eighteenth-century English society was an act of almost unbelievable presumption. If men could confront the work of God in this way and blandly appropriate responsibility for it, there was no knowing where their pride would end — why stop at society? Why not claim the further embodiment of God's handiwork? Why not claim, as indeed parts of the Lockean epistemology almost seemed to, in this paranoid vision, to have created God, or at least to have conferred on him by their recognition the attributes which made him worshipful? The whole way of thought logically implied blasphemy. The order of nature was ruptured; the great chain of being was torn apart. It was not an accident that the most insipid eighteenth-century attack on Locke's theory of government came in the writings of the flattest of eighteenth-century optimists, in a work in which Soame Jenyns sets out a peculiarly ill-considered exposition of this well-worn cosmic image.[29] He recorded the vision with still greater metaphorical assurance elsewhere.

The Universe resembles a large and well-regulated Family, in which all the officers and servants, and even the domestic animals, are subservient to each other in a proper subordination; each enjoys the privileges and perquisites peculiar to his place, and at the same time contributes by that just subordination, to the magnificence and happiness of the whole.[30]

Such a level of blandness was altogether beyond Leslie — he felt no need to rely on such tepid metaphysical certainties. The strained horror which he felt at the Lockean image of a social order whose continuing legitimacy was maintained only by the individual assents of its members is shown in the wild charge of blasphemy. But his response goes beyond this deep emotional revulsion. His criticisms both personal and intellectual are exceedingly enlightening. Even though he felt the Lockean argument to be almost blasphemous, he still could not quite believe that Locke meant it seriously. With graphic scorn he sketched a picture of how a household would be run, if the Lockean notions were to be applied to it. There was no need to discuss the matter further — the picture was emotionally inconceivable.[31] All the seventeenth-century notions of family authority were quite incompatible with it. And as for the broader social implications — what if the common people were suddenly to cease consenting — the entire civilised world would crumble into ruins.[32] And how, in any case, could it be truthfully said that consent was manifested in the existing political order? 'Would they send Men about to poll the whole nation?' he sneered, with finality.[33] Leslie's successors in this line of reasoning were on the whole men of less intellectual vigour, though not of less prolixity. But as the social threats envisaged in Leslie's most nightmarish imaginings became actual in America, in France, even in England itself, the reasoning acquired fresh emotional force and by the end of the eighteenth century Locke had become again in some men's eyes, not a slightly misguided philosopher but a social incendiary.

There were two very different contexts in the eighteenth century in which this insurrectionary threat was given social immediacy and which showed very clearly that the transposition of Locke's doctrine into a very different structure of society did indeed have subversive implications. The first of these was the relationship between England and its subject territories. The second was the development of an English working-class political movement. The response to both showed that the majority of English writers, however glibly they might cite Locke's authority, accepted his doctrine only in a very parochial fashion, as at best the intellectual exposition of the theodicy of 1688. The Irish situation is in many ways the most interesting, for here Locke's work was used and acknowledged publicly by a friend, William Molyneux, in a political controversy about the rights of the Irish parliament, in which the two had previously co-operated intensively over a period of several years.[34] Molyneux used the book and named Locke as its author at a time when Locke refused to acknowledge it even in private, and without asking his permission.[35] The reception of Molyneux's book in England was unenthusiastic. The House of Commons ordered the book to be investigated on suspicion of treason, and the investigation was still in progress at the time when Molyneux arrived to stay with Locke for the first time in his life.[36] A critic pointed out graphically that Molyneux's arguments, if taken seriously, were not a justification for the legislative independence of the Irish parliament, constituted as this was exclusively of Protestant English gentry, but rather a charter for rebellion on the part of the Catholic Irish peasantry.[37] Since the threat of precisely such a rebellion was an ever-present anxiety of the English ascendancy, Molyneux's work enjoyed a queasy reception even among those on whose behalf it had been written.[38] What Locke thought of its use of his ideas we do not know; but he can hardly have felt much enthusiasm. The policies towards Ireland which he had favoured on the Board of Trade were altogether more conciliatory and pragmatic. After the ferocious reception of Molyneux's book, his friendship for the Irishman did not lessen discernibly,[39] but he seems to have felt neither capacity nor inclination to set out any theoretical clarification of the issues at stake. The reputation of Molyneux's work survived to be taken up with each burst of

Irish national sentiment throughout the century, by Swift and Charles Lucas, by Grattan and Pollock, even eventually by Wolfe Tone.[40] But the precise application of Locke's political doctrine as such to the colonial relationship remained unexamined for the most part until the 1760s, and no particular incongruity was perceived between the idea of the legislative sovereignty of the English parliament and the conventional Whig theory of politics. The opponents of Molyneux in 1698 indeed based their argument that emigration removed the right of direct representation on the plain fact of the dependency of the American colonies upon the English parliament.[41] It simply did not occur to them that this interpretation of the constitution could be challenged in the case of America.

In 1794 Thomas Hardy, a London artisan and leader of the London Corresponding Society, the first large working-class English political organisation, was prosecuted along with several other leading radicals for high treason. The charge was based upon two allegations; the first, that the society had plotted military insurrection, and the second, that it had planned to cow parliament by nationwide petitioning into granting a wide measure of parliamentary reform.[42] The first was impossible to bring home against Hardy, and most of the evidence was probably generated exclusively by *agents-provocateurs* of the government. But the second was unquestionably true and the defence plea turned upon the issue of whether private citizens had the right to attempt to coerce parliament in this way. It turned in fact upon the meaning of the idea of representation in the British constitution, on whether the ordinary citizen had a political personality and a right as an individual to make his views felt in the conduct of politics, or whether the political rights of the populace at large were exhaustively comprised in the simple act of voting on the part of those few who were fortunate enough actually to possess the suffrage. The leading counsel for the defence, Thomas Erskine, was a lawyer of considerable skill, and the tactics he pursued were crushingly successful. The Duke of Richmond, by this date a suitably conservative peer,[43] was hauled into court to acknowledge the authorship of the bill for parliamentary reform which he had been so injudicious as to advocate in 1780 and which the society had been formed to implement in the 1790s. The past support for parliamentary reform of the prime minister himself was cited by the defence. Time after time Erskine hammered away at the same point. Mr Burke could use the language of natural rights to advocate parliamentary reform; the Duke of Richmond could use it; Mr Pitt could use it, without anyone querying their impeccable constitutionality. But if the ordinary citizen, the London artisan, were to use it, it was high treason. What possible legal justification, he demanded, could there be for such an interpretation? All that the London Corresponding Society had done was to demand parliamentary reform, and for such a demand there was unimpeachable authority. 'One of the greatest men that this country ever saw,' he said, 'considered universal representation to be such an inherent part of the constitution that the King himself might grant it by his prerogative even without the Lords and Commons.' This 'maxim . . . stands upon the authority of Mr. Locke, the man, next to Sir Isaac Newton of the greatest strength of understanding which England perhaps ever had; high too in the favour of King William, and enjoying one of the most exalted offices in the state'.[44] The authority of Locke thus stood between the first leader of an English working-class political movement and the gallows on which William Pitt and his ministers were attempting to hang him. It was not perhaps a role which Locke would have relished. And when yet more radical agitators like Thomas Spence invoked Locke's theories of property to justify the end of the existing property structure, the role might have seemed still less appealing.[45] But it was not until Thomas Hodgskin set out to assert the immediacy of Locke's natural right to property against the abstract legislative scheme of the Benthamites[46] and until Karl Marx fused these doctrines with the dialectic of Hegel that the fullest potential threat of Locke's work became apparent. In this form it is a threat which we have yet to meet today.

Apart from an isolated copy to be found in the library of the planter Ralph Wormeley in Virginia in 1701,[47] we do not even know that copies of the *Two Treatises* reached the American colonies before 1724.* Even when it does become possible to trace its availability at all widely in the northern colonies, it is in a form which can have done little to encourage the casual reader. The form in which it entered the library of Harvard College between 1723 and 1725,[48] in which as a part of George Berkeley's gift it entered Yale College in 1733,[49] and in which as part of Governor Belcher's gift it entered the library of the college of New Jersey in 1755[50] was in the *Collected Works of Locke*, three clumsy and faintly forbidding folio volumes. The men whom we can show to have read it with any care before 1745 were few. Unlike the *Essay*, no Jonathan Edwards came upon it with the enthusiasm of a miser clutching at fine gold,[51] and no Franklin recorded his early study of it.[52] As in England, the reputation of the political writing derived from the prior reputation of the philosophy. There is no evidence that the *Two*

---

* This does not, of course, mean that *no* other copies did reach the colonies, a most improbable state of affairs. The claims about evidence are based on the results of the following types of investigation: an examination of holdings of Locke works which can be traced back to a definite colonial provenance in some fifty of the major American libraries; an investigation of listings of libraries, published and unpublished, from the colonial period (Mr Edwin Wolf II and Professor Theodore Hornberger were extremely generous in helping me with this); an investigation of booksellers' lists in the colonies up to 1780, both those printed separately and those published in the newspapers (up to the end of 1775); an inspection of the entire file of the colonial press up to the end of 1775, of all magazines published in the colonies before 1776, and of a large proportion of the Evans microcard series. These were supplemented by further manuscript research, wherever secondary authorities suggested that this was likely to be fruitful. The results of this investigation certainly do not *demonstrate* that few Americans read the *Two Treatises* before the revolutionary period but they certainly call into severe question the evidential status of the received opinions about the *scale* of the book's distribution and consequent availability. For an early example of the way in which the reputation and the meaning of the book were absorbed by the colonial élite see the letter of the Quaker, Isaac Norris I, of 1707 from England, noted by Frederick B. Tolles, *Meeting House and Counting House* (paperback ed., New York 1963), pp. 171–2. The 1728 edition of the *Two Treatises* is the earliest of which I could trace copies with a definite colonial provenance.

Treatises figured in the set curriculum of any American college before the revolution,[53] though it was on the recommended list of reading at the College of Philadelphia in 1756, and William Smith was defended by his students against charges of partisanship with the claim that he never advanced any other political principles than what were warranted by their standard authors, Grotius, Pufendorf, Locke and Hutcheson.[54] This list is a decent enough indicator of the type of academic continuum in which the book was seen, a moderately unenticing academic treatise on government, a work whose relevance to political life was likely to be adventitious and occasional, but an acceptable embodiment of the current political pieties.

But this is not perhaps surprising. Its academic standing had never been all that high: it never held the unimpeachable eminence of the works of Grotius or Pufendorf. Its subject matter was too limited and it was, as a student at William and Mary College complained in 1801, so exceptionally diffuse that it almost exhausts the patience of the reader.[55] It was in its potential political utility rather than its didactic value that its enticements lay. And it was direct and focussed conflict between the colonies and England which made this potential actual.

The first occasion that the work appears on the New England political scene was superbly ironic. John Checkley, a dissident and pugnacious proponent of Anglican ideas, had long been a thorn in the flesh of the Massachusetts clergy. When in 1725 he published an inoffensive and apologetic work by the English non-juror Charles Leslie and added to it a somewhat rewritten treatise on the merits of episcopacy, their patience gave way completely.[56] He was dragged into court and accused of publishing an offensive libel and of impugning the legitimacy of the king. What Checkley in fact impugned was the Whig theory of political obligation. In a parallel which gave him evident delight he demonstrated to his own satisfaction that Congregational theories of church polity rested on as absurd a historical basis as what he called republican theories of government. When some of the more incautious phrases about usurpation which he used in this demonstration were produced at his trial as evidence of his seditious attitude, he defended the criticisms of Whig political theory at greater length. Even Mr Locke, he pointed out, had been unable to make sense out of the theory — for he insisted that the vote of each individual was necessary to constitute the populace and this was plainly an impossible requirement.[57] Checkley was convicted of publishing the libel, though the jury made efforts to shelve the responsibility for the decision. But on the charge of insulting the king they made no similar attempt at evasion. In 1724 to impugn Locke's account of political obligation and argue for the tenets of patriarchalism was certainly not enough to constitute sedition and no jury was prepared to tolerate such an equation.[58] Somewhat later in the same year the Rev. John Bulkley, completing his preface to Roger Wolcott's *Poetical Meditations*, put Locke's work to a more approving use.[59] Uniquely among the colonial applications of the doctrine, it claimed a relevance which Locke himself might well have considered and even accepted. The argument which he developed, an attempt to deny the legal or moral necessity of holding lands in New England by title from the Indians, was presumably of local and practical intent. But the discussion which draws at great length from Locke's chapter on property is remarkable for its intellectual poise. It refuses determinedly to transfer categories elaborated for a developed legal system to the more irregular social practice of the Indians. The subsistence pattern of the Indians was not in itself depreciated but, in an application which Locke would have approved, the lack of possible motive for the Indians to appropriate land and to labour upon it in the pre-monetary economy was used to destroy the idea that they could have appropriated any great area.[60] The traditional natural-law basis of property right, the right of occupation, was more remarkable when contrasted with the claims of labour for its legal convenience and precision than for its moral force. The Indian type of territorial occupation might well be held to meet the traditional criterion, but in the more morally exigent analysis which Bulkley drew from Locke its moral claim was deeply unimpressive. In what was probably the only sustained application of Locke's theory of property to American circumstances, the moral dignity of labour was deployed to give powerful moral embellishment to the expropriation of the Indians by the laborious and God-fearing people of New England.*

In the years that followed the book was distributed more widely — the first separate edition which is frequently to be found in American libraries is that of 1728. It attained a degree of casual acceptance which made it easy for Jared Eliot to refer to it in his election sermon of 1738 at one point for a single particularly dubious historical argument, without it having any noticeable impact on the doctrine expounded. Eliot's theological views were of course a trifle spineless, and it is not surprising that he should have assumed a rather Anglican assurance about the implications of the book. The doctrine of the sermon was less than incisive, a banal reiteration of the need for legality in just government.[61] A sharper insight into the radical implications of the

---

* There was nothing original in the substance of this claim. It stretches back at least as far as Thomas More. See *Utopia, Complete Works of St. Thomas More*, ed. Edward Surtz, S.J., and J.H. Hexter (New Haven 1965), IV, 136, ll. 14—17: 'nam eam justissimam belli causam ducunt, quum populus quispiam ejus soli quo ipse non utitur, sed velut inane ac vacuum possidet, aliis tamen qui ex naturae praescripto inde nutriri debeant, usum ac possessionem interdicat', etc. It justified the Puritans in their early confrontations with the Indians (see Alden T. Vaughan, *New England Frontier. Puritans and Indians 1620—1675* (Boston 1965), esp. pp. 104—21 (but cf. Chester E. Eisinger, 'The Puritans' Justification for taking the Land', *Essex Institute Historical Collections*, LXXXIV (1948), 131—43); Wilcomb E. Washburn, 'The Moral and Legal Justifications for Dispossessing the Indians', in *Seventeenth-Century America*, ed. James Morton Smith (Chapel Hill 1959), pp. 15—32), and it remained a major strain of apologetic throughout much of subsequent Indian—white relations, see e.g. William T. Hagan, *American Indians* (Chicago 1961), pp. 39, 43, 68—9, 140. For its significance in the interpretation of American history see esp. Louis Hartz, *The Founding of New Societies* (New York 1964), pp. 94—9. My point here is that this example does not show Locke imposing a new language or a new vision on the bemused Connecticut minister but rather that it records his delighted recognition that 'that Great Man Mr. Lock' was speaking in the most reassuringly familiar of accents.

work came with Elisha Williams's anonymous pamphlet of 1744. In the emotional context of the Great Awakening, Locke's dignified intellectual insistence on autonomy of judgement becomes sharply radical. The theory of government which Eliot had expounded in 1738 was no more secular than that contained in John Wise's work of 1717[62] and it was considerably less radical. The religious structure of New England might have become a trifle etiolated by 1738 in comparison with the great days of Winthrop, but the solid fabric of social order did not seem to have been noticeably impaired. Yet six years later in Williams's dazzling assault all the lineaments of authority were wrenched aside. Locke's notions of toleration were fused with a brilliant presentation of his theory of government, and a doctrine of startling originality appeared. Williams was not in any sense a secluded scholar without understanding of the lives of men in the world. He had seen the Great Awakening tear apart the staid order of New England society and he meant just what he said when he insisted that no act was a religious act without the understanding and choice of the agent, that it was every man's duty to concern himself actively with public affairs, that for the civil power to attempt to exert any influence whatever upon the religious practice of individuals was blasphemy.[63] When the cool epistemological individualism of the scholar's closet was fused with the insistent Puritan demand for emotional autonomy, the two became transmuted into a doctrine which in the radicalism of its immediate and self-conscious social vision could not have been conceived anywhere else in the eighteenth-century world. It is possible that Williams's practical political intentions were little more radical than those of Wise, but the explicit implication of his work was more radical than any society in the early eighteenth century could have accepted.

Locke's writings on toleration played a minor role in the controversies of the Great Awakening as they did later in the controversy over the taxing of the Baptists to maintain the Congregational clergy.[64] They emerged, for instance, in the course of a fracas between President Clap and a New Light student at Yale.[65] But the *Two Treatises* evoked on the whole less interest. By the time that they appear prominently in colonial controversies with England, early in the 1760s, they had become an uncontentious and somewhat unexciting work. The role they played in the ensuing controversies in the instructions which the committee of the Massachusetts General Court, including incidentally Thomas Hutchinson, drew up in June 1762 to send to their new agent Jasper Mauduit[66] and the work of Otis later in that year,[67] through the full run of the revolutionary pamphlets, to the Declaration of Independence itself, was not conceptually a very interesting one. Over the preceding century the colonies had elaborated a tradition of political behaviour in which the actual structure of social authority had become increasingly divorced from the formal structure of political authority, in which the operational control was no longer seriously dependent upon a hierarchical legal order under the crown of England. As Professor Greene has shown with great cogency,[68] the political tradition which the colonists had thus evoked was perceived by them firmly in terms of English precedent and within English legal forms, but it no longer bore any clear relationship to the English view of their constitutional status. The legal order which they saw as existing in America was superbly unLockean, almost wholly the creation of prescription as opposed to formal legality. But by the 1760s there were few in the colonies who did not see it as the legal order. Within the very general prescriptions of the Navigation Laws the lords of trade and the plantations and their local emissaries, the governors, were, on the occasions when they attempted to intrude, closer to being a diplomatic problem than an effective political superior. The cant of the disputes between governors and assemblies were belligerently constitutional in character, but the feeling behind it was seldom brought to any inter-colonial focus. Moderate English conservatives like Hawkins claimed that the only argument that was ever used to justify the American revolution was Locke's doctrine of the illegitimacy of taxation without consent.[69] But this was certainly not the only portion of Locke's work that was brought to bear in the course of the struggle. Not only was the fundamental basis of the rights of Massachusetts in 1762, or the illegality of every fresh substantive attack by the British parliament, proclaimed with the phrases of Locke; but even Hutchinson's summoning of the General Court to meet in Cambridge instead of Boston was subjected to the same assault.[70] The precise application of the book varied enormously, but the form remained identical. There existed a legal order, and the political moves of the English government or the governor of Massachusetts were in breach of this order. Endlessly the work of Locke was summoned to expound the tautology that illegality was not legal. Gradually their notion of the legal order changed and grew more coherent. At one point in this transition, over the specific issue of taxation, Locke's text was of some precise assistance, but for the most part it could only form a passage in a circular argument. And at times the phrasing was less than happy. 'I know,' complained Thomas Hutchinson, after being read a particularly severe lecture by Sam Adams, 'of no conspiracy to destroy you.'[71] It was often difficult to see the relevance of the citations from Locke at such a point. Hutchinson's irritable incomprehension was a little reminiscent of John Cary's answer to Molyneux — whatever Locke had been talking about he had clearly not been talking about the propriety of holding the General Court in Cambridge.[72]

Those who read Locke differently, and on the whole more accurately, were in many cases men with closer ties to England, and with more of a feel for the political or social world of which the intruding governors were the emissaries. Only the redoubtable near auto-didact Boucher, product of the archaic northern counties of England, felt called upon to challenge frontally the whole conceptual system within which the colonists were operating. Many of the other Tories, particularly the Anglican clergy, probably held a very similar basic view of politics to that of Boucher. But it took a man of

considerable intelligence who had both fought his own way up in a hierarchical society and then attempted to transfer the rigid attitudes thus
acquired to a very different society, to feel the emotional need to call in
question the entire structure of American political argument with such
stubborn insistence. That there was little or nothing original in his presentation of the High Anglican position he himself acknowledged and is scarcely
the point.[73] What is significant is the practical realism, emotional subservience
or theoretical paralysis which made the other Anglican clergy incapable of all
but the most superficial and tactical of reactionary polemics.

If Boucher was almost the only authentic Tory to take the Lockean argument seriously, there was at least one other man, as near to being a neutral in
the struggle as an American could well be, who took it equally seriously.
Peter Van Schaack, a prominent New York lawyer, had been an enthusiastic
supporter of the earlier stages of the colonial resistance, but by 1776 he had
begun to develop qualms of conscience.[74] Eventually he retired to his country
farm and settled down to read the standard authorities on political theory.
After deep consideration and a peculiarly close perusal of the works of
Locke, he decided that the provocations of the British government were not
in fact adequate to justify revolution, that they had indeed acted with
persistent injustice, but that it was not clear that their motives were in any
sense malicious, or threatening enough to free a subject from his duty of
obedience.[75] Van Schaack did not approach the text of the book with a
mind made up — he continued to feel emotionally close to the colonists
throughout the war and he remained a close friend of several of the revolutionary leaders. The Adamses and Jefferson, Dickinson and Franklin, Otis
and Madison, had come to read the *Two Treatises* with gradually consolidated
political intentions and they had come to it to gather moral support for
these intentions. Van Schaack came to it in conscientious indecision and
what he found in it — to hazard a wild historical conjecture — was probably
closer than any other man in America to the prescriptions which Locke himself saw in it. To most men in America by 1774 the affective force which
attached to the duty to obey social norms, the internalised structure of
social control, had become irrevocably detached from the legal order of the
English polity. The authority which they felt and responded to was an authority operative in their own society. It was not a formal symbol across the
ocean. Only a man with a somewhat abstract sense of social obligation or a
man with a great capacity to infuse emotional seriousness into an oath taken
to a shadowy entity in a distant country could feel the duty of political
obedience with any immediacy. Only such a man could feel any emotional
pressure to stand on his own for conscience' sake against the mass emotional
certitude of his countrymen.

Once the climactic point, the outbreak of revolution, was past, the book
was never again to be such an intellectual cynosure or to display such an
apparent relevance. John Adams's remark that the constitution of Massa-

chusetts embodied the doctrines of Locke and Sydney was a piece of rhetoric rather than an analytical point.[76] The analytical position was better stated by Benjamin Rush in his dismissal of the book's relevance to the formation of the constitution of Pennsylvania. It was a work of pure theory.[77] Even Jefferson, while he recommended it as being perfect as far as it went, promptly observed that if one descended from theory to practice *The Federalist* was an excellent work.[78] For the most part Americans found no need in the ensuing years to ascend to a level more theoretical than that of *The Federalist*, and by the time that they did need to do so Locke's work had become a historical curiosity. A man as sophisticated as Francis Lieber could mourn that political theory had ended with Locke,[79] and George Fitzhugh could still at times identify the philosophy of *laissez-faire* individualism which he was engaged in excoriating as the theory of Locke,[80] but the book was never again to be an emotional or conceptual focus in the discussion of the politics of the nation.

Whether the book had ever exercised causal impact upon the way men thought, whether it had ever been more than the most distinguished name that could be appended to men's prior political convictions, whether it gave to the American revolution more than a few specific phrases, remains hard to tell. But some points can now be made clearer. The claim that Locke's book exercised a great influence in America can be put in a stronger and a weaker form. The stronger form is simple — that most educated Americans derived their view of politics directly from it. This is not persuasive. The book was of no great popularity before 1750 and the tradition of political behaviour[81] within which the colonists conceived their relationship with England was already highly articulated by this date in its most general values, though not of course in its specific understanding of the constitutional relationship. It cannot have been Locke's *Two Treatises* which taught them this tradition of behaviour because there is no reason to suppose that many people had read it with care in the colonies by 1750. The weaker form seems more appealing — that the ideas were absorbed by a sort of intellectual osmosis, so that Americans could be of Locke's party without knowing it, rather as men earlier in the century could be Newtonians without having read a word of the *Principia*. The analogy seems tempting but is entirely spurious. The *Principia* achieved an immediate European pre-eminence. It was recognised as being a distinctively new achievement, a watershed in both science and philosophy. The *Two Treatises* never enjoyed such an unchallenged European reputation. It was not even particularly widely known outside the English-speaking world for eighty years after its composition and it became well known then only because of the huge influence of Locke's epistemology. It was never recognised as being peculiarly original, and in those points in which it was considered to be so, it was frequently regarded as being mistaken. Above all it was only one work among a large group of other works which expounded the Whig theory of the revolution, and its prominence within this group is not noticeable until well after the general outlines of the interpretation had become consolidated. The readiness with which many scholars have detected the influence of the *Two Treatises* in England and America is at least in part a product of the fact that they have read so little else of the English political writing contemporary with it.

The intellectual stature of the book's author can hardly have been without some slight influence in making respectable sundry of the doctrines which it contained. But the work's prominence in controversy in America was largely confined to the post-1760 constitutional writings of the highly educated, and if we wish to understand the literary influences upon the rhetoric in which the dispute was conducted at all levels but the most legalistic, and the sentiments to which this rhetoric gave expression, we need to look at works which were a good deal less demanding on the intellect and exhausting to the patience. For the American population at large the revolution may have been about many things, but in very few cases can it possibly have been thought to have been in any sense about the *Two Treatises of Government* of John Locke.[82]

The historicity of the answers

5

Practising history and social science on 'realist' assumptions

§ 1 This paper discusses a number of philosophical issues from the viewpoint of a practising social scientist and seeks to alert other social scientists to the significance of these issues for their conception of what they are attempting to do. Philosophers can thus afford to read the account of, for example, the indeterminacy of translation considerably more briskly than they would normally care to read a piece of philosophical writing. Moreover, 'relativism' and 'realism', as they appear here, are not proper philosophical terms of art. 'Relativism' is a name for the view that the truth is something which we make up (collectively or individually) more or less as we please. It is *ours* to make up. And if more or less, why not completely? 'Realism' names the view that whatever we make up less or more as we please is, it certainly is *not* the truth. This chapter attempts to throw some light on the intuitive appeal of relativism in this context, a context in which its appeal is in some ways surprising. (Nature may be any old way. But how can *we* believe that the same is true of *us*?) It also attempts to throw some light on why any coherent version of 'realism' should be so hard to state in this context.

Do history and the social sciences possess a determinate subject matter? Do they form a cognitive field about which the truth could in principle be known? If so, are there methodological principles which, correctly applied, will guarantee that we come to know some of this truth? If there are not, how can an affirmative answer to the first question be other than a barefaced fraud or an unintended confession of intellectual confusion?

The language we use to characterise our experience reflects many presumptions as to what sorts of things 'humanly speaking' there are to describe.

If these presumptions could all be made clear and if they were all valid we could conclude both that there was a determinate subject matter for the sciences of man (perhaps men as they are, acting as they act, within societies as they are, etc.) and that we knew what that subject matter was. Although we may hope that all these presumptions can be validated, it would be ludicrously optimistic to presume that this happy state of affairs must obtain. On the other hand, we plainly cannot presume that literally none of these presumptions are justifiable: to presume this would deprive us of the conceptual basis of personal identity and the instruments of rational thought. We would be unable to understand anything which we might attempt to do.

What *a priori* grounds are there for presuming the existence of a determinate subject matter for history and the social sciences? How far are these grounds in fact valid?

§2 In spite of all temptations, always and everywhere, people behave exactly as they do and not otherwise. This, at least, is not a miracle. It is indeed, we may initially presume, nothing more exciting than a tautology. Not only is it the case that this striking 'regularity' obtains; better still, we can *know* that it is true that it obtains. And, even better, we can *know* that any theory of knowledge on which this 'regularity', and our knowledge of it, comes out as a standing miracle is shown to be inadequate by this result. But from this superficially promising beginning epistemologically it is downhill all the way.

§3 Can we *know* why we ourselves or anyone else at all did, are doing, or will do anything? (In our own case, we are certainly in a different boat: you are by no means me. But is it necessarily a less leaky craft?) Can we even know *what* we ourselves or anyone else did, are doing, or will do?

Reports differ from descriptions in that competent observers in the face of identical stimuli will report them (roughly) identically, or else will misreport them, while no such starkness of choice between approved format and dereliction of duty obtains in the case of descriptions.[1] Quine's thesis of the indeterminacy of translation* implies that even reports, the stuff of knowledge, cannot provide determinate specifications of psychological states or of intended meanings and therefore that the latter are not *objects* of knowledge. People behave exactly as they behave and not otherwise. But is it true for example that people always *act* exactly as they act and not otherwise? Is there a 'fact of the matter' as to how they act? The answer to this question presumably depends upon the type of account given of what it is for something to be a 'fact of the matter'.

§4 People behave exactly as they do and not otherwise. Part of the explanation of why they behave exactly as they do is *often* that thus, in some respects at least, is how they had it in mind to behave. Human beings (most

* See § 15 below.

of them) can and do act upon the world. They also describe in a language both this world on which they hope to act and the acts which they hope to perform. Hence the suspicion that the linguistic capacities of human beings stand in some constitutive relation to their capacity for agency. (It is evident enough too, from an evolutionary viewpoint, that linguistic capacities form a necessary condition for much of the present human behavioural repertoire. Among non-human animals matters are somewhat different. To know as a matter of fact just how different would be to know vastly more than we at present know about both human and non-human animals. To know in principle how to determine precisely how different would already be to have solved an impressive array of fundamental philosophical problems.)

Always and everywhere people act exactly as they do and not otherwise. This too at first sight appears nothing more exciting (or hazardous) than a tautology. But how should we picture the relation between this impressive 'regularity' in the precision of their action and the equally impressive 'regularity' in the precision of their behaviour? It is fairly widely agreed by philosophers of action that one could be perfectly informed on how someone is behaving at a particular time without knowing what he *must* be doing (since any specification of behaviour is compatible with the performance of many different actions). It is perhaps equally widely agreed that one could be correctly informed of what someone is doing on some occasion and yet be unable to determine exactly how he must be behaving on that occasion (since any action can be executed by a variety of items of behaviour). To accept that such an epistemological gap exists will appear to some an ignoble capitulation to Cartesian dualism. But whether it is ignoble to capitulate to dualism or absurd not to recognise its validity or possible, in lieu of either option, to adopt a version of anomalous monism[2] the recognition of this epistemological gap cannot without much further argument be judged to imply the falsity of 'realism'. The sentences of history or tenseless human science are true or false in so far as they mention truly or falsely the exact actions which people perform as they do perform them and not otherwise or, similarly, in so far as they mention truly or falsely the exact behaviour which people exhibit as they do exhibit it and not otherwise. (To be true in either case, they must assert nothing which is false and deny nothing which is true. They need not assert everything which is true or deny everything which is false.) The true sentences of the history or tenseless human science of human behaviour will differ widely from the true sentences of the history or tenseless human science of human action. But the truth of the true sentences of the one must *ex hypothesi* be compatible with the true sentences of the other.

§5 Where does this leave the indeterminacy argument? It all depends what 'matter' you take the facts of seriously. If we took the 'facts of the matter' of behaviour less seriously, why could we not read the Quinean indeterminacy argument as proof of the ambiguity of behaviour? (If you cannot specify action from behaviour, so much the worse for behaviour knowledge as a *general* cognitive vantage point.)

Always and everywhere people mean exactly what they do mean and not something else. Now at last we have an *evident* falsehood. It is the vagueness of meanings and the difficulty of assigning to them a clear theoretical status which really menaces the coherence of our *a priori* presumptions. Meanings infect intentions and thus actions with their distinctive haziness. Does anyone *ever* know exactly what he means? (Exactly what I mean may be a pretty inexact affair, may be much vaguer than I hope.)[3] Do I *know* even what my present arguments mean? Do I even know exactly what I am saying? (My ears may be deceiving me. My tongue may slip. My grasp of my own language as spoken by other speakers may be systematically or randomly in error. If I did know exactly what I *was* saying, perhaps even I would scarcely have the folly to maintain it.) All these hazards seem real possibilities. If I expressed what I mean as it would be expressed by a perfect speaker of a perfect language, even *I* might be able to see that it is false. Can one ever *mean* (fully intend to assert, with a full grasp of the implications of asserting it) a proposition which is in itself false?

I assert A, not-A, and the law of non-contradiction. I intend to assert what I assert. Could I sincerely intend to assert, to hold to be true, something so *evidently* false? Either my intention must be radically incoherent or my understanding of the sentences must be spectacularly confused. Most of our brushes with the law of non-contradiction are more spaced out: the product of amnesia, inattention, congenital intellectual indolence, sheer feebleness of mind. We affirm A, forgetting a past commitment to its negation to which (if reminded of it) we would still feel deeply committed. We do not recognise quite what it is that we are saying and quite how it relates to our other assertoric inclinations. It is a permanent condition of the thought of most men that they do not and cannot think in the full light of all their best reasons. There is a full cognitive equivalent to akrasia[4] and it is at the heart of the experience of thinking. Like acting, reasoning and talking involve intentions. I can fully intend to assert a proposition which is in itself false; but only by dint of not fully understanding what I am asserting. But does not meaning X imply knowing that X and not something else is what I wish, as of now, to assert?

The intentionality of action and assertion here clashes with the meaning of speech. You may mean A (namely intend to assert A). But what you have said means (namely implies the assertibility of) not-A. The question is whether intentions or meanings are to be master. And yet intentions and meanings depend conceptually upon one another.

§6 If there is such a field of potential knowledge as historical, political, social etc. truth, what does it consist in? It is unnecessary to draw the boundary of such a field to establish its reality. At its core we find, in a somewhat shop-soiled but still serviceable phrase, 'real living men', past, present and future, or, more broadly, human acts taken under intentional descriptions,* past, present and future, and the causes and consequences of such acts. Human agents *are* the subject matter of human history and the constituents of human society. We need to augment the ranks of human agents with other entities, if we are to provide a full specification for the field of history or social science. But human agents must remain at the centre of this field and the conditions for valid knowledge of their situation and performance are the central question for the philosophy of history or social science. In practice the conditions for acquiring knowledge about the past are very different from those for acquiring knowledge about the future; and these differences suggest the prospects for acquiring much very interesting knowledge about the human future to be poor. How can we sanely expect to be able to characterise adequately the circumstances in which men at all far in the future will have to act? Most human scientists who have supposed knowledge about the future obtainable in principle have been more or less self-consciously behavioural in approach, seeking to render human performance in an idiom in which replicability and inter-observer reliability are at a premium, in which performance can be reported and not merely described.[5] Historians, by contrast, have felt little temptation to desert the categories of action, seeing few opportunities for systematising their inquiries in purely behavioural categories. Even the stalwart advocates of a covering-law account of historical explanation have felt no obligation to eschew a data language of highly interpreted human conduct, though their opponents have sometimes used the omnipresence of such language in historical writing and the types of conceptual connection which historians use in explicating the conduct of their subjects to argue for a radical discontinuity between history and generalising social sciences.[6] More recently there have been strong defences, notably by Charles Taylor and Alasdair MacIntyre, of the central role of hermeneutic considerations throughout the human sciences.[7]

§7 Perhaps there could be a non-human science of man of a strictly behavioural (matter and motion) kind. It would involve entry into an anti-hermeneutic circle within which intentional categories were never admitted. There do not appear to be clear principles of translation from action to behaviour categories or from behaviour to action categories. There are strong

---

* Why exactly? Is it simply a moral injunction: 'That's a man and you (morally) ought to conceive him in conceptually appropriate (human) terms'? ('Hath not a Jew . . . ' Even the Nuer think. Even the British feel. Even behaviourist psychologists require and are entitled to interpretation. Etc.) Or is it a pragmatic claim: 'That's a man and if you don't recognise it as such, you'll be making a grave mistake'? In pragmatic terms the proof of the scale of mistake should be simply the gain or loss in predictive power. There seem sound pragmatic reasons for such insistence. But there are also sound moral reasons for it. The possibility of doing the data an injustice is hardly a major epistemological hazard in most of the sciences of nature. But in the human sciences it is perhaps always the most pressing aspect of the scientist's situation.

reasons for doubting the capacity of men even to *attempt* to construct such an anti-hermeneutic science (despite their amply proven capacity to believe that they are making such an attempt), and even stronger reasons for doubting their chances of succeeding in any such attempt. There are also reasons for viewing the making of any such attempt with strong moral resentment. All efforts thus far to constitute human sciences of behaviour plainly rest on the covert use of action categories. There is evident economy to such use. Furthermore, since our interest in the results of the human sciences is a human interest, it seems unlikely that the results of such an anti-hermeneutic science would remain unincorporated into human practice. If it were to be so incorporated, all the difficulties of the relation between behaviour and action categories would presumably resurface. In practice there seems little danger that humans will create or encounter such a superhuman 'human science knowledge machine'. But it appears to be an empirical question whether such a machine is or is not naturally *possible*. And it is difficult to deny at least the logical possibility that a learning machine which adopted behavioural categories of a degree of purity which no human being would be at all likely to opt for and which kept rigidly within such categories (and which kept its learning firmly to itself) could become highly prescient of the human (behavioural) future. There may be in principle no mechanical way of recording precisely what is humanly going on. But there are mechanical ways of recording non-humanly pretty precisely some of what is going on — light, heat, sound etc. — and what can or cannot be predicted on the basis of such a mechanical procedure seems as hard to foreclose on in principle as the limits of what will be successfully predicted on its basis might be easy to predict in practice.

Perhaps a *discreet* anti-hermeneutic human science could in principle even know the entire human behavioural future. But the tragedy of anti-hermeneutic human science thus far is that it has been conceived in indiscretion and nourished in some little flagrancy. And even a *true* science of human behaviour could not tell human action where it gets off. So far from being able in general simply to replace our own characterisations of our actions, an anti-hermeneutic human science can retain its epistemological respectability only by the consistent refusal to say anything about what we are *doing* and why we are doing it.

§8 Human beings speak, think, feel and act; and they do so within a frame of natural causality. Language, a social practice, enjoys a dominant role in speaking, thinking and acting, a somewhat more subservient role in feeling, and (ideally) a wholly subservient role in the analysis of natural causality. Approaches to the analysis of natural causality which prove to be sound will not necessarily transfer felicitously to a subject matter in which the status of language shifts from the instrumental to the constitutive. Keeping in mind the difficulties which these disparities may pose, we may sketch a broader specification of the field of potential knowledge of human agents. This might consist of (1) a set of texts; (2) a set of speech acts; (3) a set of actions; (4) institutional persistence and change; (5) material factors which can be seen to have some direct reflection in human consciousness;* (6) material factors which cannot be seen to have any direct reflection in human consciousness but which exert some causal weight on categories 1 to 5. (This last category might turn out to be coextensive with the totality of facts about nature. It is natural to present all of these categories in past or present terms; but category 6 at least could certainly be rephrased in principle to make whatever truth claims are regarded as epistemologically or ontologically respectable about the future.)

There are matters omitted from this list which might pose severe problems. What, for example, of states of consciousness which are not ever reflected in any speech act or action or which never will be so reflected? (We all have lots of beliefs which we never have asserted and which we never will.)[8] History, on any realist account, must be epistemologically confined to what can be *known* — to what took place in (in the broadest of terms) a public domain. In practice, of course, it is more restricted still — confined indeed to what has *remained* in a public domain, what has left a record. But it seems natural, again, to suppose that in this respect the future is exactly like the past except that in the case of the future we are better placed in the short run to choose what sorts of potential phenomena will achieve the status of (however evanescent) record.

§9 There is one philosophical tradition which does focus on the centrality of language in human experience, the rather disparate tradition now customarily referred to as hermeneutic, the tradition of Dilthey and Gadamer in Germany and in part, though only in part, that of Max Weber.[9] Hermeneutics in origin was an inquiry into interpretative criteria for sacred texts for which truth-guaranteeing criteria of interpretation *ex hypothesi must* exist. But, God now being dead, we have no reason for supposing that truth-guaranteeing interpretative procedures for learning how to understand anything (least of all one another) are in fact naturally available. Hermeneutics is an admirable name for the good intention of attempting to understand one another. But as a name for an epistemology and its implied set of methodological precepts, it is perhaps merely a verbal placebo. If we wish to under-

---

* As is apparent from the epigraph, the present account is in some ways deeply inimical to the materialist theory of history. Much of what is claimed, politically and historically, by exponents of various versions of this theory is certainly true, and its heuristic merits are unmistakable. But if it is presented, as for example by Althusser and some of his followers, as a rigidly anti-hermeneutic theory, the empirical truth of many of its contentions could not serve to vindicate its truth. The key question is what would constitute *showing* that it was true. The position adopted here is that no theory of human social action can be shown to be true in a rigidly anti-hermeneutic fashion. Materialist theories of history of an anti-hermeneutic bent might indeed be right in what they maintained; but they must be so for the wrong reasons. They must be necessarily theoretically false, even if they were contingently empirically true.

stand other people and propose to claim that we have in fact done so, it is both imprudent and rude not to attend to what they say. But whatever heuristic procedures we adopt, we have no reason to believe that they can guarantee our success.

Language is the star of a hermeneutic conception of the human sciences. Human action and human experience aspire to the perspicuousness of human speech. A full explanation of an action might be represented as an extended text, representing the pattern of attention of the agent, the set of beliefs conceived as relevant by the agent, a set of identified preferences and capabilities and the act as a rational outcome of all these. If what we wanted to explain was why an agent had performed a particular act and not some radically different act (why Caesar crossed the Rubicon rather than settling down to a life of writing bawdy poems), such a text would not be an economical statement of the explanation for which we were seeking, though it is not easy to see how it could fail to contain this explanation. And if we wanted to fit the precise action which was performed firmly and precisely into natural causality, to explain why exactly Caesar did cross the Rubicon exactly there and exactly then and not somewhere else or some other time or never, it is hard to see how we could do so, in the light of the anomaly of the mental, without conceptual access to the Telex record of such a stream of consciousness. Such a text might be improved (or impaired) by the sensitive or sardonic commentary of bystanders or psychiatric experts. If the act displayed imperfect rationality even after sustained co-operative effort and the vigorous exercise of the agent's memory, the gap between rational performance and actual performance might be explicable causally in the same way that a linguistic error or a mistake in arithmetic or even a gratuitous stumble in the street might be so explained. If we proceed in reverse, texts may be presented as composite speech acts and features of them explained accordingly.[10] What speaks to us clearly and honestly we truly can know. But is language so perspicuous, compared with nature? Do I really apprehend any other person (or even myself) more clearly and with more assurance than I do sundry features of the physical world?

§10 There are a number of different grounds for doubting the perspicuousness of language. Human mendacity and incompetence, technical problems in the theory of translation, the sparse and somewhat randomly selected records of states of consciousness which ever enter a public domain and the far sparser set of such records which remain at all durably within one. If what persons could have said under perfect interrogation forms the perfect text of human history (at the Last Judgement) what we can rationally and justifiably believe that they *did* say is likely to be a nastily mangled palimpsest. It will certainly underdetermine drastically what we have good reason to believe them consequentially to have brought about.

There are also a number of different grounds for doubting the opacity of nature. One of these, self-evidently, is the striking progress in mechanical control engendered by the development of natural science. Another is the commonsense experience of living within a naturally fairly unsurprising everyday world. Extreme scepticism about the knowability of nature seems strained and silly. And if we can know about nature at all, why not in some measure about men within the same frame of knowledge? We make many predictions about what persons will in practice do (whatever they pretend or the rules say) and a fair number of these predictions are not disappointed. To reverse Alasdair MacIntyre[11] we are all of us unsurprised in our social life for a great deal of the time. There are worse epistemological predicaments than that of the ordinary agent.

§11 Supposing that we accepted for the moment a strongly hermeneutic conception of the conditions for valid understanding of speech acts, texts and individual actions, what implications might this have for a view about the conditions for a valid understanding of (and even for the possibility of explaining) institutional persistence and change? There are two possible ways in which such a conception might require us to extend a hermeneutic approach into the analysis of institutions. The first of these seems a serious restriction but implies in its terms the existence of a quasi-empirical boundary between the hermeneutic and the strictly external domains of understanding. As MacIntyre puts it: 'it is an obvious truism that no institution or practice is what it is, or does what it does, independently of what anyone whatsoever thinks or feels about it. For institutions are always partially, even if to differing degrees, constituted by what certain people think and feel about them.'[12] (One may doubt whether it is either in fact or in principle at all easy to draw the line between those whose thoughts or feelings are accorded the status of (partially) constituting the institution, and the totality of those who stand in any conscious or causally consequential relation whatsoever to the institution. Is the British state constituted by the thoughts and feelings of all its citizens or only by those of some comparatively small proportion of them? (It manifestly is not constituted *solely* by the beliefs and attitudes of its own citizens. Other states, at the very least, play a leading role in constituting it.) Just which thoughts, beliefs and attitudes can indeed be said to *constitute* it, rather than simply to happen to be externally related to it, may depend upon what precise characteristics of it are being inquired into. There are such matters of fact as the current military capability of the British state, its Gross National Product, its population, its membership of international agencies, even perhaps the extent of its legitimacy in the eyes of the electorate of a particular constituency. There is no such thing as the British state *tout court*. One of the severest practical difficulties of the social sciences is the gross vagueness of reference of many of their more important terms.)

The second, more radical, obstacle to keeping hermeneutics out of the assessment of institutional causality is the claim that institutions are sustained or altered by (persist or change as a result of) actions which are contextually, dispositionally and credally rational for their agents (or defectively so, only in naturally explicable ways). We might well hope to uncover by study systemic properties of institutions of which their participants were imperfectly aware. (We often have the same hope at least equally keenly in our practical life.) But once uncovered, such systemic properties affect what it is contextually and credally rational for agents to do. In politics particularly the uncovering of such systemic regularities is frequently a cue for endeavours either to change them or to prevent others from attempting to do so. Even quite rigorously tested causal understanding may thus be more dependably available in principle in relation to the past, since in the past there is at least no direct possibility of the theory contaminating the data. The more important the discovery claimed, the more likely that the theory will (as one might put it) enter into history. Such contamination results from an alteration in the agent's beliefs and hence in what it is (on the basis of these beliefs) rational for him or her to do. It does not imply any likelihood of the actions in question having anything resembling their intended consequence.

The simplest way of resisting this line of thought is to point out that it begs the question which it claims to resolve. The fact that history is made by men acting does not necessarily mean either that its course can be fully explained by stitching together explanatory observations about individual actions (a denial of some forms of methodological individualism) or that no aspects of its course can be validly explained in any other terms. Is there in fact any sound reason for rejecting the view that there are or at least may be some knowable regularities in the persistence and change of institutions considered simply as part of a knowable causal order? It is likely that such regularities will be hard to specify correctly in practice and even harder to assign an appropriate chronological scope. But the idea of weak probabilistic laws, valid for a limited duration, does not seem fatuously optimistic. If we accepted realism for natural science, as does Putnam,[13] on the premise that natural science shows convergent theoretical understanding (because otherwise the efficacy of natural science becomes a standing miracle), we might reasonably seek to extend such a view to the *possibility* of our identifying causal relations within institutions and knowing that we had done so. Few, if any, of the most evanescent 'miracles' have yet occurred in social science; but perhaps some could. The claim that such knowledge is in principle possible does not depend necessarily on its ever having been attained in the past nor on its ever in fact being attained in the future. No one has much experiential occasion yet for being a 'realist' in the human sciences, has 'realism' in this instance thrust upon them. But one might optimistically, if perhaps gratuitously, *choose* to be one.

An initially more manageable line of thought, trading on the success of common sense theory of material objects etc., would investigate the possible dependence of a hermeneutic explanatory scheme for actions on agents' possession of at least some true beliefs about regularities (linguistic, behavioural etc.) in their social as well as natural environments. Much of any agent's consciousness of their social environment does in fact take the form of not very self-conscious but epistemically quite well-founded expectations as to what will or will not occur. I, as a middle class British white citizen, expect not to be assaulted by most of those dressed as policeman whom I see (unless perhaps while taking part in an importunate political demonstration). I have this expectation not because I am particularly credulous about the normative coherence of British society or the effective incorporation of the police force into this supposed coherence, but because I have had good reason over the years to form the expectation that there is very little statistical risk of persons so dressed electing to asault me under most circumstances in this country so far. Such expectations might well not extend, for example, to younger working class black British citizens, or to many other police forces elsewhere or, necessarily, to the police force of this country in ten or twenty years time. But they seem (inductively) little more precarious so far than my belief about the solidity of chairs or tables or the lack of solidity of air. (One can get a nasty shock from attempting to walk through a plate glass door.) It is hard to imagine what living in a society would be like if many such expectations were not entertained by all humans and a fair proportion of them did not fail to deceive.

§12 Let us take as an example an area of social inquiry over which many behavioural scientists have been confident that important regularities can (or might) be identified: the conditions for the occurrence of revolutions. It has been proved extravagantly difficult to state plausible non-tautologous candidates for such regularities; but it has certainly not yet been *shown* that there are no such regularities to be found.[14] One major difficulty in such inquiries is the issue of how to distinguish clearly between candidates for the *explanans* in such explanations and the *explanandum* itself. An explanation of a particular revolution would state sufficient conditions for the occurrence of that revolution broadly as it in fact occurred. But the explanations of all revolutions would not necessarily uncover (and in practice would *not* uncover) a common set of sufficient conditions which could be conceptually distinguished in their entirety from those revolutions whose occurrence they explained. What might be available is a non-trivial list of necessary conditions for a particular sort of revolution. A second difficulty, plainly, is terminological. There is little agreement even on the necessary and sufficient conditions for entitling a set of happenings a revolution. Instead there are the usual plethora of vague typologies generated by social scientists in the face of *questions mal posés*.

Suppose that we define revolution as a drastic transformation of the class structure and productive capabilities of a designated populace, following extensive and violent civil conflict and the destruction of an existing state power, and guaranteed some durability by the constitution of an effective new state power. This definition in practice excludes the French Revolution and is probably only satisfied by political upheavals in the twentieth century (a historical claim). The French Revolution created the main outlines of the modern concept of revolution, though it appears in itself to have had little direct impact upon productive capabilities. It created the role of professional revolutionary and, in addition, at least two broad causal conceptions of what revolutions are and hence of what role individual human intentions play within them — the natural process image of revolution as humanly undirected natural catastrophe, along with the image of revolutions as the outcome of the evil (or benign) machinations of small groups of politically motivated men.[15] The Ancien Regime was over before it knew quite what had hit it; but all subsequent anciens regimes have lived with a nasty suspicion as to what might well come to strike them in their turn. Many of them, a proportion increasing throughout the last sixty years, have also had to live with subjects who saw themselves as professional revolutionaries and aspired to strike the fatal blow. Theories about the incidence of revolution, about the necessary and sufficient conditions for their occurrence, have formed part of the credal rationality of vast numbers of (in some cases clearly consequential) political actions since 1900. It is possible that literally none of the beliefs of any of these agents which directly concerned revolution were in fact true (though this is singularly implausible, for instance, of Lenin's conception of the conditions of regime fragility or effective revolutionary organisation). But it seems very odd to presume that there is nothing for such beliefs to be true of.

It would be fairly easy to produce plausible candidates for the role of necessary condition for revolutions, though their plausibility in the face of past experience would not, of course, guarantee that they were in fact necessary conditions. More interesting would be an attempt to produce a list of factors the presence or absence of which would make revolution very probable or very improbable. Circumstances in which a revolution has become sufficiently likely for them to resemble conditions sufficient for its occurrence will certainly figure extensively in the credal, dispositional and contextual rationality of large numbers of agents. As an example of circumstances which would make a revolution highly improbable we may take a combination of steady gains in real wealth throughout a population and the presence of a state apparatus not effectively disrupted from outside the society in question. Few societies satisfy such a description continuously for long; but it is a safe bet that none which has done so has yet experienced a revolution (as here defined) at a time whilst it was still doing so. For the view that severe disruption of an incumbent state apparatus from outside a society is a necessary condition for revolution we have the authority of Lenin[16] (maker's knowledge?) and what initially appears some inductive support from the twentieth-century historical record: Russia, China, Vietnam, Yugoslavia, Indonesia etc. But any claim that such disruption might truly be a necessary condition encounters several reasonably clear counter-examples: Algeria, Guiné-Bissau, most importantly Cuba.

There are not sufficient instances of revolution even in the twentieth century to press these thoughts much further, though one can, of course, amass a great deal of descriptive material in relation to them. It seems more instructive instead to take a twentieth-century phenomenon which partially overlaps with the experience of revolution in the same period and about which much clearer causal relations have perhaps emerged, not simply in the form of inductively derived regularities accumulated by social scientists. Much of the land area of the world in 1900 consisted of colonies of western European countries. Rather little of it still does so. A few instances of decolonisation took the form of anti-colonial revolutions (Vietnam, Algeria, Guiné-Bissau, Indonesia, less clearly Mozambique and Angola). Most did not, because they did not have to. Why did they not have to? Very crudely, the answer appears to be that all western European colonial powers realised in the aftermath of the Second World War, some appreciably faster and more clearly than others but all in the end, that the costs of fighting anti-colonial political forces in their colonies would outweigh any gain of retaining these countries as formal colonies. Anti-colonial political forces inside colonies have been emboldened progressively by this understanding and professional colonial rulers correspondingly disheartened, in both cases, at least within this context, rationally enough. What has been uncovered with increasing clarity is what can or cannot be brought about by the deployment of a certain range of political resources within a particular structural relationship over a particular time span. To explain this (a regularity of *power*, it might be called), it might be necessary to explain what about the preceding time span or the distribution of political resources or structural relationship prevailing within it, made it possible to bring about and maintain in relative stability a very different balance. But to explain the full set of outcomes, their pace, sequence etc., it would also be necessary to explain why anti-colonial revolutionaries and colonial rulers came to make the judgements which they did about the political vulnerability of these regimes. The judgements themselves would include beliefs, true or false, about power-regularities. One might explain why each believed exactly what they did believe on every occasion and explain situationally and naturally, genetically and biographically (some are cleverer than others), why some learnt faster or more accurately than others. What one could not expect to do — because of the structure of states and political groupings which contest with these — is to provide adequate explanations of the precise pattern of outcomes which were not mediated in many instances through interpretations of the consciousness of agents. MacIntyre's nebulous line between institutionally constitutive and non-constitutive thoughts and feelings of agents relates to the way in which historically consequential chosen interventions in the course of nature are grounded in a variety of more or less elaborated rationalities. Not only do men make their own history; but some men make far more than their fair share of the history of others. It is hard to see how one could in principle make sense of this conclusion within the practice of history or political science without acknowledging the existence both of humanly constituted natural regularities in human environments (impossibilities, improbabilities, high probabilities, even certainties) and of consequential interventions in the course of nature which require characterisation in terms of agent belief, disposition and rationality. Heuristically the only plausible approach to the latter is, broadly, hermeneutic. There are few, if any, natural regularities in human affairs which do hold within a certain chronological or spatial range which might not become superannuated as a result of future beliefs. But one can hardly give a coherent account of the beliefs of an agent without making presumptions about the truth or falsity of any of his beliefs about social reality. Heuristically in the human sciences it is wise to be as vigorously hermeneutic as one can stand being. But credally, either in the human sciences or simply in life, it would be barely sane to discard the view that some beliefs about what is likely, socially and individually, to occur are considerably closer to the truth than others.

§13 Describing is the primitive cognitive act of all sciences. The sciences of nature contain many other components besides descriptive statements. But what makes it possible for them to be sciences *of* nature is their inclusion of true descriptive statements. In the sciences of nature many such statements at particular times show the inter-observer reliability of 'reports'. Some epistemological suspicion in the philosophy of natural science has recently been focussed on the social explanation of this fact. Are 'reports' a synthetic product of social complicity? Their failure in particular to show a corresponding inter-observer reliability over spans of time (unless heavily doctored to do so) raises severe technical difficulties for anyone attracted to the project of giving a realist account of the status of natural science.[17]

The sciences of man differ from the sciences of nature in at least two respects in the part played in them by descriptive statements. The first is in the relative proportions of reports to less formalised descriptive statements. Some social sciences record data largely in the form of mechanical reports, with strikingly jejune intellectual profit (except at a physiological level). Most social sciences sensibly make no attempt to do anything of the kind. The prevalence of descriptive discretion is not in itself epistemologically alarming, though it does weaken the prospects of any very crisply incremental development of the social sciences. In itself it comes no closer to imperilling the reality of human performance than variations in the taste of landscape artists come to altering the physical properties of mountains. To make it epistemologically alarming and not merely methodologically troublesome, it would be necessary for it to extend to the assertion and negation of the same description (identically interpreted) of the same phenomena by two different competent, sincere and attentive observers. Philosophers of the human sciences often write as though such encounters are frequent affairs. But in the case of a species which frequently slips below the highest standards of competence, sincerity and attention, we may take leave to doubt whether they really *are* very common, and we are on still firmer ground in insisting that their frequency is certainly not *known* by those who invoke them.* (Quite insufficient attention has yet been paid in the philosophy of the human sciences to the possibility that the major cause of the snail-like cognitive advance within most of these most of the time is simply the insensitivity, greatly exacerbated in professional training, of very many social scientists.) Descriptive discretion is simply not absolute.

§14 The second respect in which the status of descriptive statements within the sciences of man differs from its status within the sciences of non-human nature is more striking, and it is a formidable task to assess what its significance may be. Describing is picturing in words, verbal representation.[18] The rest of nature is a helpless victim of our representational enthusiasms: man can answer back. Describing men is picturing in words a type of creature for whom it is already a constitutive characteristic, at least in adults, that they picture themselves in words of their own choosing. Between a describer and a self-describing object there exist relations which are peculiar not merely epistemologically or even perhaps ontologically, but also morally. Confronted by interlocutors of exquisite sensitivity and awesome patience, persons possessed of formidable initial participant-observational grasp of our own culture and society and facility in our own natural language, perhaps we might be fortunate enough never to need to answer back to others' characterisations of ourselves. But if the need did arise, to be able (conceptually, not necessarily acoustically) to answer back is part of what it is to be fully a man (perhaps even the core of what it is to be *fully* a man).

The history of human beings cannot exclude the history of men as agents and as the possessors of intellects. It cannot happen 'behind the backs of the consciousness of real men'.[19] To every man, then, his own truth — not a *private* truth, but a potentially public truth which truly is his. Two main difficulties follow from this centrality of the human capacity for self-description in specifying the field of the sciences of man, either or both of

---

* It would in fact be extremely illuminating philosophically to be offered the opportunity to inspect a really full and convincing description of such a disagreement. Could it in fact be a convincingly full description without disclosing how the mishap occurred? Charles Taylor ('Interpretation and the Sciences of Man', *Review of Metaphysics*, 25 (September 1971), 3–51) refers to the possibility of encountering such irreducible gaps in intuitions. But the epistemological resolution which he offers for it (esp. pp. 46–7) is suspiciously reminiscent of Mill's argument for the superior eligibility of the higher over the lower pleasures (that he had sampled both and preferred the former). On such questions, one must surely be either more of a 'realist' than Taylor here perspicuously declares himself or else be less of an (epistemological) egoist?

which may preclude the giving of a realist account of the status of these sciences. The first of these is the problem of providing clear criteria for the valid description of meanings (the problem of the determinacy of translation). The second is the related difficulty of providing a clear account of the character of human consciousness and any plausible criteria for its true or false description.

§15 The claim to know exactly what other persons mean or meant (and thus perhaps the claim to know what other persons are doing or have done) depends upon there being in principle specifiable truth conditions for correct translation. The existence of such truth conditions has been challenged and a 'realist' attitude to psychological states impugned by Quine's thesis of the indeterminacy of translation. Indeed, since radical translation, as Quine himself puts it, 'begins at home',[20] it is not only the meanings and actions of others which are rendered indeterminate on this theory, but equally our own. This challenge is certainly the most formidable threat yet identified to a realist view of the subject matter of history and the social sciences. The core of Quine's argument is the claim that

manuals for translating one language into another can be set up in divergent ways, all compatible with the totality of speech dispositions, yet incompatible with one another. In countless places they will diverge in giving, as their respective translations of a sentence of one language, sentences of the other language which stand to each other in no plausible kind of equivalence however loose.[21]

There is no question of one of these theories (translation schemas) being true and the rest false. There is no 'fact of the matter'. If we lack a pragmatist definition of synonymy, we ought not to adopt a realist attitude to the theory of meaning. Actions do not have determinate intentional descriptions, except relativised to particular theories of interpretation. (If there cannot be a pragmatist definition of synonymy, what exactly does it mean to assert that persons mean exactly what they do mean and not anything else?) These difficulties extend from the case of radical translation into a wholly alien language in chronologically or culturally very alien societies, through alien languages in contemporary or culturally very similar societies, or our own language in chronologically or culturally very distant societies, to our own language spoken by other persons in areas of our own society with which we are culturally familiar now and perhaps even to our own language spoken by ourselves on other occasions.

Homophonic translation theories work astonishingly well on ourselves, at least over short periods of time, and reasonably well among the speakers of our own natural language within culturally and structurally similar social niches over longer periods. If they did not work reasonably well in these circumstances we could hardly learn (be taught or teach ourselves) to get them to work so splendidly for ourselves in the short run and could scarcely formulate philosophical dilemmas, let alone decide whether we had solved them. But in the very long run for the inhabitants of very different societies speaking very different languages there simply cannot be empirically validated translation theories with unique authority in this way. Even within our own language a homophonic theory works increasingly poorly as we get further away from ourselves culturally and temporally, as historians of ideas are painfully aware.* When it comes to radical translation between languages, interpretation appears to presuppose the assigning of theoretically structured beliefs and the imposition of standards of rationality on the alien subjects before it can even commence.[22] There seems no way of vindicating the choice of a unique set of presuppositions.[23] A translation manual, empirically adequate in the past and even in the future, could be set up to maximise the ascription of true beliefs (credal charity) or of readily intelligible desires[24] (libidinal complicity) or a number of other possibly more practical objectives, with substantial consequent divergences in the interpretation of the contents of translator/native conversations. It *might* still be correct to dispute whether this really is a natural possibility, whether more ingenious and patient testing of the empirical accuracy of the translation might not in every instance eventually offer some decisive criterion for favouring one rather than another. (This seems to be Jonathan Bennett's expectation, and in a fideist manner it seems an operating presupposition of the finer-grain hermeneutic inquiry in history or other human sciences.) But even if it is a persisting natural possibility, it could license only the most restricted form of 'relativism'. If we cannot know exactly what those noises which he made meant or exactly what he was then doing, there is a rich abundance of things which we can have strong reasons to believe that he was certainly not doing and certainly did not mean. The notion of empirical adequacy, the point at which Quine's thesis is least intuitively plausible, is also its firmest protection against serving as a shield for heuristic indolence. The day when a social scientist is forced in good faith in his interpretation of his subject's discourse or action in the *present* into a choice between one or other of several incompatible translation schemas, all empirically adequate to all practically available evidence, has yet to arrive; and we need not expect it soon.

§16

Seldom, very seldom, does complete truth belong to any human disclosure; seldom can it happen that something is not a little disguised, or a little mistaken.

(Jane Austen, *Emma*, ch. 49)

---

* Consider, for example, the disastrous effect on the interpretation of Locke's social and political theory of the assumption that when Locke used the word 'property' (as for example when he used it to define the content of justice and the ends of government) he meant normally what we normally mean when we today use the word 'property' outside philosophical contexts. For the most glaring example of this error see C.B. Macpherson, *The Political Theory of Possessive Individualism* (Oxford 1962). For a conclusive demonstration of just how deeply erroneous a view it is see James Tully, *A Discourse of Property*, Cambridge 1980.

The great strength of the hermeneutic approach is that it takes consciousness and action as the core subject matter of the human sciences and treats these as essentially linguistic phenomena, the possibility of characterising which in language is constitutive of them in a sense in which it is not in the case of non-human nature. Its great — and, as perhaps we can now see more clearly, its *corresponding* — weakness is that anyone who practises it, as Schutz complained of Dilthey, 'opposes to rational science another, so-called "interpretive" science based on metaphysical presuppositions and incorrigible "intuition" '.[25] How far it is necessary to settle for incorrigibility of intuition and what metaphysical presuppositions it is appropriate to presuppose are by no means easy questions to resolve. Here we come to the second difficulty mentioned at the end of §14.

Is it possible to understand even ourselves? — and other people? — even those with very different languages and systems of belief? Anthropological understanding of an alien community seems possible only if we make questionable assumptions about the extent and nature of their rationality. Even if one could legitimately presume that the members of another society are rational agents and had a clear conception of the necessary and sufficient conditions for being a rational agent, within what frame should such agency be located,[26] and how perfectly or imperfectly rational should such agency be presumed in practice?[27] If being a good anthropologist means successfully infiltrating an alien belief system without abandoning one's own, might not being an even better anthropologist amount simply to going native — deserting one's own belief system completely? (*Credo ut intelligam*: better anthropologists would not just translate but would try to believe.[28] Ideal anthropologists would succeed (fleetingly or permanently?) in believing.)

§17 One might claim that access to a full verbal transcript of conscious experience holds the key to understanding another person. This notion presents myriads of difficulties. We certainly do not formulate all of our experience in words — chattering incessantly to ourselves. Moreover, it is not obvious that all our experience is conscious. If available, such a transcript would be a valid description of an individual's experience: it would characterise all the relevant experiential states of which the described person was conscious for a particular auditor who could grasp all the assertions made in the description. Sentences which he customarily used in his own language would be relatively easy for him to grasp clearly. Sentences (particularly sentences reporting feelings or conceptually novel thoughts) which he had never had occasion to use would be relatively hard and in some cases probably impossible to grasp. They would need more imagination, and imagination has its limits. It simply is very difficult to understand even in outline the feelings of those with very different temperaments from oneself and, as every schoolboy knows, there are plenty of intellectually respectable concep-

98

tual structures (mathematical, logical) which cannot successfully be taught to many people.

It seems more promising to abandon the search for a total transcript, seeking, rather, a complete, accurate and fully intelligible description personalised to a particular auditor. (In one's own case this might resemble the transcript.) The idea of better or worse, even true and false, descriptions of any experience to anyone interested for some reason in understanding it at a time lacks the prima facie absurdity of the idea of a *total* transcript. It should be possible to systematise around such a conception the more obviously hermeneutic units of human history and social practice: texts, speech acts and individual or collective actions or sequences of actions. No one in practice, for reasons of economy, would attempt to grasp individual or social happening at this radically individuated and extended level. It would still be necessary to simplify enormously in order to think about society at all, let alone to live in it. But at least this can serve to set a standard, designating what there is minimally for the human sciences to understand, by which to judge the necessary deviations of more practical understanding. It would serve to specify what would count as their having understood it and hence what forms of simplification for practical purposes must be considered false because they are incompatible with it — and not merely and mercifully less interminable.

§18 The core of such a conception of 'what is or is not the case' is the idea of full true descriptions individuated to particular auditors on particular occasions. In the case of descriptions provided by agents themselves, we may employ Jane Austen's term 'disclosure'. Actual disclosures to particular auditors are seldom wholly true and perhaps never complete, though practically they often serve very adequately. Life is much too short for perfect disclosure. Nor is it any longer for practising historians or social scientists who aspire to complete their inquiries or to have their books read. All human scientists, even the most behavioural, practise in the fond hope that the deficiencies of description or the errors and gaps in the intelligibility of record will all come out in the wash. Social complicity (the taking in of one another's washing) has much to do with the maintenance of optimism among social scientists.

By this means one might characterise the set of human public acts: texts, speech acts, actions. These stand in close, though complex, conceptual relations.[29] The primitive cognitive professional acts of the human sciences are the formation of perspicuous, true one-auditor-at-a-time individuated descriptions of such acts or patterns or sequences of action. This states (very crudely) the standards in relation to which the *truth* of professional statements in the human sciences are to be measured. Their role as standards is presumed in epistemological criticism and in professional self-justification in response to this.

§19 Simply to provide such descriptions is no easy task. But it cannot be denied that it falls in some ways drastically short of the bold cognitive ambitions of most practising social scientists and even perhaps of many historians. Even *perfect* descriptions of all individual acts would not constitute a very well explained, even perhaps an intelligible, history.* Such a history would omit the causal impact of all material factors not 'mentioned' in human consciousness. It would misjudge the causal force and direction of many material factors which were so 'mentioned'; and it is at best unclear how well it could be expected (even if supplemented by complete knowledge of these two types) to articulate such central aspects of the human condition as the unintended consequences of individual human actions and sets of such actions. There is plainly plenty of natural, non-intentional causality within human history and around human actions. History cannot be adequately explained at the individual level (omitting mention of social wholes, or of social wholes except as reflected in individuals' beliefs; omitting mention of material factors unrecognised by any individuals; etc.). But what counts as an adequate explanation of human history includes at the very minimum an explanation of all human acts. This specifies a necessary component of the explanandum, even if it offers little guidance on how precisely successful explanations can or might be constructed.

Social scientists certainly describe more extended objects than individual actions; but this capacity in itself could hardly militate against the view that describing human actions intelligibly and non-falsely was their main cognitive assignment. What might be thought incompatible with that view is the fact that social scientists aspire to formulate regularities (which they sometimes call laws) and that they aspire to explain social processes and outcomes. Describing plainly does not preclude the identification of past regularities (indeed the latter presupposes it). The identification of correctly (non-falsely, not necessarily completely) described past regularities and the correct (non-false) description of such past regularities is the making of a historical record. Describing does not preclude in principle the formulation of true law-like generalisations of the form: If A occurs within S conditions, then B will occur. But emphasis on the epistemological primacy of description makes plainer why few, if any, candidates for true law-like generalisations of this character appear in the human sciences. If identifying regularities is to be more than accumulating a historical record (and if it is to explain occurrences in the world), the identification of these regularities must take the form of a conditional law-like generalisation: this generalisation must hold over a determinate range for a determinate class; it must at least implicitly mention some true descriptions of actions, with the truth of which it is compatible (otherwise it would be vacuous); and it must be not actually incompatible with any true descriptions of actions (otherwise it would be false). This would need drastic rewriting for probabilistic candidates; but

* They might contain all the intelligibility that history can be *guaranteed* to contain.

such rewriting would not alter the point. On this account there are probably not any serious candidates for such law-like generalisations of any scope or interest in the more descriptively orientated social sciences (sociology, social anthropology, quite certainly political science), and where there are such candidates — as in economics — they can maintain the status (if they can do so at all) only within a tautologically defined, if elaborately articulated, theory and falter, alas and notoriously, if applied to the world. Plainly in fact economics (somewhat unlike sociology and hilariously unlike political science) can and perhaps even often does improve agents' judgement of what is likely to occur. It seems intuitively plausible that there must be enormously many such law-like generalisations in relation to human social and political situations which are true (some of them at least not trivial) and which could in principle be rationally believed as a result of painstaking inquiry. The trickiest part of identifying them is not specifying the conditionally related A and B but specifying the precise range within which they hold — the conditions of application. Much self-protective energy in the human sciences goes into fudging this issue: no one likes to be shown to have been a fool. Such considerations have led MacIntyre in one recent piece to argue against the possibility of a social science.[30] But it seems more sensible to read them as demanding that those who aspire to construct any such science should impose on themselves cognitive morals more austere than they have yet had either inclination or externally provided motive to adopt, and appreciably more austere than those which natural scientists by now have socially thrust upon them.

§20 There are two important ways in which this very individualist characterisation of the field of the human sciences is certain to be challenged. A defender of social holism might contend that propositions about social wholes can be known to be true or false irrespective of the truth or falsity of the description of any individual actions at all. I strongly doubt the possibility of this, but cannot see how to offer a general argument against it. Social holists may also complain that this characterisation presupposes falsely that all statements about social wholes can be decomposed into statements about individuals. It is unclear quite what such a claim implies and therefore difficult to tell whether such a presupposition is in fact false. But in any case the view stated here is not intended to presuppose anything of the kind, and it is not obvious why it should be thought to require any such presupposition. All it does trade on (rather heavily) is the conviction, common to most hermeneutic thinkers, that human beings are better placed to sustain cognitive claims about some individual persons than they are about any institutions, let alone societies, economies or polities.

The second challenge is more mundane. We are frequently able to explain human action and human social relations without being in a position to provide perspicuous, true auditor-individuated descriptions of any actions at

101

all. Adopting such preposterously strong characterisations of what may justifiably be believed true of the human world simply ignores the vast amount of less fastidious cognitive exchange and complicity which clearly provides a viable foundation for practical life and might plausibly serve to do so in the fulness of time even for the human sciences. Human life is no bed of roses; but it is on the whole, on balance, livable. The conclusion urged here, by contrast, may well be thought to teeter on the verge of absurdity, to violate ordinary English usage and to offer no compensating advantages of lucidity or conclusiveness to compensate for these gross defects.

These criticisms assume that the role of true, perspicuous descriptions in this account is methodological in the sense in which the role of observation sentences or perhaps sense data might be thought methodological in some philosophical theories. But whereas the great charm of observation sentences or sense data for those who find them charming is the idea of their uniting incorrigibility with practical availability, it should be clear that perspicuous, true auditor-individuated descriptions derive such conceptual vestiges of incorrigibility as they are accorded from their extreme distance from anything directly furnished (*given*) by an observer's experience. Any incorrigibility which they can muster is a conceptual construction from the idea of a very extended range of inquiries. And their role is not to dictate a helpless passivity in the face of the unknowable to hitherto active human scientists, but to serve as an ultimate conceptual standard of whether what they believe to be true as a result of their inquiries is in fact true.

§21 How should we picture such perspicuous, true auditor-individuated descriptions of actions in the context of historical practice? How closely would they resemble Collingwood's famous specification of the historian's project in terms of rethinking the thoughts of past agents? One major difficulty which has arisen in relation to Collingwood's analysis is the obscurity of what should count as the criterion of identity for the thoughts in question. How can we distinguish rethinking the thoughts of Caesar from foisting our own thoughts on to Caesar? Caesar presumably thought in Latin. Few of us are in a position to emulate him. Even waiving the indeterminacy of translation, the purely practical difficulties of translating perspicuously from the language of a very different (and ethnographically in some respects very poorly recorded) society without anachronism or other forms of misleading implication are huge. Rethinking Caesar's thoughts has some resemblances to Winch's conception of anthropology as (at least temporarily) going native. But there is no practical possibility of actually joining (infiltrating) a *past* culture. We cannot literally become first-century-B.C. Romans. Furthermore, if the thoughts which we were rethinking *were* the thoughts of Caesar, they should be no less complex, involve no fewer considerations, mention no fewer terms, than Caesar's; and it seems possible that they should even take much the same time to think as they did for Caesar himself. (It would be realistic to suppose that Caesar thought about the action which we now call 'crossing the Rubicon' for some considerable time.) This is not a point simply about heuristics. A historian, unlike Caesar himself, could lavish his entire life on thinking *about* Caesar's thoughts in relation to 'crossing the Rubicon', and after so doing he might well be in a position (having had more practice than, and being perhaps smarter than, Caesar and having less at stake than the Roman Empire) to rethink Caesar's thoughts appreciably faster than their first thinker. Superior history, then, would amount to re-thinking the thoughts of Caesar with our own incomparable advantages. But any such example of historical progress would risk violating the identity criterion which serves to *constitute* the subject matter of history. Caesar's thoughts, to be rethought perfectly, should be rethought as unpractisedly (as freshly) and as unsmartly as Caesar himself thought them. There seem con-clusive barriers to vindicating any claim that the thoughts which we aspire to rethink can be *known* to be Caesar's thoughts, Caesar's whole thoughts and nothing but Caesar's thoughts. And even this may understate the difficulties. Can one rethink Caesar's thoughts around such a consequential issue of prac-tical reason without troubling to refeel Caesar's feelings, a matter in which the identity criterion would clearly become an impassable barrier to emulation?

Two conclusions may be drawn from this. First, the historian's practicable project of analysing past actions is not happily represented as the execution of a deliberate metempsychosis, the success of which is guaranteed by intuitions, corrigible or incorrigible. Even those who wish to characterise historical and social inquiry in exclusively hermeneutic terms would be better advised to abandon the language of empathy and projection for a clear recognition that what can be practically attained are hermeneutic sketches, standing to full hermeneutic representations roughly as Hempel's 'expla-nation sketches' are intended to stand to a completed positivist explanation (full subsumption of the explanandum under the requisite set of covering laws). Secondly, the idea of description of thoughts or feelings is distinctly less mysterious than the idea of re-enacting or re-experiencing them. If there can be knowledge of other minds at all, and if this possibility can be character-ised clearly in philosophical terms, there should be no insuperable difficulty in the idea of true auditor-individuated descriptions of the thoughts and feelings of others.

§22 One could not perspicuously understand anything which persons do at all without recognising that they have at a minimum both beliefs and desires. Full perspicuous descriptions would have to include full descriptions of all beliefs and desires to which an agent would have referred in candidly and carefully describing his action. This might seem too weak a requirement, because we might wish and hope to know matters about both the causation and the consequences of the action which the agent himself might omit but which it would be natural for any historian or social scientist to include within their description of the action. Persons may have some measure of privileged access to their own consciousness. But, being of limited intelligence and having other purposes besides that of understanding themselves, they do not always or perhaps ever understand themselves perfectly. Hence even if full descriptions of an action must include full descriptions of all beliefs and desires which an agent would have mentioned in describing the action himself as well as he could have described it in relation to some potential cognitive interest — and their doing so would be required for their being judged *full* descriptions at least in relation to that interest — they would not constitute a sufficient condition for being so judged. On the causal side we would need and wish to *supplement* an agent's account of what had brought him to act in a particular way with any considerations of a sociological or psychological character which we could *know* to be relevant but unmentioned, gently but firmly assisting the agent to transcend his own cognitive and moral limitations and avoid both error and deceit. We might think of this part of the inquiry as a particularly gentle and sensitive interrogation — a co-operative confessional which somehow combined charity of attitude and justice of result. (The model of psychoanalysis perhaps lurks behind this picture.)

There are two difficulties raised by this concession. The first is apparent. Can one acknowledge the possibility of *replacing* some part of the agent's description in this fashion with our observer's description? No theorist could hope to make the criterion for the validity of the supplement as strong as its compatibility with all the components of the agent's description, not all of which, because of error, are necessarily even compatible with each other. But to defend a conception of the knowledge of human action that is as strongly hermeneutic as the one advanced here, it is certainly necessary to defend the view that supplementation cannot amount simply to replacement. The most obvious way of expressing this constraint is to insist on the necessity of *mentioning* all the terms in the agent's own description (even if only in some cases to negate them). The second difficulty arises from the lack of agreement about what is at present *known* in the way of psychology or sociology. Very few, if any, laws of psychology or sociology (and none at all of political science) which might possibly relate to the motivation of action are in fact *known*, though of course many propositions of all three 'sciences' which relate to motivation are sensibly and justifiably believed by individual human scientists on occasion, as they are by the rest of us in the course of daily life. Epistemic supplementation of an agent's intentional characterisation of his action depends simply on the possibility of external observation of the particular agent in question and of other agents through time. But replacement of an agent's characterisation of his action requires a title the very possibility of which has hardly as yet been vindicated in any general way.

On the consequential side, the possibility of supplementation raises no such problems. The consequences of an action are an externally related matter of fact. As Danto has emphasised,[31] it is a conceptually important stylistic feature of historical narratives that they contain many descriptions of actions which could not have been given by the agents themselves (for example, commencing the First World War or the Thirty Years' War or, absurdly, the Renaissance). But it would be absurd to regard these as *replacing* the intentional characterisations.

Perspicuous auditor-individuated agents' descriptions of actions and the beliefs and desires mentioned in these descriptions can thus be supplemented without weakening their ability to specify the hermeneutic component of the field of the human sciences. However, psychological phenomena such as denial, self-deception and rationalisation, as well as ideology and the social determination of belief, suggest that some terms which appear in the agent's description can be discarded as redundant for explanatory and perhaps even descriptive purposes. But the claim or even the *demonstration* that some terms within an agent's description were redundant would not in any way enhance the status of theoretical claims to *replace* parts of an agent's description with other terms not mentioned (except for what he and anyone else would agree to purely for purposes of representation: economy, clarity of outline etc.). The explanatory force or status of psychological or sociological concepts of this character in relation to a particular action must be shown within an agent's own mapping of his 'problem situation' or 'set of problem situations' (action context). They must remove anomaly within, or add information to, the best description which he himself is able to offer; and it is because they must do so that it is tempting (though plainly wrong) to insist that they must provide characterisations which an agent could or even would in practice accept. When we have the best description which he is able to offer, we may well be able to illuminate him to himself, perhaps even to show him that some of his initial statements are the reverse of the truth; and our potential ability to do so will not be impugned should he not in fact wish for further illumination, wish to understand himself any better. What we cannot properly do is to claim to *know* that we understand him or his action better than he does himself without access to the best descriptions which he is able to offer. (We may, of course, believe that we have a better grasp of some aspects of it — its consequential cruelty, its extreme imprudence — than he does, even on comparatively superficial observation.) There is no doubt much redundancy and not a little error of one kind and another in agents' characterisations of their problem situations. But to know that some item is explanatorily redundant is to know the full description and to see that the part which it plays in this full description is not in any way reflected in the determination of the action. The best evidence for the redundancy of a term in an agent's description would be his truly reported true agreement (recognition) that the term was indeed redundant. If self-deception characterises a psychological process, rather than merely conveying a moral rebuke, agents ought to be *able* to know that they are or have been deceiving themselves. *Knowing* better than other people about the character of their actions must be knowing more than they do; it cannot consist in knowing less than they do but knowing it more deftly, honestly, realistically, dogmatically etc. The criterion of proof for the validity of a description or interpretation of an action is the economy and accuracy with which it handles the full text of the agent's description. The arrogance of ideological explanation of the thought of others lies in the claim to understand another's thinking more deeply than he does himself, without being in a position to provide true descriptions of almost any of it. It is a routinised claim to authority where routinised claims must be false, where all authority must be earned in detail and where the mode of its earning is by explaining persons (and their situations) more lucidly to themselves.[32]

§23 Is false consciousness, then, a literal impossibility? In so far as it involves consciousness of oneself at other times than the present or of matters external to oneself or to one's place in society or in nature, this is not entailed. Whether it can be allowed with respect to the consciousness of oneself in the present is more complicated. Not all the beliefs which we have can be second-order beliefs; but sometimes we do need to form beliefs about our beliefs in the present. For an agent A to believe at time t that he believes that P does not guarantee that agent A at time t believes that P. But (simply as a proposal about how we might recover our capacity to talk clearly, not as a conceptual claim about an agreed subject matter) we may reasonably treat it as a necessary condition for the truth of this proposition. Unless we can establish a coherent title to employ the verb 'believe' in the first person singular present indicative active, it is hard to see how we can establish any title at all to litter the past and future with firm ascriptions of beliefs to others.

Do I know what I believe? Well, I certainly have a shrewder (as well as more extensive) *general* set of suspicions on the subject of what I believe than you have on the subject of what I believe.

It may be a wise man that knows his own beliefs. But it cannot be only a wise man who experiences his own experiences. That privilege is open to all creatures which can experience at all. I have beliefs, experiences etc. I now believe I am in England rather than in Bulgaria. I now (conveniently) feel sick. If questioned by myself or others as to what I do believe or feel in these respects, I will, if speaking sincerely and attending to the matter, confirm that I *do* believe that not Bulgaria but England is where I am and that sick is among the things which I feel. Philosophers have emphasised many possible dimensions of mishap in such confirmatory avowals of belief or experience. I may not be as sincere or attentive to the matter as I need to be. My customary command of the English language may fail. The standard

106

motive for attacking the status of avowals is the wish to deny that any description of experience is incorrigible. It is not necessary to establish that any avowals are incorrigible in order to claim that we certainly do experience our own experiences and that these differ from one another and differ from all the experiences which we do not have.

§24 Full descriptions of actions, then, are descriptions which characterise an agent persisting through time, the possessor of beliefs and feelings (desires, fears, hatreds, shames, aspirations, all that goes to make up a temperament), confronted by a context at a time (characterised in terms of the beliefs and desires of the agent at that time) and responding to it, for what seemed within the frame of consciously present feelings and beliefs sufficient reasons, intentionally, in a particular manner or, by naturally explicable mishap, in some other distinct manner. (It is realistic to assume that former President Ford entered few helicopters in the course of his presidency which he did not intend to enter. But it would not be realistic to assume that he struck his head on the door-frames of few of these conveyances on which he did not intend to strike his head.) Full descriptions of actions by agents may well require supplementation before they can furnish *the* explanation of the action (Why exactly *this* act? Why exactly then? etc.). Anything less than full agent descriptions cannot provide *the* explanation, though much less saturating types of record can serve very adequately to remove anomaly from and restore intelligibility to the record for most practical purposes. What to emphasise in such explanatory representations is perhaps partly a matter of philosophical taste. Some would prefer to translate all the terms into the idiom of beliefs (expected utility, subjective probability, etc.). Others might prefer to transpose all belief statements into some intricate form of desire.[33] Others will prefer to set the notion of sufficient reasons within the set of beliefs and feelings at the centre of their account. Provided that no material is simply omitted, the choice of format may be left to taste.

There are still no cheap ways to deep knowledge of other persons and the causes of their actions. There are no simple methods which will make the insensitive perceptive, and there are no guarantees, any more than in the sciences of nature, of making real progress at all. But if *knowing* about other persons in small or large numbers over short or lengthy periods of time is a very steep project indeed, the project of trying to understand and assess how they are likely to behave simply shades off into the living of practical life. We all hold more or less well-justified beliefs about the beliefs and senti-ments and practical situations of others. We all can and indeed *must* attempt to judge methodologically how it is sound to attribute beliefs or feelings to others. Within a common physical world we are all radical interpreters of one another, assigning beliefs, desires, intentions and meanings simultaneously to one another and trying to make sense of conduct by solving the resulting simultaneous equations. A clearer understanding of the need to solve the equations for *all* of these values simultaneously would enhance observance of empirical adequacy as the criterion for valid translation manuals. A clear grasp of what principles govern our setting up of our own manual will make it easier to distinguish empirical inadequacy from variations in foci of interest. (All understanding is understanding in relation to a set of interests.) The criterion of empirical adequacy by itself establishes a domain of public co-operative and mutually corrigible endeavour which can more than absorb the efforts of all possible future human scientists. It also has the merit of licensing no cognitive claims more sweeping than could in principle be licensed, and of prescribing the most exacting and patient attention to *all* that the subjects of the human sciences do or say.

§25 This may seem superficially reassuring. But is it able to reassure merely because it *is* so superficial? What excuse could there be for using the anomaly of the mental as a flag of philosophical convenience in order to populate human history with philosophically disreputable entities and in particular determinate meanings where only indeterminacy can and should be found? May one not simply have to choose between accepting the anomaly (or autonomy) of the mental and accepting the indeterminacy of translation? If you accept both the anomaly of the mental and the indeterminacy of translation, the human sciences are in danger of falling painfully between two stools. Behaviour knowledge is accessible but cannot be knowledge of humans as such. Meaning knowledge could be knowledge of humans, if it could be determinately stated. But doubts are cast on its determinate attainability even in principle. Since translational adequacy on the Quinean account is a specifically pragmatic notion, a translationally adequate science of human meanings must in principle be pragmatically accessible. But is the subject matter of which it can give us knowledge real living or dead men, as we ought to be prepared to recognise them? According to the indeterminacy of translation we can never know that X and not anything else at all is what we or anyone else mean. In our own case we readily incline to the view that we can and do sometimes know that X and not anything else at all *is* what we mean. ('You may never mean anything in particular but I certainly do.' 'You can tell my particular meaning most of the time by what I assert.')

It may be the case that intentionalist theories of meaning[34] are gravely inadequate; but could it be the case that they literally never apply? Exactly what we mean is not necessarily a very exact business. Indeterminacy of translation rationally encourages us to take the view that our meanings may be a great deal less exact than they sound to us, to regard our assertoric ventures as a good deal looser in articulation than they feel at the time. The meanings of what we say certainly have different extension from our more optimistic hopes of our locutionary abilities. They fall short and they overshoot, failing to articulate what we do intend and succeeding in committing us to what we do not at all intend. But the meanings of what we mean surely are constituted by those hopes. In a world in which it was never possible to know what we meant, much of the use of the word 'meaning' would be unintelligible. ('I quite certainly did not mean *that*.' 'Of course, I *know* that *that* is not what I meant.')

The capacity to recognise an assertion as an assertion is a presupposition of the criterion of empirical adequacy for translation manuals. To assert is to perform an action. There is no reason to suppose that indeterminacy of translation can even be *stated* coherently without the at least covert employment of the concept of agency. Correct translation is translation compatible with what speakers are asserting. ('Put my meaning any way you like – use any old words – provided it catches my *meaning*: what I intend to assert.')

§26 How, then, should we picture the relation between the categories of action and the indeterminacy of translation? There appears at present to be no convincing answer to this question. John McDowell has suggested a striking relation between Quine's discussion of indeterminacy of translation and the vigorous dispute between exponents of realist and non-realist theories of meaning.[35] Neither realists[36] nor anti-realists[37] have, as he convincingly claims, succeeded as yet in showing how language and linguistic behaviour can be clearly understood. To have a coherent theory of language and linguistic behaviour would be to know how to characterise meanings. To know how to characterise meanings would be to know how to characterise the core subject matter of history and the social sciences. Until such a theory has been constructed, history and the social sciences will stand epistemologically in jeopardy. But in this predicament they will by no means stand alone.

§27 To assess the precise scope of the epistemological dilemmas raised by indeterminacy of translation and even to gauge how extreme these are likely to prove in practice is thus at present an excessive ambition for a social scientist. But the practice of the social sciences requires that we consider these issues in the context of other issues and restricts the range of options open to us by considerations which may well in themselves be (and which certainly at present appear to be) wholly extrinsic to epistemology.

Always and everywhere people act, behave, mean (intend to assert) exactly as they do and not otherwise. These are not tautologies which, in the practice of the human sciences, we can be prepared lightly to abandon. If the account which we give of what it is to know makes this come out as something which we cannot know, what this implies is that something has come adrift in our account of what in this context it *is* to know. The search for method is a search for a guarantee against error. But perhaps in most domains of knowing about humans there just are no *guarantees* against error. The fact (where it is a fact) that there cannot be a guaranteed method of discovering what is true about some matter does not imply that nothing is true about that matter.

In the theory of interpretation and translation a fine array of 'moral' principles are at present widely touted: the principle of charity,[38] the principle of humanity,[39] the principle of benefit of the doubt,[40] the principle of truthfulness (for which a more apt name might perhaps be the principle of credulity).[41] The moral tone of these principles is in one respect misleading and may render the present title of each something of a misnomer. For we display these mildly supererogatory and Christian-sounding virtues in the more or less optimistic hope of doing ourselves an epistemological favour, establishing or at least bolstering a conviction that the world is indeed populated with other persons who are persons in much the same sense as we are ourselves (or suppose ourselves to be) and drawing many conclusions from this conviction. No doubt we have good reason for seeking to do ourselves whatever epistemological favours we can contrive to perform. But in the sly and instrumental espousal of these supererogatory 'virtues' we risk ignoring a duty which is absolute and in no sense supererogatory, the duty of justice. *Justitia est constans et perpetua voluntas suum cuique tribuendi*. If we claim to *know* about other men, we must try as best we can to give them what is their due, their right. This is a simple moral duty, not a guarantee of epistemological prowess. We cannot try better than we can. Even trying *very* hard will not ensure success or indeed necessarily even make it particularly likely. If the indeterminacy of translation is shown to hold, it will enforce changes upon us in how we conceive what is due epistemologically to ourselves and to other men. What it could not do is to weaken the obligation to try as best we can to render to each man, including ourselves, what *is* their due.

In the 'sciences' of man the agent, our need for clear and authoritative recipes of heuristic procedure is necessarily a less fundamental need than our need for good intentions (the intention to understand human agents exactly as they are and were and will be and not any other way). Human beings, we might say, have a right to such understanding from one another or — less vertiginously, and if 'ought' implies 'can' — they have a right to at least the effort to attain such understanding on the part of any other human being who claims to state the truth about them.

We cannot *know* that our accounts are wholly true in the case of most human matters into which we have good reason to inquire. What we can *know* is that human matters are matters about which descriptions can be true or false (or both partly true and partly false). And as practising historians or social scientists we can reasonably believe in some cases that the descriptions which we offer, addressed to the persons to whom we offer them, convey information which is true about the human matters which they mention. Such practitioners' beliefs are optimistic in several different dimensions. The argument advanced here is that the dimension in which their optimism is best justified is in the presumption that there is something to describe. This conviction is often confused with the view that there exists some specifiable methodology which, correctly applied, would yield descriptions which would never be false or always be true. It is hard to see any grounds whatever in favour of this second view. If the arguments of this paper are correct at all, methodology *can* have no higher status than that of a counsel of prudence. ('If you want to find that out, I would not try to do so in that way, if I were you.' Counsels of prudence need not lack cogency. It is a criterion of soundness for counsels of prudence that, soundly applied, they must work for the better more often than not.) There cannot be *rules* of sociological or historical method; but there can be and are many bad historians and sociologists. And perhaps to be a bad sociologist or historian, not from genetic or cultural mishap but through the nurturing of some types of intention and the eschewing of others, may even be a category within naturalistic ethics.

6

From democracy to representation: an interpretation of a Ghanaian election*

When the electors of Asunafo constituency in the south of Ghana's Brong-Ahafo region went to the polls on 29 August 1969, they elected to Parliament a young secondary school teacher from a forest town in the constituency. When the new Busia government took office a month later, the representative of Asunafo became a Ministerial Secretary. By electing him the voters of this part of Ahafo certainly altered drastically the career of one young man and they contributed a seat to the massive governmental majority enjoyed by Dr Busia's Progress Party. What these twin effects were to amount to in future only time would tell: no study of an election could cast much light upon them. What studying elections may disclose is not an understanding of politics in general but simply an understanding of elections.

Elections are events which confuse in a very intimate and purposeful way the largely symbolic identifications of large numbers of people with their effects upon the politically effective conduct of rather small numbers of people. Such confusion is indeed their point. Their effect is to choose governments. The symbolic end of choosing governments in this way is, putatively, that governments so chosen will conduct themselves as more responsive agents of the purposes of their subject populations than governments chosen according to other fashions can be expected to do. Voting is a ritual of participation which purports to confer legitimacy upon the chosen. The mechanism by which it confers such legitimacy is by confusing the symbolic act of choosing a man with the very practical consequences of having chosen one. The point of elections is to fuse what electors attempt to bring about by choosing someone (an item of material and moral fantasy, or even, perhaps, the affirmation of a largely unconscious image of community and individual identity) with what they actually accomplish by so choosing — to touch the quotidian gloom of the political order with the gentler and more implicating light of past individual hope. In the exercise of governmental responsibilities of impossible dimensions one should not underestimate the services, for good or ill, which the re-enactment of even such exotic rituals

---

* For a full treatment of the political background to the events discussed in this essay, see Dennis Austin & Robin Luckham (eds.), *Politicians and Soldiers in Ghana 1966–1972*, London 1975.

of commitment can provide for the rulers in the strengthening of their moral nerve. In the democracies of the west, with their comparatively assured political environment, it may well be felt by the cynical that the point of elections, like the changing of the guard, is simply to be held. In African states, their point is, rather, to have *been* held. It would be foolish to imagine that the general legitimacy (such as it is) enjoyed by these states derives from the legal—rational character of democratic electoral procedure, though it remains striking how often they choose to revert to it. It is still true, moreover, that the higher political and administrative echelons of the state apparatus are filled by those whose articulated sense of subjective legitimacy (again such as it is) does take a legal—rational form. In this sense the legitimacy of the Ghanaian state for those to whom it still indubitably belongs, for those who make the laws and expound the reasons (which may be the most concrete legitimacy which it enjoys even today and the only legitimacy which it needs to enjoy in order to survive), may repose quite directly upon the ceremonial enactment of this exotic ritual of participation. But although it may be right to see elections in this way as a continuing feature of the moral dimension of the state's existence, a guarantee to the state's operators of its being in good faith, this aspect too represents merely a consequence of the actions of most of those involved. It leaves open the question of the nature of these actions in themselves.

In the days of the Septennial Act, the English (as Rousseau mordantly suggested) were free once every seven years.[1] On current showing the Ghanaians will be doing well if they are free more than once every fifteen. The election of 1969 was the first unequivocally free national political act on the part of the unorganised populace since the election of 1954, the first election, that is, in which the coffers of the state did not enter sharply into the political choices of voters. To understand what most voters were doing when they went to the polls on this occasion is to understand something as central to the politics of Ghana as the operation of the machinery of government — it is to understand what the people of Ghana attempt to do politically when they are free.* Whatever they may have brought about, the action which they performed in choosing in this way retains its moral status. No doubt the Ghanaian electorate was confused and ignorant, and no doubt its wills were as particular as the next nation's.[2] But abstract though it was and politically null as it soon turned out to have been, there is to be read in its choices, as there may perhaps be in the choices of all nations allowed the privilege of choosing, the shadowy outlines of a *Volonté Générale*. Elections in Africa by now may be closer to rituals of affliction than to concrete embodiments of freedom, but the sentiments to which they give transient

---

* This freedom is, naturally, a very limited matter, limited by scarcity of information and sheer insecurity. The secrecy of the ballot may still make it in some respects more free than that enjoyed by most eighteenth-century English electors. The scope of the franchise also is vastly wider in Ghana than it was in the England of which Rousseau wrote.

and paradoxical shape are no less profound for their failure to exemplify the blithe assurance of a mastered world. In order to recapture some vague outline of these sentiments, this chapter attempts to discuss two separate issues: the question of what happened in the election campaign in the Asunafo constituency, and the question of what was meant by what happened.

The Asunafo division of Ahafo is situated in the western rain-forest to the south of the main road linking Kumasi, the capital of the former Ashanti empire, to Sunyani, the capital of the present Brong-Ahafo region. Its most direct political and administrative ties have been shared between these two centres for more than sixty years, for the greater part indeed of the British occupation of Ashanti.[3] The balance of significance between the two towns has changed with changes in the political relationship between the central government of the country and the traditional political system of Ashanti. Ever since the British conquest of Ashanti in 1896, the central government has manipulated the political structures of Ahafo as pawns in its relationship with Ashanti. The delicate balance of conflict and co-operation between Accra and Kumasi has always been close to the centre of the politics of the country as a whole, and in the light of this national preoccupation, the politics of Ahafo inevitably appear provincial and instrumental. But whereas, from the perspective of Accra or Kumasi, Ahafo may well seem a mere instrument, a counter in a game of altogether grander scope, it is important to remember that from the viewpoint of Ahafo this grander game is apt to appear as instrumental to more local purposes, and Kwame Nkrumah or even the Asantehene have thereby seemed reduced to the status of weapons in local factional struggles. The confrontation of national élites, whether colonial or postcolonial, with local communities has tended to be described in terms of the recalcitrance of local values to national ends, but its meaning lies (as throughout the period of indirect rule which is substantively far from terminated today) at least as much in the subservience of national power to very active local purposes.

The administrative links of Asunafo with Sunyani and Kumasi are paralleled by the lines of physical communication along which the economic products of the area pass in order to reach the national markets.[4] The economic development of Ahafo and to no small degree the peopling of this densely-forested area followed upon the administrative penetration of the area by the British. As a district it represents the most recent (and currently the most spectacular) example of the Ghanaian economic expansion of this century, the process of rapid capital accumulation through the exploitation of the virgin forest for cocoa cultivation,[5] supplemented over the last twenty years by the timber industry. The great majority of the present Ahafo population has derived ethnically within the last two generations from other areas of Ghana or from abroad.[6] Except for the town of Mim with its sawmills and intermittent union troubles, the economic activities and the political structures of the area are entirely pre-industrial, though the equipment used

114

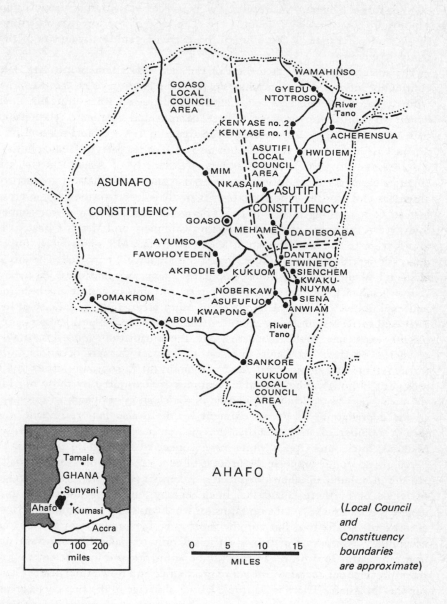

GOASO
LOCAL
COUNCIL
AREA

WAMAHINSO

GYEDU
NTOTROSO

River
Tano

KENYASE no. 2
KENYASE no. 1

ACHERENSUA

ASUTIFI
LOCAL
COUNCIL
AREA

HWIDIEM

MIM

NKASAIM

ASUNAFO

CONSTITUENCY

ASUTIFI

CONSTITUENCY

GOASO

MEHAME

DADIESOABA

AYUMSO

FAWOHOYEDEN

DANTANO
ETWINETO

AKRODIE

KUKUOM

SIENCHEM
KWAKU-
NUYMA

NOBERKAW

ASUFUFUO

SIENA

POMAKROM

KWAPONG

ANWIAM

ABOUM

River
Tano

SANKORE

KUKUOM
LOCAL
COUNCIL
AREA

Tamale

GHANA

Sunyani

Ahafo

Kumasi

Accra

0   100 200
miles

AHAFO

0   5   10   15

MILES

(*Local Council
and
Constituency
boundaries
are approximate*)

115

in timber extraction is sufficiently massive in scale to remove any suggestion of undisturbed bucolic tranquillity. A great deal of wealth is produced in Ahafo and much money is made there. The rape of the forest is an enthusiastic and participatory response to the exigencies and enticements of the world economy.

The social relations characteristic of the area are extremely intricate. The continuing inflow, now somewhat slower than twenty years ago, of those with capital to take up new cocoa land and of those with nothing but their labour to contribute, produces a very complicated economic relationship with its environment. In some ways the area is in a neocolonial relationship, not just with the world economy but also with other parts of Ghana, in that a substantial proportion of its farmers, particularly of Ashanti origin, are 'stranger farmers'. Indeed they are resented as such since they are frequently absentees and tend to export the profits of their farms to their home areas instead of reinvesting them locally.[7] The major capitalisation of the timber industry in the shape of the Mim Timber Company and Messrs Glikstens is also foreign to the area (though at least two former M.P.s now work timber concessions within Ahafo) and its profits too are largely exported. The initial character of the district as thinly-populated, largely virgin, forest has meant that it has had to import most of its capital and thus to endure a continuing and exploitative outflow of resources to other areas. Indeed, because of the increased social responsibility exhibited (under some initial political pressure) by the expatriate timber concerns, and the intrinsically more inscrutable character of their economic operations, stranger farmers occasion more direct resentment among most Ahafos than do the European interests in the area. But although the productive resources are exploited by those outside the area — as was endlessly emphasised in the election campaign with respect to the depredations of the government — Ahafo also imports, besides the greater number of its capitalists, the greater part of what the American Marxists Fitch and Oppenheimer have conceived as its rural proletariat.[8] Much of the labour supply in the process of cocoa production — and virtually all the non-familial labour involved — consists of semi-migrant foreign nationals or northern Ghanaians. Luck, energy, and good judgement may enable some of these to take up farms on stool lands and to become in effect citizens of Ahafo too. But for the most part the money which they can accumulate over a year or two is sufficient only to make them substantially richer in status and power in their home countries and insufficient to give them preferential access to the more productive and now rather scarcer land supplies in Ahafo. There is a chronic labour shortage in the rich cocoa areas, since the earnings of cocoa labourers are not such as to make the employment enticing for most southern Ghanaians even in conditions of substantial unemployment. The economic viability of cocoa production has therefore come to depend increasingly upon the continued availability of extremely cheap labour from much poorer areas. There was some discussion during the course or the campaign of non-Ghanaian business enterprise and its effects in the constituency, both European and African, particularly that of Yorubas in the retail trade, but the dependence of large-scale cocoa farmers on cheap imported labour was little mentioned.

The system of social stratification on the national level (in so far as such a thing does *exist* on the national level) played no part in the issues of the election. The sharpest conflicts of economic interest within the area also did not appear since the most economically deprived group had for the most part no local status as citizens of Ahafo and in many cases no legal title to vote in a national election.[9] It is an important feature of class relations in the area that many cocoa labourers are in a semi-domestic relationship with their employers, while even those who are employed by wholly absentee owners enjoy some degree of economic protection. The forest food crops, especially plantains and cocoyams (a byproduct of the approved method of growing cocoa), provide a diet which is plentiful, whatever its nutritional deficiencies. Few go hungry in the forest, and its most economically deprived groups — the migrants from the often drought-stricken savannah regions — are thus distinctly less deprived than they might well be at home. The politics of Ahafo have always been in consequence a politics of faction at a lineage, town, or divisional level, rather than a politics of class; a struggle between kinship groups and places rather than between geographically dispersed economic interests. Since the categories of class as such did not enter into either the vocabulary or the self-conscious political activities of the election, the intricacies of tenurial relations in cocoa production need not concern us here.[10] But two other self-identificatory roles which have come to Ahafo along with the purely economic aspects of modernity did play a part. Both the Christian religion and modern education had come slowly to Asunafo;[11] but both had appeared in a more vigorous form in the preceding ten years, and they undoubtedly had some weight in fixing the less traditional aspects of the election's meaning. The aspect of Busia's campaign which provoked most derision among some European observers and urban sophisticates, its vociferous god-fearingness, seems to have responded in this rural environment to some real needs.[12] At the same time the Progress Party's appearance as the party of respectability headed by a university professor made it the natural political vehicle in Asunafo, as in most parts of the country, for those who were admitted by the avenue of education to the participatory fruits of modernity, above all public office and the salaries which go with it.[13] The availability of post-Middle School education was a very crude symbol of the opening of modern opportunity to the people of Ahafo. The perfect candidate for the Progress Party symbolically (and the candidate whom they in fact ran) was a young man, not only Ahafo-born and graced with an Honours Degree from the University of Ghana but teaching in the local Secondary School at Acherensua in the neighbouring constituency, the provision of which had been the C.P.P. government's major local reward for political services rendered. Secondary education, in offering the possibility of dramatic social mobility through access to public office, is making an offer more resonant than that of *la carrière ouverte aux talents*. There is little bourgeois nonsense about meritocracy in the identification of the purposes of education. It is the fact that careers should in principle be open to *many*, not that they should be open to *talent*, which constitutes the progress. The symbolic offer made by education comes less as the wages of virtue than as the prize of a sort of social sweepstake. Its point is not that the rewards *will* accrue to virtue but that they *may* accrue to you. Education enshrines many of the most optimistic fantasies of Ahafo residents and in doing so it lends powerful support to the modern status hierarchy. The greatest achievement of the C.P.P. nationally, and its most concrete local service, paradoxically reinforced the political efficacy of its opponents.

In addition to the localist and ethnic categories discussed below, and the abstract categories of class, religion, and education derived from the recent social history of Ahafo, there remains one further categorical dichotomy — derived in this case from the political history of the area — which must play a part in the explanation of what happened in the election. In Asunafo, as in many other parts of the country, one way of seeing the election campaign for many of its participants was simply as a continuation of the political struggle between the former C.P.P. of Nkrumah (reincarnated uneasily in Gbedemah's N.A.L.) and the former United Party now led again by Dr Busia. At the level of local personnel the continuity was often strong enough to represent a virtual identity. But both at what could be politely termed an ideological level, and at the level of local political accumulation, it was in the interest of both parties in the 1969 election to sophisticate this crude historical distinction. Gbedemah would have been unable to don the mantle of Nkrumah overtly, even had he wished to do so — political parties had been banned by the government decree precisely for allegedly doing so — and both the circumstances of his breach with Nkrumah and his own personality presented him with little temptation to assume such an unequivocal identity.[14] At the same time it was an important feature of the rather pietistic pretensions of Dr Busia's party that it was a party of reconciliation, not one of revenge.[15] In public testimony this pacific reconciliation of all values (which of course in practice might equally well be seen as the consolidation of all interests) was testified to by a number of former C.P.P. dignitaries (among them the former Regional Commissioner, Yeboa-Afari, who had had his own difficulties with Nkrumah before the coup) appearing in the constituency to speak for the Progress Party. It is, of course, a general characteristic of politics that all parties can do with the votes of those for whose opinions or beliefs they have no use whatsoever.

There can be no doubt that the legacy to this election from the history of party conflict in Ahafo[16] (despite such purposeful blurring of the historical boundaries by the two parties) extended much further than the political *équipes* of rival party activists. Indeed the former United Party M.P. for the area assured me with some plausibility, if not with total impartiality, that the election barely needed fighting. The P.P. (he said) had as good as won before it started, since he himself had consolidated the U.P. electoral allegiance of the area in the historic battles of 1954 and 1956 when the constituency had been almost three times its present size and when he had had to lavish thousands of pounds of his own money on the enterprise. The heroic age of political entrepreneurship, it was firmly suggested, was over, the market established; and those of less innovatory skill and personal energy, to say nothing of wealth and courage, could safely expect to reap the rewards of inheriting it.

In the early 1950s Ahafo was not a politically sophisticated area. In the first national election of 1951 it was part of the extensive Kumasi West Rural constituency. The C.P.P. candidate B.F. Kusi was a young Kumasi trader from Bisease, 12 miles from Kumasi but with family connections all over Ahafo. He won the seat easily. By the time of the next election Ahafo had split off as a separate constituency. Kusi had by this time quarrelled with the C.P.P. and he stood against the party without success in his home constituency. The C.P.P. candidate for Ahafo, B.K. Senkyire came from Kenyase. He was opposed, after a contested nomination, by two candidates, one of them A.W. Osei, a former state nurse from Goaso. Senkyire won by a comfortable margin after a vigorous campaign.[17] Over the next two years Ahafo was subjected to the full ravages of the N.L.M. struggle. At its height, in the election of 1956, Osei won the seat from the C.P.P., with the assistance of a number of local chiefs, most particularly the Chief of Mim.[18] Subsequent political conflict in the area was extremely savage by Ghanaian standards. The C.P.P. reimposed its control at the local level through extensive purges of traditional office-holders and the manipulation of local separatism, notably by the restoration of the paramountcy of the Kukuomhene in the course of the creation of a separate Brong-Ahafo region. Many people were beaten up and driven away from their lands into the forest — 'to bush'. The life of the M.P., Osei, a man of striking courage and determination,[19] belied by his diminutive stature, was threatened on at least one occasion in a determined manner and numerous efforts were made to get him to transfer his allegiance to the C.P.P. He was one of the last M.P.s to remain in opposition and he continued to challenge the government intermittently (though without injudicious rudeness) in Parliament. Only the formal arrival of the one-party state and the elections of 1965, in which he was consequently unable to stand, produced his disappearance from the political scene and restored the public representation of Ahafo to C.P.P. hands. There can be little doubt that the area as a whole suffered for the obduracy of its resistance to C.P.P. control[20] and it is hardly surprising that there should have been substantial local enthusiasm at the prospect of a government of the reincarnated U.P., when the formal ban on party politics was at last lifted three years after the coup.

The official campaign for the 1969 election was naturally confined to the period after the lifting of this governmental ban on overt political activity. But in Ahafo, as elsewhere, politics never stops and there are some features of the campaign which can only be understood in the light of the entire period since the overthrow of the Nkrumah government. In one sense the most important feature of the election was that the machinery of government did not interfere in the election on behalf of either of the two major parties. Its neutrality as an organised interest may have derived more from internal dissensions along ethnic lines within the ruling N.L.C. than from the sheer force of its members' addiction to the proprieties of democratic election, but the motives for its organisational neutrality are of no significance in this instance. What matters is that it did not explicitly take sides and that any partisanship displayed by its agents at a local level was restricted in efficacy by a stringent need for discretion. The local administration, in Asunafo at least, ran the election to such high standards of propriety that despite the ebullient and far from polite atmosphere of the campaign, in which derogatory accusations were in profuse supply, for some two and a half months the writer never heard anyone allege that it had deviated from the strict demands of impartiality. Individual policemen or returning officers might have strayed from this path on occasion, but, in an exceedingly authoritarian environment, modern authority in the constituency attained impressive standards of purity in its performance of the rituals.

There is, however, a sense in which the ostentatious impartiality of the administration may have served in effect as the subtlest form of partiality. There can be no doubt that the most effective member of the local administration (the young Ga Administrative Officer) would have been happy, had not the intense rectitude of his public conduct precluded such a choice, to support the victorious party. A man of startling energy, allied with great charm and histrionic ability, he had had a very considerable impact upon the district in the two years of his administration.[21] Despite his maintenance of an elaborate mime of social distance,[22] he remained endlessly available to settle disputes, and he wrestled with *élan* against the lethargic reflexes of the central bureaucracy on behalf of the people of his district in an effort to dissipate their historical heritage of governmental neglect. The coming of piped water to the town of Goaso, the administrative capital of the district and the seat of his residence, while it was an achievement for which many claimed responsibility,[23] represented for him and indeed for the people of the town at large the consummation of his administration. As an incarnation of civic rectitude and sheer practical efficacy, he was himself for many the most reassuring political symbol — and one which plausibly united material benefit and moral purpose. If rectitude meant piped water at last, who did not want rectitude?[24]

One further sense, symbolically revealing although of small importance in this particular constituency, in which the propriety of the government's demeanour was less than impartial between the two major parties requires brief mention. Among the N.L.C.'s few specific political undertakings during the three years of its rule was the creation of the Centre for Civic Education, a government-sponsored and financed voluntary association for purveying instruction on the ethical character of the state. As one might expect with a post-colonial state, this ethical character was a pretty abstract affair, largely a question of being impartial between its subjects and of being owed duties by them. Civic education was clearly education in not voting, when the time came, for the former President (though even here the N.L.C. government showed its lack of confidence in the efficacy of the educational process by banning any party which attempted to provide this opportunity). But at least in its public dimensions it could not be asserted to have been education in voting *for* anybody in particular. The most that could be said was that earnest injunctions to exhibit virtue when voting might suggest to the innocent voter that to expend his ballot on a man whose public image was somewhat pietistic would be a more virtuous act than bestowing it on a man whose public image was distinctly more raffish. In any case it is hard to believe that the Centre for Civic Education can have exerted any very drastic electoral effect. Among the sixty or so men and women (not personally engaged in running the campaign of one of the parties) interviewed in Goaso in three months before the election, extended questioning revealed that at most four or five had *heard* of the Centre under any description, and of these none had any distinct idea of what it was for. What was more important from the point of view of N.A.L. – as Gbedemah complained on the occasion of his electoral visit to Goaso – was that the man placed at the head of this emblematically impartial body was to become, in due course, the leader of the party which eventually won the election. Gbedemah's complaint was not, of course, that there was anything inauthentic for Busia in the rôle of civic educator. (It was indeed the precision with which the rôle fitted him which served in the unsympathetic eye to blur its impartiality.) What had aroused Gbedemah's resentment was that the Centre had given the Progress Party's leader several years start in political organisation before the ban on politics had been lifted. Organisation had been the C.P.P.'s great talisman, a word of almost magical significance, pronounced reverentially even by the District Secretary of the Progress Party, and the practice of it had always been Gbedemah's forte. In his speech in Goaso he contrived to turn the start enjoyed by his opponents almost into an advantage for himself by the dramatic projection of the speed and the nationwide scope of his own organisational efforts. It was a fine performance. But the bravado rang a little hollow.

Organisation had always been an activity of slightly ambiguous meaning in Ghanaian political practice. It took in, under one of its aspects, the mastery of the modern technical aspects of political campaigning, a mastery which the C.P.P. had introduced to most of Ghana, the provision of propaganda vans, leaflets, newspapers, speakers and party paraphernalia in which N.A.L. often enjoyed something of an edge over its opponents in this particular campaign. The symbol of this modern aspect of organisation might simply be not missing the bus. In so far as it was in itself a sufficient condition for amassing votes, there is no reason to suppose that Busia's tenancy of the Civic Education platform gave him any significant organisational advantage. But, in another of its aspects, organisation always meant something distinctly less public or modernist in character: the attentive stitching together of national coalitions out of local élites, in which there remain necessarily almost as many seams along which to fray as there are strands in the local political cloth. There can be no doubt that Busia's travels around the country and his meetings with local notables had the effect of clothing the Progress Party, on its eventual emergence, in the mantle of local élite approval, making the respectable party into the party of national respectability in most areas of the country, and thus endowing with impressive political weight an ideology which had seemed to less sensitive foreign observers almost devoid of social purchase. The organisational talents of Gbedemah himself and the C.P.P. in general in this second activity had never been tested in an environment in which there existed real opposition, without the possibility of some more or less direct recourse to the coercive or economically rewarding powers of the state. The situation in 1969 demanded substantially greater political skill for their control, and Gbedemah certainly needed much more time to unpick the seams, though time alone would hardly have turned out to be sufficient. There was thus real political substance to the advantage enjoyed by Busia through his public institution, and he had in fact visited Goaso to inaugurate a branch of it. And yet the opportunity which it must have given him in Asunafo to consolidate local élite support was in practice quite supererogatory. The main seams of such a coalition had been stitched together, as A.W. Osei observed with pride, in the election of thirteen years before. The political memory of Asunafo was largely a memory of the costs of this choice, and the survivors of this élite coalition had no need of a visit from their former party leader to commit them energetically to the effort to secure the belated rewards of their past sufferings. As the bent old women who had been beaten from their villages under the C.P.P. danced in jubilation over their enemies at the Progress Party's election rallies, it was clear that the people of Asunafo had drawn their lessons from an education with roots in a soil deeper if more ambiguous than that of the civic.

The campaign which took place within the painstakingly neutral administrative framework was conducted by two different types of actors. One, a rather small group, comprised those who were overtly or covertly contenders for selection as electoral candidates for either of two major parties which alone in the end contested the constituency.[25] The other consisted of the political organisations of these two parties. The distinction between the two

122

groups was in part one of status, a social matter, but also in part one of vanity, a personal matter. Becoming an M.P. in Ghana represents dramatic upward social mobility for all except the vastly rich. A seat in Parliament, with its combination of direct and indirect economic returns, is a prize of such a scale that only one eligible man in Asunafo — a large-scale timber contractor — was plainly too rich for it to be worth his while acquiring it. Selection as a majority party's candidate for Parliament is an economic opportunity for which the ambitious might well choose to contend for purely egoistic reasons. It is thus not surprising that some of those who did aspire to the parties' nominations without success should then have failed to take any part in the election campaign. The story of the Progress Party's triumph in the campaign is largely the story of the failure of a series of vanities, ruffled in political defeat, to give rise to the customary fissions.

The party's success in preserving its unity was facilitated in part by the timing of one of the most important contests over candidacy. The eventual Progress candidate, Alfred Badu Nkansah, first attained political prominence in a tripartite competition for the nomination as a member of the Constituent Assembly[26] for the two Parliamentary constituencies of Asunafo and Asutifi (the Goaso Council area). The other two candidates were A.W. Osei, the former United Party M.P. for the area, a substantially older man, and a third rather shadowy figure, apparently an itinerant vendor of patent medicines who received little support and disappeared from political view immediately after the election. Nkansah had the advantage of a university education, important in the context of selection for constitution-making, without the disability which commonly accompanied this qualification of having chosen to live and work outside the area. He had recently played a prominent part in the successful struggle to destool the chief of his home town, Akrodie;[27] he was also an active member of the resuscitated Ahafo Youth Society, the modernist pressure group in the perennial conflict with the local state bureaucracy, a body of which Osei was probably the leading light. The electors for the representative of the locality to the Constituent Assembly were the government-appointed members of the Local Council for the area, of which, too, Mr. Osei was a highly effective member. The total number of electors was less than thirty and in no sense whatever could they have been said to be statistically representative of the area. But, whether because the prominence of officials in its composition gave it a more formalist sense of the qualifications required for constitution-making (and hence led it to put greater emphasis on youth and educational attainment), or whether for more direct reasons, the electors voted, somewhat to the surprise of a number of shrewd local observers, strongly in favour of Badu Nkansah.

In the subsequent months the latter's public performance in the Assembly was prominent enough to please the more attentive local political observers. Copies of Hansard containing speeches of his percolated through to Goaso and one or two members of the community, including the local representative of the Special Branch of the police, who observed him in action in the Assembly and professed themselves satisfied. In private, Badu Nkansah naturally aligned himself with the large group of members of the Assembly who favoured Dr. Busia and he began to attend some of the meetings of this group at Busia's private house on the outskirts of Accra. At the same time Osei was in extremely poor health for some months, and he became increasingly preoccupied with the problems of running his business and attending to his very extensive familial responsibilities. Whether or not the 1969 nomination would have been such a simple choice if he had been successful in his earlier candidature for membership of the Constituent Assembly, it was not a difficult matter in the circumstances which now prevailed to decide that he had had his fill of the travails of politics and could properly emulate Cincinnatus in abandoning public for private duties. The avoidance of any direct and embittered clash between the two men was of great significance, since the core political organisation of the party remained in essentials an inheritance from Osei's earlier campaigns.

Both the party's District Secretary (a nephew of Mr. Osei who lived in one of the rooms in his two-storey house in Goaso) and another leading member (who was not only a close personal friend of Osei's for many years but a former chief of Noberkaw, one of the premier chiefly ranks in the Ahafo division) had worked closely with Osei in the Ahafo Youth Society. There was a certain initial distrust towards these men on the part of the most active supporters and advisors of Badu Nkansah, a number of whom were not Ahafo-born, because they feared a resuscitation of Osei's candidacy and there were intermittent minor grumblings over matters like the control of campaigning funds as these became available, and over the general unwillingness to undertake the entertainment of visiting dignitaries due to speak at rallies. But, despite the general scarcity of financial resources, the atmosphere remained strikingly amicable and co-operative.

The maintenance of amity in this key relationship during the campaign did not mean that the party escaped the pains of a sharply contested candidacy. At the meeting held in the regional capital, Sunyani, some 80 miles from Goaso, to inaugurate the party in the Brong Ahafo region, another eligible figure from Ahafo appeared on the V.I.P. dais as a potential rival to Badu Nkansah. He was a man of roughly the same age as the latter, slightly more of an urban sophisticate in appearance, and he possessed the additional advantage of a British M.Sc. degree in engineering. He worked at the modern port of Tema and owned a rather new-looking Mercedes, whereas Badu Nkansah, as became important at some points of the campaign, did not possess a car and his salary as a school teacher was totally insufficient for him to acquire one. (There were, indeed, certain stages of the campaign in which the need to return to Accra to draw his allowances as a Member of the Constituent Assembly seemed to loom larger in his financial planning for the campaign than the need to participate in its deliberations did in his political planning.) This rival candidate, Yaw Podiee, hailed from Mim, the largest and wealthiest town in the constituency, and this fact, combined with his greater personal wealth, appeared to threaten Badu Nkansah with serious competition. The threat was not an entirely idle one. The fairness of the first selection meeting of the party was successfully challenged by Podiee through the regional organisation of the party; and a second meeting, summoned for the town of Sankore deep in the forest, led first to an attempt on the part of Podiee's supporters to persuade the police to close the meeting and then to an extended public wrangle before the chief of Sankore about the circumstances in which the meeting had been summoned. At the end of this dispute, the representatives of Mim marched out of the meeting and Badu Nkansah was confirmed as the candidate by an overwhelming (and clearly an absolute) majority of the delegates. Numerous subsequent efforts to settle the dispute aborted, usually because of the difficulty of assembling all the injured parties at one time and place, and it was not until a meeting (in Mim itself) shortly before the election — when the District Chairman of the party who came from Mim, and another even more determined Mim representative, grumpily condescended to take part in a rally — that the breach was publicly healed. Allegations of corruption and chicanery were passed energetically in both directions and it would be imprudent to attempt a conclusive causal analysis of the result. But it was clear, quite apart from the advantage which he enjoyed by having already appeared on the national political scene as the representative of Ahafo, that one reason for Badu Nkansah's success was that in the eyes of the electorate he was a much better candidate. Podiee, a slight figure with a quiet and rather delicate mien, who had studied in England for some years, had simply been away from home for too long. The air of urban sophistication which clung around him conveyed a powerful sense of social distance. Unlike his taller, charming, noisily articulate and slightly brash opponent he lacked the capacity to 'move with the people' and did not know how to dominate a beer bar. One could not imagine anyone saying of Podiee, as the District Secretary said over and over again with quiet and confident satisfaction of Badu Nkansah, 'The people like him.' Badu's stay away from Ahafo had left him still in possession of a reassuringly familiar local identity, and he had had the political good taste to return and find a job and make his home in Ahafo. Podiee had travelled too far and returned too belatedly to serve as a plausible vehicle for the assertive political demands of Ahafo. In the event, even the possession of the large car served, with his distant air, not to promise greater efficacy as an advocate of the interests of the area, but to accentuate the transiency of his relationship with it. What might have been seen as a testimony to its owner's effectiveness served in practice merely to emphasise the extent to which he had become exotic.

Even this account of the selection of the P.P.'s candidate represents, as will be apparent later, a distinctly tidied up outline of the shape of its campaign. For the selection of the N.A.L. candidate there is no way in which even this rather specious simplicity can be matched. It had at least always been clear that one of the parties which contested any election in Asunafo under N.L.C. auspices was certain to be some version of the former United Party. What was not clear up to the very day of nomination was what other parties, if any, might enter the lists. One reason for this was simply the much greater organisational fluidity of the other parties, a national rather than a local characteristic, though one which had distinct repercussions on the local pattern of political activity. Another was the distinctly more furtive character (it was referred to by participants quite explicitly as a largely 'secret campaign') of the N.A.L. approach in the constituency when it did in fact begin. This furtiveness was in a sense a rational response to the precariousness of the government's impartiality in the election. For while the government was indubitably impartial as a unit between the parties which were permitted to contest the election, it did actively maintain its right to determine the limits within which it *was* prepared to be impartial. Not only did it ban by decree at a national level parties for alleged complicity with Nkrumah; but, at a local level, C.I.D. or Special Branch officers attended a large number of election rallies and took conscientious notes on the proceedings, while full particulars of the secret selection meeting for the N.A.L. candidate, held in a private house in Goaso, immediately found their way into the hands of the local administration. Paradoxically, in Asunafo, the party which was assumed to enjoy most support in the senior ranks of the police force nationally was subjected locally to a certain amount of inconvenience as a result of this conscientious surveillance. On the national level the party enjoyed an irreproachable security rating. Gbedemah had not merely had the good fortune to be removed by Nkrumah from the Ministry of Finance for alleged corruption. He had also had the political prudence or personal pride to respond in due course to this treatment by leaving the country and engaging in bitter public recrimination against his former leader. But this political accreditation on the national level which, along with the economic resources at the disposal of his party, explained why in the end he was able to field the only candidate who did oppose the P.P. in Asunafo, could not suffice to provide an *a priori* charter in the eyes of the local administration for the doings of his local agents.

The N.A.L. campaign was organised by the licit residue of the former C.P.P. local hierarchy. The major organiser, and in fact the Parliamentary candidate in the neighbouring constituency of Asutifi, Kojo Bonsu, was a former chief of Kenyase and a brother of the leading C.P.P. dignitary from Ahafo, B.K. Senkyire, M.P. in 1954, and Minister in the final Nkrumah government. The latter was widely thought in Accra to have been one of the major figures behind the party organised by Imoru Egala, a party banned during the course of the campaign by the N.L.C. for its alleged intention to bring Nkrumah back from exile. Senkyire was in no position to escape from any of the versions of the government's Disqualification policies. But although he could thus, at no point, have taken an overt part in campaigning, there is no reason to believe that his brother (who used to appear in a Mercedes universally described as Senkyire's own) would not have been able, had governmental licence permitted, to swing his support behind a party which appeared to be a more authentic inheritor of the C.P.P. mantle. As it was, it was said rancorously by his opponents, that he had dallied politically and economically with at least two further parties before settling his favours finally upon the N.A.L. Such inconstancy is not a trivial matter since, if it is ignored, the insistence of N.A.L. members on the degree to which their membership of the party had been a matter of course would be seriously misleading. There is no reason to doubt the claim made by one of the most impressive local C.P.P. organisers that he had always esteemed Gbedemah, even as against Nkrumah, as the epitome of the true, pre-tyrannical (and, one may suspect, pre-ideological) C.P.P., a man whose advice, if followed, would have averted the calamity of the coup and the loss of many good jobs. Having acquired Gbedemah as a leader, the N.A.L. supporters were in no danger of being short of attributes to admire in him. But rationality should not be confused with causality: the quality of the determination of their allegiance seems to have been a largely *a posteriori* characteristic of it. One could not say that necessity had made strange bedfellows in this instance. But governmental licence might certainly have made different ones. Gbedemah's economic resources, and the character of his party as the contender least unlike the C.P.P. to contrive to survive within the limits of governmental tolerance, made him the natural inheritor of a local political *équipe* which increasingly looked to be all dressed up with nowhere to go. But although this *équipe* was an excellent example of what could be acquired for cash on a decidedly oligopolistic political market, one characteristic of it points up a general dilemma in Gbedemah's national campaign strategy.

Whereas much local political support could be picked up on a purely market basis, there were few places in which a preponderance of support could be picked up on this basis alone; while organisational support of any political weight acquired on a purely market basis tended to carry intrinsic costs above and beyond those of its political purchase. A political *équipe* authentically N.A.L. in its ideological identity (whatever such an *équipe* would have been like outside the Ewe areas) would not have been unduly embarrassed by administrative scrutiny. But a local C.P.P. apparatus, in which former C.P.P. District Commissioners were covertly promised their jobs back if the party won, might well appear to the local administration as intrinsically closer to its protracted historical identity than to the decorous political label which it had so recently adopted. In this guise it might well seem to require all the administrative surveillance which it could conveniently be given. Without the government's exclusion of a potential competitor Gbedemah, then, might well have failed to garner the political support which he did acquire in Asunafo.

It is a mark of the equivocal status of N.A.L. as a contestant in the constituency that, whereas the first public P.P. meeting of the campaign was held in Goaso on 1 May, in the immediate aftermath of the lifting of the ban on politics, no major N.A.L. activity was discernible in the constituency at all (though a N.A.L. van did drive through on 8 June) until the middle of June when a meeting was held in the smartest Goaso beer bar. The Special Branch representative in the district claimed that as late as 7 August the party had still not secured a permit for holding an official public rally some three weeks before the election was to take place. The two campaigns represented a dramatic contrast in styles. To a very substantial extent they went their separate ways, resolutely ignoring the existence of one another. The competition between them took on many different guises, but one form which it never assumed was that of a rational and explicit debate between the two parties about how the state could best be governed. The Schumpeter image of conflicting élites blandly offering their managerial talents to discriminating consumers in an assured environment was as inept a picture of the efforts of the vendors as it was of the expectations of the purchasers. The loyalties reached for were deeper and more pervasive, and the enterprise to which electors were summoned was altogether more urgent than the practice of marketing. The rewards for success and the penalties for failure were of quite a different scale both for élites and masses, and the prospects for failure were known by all not to terminate with the election results. The image of cementing unity in the struggle against a nebulous but menacing foe, captures the language in which the activity of electioneering was described much better than that of the compulsory but attentive choice between rival schemes of hire purchase. It will be more illuminating to discuss the recruiting campaigns of the two armies separately, as they happened, and it is convenient to begin with the first to appear on the scene.

The opening meeting of the Progress Party in Goaso on 1 May, summoned by the Chief of Goaso beating gong-gong, in a sense epitomised the problems of the party in the coming months. Although it claimed to be the official inauguration of the party in the constituency, it was in fact a meeting unauthorised by the central machinery of the party: it was organised by the faction in the longstanding Goaso chieftaincy dispute which opposed the faction to which Osei belonged. As far as was then publicly known, the latter was still a prospective candidate and it was assumed that the holding of the meeting at this time was an effort to preempt the political ground for another candidate. Organisationally the meeting also foreshadowed much of the rest of the campaign; it had to be closed and reconvened some hours later because of the paucity of the attendance. The subject matter of the speeches, appropriately enough, was the need to come together to represent the interests of Ahafo in view of the dreadful damage to these interests caused by past local disunity. Three weeks later, on 21 May, the national machinery of the party, in the masterful person of A.A. Munufie, a Sunyani

128

lawyer and interim Regional Chairman of the party, appeared in the constituency to reimpose some order on the proceedings. The meeting was supposed to be a meeting of the party executive, rather than the public, but it took place very publicly at the courthouse. Munufie was somewhat late and the chief of Goaso attempted to have the meeting postponed to another occasion. Munufie's powerful voice quieted the hubbub briefly and he explained that all the offices in the party were merely interim until the formal regional inauguration in Sunyani, three days later. Then a representative of the alternative faction in the local chieftaincy dispute complained that the self-selected party executive did not represent the people of Goaso and the meeting broke up noisily.

The regional inauguration on 24 May duly saw many important Ahafo figures at Sunyani. The former Paramount of Ahafo, the Kukuomhene, was among the chiefs sitting in state beneath their umbrellas, while Mr. Osei and his nephew (the aspiring District Secretary) and both candidates for the party nomination were also conspicuously in attendance. Busia arrived to speak to a substantial crowd, flanked by numerous policemen and traditional state executioners. It was a gay and festive occasion, featuring sundry party dignitaries from Accra, a band or two, some dancing, men with megaphones, party motorcyclists, a carload of girls dressed in white and red, and a good deal of genial disorganisation. If the party shrank from the distribution of bread (or its Ghanaian analogue, sardines), it clearly had no inhibitions about supplying the people with circuses. A main theme of Busia's speech was an assurance that he did not propose to dismantle the Brong Ahafo region (Sunyani's sole industry). It was in essence a denial (made rather anxiously by Munufie in Goaso three days before) of the charge of being a lackey of the Ashanti, which the former U.P. leader was clearly under strong pressure to make.

In the three weeks after this inauguration the decisively national focus of the campaign's objective, and the external political resources which this made available within the constituency, began to impose order on the ebullient particularism of Ahafo to the extent of providing it, by mid-June, with an authorised District Executive, the election of which had been duly supervised by party officials from outside the constituency. Osei's nephew, Benson Anane, duly became the Secretary and his election was made more generally palatable by Osei's own public declaration that he was not prepared to stand as a candidate. The self-elected Goaso executive was largely supplanted outside the town itself, but it swallowed its pride and continued to co-operate in the campaign. Further public meetings, at both of which Munufie spoke, were held at Mim and (in the second week of June) at Kukuom, in the immediate aftermath of Kukuomhene's acquittal celebrations,[28] a piece of timing which secured an optimal audience but which clearly irritated the chief himself. On 29 June Badu Nkansah was chosen as the candidate, Yaw Podiee having, as the Executive judged, improperly submitted his application to the regional office and thus being ineligible. The consequences of this dispute dragged on for several more weeks, exhausting most of the energies available. Taken with the unavailability of a party van for the district, and with Badu Nkansah's modest personal means and his need to leave the constituency for substantial periods to participate in the Constituent Assembly, it resulted in there being a temporary respite in the public campaign — a respite which lasted until a meeting in Badu Nkansah's home town Akrodie in mid-July to which a leading U.P. former detainee, R.R. Amponsah, came to speak.

The remainder of the P.P. campaign was more continuous and less eventful. There were a substantial number of further public meetings, held at least once in all the major population centres in the constituency, several with visiting speakers. A promised visit by Busia himself never materialised, though on two occasions leading party supporters in the constituency made extended trips outside it in order to hear him speak. The content of speeches did not vary very much, though the tone of persuasion wavered in sophistication and delicacy from the purely pietistic to the sharply and personally minatory, and from the grandly universalistic to the meanly ethnic. Apart from the intermittent character of the candidate's presence, the most striking organisational problem throughout was one of transport. The modern party van from the regional organisation was shared with several other constituencies and was thus only occasionally available. Badu Nkansah, out of the not very extensive campaigning funds raised at local rallies and made available to him by the party's central organisation, contrived to borrow or hire a motley array of decrepit vehicles ranging from a Land Rover with a wooden body to a pair of exhausted Volkswagens, none of which spent as much time available for use as they did being repaired. The constituency was of substantial size, and its population was scattered through the forest in clusters, most of which, because of the rather uncharacteristically low rainfall in 1969, could be reached by road in a fairly robust vehicle. There can be no doubt that the party organisers were compelled to devote more energy and money to actually getting to as many places as possible in the constituency to campaign than they did to any other part of their enterprise. When they actually did get to most of the more rural villages, they confined their political activities, apart from consultations with the party's local representatives where such were to be found, to a brief introduction of the candidate, an identification of the party emblem (which illiterates had to remember if they were to be able to vote at all) and an extensively mimed representation of the activity of voting. The procedure for voting was in fact fairly elaborate and the mime consequently took up most of the time available at each halt. The entire procedure was described throughout by the party organisers as 'educating the people' in how to vote. It was certainly true, too, that what was transacted was more aptly described as educating them in how to vote for those for whom it was assumed they would already wish to vote, than as attempting to persuade them to vote for a particular party. The P.P. assumed throughout (quite correctly as the results demonstrated)[29] that their problem was simply one of getting electors to the polls with an understanding of the mechanism of casting a ballot, not one of persuading them to vote for the P.P. rather than for their opponents. On occasion they pressed this exercise in civic education rather hard — as when they visited a primary school and attempted to get the Headmaster to teach the children to identify the P.P. symbol in order to assist their parents in doing so when the opportunity in due course arose. The neutrality of this undertaking was greeted with some incredulity by the predominantly Ewe schoolteachers and in fact the N.A.L. vote in this village was one of the highest in the constituency.

The N.A.L. campaign began later and proceeded in an altogether more covert and less assured fashion. A bus load of supporters from one village deep in the forest was alleged to have gone to Gbedemah's inauguration rally but the P.P. resolutely denied that this had happened. A N.A.L. propaganda van, painted in the party's striking red and yellow colours, had appeared in the constituency on a number of occasions in the first half of June. The P.P. organisers claimed to know the identity of the N.A.L. candidate as early as the middle of June, and indeed gave the (true) fact that he came from Mim as an argument against the chances of Podiee's being selected as P.P. candidate. But it was not until shortly after this that N.A.L. held their first Goaso executive meeting, presided over by one of the party's regional officials, Mr Essel, the Kukuomhene's clerk. T.N. Baidoo, a former C.P.P. District Commissioner, a relative and long-time rival of Osei's and a colleague on the first official agency for the development of the area seventeen years before,[30] spoke at length at this meeting. It was clear that the organisational talent of the party was a direct heritage from the C.P.P., though the preliminary District Chairman, a male nurse, S.K. Dontor, was a Fanti and a relative newcomer to the district. On 5 July after a series of postponements an official candidate selection meeting of the party began. There were three competitors for the nomination. One, J.K. Osei, a quiet schoolteacher from Mim at that point teaching outside the constituency at Bechem, was a member of the Ahafo Youth Society and agreed by all to be an excellent candidate. The other two contestants were an agricultural survey officer from Akrodie, said to lack force of personality and a large bull-like man, recently admitted to the University of Ghana as a mature student, who had studied meat technology in Germany and served as production manager of the government meatpacking factory in Bolgatanga. He had expressed a vehement and pungently cynical interest in politics at his University interview and was clearly a formidable figure. But, as one of the executive remarked quitely before the meeting began, he had little prospect of success since he came from Ashanti and his eligibility derived solely from his mother's ownership of a farm in the district at Ayumso: 'If we are not going to have a candidate who is Ahafo-born, then let's stop the party.' Most of the meeting was taken up with a dispute over the choice of the party District Chairman in which the geographical divisions, Kukuom side and Mim side, were reflected in a bitter conflict as to whose candidate should be selected as Chairman, a conflict in which the even balance of forces might well have foreshadowed (and was clearly expected by all participants to foreshadow) a conflict between the two localities over the Parliamentary candidature. Some of the structural problems of the party were revealed by the subject matter of the dispute — the significance of having a literate rather than an illiterate (namely, the Kukuom representative), the desirability of having a local man rather than a stranger (namely, the temporary chairman, S.K. Dontor), and the usual range of accusations of chicanery in the distribution of information. The valiant endeavour of the regional presiding officer, Kojo Bonsu, and his determined insistence on the need for unity and propriety, did not prevent the meeting from breaking up after some hours (and before the Parliamentary candidate had been selected) in what the District administration rather unsympathetically described as a riot. The one determinate result of the meeting, the election of a District Executive, by confirming Dontor as District Chairman, further emphasised the tension in the party's local identity. Since, as one of the Executive observed *sotto voce*, the party's leader was very much a stranger to Ahafo, it would have been a pointless exercise to attempt to portray itself as more indigenous than the indigenes. N.A.L. was forced therefore into the pursuit of the allegiance of the relatively large local stranger population, above all the Ewes and Krobos. But in doing so, it risked discrediting itself as an authentic representative of the locality. Even the eventual running of an Ahafo-born candidate could not quite dissipate the whiff of the alien which hung about it and any more purposeful attempt to elude this identity would have risked the sacrifice of a more or less guaranteed core of electoral support in exchange for a highly speculative (and in all probability non-existent) chance of a majority.

The day after the fracas at the courthouse N.A.L. applied for a police permit to hold another candidate selection meeting but the request was refused because the District administration thought it likely that a week of cooling off might be required to prevent further trouble. In the event a N.A.L. van returned to the constituency from Sunyani on the following day and a secret meeting was held at the house of T.N. Baidoo, rather mysteriously reported as a public rally in one of the national newspapers, at which the offer to the former C.P.P. District Commissioners that they should regain their jobs in the event of a N.A.L. victory was allegedly made by the party official from Sunyani. Thereafter the party contrived to conduct what was referred to, both by its own adherents and the P.P. with varying admiration or censure, as its 'secret campaign'. It never had the full use of a propaganda van with which at one time all constituencies were supposed to be endowed and there was some grumbling among the party's temporary employees at the non-appearance of other resources. There is no good reason to suppose

that really large sums of money ever arrived in the constituency for its campaigning purposes, though there is much reason to suppose that this came as
a considerable and disagreeable surprise to many of those concerned. Indeed
some senior members of the party were still expecting the arrival of some
thousands of pounds in the constituency on the very eve of polling itself.
The party's stylish propaganda vans drove through the main towns from time
to time, playing the same catchy religious popsongs from their speakers as
those favoured by local motorised salesmen of patent medicines, and the
party's slogans were duly broadcast at the bystanders. As campaigning it had,
as far as it went, a harder, brassier tone than that of its opponents, slicker,
more modern and more urban. But as campaigning goes, it cannot be claimed
that in quantitative terms it went very far, and the image it left behind it had
some of the meretriciousness, the urban untrustworthiness of the patent
medicine vendors, besides its protective promises. The yawning gap between
this assured and transient public advertisement and the furtive, persistent,
'organisational' efforts of the local party machine, was not reassuring. It
suggested the menace at least as much as the blandishments of modernity.

The climax of the N.A.L. campaign, by contrast, was the most dramatic
and the most public local event of the entire election campaign: the visit of
the party's leader to Goaso, Kukuom and Mim a fortnight before polling
day itself. The excitement generated by this event was intense. Whatever
may have been its causal weight (and no doubt this should not be exaggerated
since the party's total poll barely exceeded the joint attendance at its three
meetings), its symbolic significance could hardly be overestimated. As the
beautiful Ewe girls in all their finery danced on the hillside in the sunshine,
waiting for their leader, the atmosphere in the crowd was sharply expectant.
When the party vans at the head of the procession hurtled into town, blaring
out the thudding Twi rhythms, 'He is coming: He is coming: He is coming,' a
quite different level of political panache had entered the campaign however
briefly. The meeting itself in Goaso was a demonstrative exercise in the new
political respectability. Gbedemah's former Parliamentary foe and locally
prominent current opponent, Mr A.W. Osei, was given a seat of honour with
Gbedemah and his local aides on the steps of the Goaso Local Council building, while Gbedemah's speech (which took up the entire meeting) included
much stress on the virtues of opposition in a Parliamentary democracy and
the iniquity of political violence and the one-party state. A tall and powerful-
looking man, of extraordinary self-assurance and striking physical glamour,
he formed as he stood up to speak a stunning incarnation of sheer power and
success. If this was success, then it was easy to see how many might feel that
nothing else could succeed quite like it. The speech itself, although fluent
enough and undeniably forceful in delivery and sentiment, hardly matched
the dazzling quality of the physical presence. Partly this was a matter of
clashing styles. The speech was delivered in a confident Twi, but it kept
lapsing at the more aspirational points into clusters of apparently well-worn

phrases or whole sentences in English.[31] The attentive cosmopolitan 'liberal' stress on the values of Parliamentary opposition jostled against a rather cruder presentation of the meaning of Gbedemah's campaigning presence: the bringing of rain to a parched Navrongo and of a miraculous draught of fishes to the port of Elmina. The main theme of the speech was the certainty of his electoral triumph all over the country: Keta, Dodze, Cape Coast, Sekondi, Bawku, Bolga, Walewale, Wa, Manya, even Wenchi, and the consequent rationality — prudential and emotional — of joining in. The whole speech was an articulation of the party's slogan 'N.A.L. VICTORY'. The offer was plain and forceful enough and if it was made in English, rather than, as with the P.P.'s pietistic chant (P.P. Good Party) in Twi, there is no doubt that it was couched in a dialect which has become pervasively understood in Ghana. Shorter versions of the speech were delivered to smaller crowds in Kukuom (where the cavalcade paid a brief private call on the chief but the latter did not appear at the public function); and at Mim where Gbedemah was jeered by a hostile crowd. One small detail, no doubt a consequence of the strains of the campaigning tour,[32] stood out in retrospect. As the resplendent Gbedemah towered over the slight, bemused figure of the local N.A.L. candidate, whose hand he held up in introduction to the people ('if you vote for him, you will be voting for ME'), he twice, at Goaso and at Kukuom, forgot the candidate's name and was obliged to ask in an irritable hiss what it was.

When the electors went to the polls a fortnight later, they voted overwhelmingly for the Progress Party, as they did in both the other constituencies along the main road out of the Ahafo forest towards Sunyani and Kumasi.

Asunafo	A. Badu Nkansah (P.P.)	13039	81 polling stations
	J.K. Osei (N.A.L.)	2715	P.P. wins 79*
Asutifi	I.K. Osei Duah (P.P.)	6026	42 polling stations
	Nana Kojo Bonsu (N.A.L.)	1707	all won by P.P.
	Kwame Anana Obinim (U.N.P.)	124	
Ahafo-Ano	H.M. Adjei-Sarpong (P.P.)	11959	49 polling stations
	G.K. Annin-Adjei (N.A.L.)	2268	all won by P.P.

It was a remarkably peaceful and administratively well-organised poll. Before considering, however, what the electors were voting about, it is necessary to discuss a number of possibly coercive features which would make such a question otiose. If men are compelled to vote in a particular way it cannot usefully be said that they vote *about* anything. They merely do what they are told. Many Ghanaians, for convincing inductive reasons, undoubtedly do expect that electoral behaviour will be essentially an exercise in obedience.

* For polling station figures see appendix (pp. 155–6).

As one old man whom I interviewed replied testily in an answer to the question of how one should choose a political party: 'I don't know anything about that. But when the time comes I will put the paper into the box into which all the people are putting theirs.'[33] Ghanaian society is in many ways highly authoritarian and it would be naive to expect political parties as composite social realities, if not as formal hierarchies of command, to eschew the use of such dispersed authority as is available to them. But it is not a trivially definitional matter to insist, against Hobbes or possibly Marx, on the crucial significance of the voluntaristic element in electing. Fear is not the same as respect, and force without right as the basis of electoral choice does erase whatever symbolically consensual element might be thought to reside in the act of voting. It is thus a matter of some embarrassment, though one which in prevailing conditions could hardly be otherwise, that it is impossible to pronounce with complete assurance on the degree of random social coercion or malpractice involved in the election. One point which does seem clear is that such coercion as did occur was on this occasion, because of the real secrecy of the ballot, effective at an economic rather than a physical level. The fear of violence may not have been altogether absent. There were a small number of brawls in the course of the campaign — the N.A.L. candidate in the neighbouring constituency, Kojo Bonsu, was even taken to court himself on a rather tendentious assault charge — but the actual incidence of violence was distinctly lower than almost everyone expected. Gbedemah himself did feel it worthwhile to warn in his speech in Goaso that the soldiers in the constituency were not coming to threaten people but to assist the wholly inadequate numbers of the police in supervising the large number of polling stations. But only a small number of soldiers ever appeared and they certainly did not intervene in the electoral process. More graphically, the chief of one town did threaten to beat the passengers if a N.A.L. propaganda van came to his town, but it was reported later that one had done so without injury being incurred.

In general, traditional authority does not appear to have been very active in the campaign even in a non-coercive fashion, though one chief did arrive at the main P.P. rally with a busload of supporters from his town and at least two others publicly declared their support of the P.P. The average age of the chiefs in the area was rather high, most of them having been removed by the C.P.P., and then replaced by the N.L.C. under decree 112. Their formal legitimacy was on the whole impeccable, but it might be doubted whether all could have survived the threat of destoolment for so long in a more open political environment. In any case, whether because of the inertia of age and a sense of subjective fragility in their authority, or because of the strong governmental directives to chiefs to remain neutral in the electoral campaign, most did maintain some public decorum. Furthermore the P.P., which for historical reasons enjoyed the support of the majority of them, was in no position because of its unceasing public commitment to rectitude to make use of these dubiously legitimate political actors for publicly coercive purposes in any general way. Any effort to do so on its part would have risked not only an embarrassing exposure at the hands of its opponents but also, since the ballot was in fact secret, distinctly counterproductive effects when it actually came to the voting.

Perhaps the level at which the notion of coercion is relevant at all is the level of vague menace, characteristic in industrial society on occasion of some aspects of workplace solidarity in which a measure of blackmail is indubitably involved, but in which it is clearly appropriate to see the threats as largely those of moral scorn, rather than of instrumental violence.[34] There was at least one occasion when the Progress Party representatives read out from the electoral registers the names of the inhabitants of a small forest village, and warned them darkly that the election results were going to be known this time, polling station by polling station, and the party would know all too well which way they had voted. There can be no doubt too that Gbedemah, when he emphasised the secrecy of the ballot in his Goaso speech[35] against those who had been threatening share-croppers and cocoa labourers with dispossession or unemployment if they voted the wrong way, was attempting to deal with a real political threat. The reality of the threat was indeed confirmed by the explanation given by an N.A.L. organiser of the small forest wards in which it did prove successful: that the main land-holdings in the area were under the control of strong party supporters. The nagging fear, too, that physical violence might ultimately be deployed was not a total fantasy, though it was also not justified in the event. At least one prominent P.P. campaigner suggested in the immediate aftermath of its crushing victory that the party's supporters take the opportunity to repay some of the violence which they had incurred in the past at the hands of their C.P.P. opponents, though the suggestion was indignantly repudiated as atavistic and disgraceful.

It would have been absurd in a society like that of Ghana to expect an election campaign to be uncontaminated by a good deal of more or less discreet bullying. But even where the number of electors involved was low enough partially to vitiate the protection conferred by the secrecy of the ballot, it would be easy to misdescribe the implication of the directed quality of the vote. Even if the politics of Asunafo is largely to be described as a politics of patronage, and of integrating clientages for political purposes, it does not follow that such mechanisms — in conditions of genuinely secret balloting and without recourse to state power — can appropriately be envisaged as the rule of terror or as the subjection of a mass of individual wills to the antagonistic will of a single man. After all, one can only vote in an election between the candidates who present themselves, and between the two candidates who did so in this instance it would have required a more than Chinese ideological sensitivity to detect a trace of difference in the character of their class appeal. This is hardly an occasion for wonder in view

136

of the virtually complete absence of class-consciousness as such from the political mind of Asunafo. Such patronal political instruction as was put about under these conditions was certainly less likely to represent the coercive repression of the desires of individual voters to vote in a particular fashion than it was simply the provision to them of reasons for troubling to vote at all. In the particular N.A.L. village in question – a village organised by a long-term resident from the Kusasi area of northern Ghana and peopled largely by Kusasis whom he had settled there – its patronal reliability is as plausibly represented as depending on its ethnic homogeneity and the strength of personal obligations as on its susceptibility to purely economic threats. In general, such solidarism as there was in the constituency seems to have taken an ethnic and not a class form. In a multi-linguistic area of recent, but geographically dispersed, settlement the dimensions of community which are directly relevant to the structure of men's lives necessarily have more to do with the concreteness of cultural affinity than with the abstract dimensions of social stratification. Inter-ethnic trust is a necessary, and as yet unavailable, prerequisite for the experiential salience of a consciousness of class.

It is not a simple matter to capture the meaning of these events. Indeed the problems of analysing the politics of such an area substantially recapitulate the problems of, in the graphic Ghanaian vernacular, 'doing politics' in such an area. Where practice is so intricate and so densely particular, theory is in no condition to leap confidently ahead. The entire election can be aptly seen as an investigation in very practical terms of the social location of moral feelings. It would have been rash for any participant, and it would be still more rash of an external observer, to claim with confidence that he was certain of just where the boundaries of such feelings do lie for different groups. But if we are to make any serious attempt to delineate the intersection between the national and the local which such an election necessarily represents, and, above all, if we are to move towards determining the terms of trade between the national and the local which is where the internal meaning of the national politics of African states largely resides, it is essential not merely to distinguish in the current American style between symbolic identification and technical economic rationality in electoral choice but also to offer a serious account of the moral character of such identification.

The dimension of technical rationality need not detain us for long. It has been the indubitable achievement, though it may perhaps not have been the aim, of the American economic theorists of democracy to prove conclusively that no actual individual in a western democracy has sufficient egoistic grounds, by their own stringent criteria of egoism, to bother to drag himself to the polling station at all.[36] A possible incidental felicity of the study of African elections might thus be – whether through the offers of money, corned beef or sardines or the threat of blows – to provide belated instances of the vote as an economically rational act. It must indeed have been true during some elections in Ghana under the C.P.P. that electors were on occasion tried by the fearsome ordeals of Downs and Olson and not found wanting in egoistic rationality. But the secrecy of the ballot on this particular occasion, while it may have left some men with reasons upon compulsion to make their way to the polling booths, cannot have given anyone a reason actually to cast a valid vote for anyone once he had got there. It is true that for anyone who did reach the ballot box after extended waiting in the queue, because it had been made clear to him that it was in his interest to do so, the marginal cost of choosing to vote for the side he preferred over making a purely random choice might seem small; and the discrimination of rationality under such circumstances may perhaps prudently be left to those with the requisite mathematical techniques. In any case few electors had a sufficiently complex picture of the political universe, upon which they might have attempted to exert a purchase by their vote, to be in any position to indulge in such complex mathematics.

But if the rationale for voting must have been of a symbolic and not merely an egoistically rational nature, the more traditional understandings of democracy do plausibly regard some forms of symbolic identification as distinctly more symbolic than others. A traditional understanding of egoistic rationality in voting would merely require that in voting men are choosing a state of affairs which they would, in their expectation, prefer to any alternative on offer. Rationality inheres in the preference (or set of preferences) itself, and does not have to be stretched to the willingness to participate in the entire ritual. No doubt in the absence of effective sanctions at the level of expressed preferences (the ballot being clearly secret in *effect* —as it was everywhere in procedure — in all but a few small and isolated polling stations),[37] the electors of Asunafo did on the whole attain this minimal standard of rationality. Agreement on this matter, however, does not greatly sharpen the point at issue because of the virtual unanimity of the parties on what might be politely called policy issues. Not only was there no detectable difference in the class appeals of N.A.L. and P.P., a matter in which Ghanaian rhetoric may well be closer to Ghanaian reality than is true of the politics of many other countries; there were few detectable explicit disagreements on the techniques to be employed in the pursuit of agreed goals. Political rhetoric remained firmly within the bounds of the kingdom of ends, and even there it cannot be said to have taken a very contestatory form. All parties promised economic development, employment, industrialisation, the fostering of agriculture, educational advance. (You want it, we name it.) None provided concrete suggestions as to how the cargo could be inveigled down to earth. The P.P. manifesto was perhaps slightly more explicit than that of its main opponents. But whatever significance that fact may have had in Ghanaian politics at large, it cannot have had much in the politics of Asunafo since virtually no one in the constituency had seen a copy by polling day and it is doubtful whether *anyone* in the constituency had read it. Few parties in any country, of course, go to the polls on a platform of bringing about swingeing cuts in the general standard of living, and it is hardly unique to Ghana to regard politicians' public proclamations of their intentions as possessing little or no predictive value. But it is more unusual for a rational preference over social and economic politics to depend exclusively upon the relative credibility of the parties' proclaimed good faith.[38] Since there was nothing about which to choose between the parties, except the degree to which one could contrive to believe what they said, the level of symbolic identification involved in electoral choice was, on this occasion, notably high.

Two types of symbolic identification were in fact marketed by the two parties, and their purveying formed the ideological content of the campaign. The election result itself represented the decisive, if perhaps necessarily temporary, choice of one of these identities by the electors of Asunafo. But there are two other types of symbolic identification with which the election might conceivably have been concerned, but which it in practice evaded. These two require to be discussed independently of the campaign itself. The first may well have been a potentiality only at a purely mythical level, the creature of a story put about by Nkrumah and David Apter: the children of the transformational promise of the C.P.P., the youthful and pioneering protagonists of modernity. The committed *croyant* in the efficacy of political mobilisation might endeavour to explain its absence by the military government's resonant antipathy to the notion, and by the fact that the N.A.L. was almost as unenthusiastic about it as the N.L.C. itself. Since, however, its earlier appearance in the story derived directly from the even more resonant sympathy of the preceding C.P.P. government, it is not necessary to be over-impressed by the economy of this explanation: 'no political mobilisation without the risk of subsequent political demobilisation'. The state gave and the state hath taken away. Blessed be the name of the state. No one in Asunafo appeared to conceive of himself in terms in any way continuous with these. Fifteen years of submission to the ordeal of political modernisation appeared to have left local identities not merely unreconstructed but virtually unscathed.

The second potential identity which failed to appear in the campaign to any significant extent was almost the obverse of the first. Whereas the C.P.P. has been an instance of political lexical transfer masquerading as political institutional transfer, this second identity was unchallengeably concrete, historical and there. The terms of trade between national and local had been such indeed that, while the C.P.P. supplied the words, Ahafo retained a fairly unremitting control over their meanings. The history of the C.P.P.'s struggle to establish its local power by the manipulation of multitudinous local identities proved, in substance, to have lent its power to their purposes to an even greater extent. Localism is a powerful force in Ahafo and the meaning of the election might well have been purely localist, might have been confined to the reenactment of local factional conflict between town and town or between one consolidated chiefly interest and another. The first eventuality seems never to have occurred. Even such inveterate historical foes as Kenyase I and Kenyase II[39] voted firmly for the same candidate. The fact that in the Asutifi constituency N.A.L. did not even win a single polling station, and in Asunafo it won only two out of some 80, disposes conclusively of the possibility that either party contrived on this occasion to turn the election into a simple town squabble. The traditional tensions between Kukuom side and Mim side came out in an etiolated form only in the candidate selection process of the two parties. But as a shadow of its former self it was so pale as to be bereft of causal significance. The most impressive result of the election, and the conclusive testimony to N.A.L.'s failure, was the establishment of the unity of Ahafo as a political interest. A necessary condition for such unity, and one which was surprisingly in practice available, was an accepted common front on the problems of the traditional political order of Ahafo.

The difficulty of contriving this requires some little explanation. Most local areas in Ghana are subjected to regular disputes over the location of traditional political legitimacy. Enormous energy is expended on such disputes, and it requires great political sensitivity and skill (sometimes greater than is available) for the local and national administrations to control the dimensions of conflict.[40] Extensive efforts, both financial and coercive, are made by local protagonists to secure the services of the national administration for their purposes, and equally strenuous efforts in much the same currency, are made by national political forces to use local dissensions to consolidate their own national patronage structures. The monopoly of power in the hands of the state now makes it (and has made it for some time in the past) impractical for local actors to offer explicit resistance to the state as such. Biafra may dream of secession. But no such opportunity, transparently, can be open to the Dagomba or the Nzima.[41] Nevertheless, due subservience to state authority does not necessarily imply obedience to its local representatives. The King is always good, but any of his local ministers is plausibly wicked and may at least be subjected to purposeful obstruction on behalf of the King's supposed real will. (Even within the colonial theory of impassive obedience, the impassivity at the receiving end often surpassed the obedience.) This presentation is made easier by the fact that the state has not ceased to advertise the virtuous quality of its will since the time of the British conquest of Ashanti, and there has been general verbal agreement on the criterion for virtue in the adjudication of traditional legitimacy: namely, tradition. Ideologically the transaction has been one between a national near-monopoly of fire-power and a local near-monopoly of legitimacy. It has been a transaction in which each participant has been able to supply real services to the other. Indirect rule provided both agents with cheap, if intrinsically limited, increments of power. But over the years fire-power has proved distinctly easier to concentrate than legitimacy. If this is in some ways deplorable, it should not be in any way surprising. The promise of the integrative revolution is the construction of an ideological or spiritual surrogate for an armoury. But it is increasingly unclear whether in post-colonial states the spiritual component can, for some time, be much more than a legend over the armoury door. Traditional legitimacy in actuality is almost as dispersed locally as charisma. Conceptually it reposes very solidly upon history. Practically, however, history must be seen as being tastefully rearranged around it. Few statements about the history of Ahafo, however innocent in intention, can escape being politically partisan in effect. There are almost as many histories of Ahafo as there are long established settlements in Ahafo.[42] Since, too, they exist orally rather than in a written form and since politics goes on, both locally and nationally, their political availability need not be impaired even by the constraints of consistency over time. The Ancient Constitution of Ahafo has many historiographers and they display what Nkrumah, for instance, would have seen as an altogether excessive measure of feudal legalism.[43] Village Spelmans and Bradys, they are far from mute and they can enjoy their own glories without having to submit to the chastening disciplines of print.

Much of the political dispute in Ahafo is conducted in consequence, just as it was in the seventeenth-century in England or France,[44] in terms which wear, to the alien modern eye, an air of rather desperate paradox. It is not the historicist oddity of regarding a set of events in the sociologically (and indeed chronologically) distant past as the proper criterion for a set of present political arrangements, but the extraordinary logical contortions (made familiar for English history by John Pocock) which are necessarily involved in the reasoned defence of the set of past events selected to act as the criterion. When these logical conundra have been resolved in the constitutional history of Ahafo they have had to be so more by exercise of the will than of the intelligence. There has been no obvious shortage of wills, however, ready to shoulder the burden, either inside or outside Ahafo. Whatever the origins of the earliest settlers of Ahafo, it is undisputed that the area was at one time thoroughly integrated within the Ashanti empire. Both of the main constitutional traditions in Ahafo acknowledge that the proper context for its political analysis, ever since its incorporation, has been the struggle between centrifugal and centripetal forces inside the empire. The circumstances under which it was integrated serve to explain the character of its political subordination to Ashanti, while this character in its turn goes some way to account for the enduring strength of local separatism. Its initial incorporation into Ashanti followed on the pursuit into the virtually uninhabited forest area, by a punitive expedition under several of the Kumasi wing chiefs, of an invading force from what is now the Ivory Coast, which had contrived to sack Kumasi. In the aftermath of these events (the Abiri Moro war) the Ashanti leaders left behind them in the forest areas a number of small settlements manned by their followers. These settlements naturally retained their Kumasi traditional allegiances. Consequently, different Ahafo towns owed allegiance within the traditional constitution of Ashanti to different Kumasi chiefs and the Ahafo area as a whole lacked a unitary local political focus. During the last quarter of the nineteenth century, under the impact of British military and diplomatic pressure, the central political control of Ashanti weakened and the possibility of successful local political consolidation against Kumasi became a real one.[45] In 1896 the British signed a treaty of protection with one of the major Ahafo chiefs, the Kukuomhene. Shortly afterwards, with the defeat of the last Ashanti struggle for independence in the Yaa Asantewaa war, the British authorities recognised the Kukuomhene as the Paramount Chief of an Ahafo division which was rendered formally independent of Ashanti. In the Ashanti understanding of these events, this represented the recognition of a *fait accompli*, but one the status of which was exclusively *de facto* rather than *de jure*. In the separatist understanding, it was merely the recognition of the rights already secured by the Ahafo war of liberation, the Asibi Entwi war, the very occurrence of which is denied by Ashanti.[46] The British colonial authorities at this stage appear to have displayed a fair degree of moral relaxation in their treatment of traditional legitimacy. Their recognition of Ahafo's independence undoubtedly owed more to their sense of prospective administrative convenience than to their regard for the historicity of Asibi Entwi.

Over the next thirty years, the British administration in Ashanti developed, as public bureaucracies and particularly British ones are apt to do, an extremely moral conception of its own role. Partly out of guilt at its own initial callowness (evoked largely by the intractable figure of Rattray who enlightened his bemused colleagues on the spiritual meaning of the Ashanti habit of human sacrifice) and partly out of sheer exhaustion at the recalcitrance of local political identities, it acquired a healthy respect for the significance of history. Eventually, in 1935, it chose to expiate its past guilt and enhance its future power by the resuscitation of the Ashanti confederacy in virtually its pristine splendour. (Human sacrifice was omitted.) This restoration was a supposedly consensual affair. All Paramount Chiefs affected were consulted and most welcomed the proposal, though Kukuomhene did show apprehension over whether he would be permitted to retain his Paramountcy.[47] In the event, since the restoration was so complete, Ahafo towns returned to their disparate traditional masters in Kumasi and the Kukuomhene became once again merely one among the many other local chiefs. The restoration was undoubtedly effective in that chieftaincy affairs, after slight initial turbulence, remained relatively placid and uncontroversial for the next two decades, but there is no doubt that the interests of Ahafo as such, both in the costly traditional courts of Kumasi[48] and the relatively modernist exploitation of the Ashanti National Levy, were not well protected against those of Kumasi.

There was consequently extensive local separatist sentiment, of a firmly economic character, available for political utilisation. In his struggle against the Ashanti-based N.L.M. Nkrumah was consequently able to unite the economic and traditional political components of Ahafo separatism to provide a supplement to the Brong separatism of the Brong-Kyempim Federation. The institutional outcome of his strenuous rewiring of the circuits was the creation of a separate Brong-Ahafo region out of most of what had long before been the Western Province of Ashanti and the restoration of the Paramountcy over a reconstituted Ahafo division to the Kukuomhene. The lines of political division inside Ahafo thus arrayed the traditional political interest of Kukuom and the modern political interest of the C.P.P. (a union symbolised by a number of substantial favours the Kukuom State Council were prepared to do for the former C.P.P. Member of Parliament, B.K. Senkyire) against the traditional political interest of Ashanti and the modern political interest of the United Party. In the aftermath of the 1966 coup however all the chieftaincy arrangements of the C.P.P. were conscientiously undone. The former U.P. chiefs were returned to their stools, the Kukuomhene ceased to be a Paramount, the lines of allegiance to the Kumasi chiefs were restored, and the Kukuomhene in due course was personally, if perhaps rather untraditionally,[49] summoned to pay his allegiance to the Asantehene.

The political situation to which these events gave rise was as murky as it was important. Indeed it is largely the case that it remained so murky precisely because it was so important. The traditional issues were so delicate that they were at no point left in the hands of the Chieftaincy Secretariat,[50] the decorous body set up by the N.L.C. to restore belated impartiality to the State's handling of traditional affairs, but were dealt with throughout directly by the government itself. A government commission, the Bannerman Commission, was set up to consider the question of Ahafo lands, but its proceedings were shortly suspended *sine die*, and nothing more was ever heard of it. In the meantime Ahafo traditional land revenues were frozen, the area being bereft of a State Council. Chiefs failed to receive their salaries and scholarship and other development funds were rendered unusable. There was general local agreement on the imperative need for the restitution of *some* local political order, though the local supporters of Ashanti, headed by the Chief of Mim, and those of Kukuom inevitably continued to differ on the issue of what form this order should appropriately take. As the election campaign began, the Kukuomhene was appearing on a state charge before the High Court at Sunyani for refusing to obey the Asantehene's legal summons to pay his homage in person. He was defended against this charge — the penalty for which, had he been convicted, would have been a substantial jail sentence — by a Sunyani lawyer, Munufie, who duly turned out to be the interim Regional Chairman of the Progress Party and who became a Minister in the government. On 9 June the Circuit Judge found the Kukuomhene not guilty of the offences charged on the ground that the Kukuom stool was not subject to the Golden Stool of Ashanti.[51] The extended historiographical basis of the judgement did not conceal (as in all arguments of a prescriptive character, where argument has become necessary, it inevitably could not conceal), the firm basis of choice on which the verdict rested. There are, plausibly, many legal contexts in which it is not a felicitous analysis to maintain that law is what the courts decide. But this was certainly not one of them. The effort to cement the chief's allegiance persisted until the election itself. Munufie took the opportunity of his acquittal celebrations to hold a Progress Party rally at Kukuom, rather to the chief's annoyance. Gbedemah in his turn duly paid his respects on the occasion of his own visit to Kukuom. The P.P. local organisers worried intermittently over the chief's prospective support and many of the N.A.L. campaigners tended to assume the continuity of his loyalties. Even in Kukuom itself there remained doubt about his sympathies almost up to the day of polling. Given such a level of decorum and discretion, the effect of his sympathies cannot have been very extensive. But whether it remained a decorous prudence or a genuine impartiality, there is no question that it furnished a necessary condition for the exclusion of one potentially salient meaning from the campaign, that of being yet another battle in the long war against Ashanti control of Ahafo. The Progress Party in Ahafo did not need the forceful backing of the chief of Kukuom in order to win the election. N.A.L. undoubtedly did, if it was to present a real political challenge at all. Perhaps such an opportunity was closed to it even before the campaign began, and before the High Court in Sunyani brought in its verdict. After the close of the P.P. inauguration rally in Sunyani, prominent party supporters congregated at Munufie's house on the outskirts of the town. Among them, at one point, in two successive cars of drastically varying elegance, there appeared the Kukuomhene and Victor Owusu, former N.L.C. Attorney General and the only leading politician of long standing to enjoy ministerial responsibility under them. Balancing the political and economic claims of Ashanti and Ahafo had been a tricky political assignment and it must have required all the attentive governmental handling which it could be given. When the voting came, this attentive delicacy was amply repaid. Once again impartiality was to show itself to be the subtlest and most effective form of partiality.

It is possible in this way to dismiss the potential relevance of both the universalist face of the C.P.P. and the purely localist face of Ahafo's faction-torn traditionalism to the meaning of the election by noting the absence of any identifiable groups in the context who conceived it firmly in these terms. The problem of assessing the scope of the two competing meanings which must now be considered is not that they cannot be shown to be embodied in the persons of any of the contestants, but rather that it is not altogether clear how intimate is the connection between these energetically purveyed identities and the identifications of those whose electoral allegiance they secured. If the two meanings were to be offered as a causal explanation of the voting figures they would plausibly beg the question they purport to answer. Accordingly, a simple if slightly evasive causal explanation is set out as a rational debate between the effort to derive power from authority and that to derive authority from power.

The election was a contest between national élite coalitions for local mass support. In the political history of Ahafo with its extensive cocoa interests and strong, if ambivalent, Ashanti connection, local allegiance had been predominantly, even under conditions of substantial political pressure, to the former United Party. The Progress Party, being led by the former United Party's leader, inherited the allegiance of a political coalition held together by a common history of struggle and to some degree governmental neglect and oppression. In the preceding three years this local élite, with some national assistance, had contrived to begin to undo the ravages of neglect by securing the provision of supplies of clean water[52] and by an increase (claimed specifically in the course of the campaign to be a product of Dr Busia's advice) in the producer price of cocoa. At the same time, as we have seen, it had contrived to close up some of the historical fissures of localist political conflict[53] which the C.P.P. years had widened alarmingly. Its effectiveness in consolidating this historical inheritance of political support in the event of the campaign was enhanced by the distinctive identity of the party which eventually emerged as the alternative national contender for power. N.A.L. was not referred to commonly in the constituency (as it was for instance among the Legon students) as 'Ewe party'. It would certainly be false to describe the campaign locally in terms of the projective engineering of primordial hostilities. The position of Ewes in Ahafo is not one which subjects them to any obviously greater suspicion than any other stranger groups — and the Ahafo population probably has a higher stranger component than that of any other part of Ghana except the new urban conglomerations. Ewes are particularly prominent in the teaching profession, but, unlike the Ibos in Northern Nigeria before 1966, they do not represent a pervasive economic threat in petty retailing or modern craft work. It was true that Busia comes from Wenchi and Gbedemah from Keta and this geographical symbolism did play a part in the campaign.[54] But the way in which it was presented was very secular, and far from atavistic. It is safe to assume that, whereas few Ahafos identify themselves with Brongs for any, except crudely political, purposes, all would be likely, other things being equal, to feel strikingly more at ease in political union or social intercourse with a Brong than with an Ewe. Yet in Ghanaian politics other things never remain equal unless they are energetically made so and the achievement of keeping them so was not in practice lightened by any effort to invoke hostility to Ewes as such. As is suggested by the example of the Legon students, ethnic hostility was often much stronger at an élite than at a mass level, and in Ahafo at least the local élite was fortunate that it did not need to draw heavily on ethnic hostility to cement its mass following, since the requisite style of hostility was only dubiously available for it to draw on. Gbedemah's problem in

145

Ahafo turned out to be *not* that the fact that he was an Ewe counted against him, but that so little except the fact that he was an Ewe counted *for* him, and that in Ahafo, as in general outside the Ewe areas, this alone could hardly count enough. As a non-Ashanti he appealed forcefully to many of the poorer southern (and indeed northern) strangers, and as being at least more C.P.P. than Busia, he appealed to those to whose lives the C.P.P. had rendered substantial and direct services. But when it came to the count these twin appeals turned out to make little inroad into the inherited U.P. political clientages. The causal explanation of the P.P. triumph was locally (as it was nationally) the degree of political skill in its consolidation of élite support, coupled with the fact that it had as a genuinely national competitor only Gbedemah's apparat to compete against. The egoistic basis of the P.P.'s national solidarity in the inter-ethnic élite competition for power and profit may have been rational even in Olson's terms[55] (though I do not believe that its motivation can be accurately and exhaustively analysed in this fashion). And the solidarity of its local electoral clientages may have derived largely from the members doing their betters a prudent favour, rather than from any more intensely moralistic performance. But whether or not this is what it derived from — whether or not public morality is still something which their masters have to do for them[56] — it cannot be the case that this was all it meant.

What men do, the meaning of their actions, cannot be fully known, while resolutely ignoring what they suppose themselves to be doing. To uncover this final layer of meaning it is necessary to brush aside the axiomatic professional cynicism of the political scientist and attend in all simplicity to the stories which actors told themselves. For these were stories which they did tell in private or when exhausted late at night, when gloomy, irritable or excited, not just on the pompous respectability of the public platform. If they were masks at all, they were certainly masks most of the time to the men themselves. If that was not where the action was, it is hard to see where there was left for it to be at all.[57]

The commonest local account of the meaning of a political party was simply men coming together to help to choose a government. The electoral reference is plain enough. The significance of 'coming together' is its fusion of the descriptive content of campaigning (which does tie men from different localities to a common purpose, though it certainly does not dissolve them into a common purpose) with the moral content of the traditional political values of unity and harmony. It is a reflection of traditional culture as much as of recent experience that the commonest reply to the question 'what would you most like to happen in the world' among the ordinary citizens of Goaso was simply 'peace'. Both parties necessarily marketed to individual electors the benefits of uniting for peace. The dramatic difference between the two lay in their presentation of what peace meant. The essential character of the N.A.L. appeal was individualistic and pragmatic, that of the P.P.

146

collectivist and moral. The N.A.L. campaign stressed (as the party slogan implied) 'Victory' and what you could get out of it, the P.P. campaign (again as its slogan suggested) stressed 'virtue' and what it could mean for you. This is not to imply that the N.A.L. campaign was self-consciously diabolist or even amoral nor that the P.P.'s appeal could be aptly described as ascetic. Asceticism has markedly little appeal in Ghana and the most flamboyantly corrupt C.P.P. ministers were often generous to their own (sometimes *very* extended) 'families'. The polarity remained nevertheless, in these terms, astonishingly sharp.

At the N.A.L. candidate selection meeting a leading member of the party observed with stunning economy 'If power is being sold, try to sell your old lady to go and buy the power. After you have got the power you will be able to go and bring back your old lady.' When asked how support was acquired politically, all N.A.L. organisers replied in terms of the expectation of concrete benefits to be received.[58] Electoral allegiance was seen as being consolidated in whatever currency was practically available. Morality stopped at the boundaries of the party. Party unity was a technical prerequisite for party victory which, in turn, was plainly a technical prerequisite for the many good things which it would bring with it. Such moral characteristics as it did display were products of the shared history of struggle, moral artefacts in the Hegelian manner of the conflict itself,[59] not ends external to it and helping to constitute its point. Politics was a severely technical activity with its own toughly Machiavellian rationality.[60] The former C.P.P. organisers were proud of their own professionalism and scornful of what they saw as the P.P.'s bumbling amateurism. Indeed in a way this conception was at least partly accepted by the P.P. workers too; amateurs they might be, but they were also in contrast to their opponents, at least arguably, gentlemen.

Holding this unflinchingly egoistic view of political value and lacking, on this occasion, access to the coercive or incentive resources of the government, the N.A.L. organisers faced their bleak assignment with gaiety and a good deal of courage. Indeed they showed some little political imagination in the degree of symbolic identification which they did manage to evoke. The core of party organisers entered the N.A.L. campaign because of their past C.P.P. loyalties, and they entered as a political *équipe* purchased on the oligopolistic national political market by Gbedemah. Much of the support which they gathered came from those with a common history of C.P.P. allegiance or from stranger elements whose affection focussed upon N.A.L. as an anti-Ashanti party. But the most interesting group of supporters were the local members (here sometimes Ashanti themselves) of the groups to whom Gbedemah's national campaign rhetoric of inevitable victory was directed.[61] Often young and usually not very well educated, though sometimes highly intelligent, their feelings revolved very much around the image of Gbedemah himself as a conceptually diffuse, but highly cathected symbol of social effectiveness. The reason why he was certain to win the election, they felt,

147

was also the reason why it was desirable for him to win it. He knew all the big men in the country (enjoyed, that is, the support of leading C.P.P. dignitaries) and was well acquainted with and well esteemed in all the big countries abroad, especially the biggest and most exciting of all, the United States. Above all he had extensive *business* contacts, and even more business skills. A high level of structural unemployment and an increasingly steepening pyramid of educational advance threatened most young Ghanaians with a gloomy future. Entrepreneurial skills (which consist subjectively in a heady combination of magic, chicanery, intelligence and sheer efficacy) of a very high order were clearly to be required to make these clouds lift. In the face of this disagreeable and pervasive aura of *necessita*, Gbedemah's supereminent command over *Fortuna* was just what was needed. All this may sound like purely technical rationality, but it was in practice every bit as much a mode of symbolic self-identification, a participatory value, as the P.P.'s proffered virtue.

In strictly political terms it had, too, a rather dense historical rationale in the experience of C.P.P. rule. Where instrumental politics is the politics of patronage systems, the most apparent political value is simply to succeed, to associate yourself with the biggest and best. Gbedemah's appeal was explicitly pitched (apart from the totally unintelligible cosmopolitanism of his party's title) at a level of pure economic egoism. The tactical disadvantage of this was that, since no one was against progress,[62] it only constituted a reason for voting for Gbedemah himself among those whom he could furnish with direct incentives for so doing.[63] Even in the post-electoral fantasy world of the party's triumph, it would be a mistake to suppose that most of its supporters expected with any assurance to derive concrete benefits from it. What they were committed to, symbolically speaking, was a government which took their dreams seriously. Few were still optimistic enough to expect a government to realise their dreams. The value which Gbedemah represented was the value of success and N.A.L. offered, as had the C.P.P. in its later stages, symbolic participation in the most powerful patronage machine. The atmosphere of gleeful and rather naive chicanery which hung over the N.A.L. campaign reflected the self-image of those whose chance of living well could derive only from their manipulative wits along with plentiful draughts of sheer luck. For these secular and non-ethnic supporters what N.A.L. offered was a belated form of participation in modernity, the consummation of knowingness as a political value (the consummation, too, in an oddly pure form in which knowingness became its own reward). One historical consequence of the C.P.P.'s rule had been to offer a view of politics in which knowingness did become a truly participatory value, not merely one which reflected an axiomatic distrust of all social loyalties.[64] In an area with such a large proportion of relatively recent immigrants, such an offer might have been expected to enjoy a wide appeal. But in a competition between knowingness as its own reward and virtue devoid of costs, the pains of social change and geographical mobility turned out to be insufficiently searing to make knowingness a more attractive offer.

The basis of the Progress Party's success was their capacity to establish a belief, of however fleeting a character, that virtue would turn out to be devoid of costs. This belief, in practical effect, meant a belief in the moral trustworthiness of the official local status system. It is a commonplace of contemporary anthropology that many of the strains of modernisation for traditional communities are carried by individuals whose roles place them in an interstitial position between traditional village and modern city, and thus enable them to act as cultural brokers between the two. Such men reinterpret the bleak demands of modernity and the unintelligible requirements of public bureaucracies into assignments within the grasp of traditional villagers. They perform these services, on the whole, for extremely concrete rewards.[65] They tend to play a peculiarly critical role in the engineering of rural credit and may at times be well placed to exact a steep price for the indispensability of their services. The demographic history of Ahafo and its intimate connection with the spread of cocoa as a cash crop cast some doubt on the propriety of describing its villages as traditional communities at all, and the sheer frequency of geographical mobility in Ghana plausibly implies that the market for such cultural brokerage is more competitive than it was for Wolf's Mexican villages. But the demands posed by the extent of illiteracy are common to both countries, the role of mediator is even more heavily culturally approved in Ghana than in Mexico, and the need to have matters fixed is certainly often a pressing one in Ghana too. The entrepreneurial provision of such an unofficial surrogate for the Citizens Advice Bureau may not exemplify the highest standards of market freedom, but it does do the community certain services. Knowingness is the cultural value marketed by such fixers. The fact that the value has to be paid for may even, as perhaps in the case of psychoanalysis, serve retrospectively to enhance its credibility. The initial scarcity of information is such that it is far from simple to be certain in any particular instance what one has obtained in return for one's investment (even if, again like psychoanalysis, it is often apparent that it is certainly not quite what one wanted). Such brokers may not always be trusted — literacy is too great an inequality of power to be compatible with any great trust. The point of education is to avoid being cheated by literates.[66] But however equivocal their trustworthiness, no one would be likely to deny their indispensable role in the social division of labour. The fact that they are indispensable, and that they are paid piece work rates, may also make them subjectively more reliable than their publicly-salaried superiors whose direct services to individual lives are not always intelligible to the naive understanding. Social distance can breed distrust as readily as admiration. It might feel substantially safer to put one's trust in the raffish and knowing fixer than in the respectable incumbent of a social role, the rationale of which may be unintelligible (and on occasion might not even be there). Ghanaians have a

149

sharp nose for hypocrisy, and the course of twentieth-century social change has given them extensive practice in its detection.

The political achievement of the P.P. campaign was to tease out these ambivalent characteristics of the experience of modernity and the social roles around which it focussed into a sharp polarity. On the one side they set in their public rhetoric (and indeed substantively in their private conception of the campaign) the sly, knowing, undependable tricksters, explicitly hell-bent on Victory, without status to lose in their pursuit of power and with class all too much to gain. On the other side they displayed themselves, per-haps with some complacency, a stage army of the good, but one in which some warriors at least did bear the scars of real and far from forgotten battles, also modern men, men who had indeed to their credit some small achievement in the discipline of modern status and class competition, the educated, the virtuous, the wise, the brave. It is not to be supposed that this glowing transfer was in fact made to adhere in its entirety to the conscious-ness of most voters. But it does appear to have struck quite deep chords in many. It derived its plausibility from a history of guilt displayed in disunion, and the suffering generated by disunion; and the remedy which it offered was the re-establishment of union, a proposal which assimilated the moral and the practical. Most importantly of all it offered an account of how such a union could be morally credible in terms of the pledged good faith and knowledge of those in the community whose word and judgement men had most reason to trust. What the Progress Party did politically was market the moral self-image of the higher segments of the local status system, modern and traditional.[67] The consumer response suggested a stability in the status dimension of social stratification,[68] which current writings on the sociology of modernisation have totally failed to capture. In Dahrendorf's terms an abstract élite seemed well on the way locally to becoming an established élite.[69]

The moral project offered by this élite was the exorcism of a past shame by the engineering in the present of a collective moral will. Disunion had been brought into Ahafo[70] by thieves and cheats. Ahafo, as a whole, had had to pay the moral price of disunion because of the complicity of some of its citizens in this invasive immorality. It was precisely because members of the community had been ready to demand — or at least to accept — concrete rewards for the allocation of loyalties which should have been allocated on a basis of Kantian purity, that the moral integrity of the community had been violated. The fact that the violation of this integrity occasioned a history of overt and, at times, violent conflict, served both to deepen the moral squalor of the betrayal, and to provide a moral rationalisation of the sufferings in which the betrayal resulted. Having touched pitch, the men of Ahafo had only themselves to blame if they had duly become defiled. A few had done well out of these impure practices, but for the community at large it had spelled nothing but neglect and dangers. In a village a private thief, if apprehended in the act, might risk being beaten to death. Without justice, what could the state be but a great band of public thieves? The people of Ahafo were summoned to endow the state with justice by keeping their own hearts pure.

Two questions are raised by this remarkable rendition. How was it that the P.P. attempted to show that this, in some ways, rather strained story merited the belief of the electors, and why was it that they succeeded in some measure in arousing such belief? It is important to separate these issues since the form of authentication which the P.P. in fact strove to provide, while it was the only form of authentication conceptually available, may equally well not have been the cause of its acceptance by the electorate. That the problem of credibility was at the heart of the election no one who listened to the gloomy private responses or the ribald public challenges at the party's rallies could well doubt. As far as promises of improvement went, the long suffering electors had heard it all before and they were not slow to inquire how they were supposed to tell whether it meant anything more on this occasion than it had before. The P.P.'s dialectical response to this challenge was not in detail impressive. (It is hard to see how anyone's response could have been.) But it did attempt intuitively to forestall it by one feature of its campaigning. In that representative democracy necessarily implies the choice of a single man by a large number of men, and in that the chosen individual in Ghanaian politics is legally required to be somewhat unrepresentative in a statistical sense[71] (and in all representative politics he is sociologically likely to be highly unrepresentative) the question of what reason electors could have to choose someone to represent them is a very acute one. If democracy is indeed a choice between competing élites, in a country in which the class, status and power gaps between élite and mass are as yawning as they are in Ghana, it is not at all obvious what the point of democracy is supposed to be for the mass of the population, while it is abundantly clear that its point, as far as the élites are concerned, might readily take on the character of a Conspiracy of Unequals. All that could be provided to avert the risk of such conspiratorial betrayal was a set of character references from those who did not obviously stand to gain too directly from the upward mobility of the successful candidate for inequality. Thus the former United Party M.P., Mr. Osei, spoke eloquently at the Akrodie rally of how he had known Busia since their schooldays together in Kumasi and how he had never known him perform a discreditable act, while at the Progress Party's candidate selection meeting at Sankore, a former school fellow of Badu Nkansah also talked at length of how long he had known him and how sterling had been his conduct throughout this time. The intimacy of the recollections offered a trajectory across the massive social chasm between state and people without submission to mere fantasy. It provided, however evanescently, an image for the unimaginable, how the subjects could also become citizens, the ex-colonial state become a nation. To be a

151

credible representative, their candidate had to be a man with a firm local identity and a man for whom others with firm local identities would stand surety; and the leader of their party, while it certainly helped that he had a geographical identity which was not too distant, also *had* to be vouched for as a man by those with firm local identities. The coalescing of local political élites was not just the mechanism of party integration on the national level; it was also the most eloquent vehicle of party propaganda on the local level. It was on the knowledge of men whom they themselves knew and respected that the rationality of the choice of the majority had necessarily to depend.

The moral credibility (such as it was) of the leaders' presentation of themselves in this role depended, in part, upon adventitious historical factors. The local élites had been rather unusual by prevailing standards in the extent to which they had resisted the blandishments of the C.P.P. government, to say nothing of its less gentle approaches. This meant both that their own hands were comparatively clean, and that the area as a whole had undergone a rather more than average share of governmental neglect. Uniting for peace in this instance, and behind these leaders, could be plausibly presented as uniting against neglect and oppression. Furthermore, the image of the local community as the moral victim of an immoral government was paradoxically strengthened by the extent of local prosperity. Such prosperity was, to be sure, relative; there was continued and vociferous economic discontent. But it was nevertheless indubitably there. The Ahafo production of cocoa and timber remained as high as anywhere in Ghana. Wealth was unquestionably produced in the constituency and it required little political or economic sophistication to grasp just precisely how large a part of the surplus was extracted by the government. The low level of government development expenditure, the high level of local production and the history of extensive governmental taxation on the production of cocoa and timber, served together to confirm a simple physiocratic image of the location of economic virtue. A set of parasitic public thieves had battened on the virtuous and productive forest. The time for justice to be done had come at last. Since the local élites had, however, failed to collaborate with this brigand invasion, it was in fact they who (to sharpen a historical irony) were the 'natural leaders' of the exploited peasants in the effort to secure this belated justice.

All this is very much taking the Progress Party at the value of its own moral face. It had naturally other and less moral faces. Once in possession of state power, no party in Ghana today could well retain such purity of moral outline, let alone act out in a neo-colonial setting, the simplistic fables of physiocratic economics. If the dreams of Frantz Fanon could not be realised by the Algerian war of National Liberation, they were in no danger of being fulfilled by the electoral triumph of the Ghanaian bourgeoisie. Indeed the constraints of social structure made it all too probable that, while the élite campaigners of the P.P. might derive fairly direct benefits from their share in the marketing of virtue, having voted for virtue would turn out for most voters to have been its own sole reward. If would be unjust to the Progress Party to suggest that the second of these considerations loomed large in their consciousness. But it would be naive to suppose that the first had not occurred to a fair number of them. Discussion of the fruits of electoral victory was often as directly egoistic and as uninhibited in its gusto among them as among the N.A.L. supporters. But these fruits were seen as rewards for having invested in virtue, not simply as returns on having invested in investment. The moral image was closer to that of the spiritual churches than it was to either the unbending principles of Kant or the crude importunities of the National Lottery. Rewards were genuinely rewards, prizes for having been virtuous, not merely adventitious windfalls. Even if the point of being virtuous (in the sense of the sufficient motive) was the prospect of its resulting in concrete gains, it would be an error to imagine that many inhabitants of Ahafo had the poise to conceive their lives unflinchingly as a market enterprise. Early socialisation, however variegated, had certainly served to accentuate for many the subjective probability of rewards accruing to virtue. Whatever history may have done for the inhabitants of eighteenth-century Königsberg, it has not left those of Ahafo today in any condition to make sense out of the bleak requirements of Kant. To say that they did not sense the deprivations of altruism in the attachment of political virtue to public goods, is thus only to observe that it remains a psychological possibility in Ahafo to have reason to attempt to live virtuously. Whether it remains a philosophical possibility is not a question which can be answered here.

Even in the extensively studied societies of the industrial west, elections cannot plausibly be claimed to be events which are particularly well understood. Their position in the ideology of representative democracy is well established, but their precise character as social events, their social meaning, remains imaginatively opaque. In the thinly studied societies of contemporary Africa it would be remarkable if their meaning was not even more opaque. Along with their abandoned state apparatus, the departing colonialists left behind them the recently introduced formal prerequisites for egalitarian democracy. It could thus be argued that what Africa is stumblingly in search of is not democracy (which at least intermittently and unstably it perhaps enjoys or at least *experiences* already), so much as representation. Elections as a mode of choosing rulers are tied historically not so much to democracy as such as to *representative democracy*, a theory of how democracy could be made a reality in a territorial rather than a city state. In the territorial states of western Europe the practice of representation long preceded the achievement of democracy. Indeed it long preceded the establishment of anything resembling a nationally self-conscious system of social stratification. Representative Assemblies were summoned by existent state power, the monarch and his court, largely in order to enhance his tax-gathering effectiveness. Naturally such local representatives were for the most part men of high status in the local community. Had they not been so, they could hardly have

153

served to bind the other inhabitants of their community by their choice. Despite its origins as a device for increasing the central power of the state, representation did not (where it was permitted by the state power to remain at all) remain restricted to the service of this purpose. Indeed over time, and largely before the advent of democracy, it became the device by which society acquired such control as it has over the state. With the (causally linked) advent of democracy and a self-conscious national system of social stratification, representation became the instrument for securing the level of social equality and individual freedom, such as it is, now characteristic of western societies.

If the account which has been given of the election in Asunafo is to any significant extent veridical, it raises an interesting question. In the current absence of a nationally self-conscious class stratification in Ghana, what authentic forms of representation are possible? The possibility of representation stops at the boundary of the moral community. Socialist theory in nineteenth- and twentieth-century Europe attempted to stretch these boundaries first to the national and then to the international proletariat. Although it cannot be said that it was very successful, it does seem likely that the electoral transposition of a measure of proletarian solidarism was a necessary condition for such internal political rationality as the political systems of the western world currently display. When it comes to interpreting African politics, however, western observers seem for the most part to have left behind such feeling as they possess for this painfully slow extension of the moral community. Taking their cue from the legalistic universalism of the electoral systems left behind by the colonial powers, they have seen the insistent recurrence of localist values, 'tribalism', as a reversion to primitive barbarism. By insisting on peering irritably at the national level and noting how badly the states have managed to cope with the problems left to them by their former masters, they have failed to perceive most of the extended political achievement involved in beginning to deal with the difficulties which they actually face. 'Tribalism' is undoubtedly a danger from the point of view of the state, but it may also represent the painful construction of a political community. Whilst it was simply a matter of sharing out the contents of the public coffers among the successor élites such a perspective might seem perverse. When it can be shown, however fitfully, at work in the processes of a democratic election campaign, it may be easier to understand the moral substance which, along with its immoral and its dangerous characteristics, it does beyond question display. The Progress Party in Asunafo advanced an image of Ahafo as a moral community. They elected a man from Ahafo who had grappled with modernity but returned to live within Ahafo to stand for them in the national tourney in which community struggles against community for the goods and evils which the government distributes. Under the C.P.P., as the chief of Sankore bitterly observed, a black man had forgotten that he was black, but after the coup 'People who had made themselves white men came to understand that they were black men like us.' The anxious image of the future which the Progress Party campaign attempted to allay, and at the same time the eventuality which it attempted to avert, was that once again black men should think they had become white men. In the election, what the Progress Party offered was an image of virtue predicated on a moral community. The story of how the electors of Asunafo, perhaps rather bemusedly, chose virtue is a story which deserves a share of honour even outside its own country. What else better, in all innocence, could they in fact have done?[72]

Appendix Asunafo poll figures, August 1969 (by polling station)

Polling Station	N.A.L.	P.P.
Special Voters (Army & Police)	17	35
Mim R.C. Primary School	50	352
Mim Methodist Primary School	55	363
Mim Co-op Shed No. 1	52	297
Mim Post Office	37	286
Asukese Cocoa Shed	9	88
Asuadei L.A. Primary School	7	16
Biaso L.A. Primary School	17	102
Gambia No. II L.A. Primary School	15	186
Asamoakrom Co-op Shed	48	162
Bediako Co-op Shed	9	120
Central Bitre Co-op Shed	13	118
Nsuta Primary School	11	68
Kensere L.A. Middle School	13	173
Dominase Co-op Shed	11	78
Kasapii Cocoa Shed	31	213
Wam S.C.M.B. Shed	5	114
Peprakrom Cocoa Shed	4	101
Kaniago Cocoa Shed	11	89
Goaso Methodist Primary School	74	309
Goaso Local Council Hall	97	300
Goaso S.C.M.B. Cocoa Shed	59	219
Kamirekrom L.A. Primary School	15	57
Kantukwa Cocoa Shed	5	34
Fawohoyoden Methodist Primary School	31	360
Ayomso Methodist Primary (i)	50	287
Ayomso Methodist Primary (ii)	37	240
Dotom Cocoa Shed	44	173
Kwakuduakrom S.C.M.B. Shed	13	124
Kumaho Cocoa Shed	38	208
Minkakrom Co-op Cocoa Shed	9	196
Kukuom United Primary School	220	278
Kukuom Co-op Cocoa Shed (i)	123	144
Kukuom Co-op Cocoa Shed (ii)	119	160
Yankye L.A. Primary School	76	41
Dantano Methodist Primary School	40	129

Polling Station	N.A.L.	P.P.
Domiabra L.A. Primary School	55	99
Noberkaw Catholic Primary School	86	233
Asufufuo L.A. Primary School	26	153
Anwiam Catholic Primary School	59	156
Sienna L.A. Primary School	32	131
Manhyia No. III Co-op Shed	32	115
Kwapong Co-op Cocoa Shed	55	429
G.W.A.8 Camp Co-op Shed	32	101
Pesewukrom S.C.M.B. Shed	84	67
Adwumakase S.C.M.B. Shed	15	203
Atotrom S.C.M.B. Shed	12	106
Asante Dodowa Co-op Shed	18	51
Asibrimu S.C.M.B. Shed	4	58
Sankore S.C.M.B. Shed	32	173
Sankore L.A. Middle School	40	159
Camp No. I S.C.M.B. Shed	66	195
Mamfokrom S.C.M.B. Shed	63	136
Manhyia No. 4 S.C.M.B. Shed	19	151
Kokooso No. I S.C.M.B. Shed	9	136
Asaweneso S.C.M.B. Shed	13	186
Opongkrom S.C.M.B. Shed	49	358
Beposo Co-op Shed	8	192
Durowaakrom L.A. Primary School	19	64
Afodowa S.C.M.B. Shed	63	162
Asempaneye L.A. Primary School	7	45
Mintumi L.A. Primary School	12	57
Akrodie Methodist Primary School	34	383
Akrodie Co-op Shed	33	380
Nyamebekyere No. 3	26	97
Ahenkro Cocoa Shed	13	140
Ahantamo Cocoa Shed	2	101
Kankyiamoa Cocoa Shed	13	97
Mensakrom Cocoa Shed	12	104
Asarekrom Co-op Shed	11	107
Asantekrom Co-op Shed	7	72
Manhyia No. 1 S.C.M.B. Shed	15	106
Aboaboso Cocoa Shed	2	103
Mintumi No. 1 Cocoa Shed	6	11
Oseikrom	5	12
Asumura Cocoa Shed	20	215
Pomakrom L.A. Primary School	12	162
Denyasi L.A. Primary School	18	143
Abuom Catholic Primary School	43	224
Tipokrom Primary School	10	77
Sakyikrom Co-op Shed	39	145
Sikafrebogya	19	73

7

'Hoc signo victor eris': representation, allegiance and obligation in the politics of Ghana and Sri Lanka*

I

Interpreting the meaning of political structures and processes is an enterprise distinct from the attempt to give causal explanations for political outcomes. It is not, however, irrelevant to the latter enterprise. Even if one supposed that the only thing worth knowing about politics was what was likely to happen in specific conditions, it is hard to know how one could begin to select promising materials for deriving such expectations except from a political world which was already fairly elaborately interpreted. This paper is an attempt to interpret differences between the politics of Ghana and those of Sri Lanka in terms of the social basis of political allegiance. It deliberately sacrifices the selection of a neat set of *explananda* in pursuit of what is intended, perhaps optimistically, to be a greater evaluative richness.

II

It is helpful to begin by conceiving of both representation and obligation as ideological categories. Allegiance by contrast may be seen, at least for the moment, as a social fact, though one of indeterminate scope. States and citizenship, in the world as it now is, we have everywhere with us. State ideologies are almost everywhere ostensibly democratic (hence the near omnipresence of citizenship) and state pretensions to authority correspondingly overweening (if we are for the people, who among our citizens can possibly be against us?). Representation, ideally, is what the citizen is offered in exchange for his civic obligations and these obligations are the price he must pay for such opportunity as he is given to get himself represented. Representation and obligation thus link two realities which are indeed

* This essay was prepared for a seminar organised by Professors Dennis Austin and Jeyaratnam Wilson at the University of New Brunswick in Fredericton in the summer of 1975. I am extremely grateful to all participants in the seminar for their comments, to Dr Janice Jiggins and Dr Dennis McGilvray for their help in relation to Sri Lankan affairs, and to Quentin Skinner and Geoffrey Hawthorn for their very helpful and careful criticisms. Dr Jiggins's views are now available in Janice Jiggins, *Caste and Family in the Politics of the Sinhalese 1947–1976*, Cambridge 1979.

indubitably there: individuals and states. But the relations which they allege in forming these links are eminently disputable. It is not necessary to be either an anarchist or a particularly fastidious moralist to suppose that few if any state powers represent even the majority of their citizens very well and that in few if any states does a citizen have a moral obligation to obey all the orders which his government might well choose to give him. Some states seek to justify themselves doctrinally by works (pig iron production), others, more brazenly or more prudently, prefer to do so by something much closer to faith alone (as it might be, cultural revolution). A third group of states (to which the U.S.A., the United Kingdom and Canada all belong), while in no way eschewing such justificatory services as they can derive from the first two modes, seek primarily to justify themselves not consequentially nor apodeictically but procedurally. Representative democracy is a device for determining the objects of obligation by a procedure which gives each adult individual some say in their selection and hence some personal reasons for recognising an obligation to them once they have been selected. The procedural legitimacy devised for representative democracy takes the existence of an obligation-exacting state (realistically enough) as given and seeks to bridge the gap between fact and value created by the material viability and moral implausibility of such states by a bold synthesis. Since allegiance is going to be exacted from citizens in any case, this exaction will at least be less of an affront if those who do exact it have been selected by the collective citizenry as less inept foci for their allegiance than any others on offer. There is a large element of myth, plainly, in any such presentation of democratic politics, especially in its resolute treatment of the citizenry as a composite category all of whom choose and all of whom consequently end up obliged. But despite this resolute disregard for social and political differentiation, the credulity demanded by this myth remains on balance less bleak (and closer to the credulity demanded simply by ordinary human life) than the more ambitiously pure theologies of faith or works alone. In representative democracies, professional politicians compete to serve as representatives for individuals. The medium of their competition is the presentation of themselves as more *appropriate* representatives for individuals than any other competitor. Devices for this self-presentation vary from the crudest sanctions of physical threat, through individual payment to the most nebulous of appeals to the individual's sense of social identity. We may certainly presume in the cases of both Ghana and Sri Lanka that even in their competitive elections there have been substantial elements of intimidation or bribery in the determination of electoral allegiance. But in these competitive national elections, perhaps five now in Ghana in all and rather more in Sri Lanka, it is perfectly clear that the majority have voted as they have neither out of extreme fear nor on an immediate 'fee for service' basis but as their (perhaps slightly nervous and undoubtedly unascetic) sense of social identity suggested that it would be most appropriate for them to vote. The skill of a politician in competitive

158

electoral politics is largely that of knowing how to symbolise most effectively his identification with the social identities which prevail amongst his electors.

It is important to emphasise that these considerations concern the requirements of the political craft, of political competence, not the basis of political motivation. Leaders in politics, potential representatives, no doubt commonly cast their eye over a range of symbols, seeking the most prospectively efficacious. Symbols for them are often simply (and perhaps always quite importantly) instruments with which to persuade, or at worst dupe, their followers. But if, as sophisticated bystanders, we may agree that political leadership consists largely in the propagating of more or less noble lies, it is a mistake to adopt too Platonic an image of the psychology which goes with the exercise of such leadership. The model of manipulated and manipulator, deceiver and dupe, gives too rationalist a picture of political agency. Leaders sometimes need lies in order to deceive their followers, actual or potential. But they do not have the status in political theory of unmoved movers and it is plain that they also often need lies to deceive themselves. (They too must rise in the morning and sleep as best they can at night.) No lies will deceive either speaker or audience so effectively when necessary as lies which are largely or usually true; and no one would long believe the lies of someone who never in fact told the truth. When the emperor Constantine the Great saw in a vision one evening an illuminated emblem in the sky and read the legend that he would conquer in that sign, it would take a very bold historian to be wholly certain of the precise character of his experience or of the nature of the motivation with which it subsequently furnished him.[1] But when he put the emblem, the monogram Chi Rho, on his soldiers' shields, on his own helmet and on the imperial *labarum* before the battle of the Milvian Bridge and proceeded to win that battle, the subsequent career of the emblem (and of what it stood for) was sundered neatly from the obscurities of Constantine's psychology and sent on a notable (and unmistakably public) career. Even the materialist theory of history, one might say, is now semi-officially on record as admitting that this somewhat inconsequentially incurred symbol changed crucially the subsequent history of the world as a whole.[2] To make the Roman empire Christian was a larger gesture than rendering the politics of Ceylon 'swabasha'.[3] But both performances are better reflected on in terms of the social *possibility* of their being performed than in terms of the private mental states (dispassionate and manipulative or passionate and credulous) of the historical actors who conceived and executed them. It is always possible to look at political allegiance in two ways, ways which can even, as in the case of the famous rabbit/duck illusion,[4] serve to exclude one another. Followers can be seen as what leaders are for. Leaders then are use values for their followers and the Pope, humbly, is *Servus Servorum Dei*. By contrast one may take the view of Thrasymachus, prototype of the hardnosed political scientist, that leaders are what followers are for. Followers here are use values for leaders and the Pope may well prove to be Julius II, amoral manipulator of the material and ideological resources of his incomparably humanly arrogant role. But although these two conceptions can be (and often are) developed in such a way as to exclude each other, furnishing the strongest axiomatic principles of interpretation, in the messy reality of the political world neither looks much like the complete story. Both leaders and led try as best they can to do their own thing; but neither is likely to be orientated towards the other in all circumstances in a purely exploitative or purely self-abnegatory fashion. Followers betray and serve leaders, just as leaders serve and betray followers. The conduct of political life is neither a charity fête nor a zero-sum game.[5]

III

In setting out an analysis of representation, then, it is essential to acknowledge a certain imputed psychology and preferable to explain the choice as well as outline the character of the psychology which has been imputed. The psychology imputed here is one which takes as given the demonstrated capacity of human beings to co-operate with one another and which attributes this capacity stipulatively, in the tradition of David Hume and Adam Smith,[6] to a mechanism of sympathy which links individual egos with varying emotional force to the social situations of a variety of other social actors. With such an imputed psychology, such acknowledged representation or obligation as we encounter in our consideration of these two societies does not have to be explained away or conjured theoretically out of thin air. An unrestrictedly egoist philosophical psychology may permit theoretically of the possibility of non-illusory representation; but, despite Hobbes's valiant efforts, it is hard to see how it can generate any valid social obligations at all. The sole obligation of the true egoist is the obligation of prudence, the duty to oneself to take due account of the future when selecting present actions. A second possible imputed psychology would be one of unrestricted altruism, a psychology in which universal values are the focus of all obligations and the content of my duties is only very thinly and contingently related to who I happen to be. The Platonic polity in which representation, obligation and universal value are logically interdefined is a fine sketch of how these conceptual relations would operate with such an imputed psychology, conflating as it does (and indeed must) perfect altruism with perfect egoism. But, whatever its merits in the rhetoric of moral edification, the project for which Plato himself plainly wrote the *Republic*, the philosophical reach of unlimited altruism as a philosophical psychology grossly exceeds its empirical grasp. No political scientist could be at ease with a conceptual scheme so much at odds with casual introspection and equally casual observation of the conduct of others. The mid-point in this continuum, a psychology of extended egoism or restricted altruism, seems considerably more promising. Most persons, one may presume, are behaviourally altruistic quite extensively within what may be thought of as their identity-defining groups. There are likely to be a number of identity-defining groups for any one individual, concentric or overlapping; and the sentiments which link them are almost certain to be of widely varying strengths. Their interests are also likely to conflict on many occasions: those of my tribe as opposed to those of my church, my family against my friends, my caste against my class. Conduct is explained purely egoistically when orientated *outside* identity-defining groups and it is explained as impurely egoistic (as the product of a socially extended ego) *within* these groups. Unrestricted egoism, it has been shown, is theoretically inadequate to explain even individual political action, let alone group political action.[7] It is also empirically false in many cases. There are some psychopaths in politics and the highest-minded are liable to malice or greed on occasion. But most people most of the time exhibit a very moderate and restricted altruism; which is merely to say that not all socialisation is a failure. Some people treat all associations into which they enter in a detached and instrumental fashion. The only nexus of solidarity which they can permit is a fee-for-service arrangement, a cash (or, as it might well be, threat) nexus. A few people (the Lord Buddha, Jesus Christ, Chairman Mao, as devotees would see them) render their egos simple instruments of external and higher purposes. None of their acts are acts for self. But most people most of the time, and above all in politics, act with restricted altruism. Insofar as they assess their behaviour from the viewpoint of its cost-effectiveness, they treat the benefits of such behaviour for valued others as a good just as they treat its benefits for themselves. Few perhaps intend and fewer still positively hope for their political participation to represent a net personal cost. But very many, plainly, are prepared to accept with good enough grace a modicum of net cost fairly often in return for significant benefits to those whom they hold dear. If this were not so, it would indeed be true, as Olson has argued, that only the smallest groups of politically motivated men could have sound reasons to act collectively.[8]

Potential political action groups are groups as a member of which it may make good sense for me to secure my representation; and the interests of such groups are interests which, with greater or less vigour, I am likely to see myself as obligated, *ceteris paribus*, to promote. Since representation in electoral politics has much of the character of a public good, even voting — let alone more protracted political commitment — is likely to seem rational only insofar as men value the success of broad groupings with which they in part identify themselves, whether or not the success of these groupings necessarily brings any direct increment of material value to themselves. But it is not merely the psychological drift involved in this social expansion of the individual ego which nudges the process of political representation away from individual idiosyncrasy and towards potential political action groups of significant scale. It is also, of course, the practical preconditions for securing effective political representation which serve to do so. Any individual has a

161

very large number of attributes which serve to determine his interests and almost any of them might determine his interests on occasion in a way which would make it rational for him to wish for their effective representation in the political sphere. An individual may have reason to seek representation for himself under many different descriptions: red-haired, no-haired, left-handed, frequently inebriated, teetotal, under 5 ft 2 inches in height, fat, British, European, shop-owning, East Anglian, epileptic, Cambridge graduate, illiterate, Anglican, male, juvenile, untouchable, starving, nicotine-addicted, Puritan, promiscuous, pessimistic and so on. But his chances of securing representation under these descriptions depend heavily both on the costs to others of servicing interests of those appropriately described in these ways and on the distribution and the numbers of the persons who can be so described. In electoral politics voters may long for those who will represent them perfectly as individuals; but in practice they must put up those who are attempting to represent them as components of rather blearily perceived potential action groups.[9] Elected members of a legislature may like to claim or even to believe that they serve all their constituents all the time. But in reality no such option is open to them, since the interests of their constituents conflict drastically with one another and since the representatives necessarily cannot even know what most of these interests in fact are. Even when offering themselves more or less blandly for this public service, those competing for election are compelled to gamble largely blindfolded on a presentation of themselves as effective instruments of what they hope will prove to be the more insistently identified interests of a majority coalition of those who actually vote.

IV

Both Ghana and Sri Lanka are export economies, dependent for the greater part of their foreign exchange earnings on the export of a single food crop. Both had large foreign exchange balances and substantially higher standards of living than most of their neighbouring countries at independence and both had dissipated these balances without very impressive augmentation of their per capita productive capacities by the mid 1960s.[10] Neither has had the good fortune to discover and exploit large indigenous oil deposits and both in consequence have been caught by the debt trap in recent years.[11] Both also were British colonies for a good many decades and both display very large regional variations in the extent of the social change induced by political incorporation into the colonial and post-colonial state structures and economic incorporation into the world market. Against these structural and historical similarities, there are at least three clearly fundamental discrepancies: one in terms of economic structure and two which it is probably more helpful in the first instance to conceive as cultural. The difference in terms of economic structure is simple. The tea exported from Sri Lanka is

162

produced predominantly in large plantations, managed as economic units and manned by a labour force almost all of whom are culturally alien to the island and a majority of whom are today potential citizens of a foreign country or even stateless persons.[12] Until recently, indeed, much the greater part of these plantations has been owned by foreign companies, most of them British. Ghanaian cocoa by contrast is produced by much smaller units, units which are small even in contrast with some of those in the neighbouring Ivory Coast. None of the production units are owned by foreign companies and, although a substantial proportion of the labour used in its production is contributed by foreign nationals and although the position of these foreigners in its production has been of political importance in the last decade, it is still true that the political relation between the settled population of the rain forest cocoa zone of Ghana and the government of Ghana on the other hand is wholly different from that which obtains between the settled population of the teagrowing highlands of Sri Lanka and the government of Sri Lanka.

The two major cultural differences are substantially more complex and one of them, the Sinhalese/Tamil communal division, is of considerable potential importance in the context of the economic discrepancy. There are communal divisions of a kind, of course, in Ghana, as there are notoriously in the United Kingdom. But even the Orangemen and the horrors of Belfast appear historically epiphenomenal when set against the millennial depth of the Sinhalese/Tamil dichotomy. When the villagers of Marguerite Robinson's pseudonymous 'Morapitiya' told her in 1963 the myth of the residence of the Sinhalese national liberator Prince Dutthagamani in their village, they may have been preoccupied by the issue of their own social status but they plainly did not have their minds on current politics, a confusing mêlée in which at this stage they appear to have identified little of relevance to their own lives.[13] The occasion for Dutthagamani's coming to the village was his refusal to swear to the King, his father, that he would not attack the Tamil King without paternal permission. Enraged by this nationalist obstinacy, Dutthagamani's father determines to kill his son and is only frustrated by the latter's mother coming to him as he lay asleep to warn him of the need to make his escape. She finds him in his room, sleeping curled up, and asks him (with mythic presence of mind) why he is doing so; and he replies with what in the circumstances must have been at least equal presence of mind: 'How can I sleep straight when the Tamils are at my head and the sea at my feet?'[14] Being an island Ceylon has for long had more the appearance of a bounded unit than Ghana and since its historical identity is still focussed on Dutthagamani's triumph over the Tamil enemy more than two millennia ago and the consequent cultural and linguistic survival of the island as a Sinhalese cultural domain, it is hardly surprising that Tamil/Sinhalese communal divisions should be of major political importance. Nor is it surprising, given such political importance, that Dutthagamani's waking image should have remained markedly evocative. With the sea still at their feet, with their 'Indian' or stateless Tamil foreign exchange earners in the highland tea plantations, with the tens of millions of Tamils in southern India organised with increasing fervour in communalist organisations with blatantly separatist dreams, and with a substantial Tamil beach-head in the northern Jaffna peninsula, a large Tamil-speaking zone on the eastern coast, and an impressive Tamil fifth column among the civil servants and professional men of the great city of Colombo, it is scarcely surprising that Sinhalese politicians should have succeeded so handsomely in evoking a sense of threat to national and cultural identity in Sri Lankan domestic politics. Both language and ethnicity and the historical experience of rejecting a socially entrenched coastal educated elite have been of some importance on one particular occasion in Ghanaian politics. But there simply is no authentic and unitary Ghanaian culture sufficiently integral for a presumed threat to it to serve as the fulcrum of national politics for a decade.

The second major cultural discrepancy between the two countries relates to the Sinhalese/Tamil communal split but it is by no means coterminous with the latter. Prince Dutthagamani, a Sinhalese Prince, reconquered Sri Lanka from the Tamils and is thus a Sinhalese national (and communal) hero. But what he reconquered Sri Lanka *for* was Buddhism (in the end after some ups and downs Theravāda Buddhism).[15] Sinhalese national identity looks a fairly sturdy plant when set against even the Akan solidarism which is the best (or worst?) that Ghana could muster in reply. But Buddhism, of course, is a Great Tradition in the most exacting of both theological and sociological senses.[16] Not only has Buddhist commitment arguably had consequences as deep for the structure of modern Sri Lankan politics as the profound effects of the Tamil/Sinhalese rift, it has also had consequences of a somewhat different kind. Most Tamils in Ceylon, both 'Ceylon' Tamils and 'Indian' Tamils, are Hindus and most Sinhalese are Buddhists. If the religious affiliations of Buddhists had been politically defined in the same terms as the communal affiliations of Sinhalese, they would thus have been anti-Hindu in essence. In fact, however, they seem to have been decidedly more anti-Christian and in particular anti-Catholic than they have been anti-Hindu in their practical expression.[17] Moreover, it is at least arguable that this anti-Catholic orientation has lent to Sinhalese populism an organisational base and a cultural urgency in contrast to which the Ghanaian populism of Nkrumah's Convention People's Party was a plant with very shallow roots indeed.

What the prevalence of Buddhism in Sri Lankan society has certainly not done, however, has been to infuse Sri Lankan politics with a calm and pacific otherworldliness and self-abnegation in contrast with the violent and thrusting greed of the Ghanaian warrior village.[18] The social relations of an insulated, one-caste, highland Kandyan village like 'Morapitiya', do appear markedly serene and ritually unaggressive when compared with those of any

Ghanaian community of which we have a comparably sensitive ethnographic record.[19] But even inside 'Morapitiya' this seamless and factionless web of (somewhat self-congratulatory) high-caste mutuality was torn apart within a few years by the intrusions of Sri Lankan national politics. Outside such insulated communities and above all in the domain of national politics itself the levels of political violence in Sri Lanka, especially in communal riots or in the 1971 rising, make Ghana's Watson riots, or its Kulungugu bombing or Yendi massacre look like vicarage tea parties. The Five Precepts of Buddhism certainly prescribe the avoidance of violence in a very strong sense. But it is unwise to predict the conduct of those who hold any beliefs directly from the programmatic statements of their belief. Constantine the Great perhaps conceived the *signum* on his banner and helmet as a magical device for expediting military triumph. He can hardly in any case have placed it there on account of a sensitive grasp of the felicity of going into battle to win an empire under the sign of a faith whose kingdom was not of this world. When Dutthagamani put a Buddhist relic in his spear and sallied out to do battle with the Tamil King,[20] he was employing a magical device for what in the teleological perspective of secular history a Buddhist might judge to be a good end, giving a much needed historical hitch to the Great Tradition which he represented. But in placing the relic in his *spear* and setting out to *kill* the Tamil King in single-handed combat at the gates of Anurādhapura he was hardly conforming very adequately to the ethical intimations of that tradition. Formal Buddhist ethics are strikingly demanding; but in a moral culture ingenious enough to devise the notion of 'Buddhist eggs', pre-cracked and thus murder-avoiding for the consumer, on sale on the shelves of Colombo stores,[21] the accommodation of precept to a less constricting practice presents no insurmountable challenge. The role which Buddhism has in fact played in Sri Lankan politics, culminating in the assassination of its greatest political impresario, Solomon Bandaranaike, on his own verandah by a *bhikku*, may perhaps be offered without too much elaboration as a simple refutation of Professor Owusu's normative cultural explanation for the appropriative vigour of Ghanaian political practice. It is not because they are insufficiently furnished with self-abnegatory precepts that Ghanaians treat politics as an opportunity to dip their hands into the great bran tub of the state, but simply because they have been given so little experiential reason to view the state as anything morally more commanding than a huge, if also an especially treacherous, bran tub.

V

It is unlikely that anyone will wish to dispute the significance of the structural dissimilarity between the two countries in the relations of production which generate their major export. But the two cultural discrepancies mentioned here might appear to some to be less contentiously politically epiphenomenal — for example, simply because they *are* cultural discrepancies.[22] It is obvious enough, too, that millennia of historical communal antipathy are far from being a necessary condition for the most vivid of contemporary animosities. Ibos could get lynched in the streets of Kano in the bad days of 1966, even though there had been no significant historical relations whatever between the ancestors of lynchers and lynched a century earlier. But although it would be silly to attempt to assess at this level of generality the precise weight of these cultural factors in Sri Lankan politics over the past quarter of a century, it does seem worth underlining even in this preliminary fashion the *causal* significance which their very prevalence as symbolic vectors, reaching potentially deep into the society, must have had and indeed still possess today. We need to keep our attention on the career of Constantine's *signum* after and not before the Milvian Bridge. The insignia under which conquest can plausibly be attempted in the politics of Sri Lanka include, of course, as they must everywhere, the promise of material benefits. But if potential material beneficiaries were the only groups to whom representation could be offered, political entrepreneurship would be a comparatively two-dimensional business, a matter of long purses and illusionist chicanery. There is much else to represent (or present oneself as representing) in Sri Lankan politics besides consumers and producers. We may take three brief examples to underline this. Firstly, the derogatory category of 'Donoughmore Buddhist'[23] a category to which Sri Lanka's most important modern political leader, Solomon Bandaranaike, has been allocated by some scholarly commentators. It is unimportant how far from or how close to the truth about Bandaranaike's motives for committing himself to the Buddhist faith this sneer may have been. What *is* important is the sheer impossibility of imagining a perceptive young Ghanaian politician at any stage arriving at the judgement that the adoption of any local confessional allegiance might prove the launching pad for a dazzling political career. It would be considerably harder still to imagine such an expectation, if acted upon, turning out to be fulfilled.* It is not that the presentation of one's political self as authentically indigenous cannot prove an asset in Ghana or an air of being imperfectly at home in the society something of a liability. But indigenous authenticity is hardly any longer a transparent category and Nkrumah's platform sycretism of hymns, libations and modernist political phrases, sails set to catch every passing breeze, probably reflects it better than any more purist conception could do. The confessional political identification which has perhaps come closest in Ghanaian politics to the force of the 'Donoughmore Buddhist' gibe (and perhaps in comparably restricted circles) would be that of Dr Busia as a primary school Methodist: an example of fate rather than choice, since primary school is plainly beneath the age of cultural consent, but plainly for some of his more sophisticated opponents a disagreeable

* Nkrumah may have chosen to pay his respects to Kankan Nyame. But he certainly did not do so as a means of publicly ingratiating himself with the electorate.

residue of colonial deformation and an affront to indigenous culture – not
at all what a Ghanaian leader ought to be like. But Dr Busia, it should be
remembered, did not founder because of any demonstrated desertion on the
part of the electorate.

Another frivolous but rather charming example is provided by Sir John
Kotelawala's attempt during the 1952–6 government to present the threat
from the left in linguistic terms:[24] 'if either the Communists or Samasama-
jists get into power you will not only lose the personal liberties you now
enjoy but as a consequence of their policy of opening the door to foreigners,
you will be forced to give up your mother tongue of Sinhalese or Tamil and
be compelled to adopt the languages of the Indians or the Chinese or the
Russians'. It is a safe assumption that politicians will tend to present the
prospective consequences of the victories of their opponents as being as dire
as they judge their electorates to be at all likely to credit: a fate, if the
credulity market will bear it, much worse than the loss of personal liberties
now enjoyed. No doubt Sir John took a more optimistic view of the
credulity of the Sri Lankan electorate than Mrs Thatcher or Mr Callaghan
would permit themselves for the British electorate. But it seems unlikely that
either of these last, even if they supposed the British electorate to be
infinitely credulous, would hit on as the direct menace of the triumph of the
British Communist Party, the compulsory speaking of Russian or Chinese.
The final example is far more complex and more important; but it can be
presented here quite perfunctorily because it comes out so clearly in
Professor Jeyaratnam Wilson's study of the 1970 election.[25] The key strategic problem for both the S.L.F.P. and U.N.P. in these elections was very
simple: how to present themselves to the Sinhalese electorates as authentically bigoted against the Tamils (and hence dependably unyielding in their
hostility towards Tamil interests), while at the same time (if hardly on the
same occasions) presenting themselves to the Tamil political parties, with
whom they might well need to ally immediately after the election in order to
form a government, as honest and trustworthy political partners. No political
party in any election anywhere would be likely to relish a systematic and
simultaneous comparison between all the undertakings which it gives to all
the audiences which it addresses. But it is not easy to imagine how any major
Ghanaian political party should ever have occasion to get itself in public into
such a deeply unpromising posture – let alone how its main opponent could
be led to join it in an identical posture of its own free will.

VI

The practice of representation in Sri Lanka is thus a more intricate matter
than it is in Ghana in several distinct respects. Not only are there, as already
emphasised, numerous politically consequential categories of social differentiation there which have no real Ghanaian equivalent: religious, linguistic,

communal, caste. There are also many more relatively autonomous representative agencies: parties, trade unions, religious organisations. Civil society in
Sri Lanka has a more substantial weight vis-à-vis the state than it has in
Ghana; and this relative weight is exemplified in the comparatively uninterrupted practice of competitive representation which Sri Lanka has experienced. Representation in Ghana is localist as well as highly intermittent, a
drastically less important mode of relation between individual and state than
the variety of private transactions. Few groups of economic actors have had
occasion to treat public electoral politics as a promising vehicle for advancing
their collective interests and none has succeeded in generating political
organisations which can be relied on to serve as their representative agencies
over any lengthy period of time. Interest representation, in short, is very
poorly institutionalised in Ghanaian politics. In Sri Lanka by contrast more
or less distinct party affiliations have been alleged for numerous economic
categories: Sinhalese petty clerks (S.L.F.P.), urban proletarians (L.S.S.P. &
C.P.), rice-growing peasants (U.N.P.),[26] large-scale landowners (U.N.P. –
but also, in political abuse, U.F.),[27] wealthy professional and commercial
groups (U.N.P.), youthful rural unemployed (P.L.F.). There have even been
national electoral contests fought at least partially on the basis of disagreement about the appropriate strategy for economic development: the maintenance of a high level of welfare distributions or their sacrifice, at least in
the short run, to promote a more rapid rate of economic growth.

There are three reasonably plausible ascriptions of political agency to
defined economic groupings in Ghanaian representative politics, as well as a
number of broader imputations of differential economic benefit to various
groups. The initial cadre of Nkrumah's C.P.P. has been plausibly portrayed as
a group of ambitious entrepreneurs excluded from markets in the postwar
colonial order and taking to electoral politics as a novel vehicle of market
access.[28] (Later, and much less clearly, the factional squabbles within the
C.P.P. government were presented as a tussle between the now relatively
established capitalists and a more purist (and unestablished) grouping, the
custodians of Nkrumah's ideological conscience, who wished to supplant
private capitalism with a greatly expanded state sector.)[29] Far more significant for the issue of political representation was the extent to which the
N.L.M./C.P.P. struggle of 1956 came to be seen in the cocoa-growing areas of
Ashanti as a conflict between the interests of cocoa producers as a whole and
the controllers of the state apparatus, along with their local clients. The scale
of the effective cess on cocoa production, levied through the government
monopsony, was at this time dramatic enough to make this perception of the
nature of the struggle eminently plausible; and the stability of the structure
of economic rewards within cocoa production meant that the level of producer prices served to set the real incomes of virtually all groups involved in
producing cocoa, from day labourers to large landowners. (A qualification to
this producer economic solidarism in the face of government, in addition to

the normal individual qualifications generated by side-payments and party clientage, was the mitigation of local cocoa land dues enforced by the C.P.P. in its vendetta against chiefly opposition, a measure reversed by the N.L.C. government.)[30] The third important essay in collective interest representation, commenced under the N.L.C. government, pressed forward by the Progress Party government in office and little modified in essence by its military usurpers, was the indigenisation of economic opportunities in Ghana. The sluggish condition of the economy in 1966 and the constrictions imposed by the level of foreign debt meant that economic distribution for the immediate future had to be conceived in strictly zero-sum terms. The N.L.C. government and its advisers lacked the political will and in most cases the inclination to expropriate western capitalist interests, as they did to repudiate the debt. Apart from the disgraced C.P.P. dignitaries they could not afford to incur the odium of injuring other indigenous interests. In these circumstances the only direction in which they could hope to lay their hands on fresh assets for distribution was by expropriating those foreigners who lacked powerful friends in the World Bank or the I.M.F. Thus Lebanese and foreign Africans were legally precluded from (or in some cases precluded from legally) owning or participating in many areas of business. Large numbers of them were in consequence deported under the terms of the Aliens Compliance Order after the 1969 election. This measure caused considerable unintended labour problems in the cocoa-growing areas;[31] but its main (and intended) consequence was to increase the extent of indigenous control of small- and medium-scale capitalist enterprise. The Progress Party fought the 1969 election as the authentic representative of indigenous capitalism, with powerful support from business interests, especially in Ashanti and Kwahu. Whether their main opponents, Gbedemah's National Alliance of Liberals, would really have proved any less authentic representatives for indigenous capitalism is a fairly moot point. But what is clear is that the Progress Party had little difficulty in presenting itself ingratiatingly as an exponent of economic nationalism in comparison with the later years of the C.P.P.'s rule and that economic nationalism remains today as uncontroversial a political value as one can find in Ghana. One further economic constituency for which the C.P.P. government may be said to have catered was the rural and urban unemployed. Both by its drastic expansion of the state payroll in import-substitutive manufacturing in the urban areas and by its establishment of large state farms in selected areas of the countryside, as well as by its creation of the Workers' Brigade, the C.P.P. created employment for many who might otherwise have found it hard to enter the labour force at all. The economic development strategy implicit in these policies, however botched in the execution,[32] was by no means absurd in itself;[33] and the service to individuals employed was real enough to render them genuine economic clients. But the C.P.P. provided this service, unlike for example those other instruments of clientage development the Cocoa Purchasing Company loans,[34] at a time when it no longer expected or intended to have to face electoral competition. Hence the promise to offer the service was never a promise dangled before wavering voters and never consequently a promise which led voters to select the C.P.P. as their representative agency in preference to other and less concerned competitors. The evanescent character of the representative process in Ghana and the fact that it has never given rise to more than two genuinely national political parties at the same time have served to discourage exploration of economic differentiation as a potential basis for party allegiance and driven the two national political parties, whenever real political competition was in train, towards what they perceived as the centre of the continuum of economic policy. Being so driven, Ghanaian parties have in effect enacted Hotelling's model of spatial competition[35] and thus rendered effective entry for any third political grouping purely through the representative process excessively difficult.

A number of factors have prevented the public politics of Sri Lanka from developing in this over-simplified and one-dimensional manner. One stubborn cause for the plurality of parties in Ceylon has been the persisting salience of communal division. Perhaps the most important of the remaining factors may simply be the much greater chronological depth of effective representative politics in Sri Lanka. The pre Second World War nationalist movement was far from being a mass party like the Indian National Congress and the U.N.P. which succeeded to its mantle at the time of independence was almost equally a party of notables. But even if the U.N.P. was thus very much a political beneficiary of the vigorous mass nationalism of the subcontinent to the north, it was nevertheless effective enough actually to acquire state power at independence and even at independence it did have to confront opposing parties with some real institutional identity of their own. In Ghana the elite United Gold Coast Convention could neither stand up to the political impact of their returned Secretary nor (unlike the populist party which he proceeded to found) force the colonial government into conceding a hasty independence. The notables in Ghana had to learn how to 'represent' localities before they could even compete for, let alone win, control of the power of the state. The year in which the Ghanaian notables first seriously challenged their insolent supplanters, 1956, was the very year in which the notables of Ceylon first lost their grip on the power of their independent state. At the other end of the Sri Lankan political spectrum the L.S.S.P. is not merely the only politically important Trotskyist party (or ex-Trotskyist party)[36] in the world, it is also the oldest institutionally continuous political party in Sri Lanka and one whose influence had never been higher than it was initially under the last Bandaranaike government.[37] The contrast with Wallace Johnson's ventures in the pre-war Gold Coast is instructive. In both cases the bad news was brought very much from the outside, from Moscow or expensive foreign educational establishments like the L.S.E. But in Ceylon the bad news rooted itself firmly in local dis-

170

contents, while in the Gold Coast simply deporting Wallace Johnson was sufficient to cause it to wither almost instantaneously.[38]

The substantial reality of representation in Sri Lanka, the extent to which real discrete social identities provoked the formation of active political groupings, has in this way served to fashion the most progressive and cosmopolitan features of Sri Lankan politics as well as the most atavistic and particularist features. The opportunity to domesticate the full intricacy of left-wing factional conflict, a panoply of left-wing political organisation of almost Parisian comprehensiveness,[39] is the other face of a political realm in which much politics aspires to the condition of a race riot. The symbolic universality of political parties of the Fourth International or the Moscow or Peking dispensations coexists with a plenitude of what to a Marxist eye must appear as indisputably localist bigotries. But the very multiplicity of these vehicles of universal value calls into some question their success in transcending a local particularism.[40] It is no doubt historically a little retarded for Ghana never to have mustered a single party of the working class; but there are embarrassments of equal strength if somewhat different character in the fact that Sri Lanka has at times been in a position to field four or five such parties at a time. For a class whose world historical destiny was firmly attributable to its inherent propensity for unity[41] such efflorescence is plainly rather too much of a good thing. It encourages, too, the suspicion that the universal terms may not in fact correspond to structural realities of Sri Lankan society, let alone of world historical process, but that instead they may simply represent labels of ideological convenience behind which the manipulators of factional groupings can muster their followers very much for their own ends (or at least for ends which require a very different type of description). The electoral viability of these parties has always been very firmly localised in a small number of urban and industrial areas or in long established family seats.[42] On the one occasion on which one of the Marxist parties, the L.S.S.P., did make a real bid for national political power by electoral means it burnt its fingers very badly indeed. Since then it has been careful to adhere closely, at least at election times, to the tactics of electoral compact dictated by the elaborate log-rolling coalitions required to win national political office. Its political star, which in early 1975 stood as high politically as it had ever stood,[43] seems indeed to have done so in fairly direct consequence of the probability of the process of electoral representation being abandoned by the then government of Mrs Bandaranaike.[44]

In the case of political parties of the working class the contrast between Ghana and Sri Lanka is marked neatly enough by their absence in the former and their over-supply in the latter. A more illuminating, though less sharply defined contrast, is apparent in the case of those other and (despite Lenin) less equivocally representative working class political agencies, the trade unions. In Ghana, trade union organisation until recently had relatively little autonomous history.[45] The workers in the gold mines did manage to create a

171

moderately effective union before the Second World War, and the relatively solidary occupational community of the Sekondi-Takoradi railway yards played an important role in post-war nationalist agitation; in 1961 it posed the most effective political challenge to Nkrumah's claim still to represent the Ghanaian working class which he was to encounter before his downfall.[46] But the trade union movement as a national entity was largely the creation of the colonial Labour Department, verbally refurbished but rendered politically still more firmly dependent by the C.P.P. state. Since the C.P.P. represented the whole Ghanaian people (at least in its own eyes), any hint of autonomous 'trade union consciousness' was an instance of moral error and corrected accordingly. The C.P.P. greatly inflated the numbers of those enrolled in trade unions and it ensured that they were fully instructed in what was *not* to be done (striking for higher wages for example). Possibilities of a more complex representative role appeared with Nkrumah's overthrow in 1966, when Bentum's T.U.C. was for a time less effectively controlled by the N.L.C. military government or its 'liberal' elected successor, the Progress Party government of Dr Busia. But the P.P.'s liberalism soon wore fairly thin and its military supplanters, the N.R.C., while they at one point considerably raised the minimum wage, certainly did not encourage the energetic representation of anyone's political interests in public by anyone but themselves.

The position in Sri Lanka is thus far markedly different. There are many more self-established unions of moderate size and they have a record of much greater militancy than their Ghanaian counterparts.[47] The labour movement as a whole is in no sense a creature of either the colonial or the post-colonial state. The plethora of Sri Lankan political parties has generated a number of independent union groupings tied to particular parties. No less than seven political parties have had their own separate labour organisations. Many Sri Lankan unions were initially either founded by or effectively rendered viable by the services of wealthy professional men with political commitments, and in some cases political ambitions, of their own. Many unions thus have much the character of personal clientages in which the economic interests of the members have over the years been handsomely advanced individually or collectively by the brokerage services of a leader or leaders who were in no sense part of the members' occupational community;[48] and the political standing of these leaders in its turn has been handsomely augmented by their possession of impressive personal clientages. These exchange relations have served as the focus of considerable projective hostility, particularly on the part of political opponents; but there is no reason to doubt that the services provided in both directions have often been perfectly genuine and palpable.[49] The element of clientage is organisationally important in the case of party unions too and has naturally been affected directly by the capture and loss of state power by the political parties in question. The membership of U.N.P. unions increased drastically between

1965 and 1970, while the U.N.P. victory in 1965 led its defeated opponents to call out their union members in the effort to inflict a little retaliatory discomfort, seeking, as Dudley Senanayake saw it from the self-righteousness of his new majority, 'to nullify the people's verdict by undemocratic means'.[50] In its several economic roles the Sri Lankan urban working class may reasonably be judged to have been rather vigorously represented by this multiplicity of agencies. The process of being thus represented has plainly helped to generate considerable work group solidarity in the face of their various employers, public and private. Perhaps, too, the capacity to act in this way for itself may be held to offset in some degree the infelicity of its organisational disunity and the appreciable practical disadvantages which such disunity has brought it.[51]

What cannot be so readily or blithely discounted, however, from an oecumenical Marxist viewpoint is the salience of communal divisions among union boundaries. Some supposedly non-political groups such as the teachers simply have different unions for the two communities.[52] In other cases vigorous independent leadership, such as that of Bala Tampoe's Ceylon Mercantile Union[53] has enabled unions with relatively homogeneous memberships to survive the desertion of their interests by their party sponsors without sacrificing their organisational effectiveness. Being above communalism is plainly much in the interests of some vulnerable minority groups of workers. The Communist Party and L.S.S.P. unions all naturally began by taking a very lofty view about such atavistic bases of political or industrial solidarity, seeing in them the sway of reactionary ideology and the machinations of imperialism. This fastidiousness had the advantage of enabling them to group together Tamil and Sinhalese workers and organisers and, in the case of Tamils in the southern and western coastal areas, gave them what was in effect a substantial and often talented clientage with nowhere else to go. But between 1963 and 1965 the strains of party factionalism among the parties of the left and the imperatives of party advantage in national conflict had introduced severe communal tensions into even the left-wing unions and in many cases had led Tamils to abandon their previously non-communal unions in disgust.[54]

For the S.L.F.P. their alliance with the Trotskyists in 1964 was conceived quite explicitly as an expedient for keeping the organised working class under some measure of control.[55] The electorally more marginal L.S.S.P. in return stood to gain the opportunity of access to public office and no doubt anticipated that such access would in due course enable it to secure for its working class constituency some concrete rewards in return for their now dutiful docility. Deferring to the susceptibilities of its linguistically and ethnically chauvinist Sinhalese partner was a small price to have to pay for this opportunity. From the European perspective of the Fourth International's headquarters the accommodation might look very like the surrender of its political integrity for a fairly meagre mess of pottage. But to the residual L.S.S.P. leadership it no doubt appeared simply the reconciliation of theory with the requirements of effective practice.[56]

Two further aspects of economic differentiation which have received a measure of active representation in Sri Lankan politics and which have as yet no clear equivalent in the politics of Ghana require a brief mention. The first aspect is simple enough. Like Ghana, Sri Lanka was at its independence one of the wealthier countries in its geographical zone in terms of per capita income. Its foreign trade balance was markedly favourable and it possessed large foreign currency reserves. Again like Ghana, Sri Lanka today has by contrast appalling problems of foreign debt and in its balance of payments and no realistic prospect of escaping from these in the near future. The only major recent improvement in this foreign trade position, once again like Ghana, has been a sharp increase in domestic rice production (partially reversed again by the policies of the present government), and a consequent marked decrease, albeit temporary, in its need to import this grain in bulk. The long-term tendency of most other economic indices in both countries has been gloomy in the last decade. But both have at least shown a greater potential capacity to feed themselves with rice. In both countries the independence economic reserves were spent by the government and in both the decline in the prices of their major export commodities prevented the replacement of these large initial public resources. In each case a considerable proportion of the reserves was spent on expanding welfare services which might in due course augment productive capacity but which could not be relied upon to do so automatically — particularly the expansion of primary education in Ghana under Botsio's Accelerated Education Plan and the improvement of both health and education services in Sri Lanka. In Ghana under Nkrumah this expenditure was matched by heavy (and unfortunately very ill-planned) investment in productive facilities in the public sector. In Sri Lanka there was at first less public investment in productive facilities (though perhaps eventually an equally drastic expansion in the public pay-roll)[57] but there was throughout much more direct subsidisation of individual consumption, especially through the provision of a substantial individual rice ration for the population as a whole. This distributionist policy, along with a variety of measures of progressive taxation, seems to have had much greater redistributive effects on current per capita income than can possibly have been attained in Ghana in the same period.[58] It appears to have done so too, at least up to the early 1970s, without crippling effects on the rate of growth. But whatever the comparative felicity of the two development strategies (and it seems clear even in the case of the largest proportional beneficiaries of Sri Lanka's distributive arrangements that it would have been to their advantage over quite short periods of time to have had their increments saved and reinvested on their behalf, rather than handed out at once)[59] the main point in this context is the much greater degree to which the issue of savings as against consumption has been politicised among the population

174

at large in Sri Lanka than it has in Ghana. During the 1970 election campaign the U.N.P., in defence of its development strategy of cutting government expenditure and expanding local food production, attempted to persuade the rural electorate that these measures so far from being an unprincipled attack on their standard of living were in fact clearly to their advantage.[60] Large-scale government distribution of rice, it argued, was linked to the practice of massive rice importing and even if in the future it were to be detached from this link, it would necessarily cause domestic rice producers to receive a lower price for their product than a domestic free market in grain would guarantee to them. This attempt to portray the relevant division of interest as one between rural producers and urban consumers in which all rural rice-growing households which were not actually in deficit on the reduced ration ought rationally to be solidary in the face of the feckless urban urge to squander public assets in this way naturally provoked a riposte from the S.L.F.P. High market prices for domestic rice were of interest, they claimed, largely to middlemen or to those producers with large surplus stocks of rice to sell on the home market, that is to say to large-scale landowners and relatively modern agricultural capitalists. The U.N.P. in this way attempted to evoke a community of interest for the countryside as a whole against the town, while the S.L.F.P. in reply stressed the significance of class differentiation within the countryside itself and strove to elicit, as it had done with such success in 1956, a solidarity of the poor, above all the rural poor, against the rich and culturally alien. Both parties had little difficulty in identifying the presence of feudal motes in each other's eyes[61] and neither's conception of the ideological merits of their candidature needs to be taken at face value. But on balance, whatever the local plausibility of the S.L.F.P. campaign, it is clear enough that the U.N.P. in 1970 held little conviction as a representative of the collective virtue of rural producers against urban consumers.

A final aspect of economic differentiation which has appeared tantalisingly from time to time in the politics of Sri Lanka, in a manner in which it is scarcely yet relevant in Ghana, is land scarcity. There is little systematic nation-wide information about rural social stratification in either country. But even in Ghana where there are still very large reserves of potentially valuable land it is clear that control over virgin cocoa land in any quantity now represents control over a very scarce and valuable factor of production. Ownership of cocoa farms has long been a secure and recognised form in which to store individual wealth. Even in the cocoa areas it is unclear that concentration of landholding has yet increased substantially. But, matriliny notwithstanding, it seems unlikely that with rising family cash needs, fluctuating returns from cash crops and a closing cocoa land frontier that a greater concentration of holdings and a consequent worsening in the terms on which non-owners can obtain access to cocoa land can be avoided indefinitely.[62] But if land suitable for high return cash crops without very heavy

initial investment is not scarce in many areas, access to land for family subsistence farming presents few difficulties in most.

In Sri Lanka by contrast there is marked land shortage in many areas,
especially of the heavily eroded highland plantation fringes.[63] The hoarding
of lands by tea and rubber plantations in particular, whether or not this is
economically advantageous from the viewpoint of the economy as a whole,
has long been bitterly resented by Kandyan Sinhalese villagers in the highland zone. In her last government Mrs Bandaranaike, daughter and widow of
great landowners though she was, imposed a ceiling of 50 acres on private
landholdings in her 1972 Land Reform Act, thus transferring about a seventh
of all agricultural land to the custody of the State Plantations Corporation.[64]
But this Act does not appear to have been clearly envisaged at the time of
the 1970 election campaign and cannot plausibly be claimed to have resulted
from massive popular pressure on the part of those whose interests were
most directly affected for the better. The main context in which land
scarcity has entered directly into the process of representation has been the
series of government colonisation schemes for resettling highland or coastal
Sinhalese on newly irrigated lands in the dry zone of the island. Dudley
Senanayake, following in his father's footsteps, invested much of his political energy and a substantial proportion of the development expenditure
undertaken by his government in these schemes, seeing himself as continuing
the great irrigation programme of the ancient Sinhalese monarchy.[65] The
economic returns on these public investments appear to have been exceedingly meagre and it is not clear that the political returns over time have really
proved any more handsome. Some durable clientage building has no doubt
been accomplished, if not perhaps in a particularly cost-effective manner.
But in the construction of clientages it is a crucial consideration who is in
fact wielding the mason's trowel. In a number of cases under the U.N.P.'s
main opponents, for example, the effective patron in such colonisation
schemes seems not to have been even a durable member of the party and
seems to have used the colonisation opportunity to transplant his own caste
members in sufficiently large numbers to disrupt a previously assured
S.L.F.P. Goyigama vote.[66] To add one injury to another, it was the same
politician C.P. de Silva who by withdrawing the support of his Salagama bloc
brought down Mrs Bandaranaike's government in 1964.[67]

In addition to these economic groupings (and it does not seem too strong
to say, thus far more importantly) a variety of culturally and socially defined
groups have been wooed by aspiring representatives in the two countries. In
Sri Lanka at the national level these have been above all communal, linguistic,
religious or caste-based, except in 1956 when the process seems better
envisaged *en gros* as a broad political rejection of an incumbent elite by the
rest of the population which it purported to represent. In Ghana there have
been elements of ethnic and linguistic mustering in several of the elections.
But for a variety of reasons the ethnic or linguistic units involved have been

too shallow or too diffuse for the project of representing them to seem other than factitious over any length of time. Enduring representative enterprise in Ghana has in consequence been very localist indeed, cast firmly in the idiom of utilitarian patronage and linking local factionalism with great intimacy to a persisting national tussle between two political parties, whose main ambition in practice was explicitly enough to represent their own members.[68] It is important not to misinterpret this contrast between the politics of the two countries as simply an organisational contrast. There is very little available information about the process of representation in Sri Lanka from the perspective of the represented. But what little information there is, especially that assembled by Dr Jiggins,[69] suggests strongly that the mechanisms of constructing electoral clientages in Sri Lanka have much in common with those deployed in Ghana. What is very evidently different is the set of categories in terms of which such clientages are publicly identified by representers or represented in Sri Lanka and thus, we may assume, in some measure the terms in which they are actually envisaged by both types of actors.

VII

The place of ethnic and linguistic identifications among these categories has been much stressed by students of Sri Lankan politics and there seems little dispute about their instrumental role and little mystery as to how they came to play it.[70] The potentiality for activating such categories as banners behind which to assemble political followings has been extensively stressed by recent students of the political development of many countries. It is no doubt correct to see the propensity of different groupings to adopt these self-identifications for political purposes as being in part produced by relative rates of social mobilisation. But, as Paul Brass has recently emphasised with great cogency,[71] it is essential also to recognise the major role of the political choices of candidates for leadership in determining the extent to which either language or religion become effective bases for political conflict groupings. The choice of devices for the leader's banner at one time has drastic consequences for collective political perception and in this way helps to *make* political history. It does not simply reflect in a passive manner the pre-existing contours of social and cultural differentiation.

The part played by religion in Sri Lankan politics is somewhat more controversial. It is agreed on all sides that politicians have made at least ever since 1956 strident appeals to their electorates on the grounds of their own suitability to represent the latter's religious interests or on the grounds of their opponents' manifest lack of such suitability. The 1956 election campaign, in which it seems reasonable to suppose that such appeals, positive and negative, secured their greatest impact, saw the religious issues superimposed with more or less exactitude upon lines of ethnic, linguistic and, in

177

the broadest of senses, class division. Because the groups in conflict at this point in time were virtually coterminous in the case of these varying criteria, it is hard to show conclusively that the religious division was of any great causal weight. But descriptions of the campaign and its immediate aftermath make it apparent that virtually all observers at the time were entirely clear as to its eminently causal role and the sheer persistence with which politicians have attempted to evoke its aid on subsequent occasions serves as testimony at least to the enduring plausibility of its impact in 1956. Sir John Kotelawala and subsequent U.N.P. propagandists have devoted immense energy to attempts at portraying themselves as more authentic bearers of Dutthagamani's *signum* than their S.L.F.P. foes, insisting as they had always done on the dogmatic atheism of the Marxist parties and demanding how an authentically religious party could safely ally itself with such satanic agencies. (This emphasis perhaps betrays a residually Catholic conception of what a religion must be committed to. Buddhists may not conceptually be *obliged* to be atheists; but the specifically Buddhist aspect of their beliefs can hardly be thought to preclude them from being so.)[72] The electoral fate of the U.N.P. in 1970 (to say nothing of that of their alleged catspaw the irreproachably devout S.M.P.)[73] suggests a diminishing efficacy in the development of this particular *signum*, as on a much smaller scale does Richard Gombrich's report of the complete lack of impact produced by strenuous monkish propaganda in the area which he was studying in 1965.[74] There is, therefore, room for considerable variation of judgement on the issue of how consequential the prominence of Buddhist paraphernalia or Catholic commitment have in fact been in Sri Lankan politics. What is not open to dispute is the simple fact of how very *prominent* religious categories have been in Sri Lanka in the course of political dispute in comparison with their virtual absence from Ghanaian political controversy. At one point, it is true, Nkrumah's magpie zest for symbolic accumulation and his taste for public adulation did cause him to fall out with a prominent Anglican cleric and there were at least reminiscences of Low Church religiosity in the Progress Party's iconography of itself as the party of virtue. But at no point were these plausibly of the least practical significance in real political conflict. By contrast, the conflict between the S.L.F.P. and the Catholic Church over religious control of educational privilege at one point came as close to threatening constitutional government in Ceylon as the country has come since independence, while massive civil disobedience on the part of the faithful was only avoided after a Cardinal had been flown in from India to negotiate less inflammatory treatment of the Church's schools.[75] Less importantly but in its own way equally revealingly, the sheer ebullience of the representative process in Sri Lanka, the extent to which at least up to 1971 political power has really depended upon popular credence in the representative plausibility of candidates for office, has led to the issuing of political appeals to other and much smaller groups in specifically religious terms. Since most of the population of Sri Lanka (including for example a majority of prominent L.S.S.P. politicians)[76] are nominally Buddhists it is unsurprising that candidates for office should offer themselves modestly as fit instruments for the service of Buddhist goals. But the fact, by contrast, that the United Front should bother to deploy Mrs Bandaranaike's nephew to throw doubt on the suitability of the U.N.P. to represent even the interests of Catholics,[77] or that parties should undertake to trim their foreign policies to suit the susceptibilities of the Muslim community,[78] who are thought to hold the electoral balance in a number of seats, shows a more inventive attempt to identify public goods which electors might judge it to be worth voting for than Ghana has yet to cast up. It is not simply that there are more social cleavages in Sri Lanka for political entrepreneurs to claim to represent than there are in Ghana. A single Ghanaian community, little more than an overgrown village, can muster a range of Christian denominational allegiance which it might be hard to match in the entire Republic of Sri Lanka,[79] to say nothing of Muslims, local animists and secularised agnostics. Nor is it necessarily the case that cleavages between Christian denominations in African countries,[80] let alone those, as in Uganda recently, between Christians and Muslims, are politically inconsequential. But in the macrocosm of the Ghanaian nation as in the microcosm of Goaso township, religious development in the present century has failed to generate a social transposition of *odium theologicum*;[81] and the relative infrequency and lack of urgency in representational entrepreneurship has meant that there has been little external pressure to invest the bonds of confessional comfort with adventitious external animosities.

Apart from its role in bringing about and directing the policies of the first Bandaranaike government and apart from such consequences as this government passed on to the coalition of 1961, the effect of religious categories in Sri Lankan political conflict may thus have been more symbolically prominent than effectively determinant of real allegiance. The same, however, could scarcely be thought to be true of the communal and linguistic feud between Sinhalese and Tamils. That this should be so is in no way remarkable. The history of Sri Lanka and of the Sinhalese, the large majority community of the island, has revolved for two millennia around the theme of keeping the Tamils in their place. The British Raj in South Asia required that such millennial animosities be set aside and that conquerers and conquered should in practice tolerate the existing balance of power and wealth, however little they liked having to do so. But, for a variety of reasons, the balance existing at the time of independence was extremely unfavourable to the majority community. Having become a nation once again — and a nation which took the political form of a representative democracy — it was natural enough for the Sinhalese people to do their best to put the Tamils back into their place at last. Race riots aside, not all of what they have elected to do since even through the official channels has been wholly admirable from a cosmopolitan standpoint. The treatment in particular of the 'Indian' Tamils, the very large numbers of South Indian Tamil workers who moved into the highland areas of the island to work on the tea plantations in the last decades of the nineteenth and in the present century, has not been handsome.[82] There was perhaps no good reason to consider giving the more recent arrivals among these full citizenship in Sri Lanka, a substantial prize in terms of per capita income by Asian standards at the time of independence. But in some cases the families in question had been living and working on the estates for two generations or more. Rather over a third were eventually awarded or promised Sri Lankan citizenship and, after many protracted squabbles, a further 525,000 were grudgingly recognised as being its citizens by the Republic of India. But even these have only been permitted to repatriate at a slow rate by the Indian government, while the rate at which the combined convenience of both governments has in fact enabled them to do so has been appreciably slower still. A substantial residue has in effect been rendered stateless and thus deprived of all political rights which in any way depend upon citizenship in any country in the world.[83] Three main points need to be made in this context. The first is that, as already noted, the development of more restrictive nationality laws has been a weapon for spreading a fixed sum of economic benefits more handsomely among a reduced number of authentically indigenous beneficiaries in Ghana also. Such zero-sum competitive tactics are not all that representative democracy is normatively about; but they are an unremarkable occurrence in its course and one which has certainly had resonances in the recent domestic politics of, for example, the United Kingdom, France and the United States of America. Those who can, get themselves represented. Those who cannot, may unfortunately in the long run find themselves deported (or at best prohibited immigrants).

The second point is equally distasteful and even more important. The power of the Sri Lankan government and its capacity to distribute the proportionally huge portion of national income to individual consumers in the form of education, health, subsidised transport, and free or subsidised rice rations depends directly upon the substantial foreign exchange earnings of the tea growing sector. It was plainly an important factor that until recently so much of this was foreign-owned. But it was and remains an even more important fact from the point of view of representative agency in Sri Lanka that the labour force which produces the tea is to such a large extent alien also. The Sri Lankan state, notionally a representative democracy, distributes resources produced predominantly by a grouping which is formally ineligible for representation within it and which does indeed receive markedly little attention for its interests from those who control the state. Not only are the working and living conditions of the plantation workers quite notoriously dreadful.[84] But their major threat advantage has remained virtually unexploited in Sri Lankan domestic politics on all but a handful of occasions.

Insofar as they have been effectively represented at all they have been represented not by a political party but by a trade union, the Ceylon Workers' Congress. An ironical mark of the vigour of representative competition in the island has been the emergence of a second union, the Democratic Workers' Congress, to dispute this representative role.[85] The importance of the role of aliens in producing this politically crucial portion of the surplus is difficult to exaggerate. Many wealthy capitalist societies, of course, have recently found that the *gastarbeiter* can offer them a number of advantages.[86] An admirably 'flexible' component of their labour force, the supply of which can be expanded or contracted extremely rapidly with the rhythms of the economy as a whole, they are also, naturally, cheap to hire in comparison with domestic labour, exceedingly economical to house, altogether less fastidious in their work preferences, and splendidly modest in the demands which they impose on state welfare provision. The costs of 'reproducing' a labour force at current western European standards of social expectation are substantial and the appeals of importing a flexible supply of labour for which the costs of its rearing and post-retirement maintenance are borne by another economy are evident enough. But no western European country has yet approached a situation in which such a crucial component of its national production is almost exclusively created by the direct labour of foreigners.

The contrast with Ghana, already mentioned, is particularly revealing on the implications of this structure for political representation. The sheer infrequency and comparatively shallow chronological depth of representative politics in Ghana has led to a much less systematic exploration and a much less highly orchestrated arrangement of potential bases of social cleavage than the continuity of Sri Lankan electoral competition has promoted. But even in the relatively disaggregated political process in Ghana the potential solidarity of Ghanaian cocoa producers vis-à-vis the government monopsony has proved second only to the aversive stimulus of incumbent colonial power as a basis for political consolidation. Unlike the incumbent colonial power, it has also lasted. Even before the Second World War the interests of cocoa producers had generated on occasion an impressive level of organised political and economic action.[87] A more sustained process of electoral competition in the mid 1950s would plausibly have produced a more explicit representative agency of cocoa farmers as such and such a party in its turn would have powerfully affected the subsequent contours of Ghanaian political conflict. It is scarcely likely, for example, that cocoa producers would for long have tolerated as their representative agency for old times sake, as they appear to have done in 1969, a party which sacrificed, as virtually every Ghanaian government had done since 1945, their short-term interests to what it identified as those of the economy as a whole. It is tempting, for example, to attribute the prevalence of tax riots among the Yoruba farmers in Western Nigeria[88] and the absence of analogously dramatic protest among their Ghanaian counterparts not simply to ethnically based cultural differences nor to a greater level of exploitation among the Western Nigerians (which can hardly be maintained with plausibility) but rather to the much more sustained efforts made in Western Nigeria up to 1966 to organise the latter in overtly representative politics. The process of political representation is not merely the selection by electors of an instrument to serve a variety of interests all of which they have already clearly identified. It is at least as much a competitive process of exploration by political entrepreneurs of just where the interests which electors hold dear do in fact lie. In this active process of exploration electors plainly often learn to identify their interests in quite new ways and hence may learn, for better or worse, what may be quite novel conceptions of what their politically relevant interests in fact are. In the cocoa forest zones of Ghana, it is true, a significant proportion of cocoa is in fact produced by those who do not possess Ghanaian nationality, Mossi-speakers from Upper Volta in particular; and in Ghana, too, under the terms of the Aliens Compliance Order, many of these were in fact deported under the Progress Party government. But the Aliens Compliance Order was in no sense aimed at such producers. The position which they hold in the relations of production does not differ in any way from that of many northern Ghanaians, nor can it be claimed in itself to have been affected by their nationality. Nor finally does it appear likely (although there is little systematic information available about the present state of affairs)[89] that the Aliens legislation will prove to have had much lasting effect on the part which such labourers play in cocoa farming. (What may well prove to have a lasting effect, however, is the extraordinary level of economic devastation produced by military mismanagement between 1972 and 1979.) In this sense the fact that non-Ghanaian nationals were (not unreasonably) not now eligible to vote in Ghanaian elections (though many Mossi immigrants in Ahafo, for example, had certainly voted early and often as instructed in the days of the C.P.P. elections) has probably had only rather temporary effects on their own interests, while the proportion of total cocoa production for which non-Ghanaian labourers were responsible has never been overwhelming. By contrast the Sri Lankan deployment of nationality law to remove from the arena of competitive representation those who produce the greater part of the publicly mobilised surplus of the Sri Lankan economy is arguably the most important structural factor in Sri Lankan politics as a whole.

The third and more tangential point about the role of 'Indian' Tamils in the Sri Lankan representative process is also of great practical importance but much less substantially related to the actual behaviour of the Tamils themselves. From the beginnings of electoral competition in colonial Ceylon constitution makers and electoral commissioners have gone to some length in their demarcation of constituency boundaries to allot seats to communal (and in some cases even to caste) groupings, recognising the extent to which the present state of Sri Lanka constitutes a plural society and seeking to avoid even at some costs to the rights of majorities a clear exclusion of distinct communal groupings (Muslim, Burgher, 'Ceylon' Tamil etc.) from effective representation. In the case of the 'Indian' Tamils, if perhaps for political motives which had little to do with these, the electoral commissioners had paid the homage which vice pays to virtue by recognising their demographic presence in the constituencies in which they resided, while placidly accepting their exclusion from any opportunity to represent themselves. The implication of this arrangement was morally as paradoxical as it was politically consequential. Most of the 'Indian' Tamils could not represent themselves because they were not Sri Lankan citizens. On the other hand they could not simply remain unrepresented because of the formal injury which this would do to the majority principle and the more substantial absurdity which it would create of leaving heavily populated and economically crucial sectors of the countryside very thinly represented in the legislature. The solution, a firm sundering of the Gordian knot, was to allocate seats to the Kandyan highland areas in extremely generous proportion to their total effective population and to restrict (as the nationality laws required) the right to elect the representatives of these constituencies to the comparatively small number of Kandyan Sinhalese (mainly high caste Goyigama) who resided in them.[90] It is common enough in representative democracies for votes in some places to count more heavily than votes in other places.[91] But it is hard to find parallels in the modern world for a situation in which votes in one area are heavily weighted in order that one large group of those resident there may be 'virtually' represented by a much smaller group whose interests are directly and very consciously antagonistic to those of the group whom they 'virtually' represent. Not even the Union of South Africa, it may be thought, has been reduced to quite such ideological contortions in the explicit legal structure of its system of political representation.

This same pattern of over-representation naturally affects the balance between the Sinhalese population in the highland zone and their ethnic and linguistic counterparts in the lowland areas. The precise implications of this overweighting of highland Sinhalese votes remain in some dispute. All commentators appear to agree that there are pronounced cultural differences between highland and lowland areas, a product of the very much longer and more intense period of social and economic interaction with foreign and particularly European influences in the coastal areas and the virtually complete insulation of the highlands in the Kandyan kingdom up to the latter's demise in 1815. The social relations of these highland areas were certainly affected by their incorporation into the British colonial state, notably by the abolition of a pattern of explicitly 'feudal' land tenure; and the development first of coffee and chinchona planting and then of tea planting in the highlands[92] brought the area into direct and very active economic relations with

183

the world economy. But despite these changes it remains true that up till very recently indeed, as Marguerite Robinson's perceptive study of 'Morapitiya' makes clear, many of the Sinhalese village communities in this area remained to a great extent closed in on themselves both socially and culturally and indeed in large measure even economically.[93] ('Morapitiya's' most drastic encounter with the world economy seems to have been the uncompensated destruction of most of its livestock by the neighbouring plantation after they had strayed into the latter's lands.)[94] The heavy representation of highland interests initially prescribed by colonial officials was designed overtly to provide political protection for backward areas, socially less mobilised, economically less organised and thus prospectively (it was assumed) liable to be less effective at securing their own representation. The precise determinants of this pattern's continuation in more recent decades are also disputed, though it is reasonable to assume that they included a fair degree of more or less accurate calculation of political advantage.

Three main groupings have been identified as major beneficiaries or victims at different times of this persisting over-representation. At the time of the 1956 election in particular Solomon Bandaranaike's S.L.F.P. was seen as winning its overwhelming triumph as the representative of Sinhalese Buddhist non-élite segments of the population (the vast majority) against the small, *déraciné*, English-speaking, often Tamil or Burgher, and sometimes even Christian élite groups, in commerce, the civil service, the professions and among major landowners who had dominated the electoral process in the colonial period and retained this domination and the consequently persisting near-monopoly of social privilege for almost a decade after independence. It is most unlikely that the highland Sinhalese benefited from Bandaranaike's electoral victory to anything like the extent to which his more active lowland supporters did so. But as the most firmly rooted, traditionally Buddhist, least educated and furthest excluded groups, it is not surprising that the victory won by the S.L.F.P. under the *signum* of returning Ceylon to the authentically Sinhalese should have been seen as their victory above all. The failure of the various Marxist parties has also been attributed by some partly to the inertial force of this large, atypically reactionary and traditionalist mass.[95] The attribution, however is not especially convincing. The extent of electoral penetration elsewhere by the left wing parties has hardly been massive enough for the overweighting of the highland areas to constitute a crucial margin of disadvantage. The third political grouping, which has been seen as benefiting from this over-representation, has been a caste group, the highland Goyigama.[96] To assess the significance of this last identification it will be necessary to attempt a slightly fuller sketch and evaluation of the general claim for the political preponderance of caste advanced by Dr Jiggins, an attempt which must be postponed for the moment.

Instead it will be more helpful to turn first to the question of the more direct beneficiaries of the 1956 victory. It is appropriate enough to see those

184

whom the S.L.F.P. aspired to represent in 1956 as a continuation of those whom Bandaranaike's Sinhalese Buddhist cultural association had aspired to serve from its inception: the Sinhala-speaking, Buddhist and on the whole impoverished majority of the island's population. Nor should the evocativeness of this claim to represent the poor and weak against the wealthy (if by the wealthy) be underestimated. A hint of its disruptive and inspiring power can be gathered from noting the speed with which it became domesticated in the strikingly socially homogeneous community of 'Morapitiya' between 1963 and 1967.[97] Symbolically in 1956 the S.L.F.P. fought (and was seen by most of its followers to be fighting) to put down the mighty from their seats and to exalt the humble and meek, a project which lost none of its attractions from the fact that many of the mighty were in fact Christians. In most of the rural areas in 1956, as again in 1960, the humble and meek plainly found the S.L.F.P. a vastly more plausible representative for their aspirations than any of the Marxist parties. But if it may thus genuinely be claimed to have represented the rural Sinhalese poor by its example, it is less plausible that it was on balance these whom it represented by its exertions once in office. Those who suffered most on balance as a result of the 1956 S.L.F.P. government were probably for the most part English-speaking Tamil clerks and those who benefited most, correspondingly, non-English-educated Sinhalese literates. This, of course, is by no means an exhaustive summary of those affected for better or worse by the change in the status of the Sinhalese language. The use of one's own language as the language of administration and justice in place of that of a foreign conqueror is a real public good and it is in no way sentimental to see its effects for the majority Sinhalese community as marking simply another element in the breaking down of the barriers between alien state and indigenous society which the S.L.F.P. had set itself to achieve. In the same terms, the adoption of Tamil as the language of administration in the 'Ceylon' Tamil area, insofar as this has been implemented after years of savage struggle, is in itself a genuine public good for the Tamils also. But neither the intensity on both sides of communal commitment to this goal nor the consequent animosity created by more monopolistic arrangements in the interim suffice to explain the full bitterness of the conflict. At times the language struggle has certainly been marked by the vigorous effort to give the Tamils much less than justice. But the initial aim of the language legislation (and what is likely to prove to be its most durable consequence) was concerned with a less symbolic and more palpable matter, the communal distribution of employment. Here the crucial factor was education. It was the educational factor above all, the struggle for the control of schools, which caused religious affiliation to be linked so directly with language and communalism in the course of the conflict.

The broad outlines of the relation are simple enough.[98] The home province of the 'Ceylon' Tamils, the north and especially the Jaffna peninsula, was both agriculturally unrewarding to the majority of its dense population and extensively penetrated by mission influences. The expansion of education and Christian allegiance were mutually reinforcing processes, leading to large numbers of Tamil clerks being employed in government and private commercial roles throughout the island and especially in the great western metropolis of Colombo (to say nothing of their employment outside the island in Malaya). Tamils were not proportionately the wealthiest or best educated communal grouping at the time of independence, being clearly surpassed for example by the. Burghers. But they were on average strikingly better educated in English (and in consequence much better represented in modern literate employment) than the other really large communal grouping, the Sinhalese majority. This ratio of advantage was potentially inflammatory in itself, as soon as an effective process of political representation had commenced. But it was rendered much more inflammatory by another striking discrepancy between the Sri Lankan situation and that of Ghana. Besides being heir to a literate cultural tradition of more than two millennia going back to the Buddhist Pali canon, Sri Lanka is also today a much more functionally literate society than Ghana. In Ghana virtually anyone who is literate is literate in English; and although virtually everyone, literate or illiterate, can and does speak at least one of the vernacular languages, very few people in practice communicate much in writing in anything but English. Most education after the earliest years of primary school is still administered in English, virtually all newspapers in recent years have been published solely in English and most letters, private as much as commercial, are written in English. The social gap between literates and illiterates is one of great political and social importance; but there is no social gap between literates in English and literates in vernacular languages because there are virtually none of the latter who are not also the former.[99] The products of the 'swabasha' schools of Sri Lanka by contrast, literate in Sinhalese but not in the language of their erstwhile colonial masters, stood to gain from the Sinhalese supplanting of the English language not merely a public symbolic recognition that the state of which they were citizens was now at last well and truly their own state but also the opportunity, previously denied to them on grounds of functional incapacity, to administer this state in person and to draw the appropriate clerkly salaries for doing so. As an incidental bonus they could also have the pleasure of depriving of these salaries a fair number of the all too successfully collaborating Tamils who had previously enjoyed them, as a reward for their community's privileged complicity with the British. It is not surprising that this heady combination of symbolic communal triumph and prospective individual economic advantage should have proved to display great electoral *éclat*.

VIII

The importance of electoral *éclat* for the development of representation in

Sri Lanka may be seen readily from a further comparison with the Ghanaian case. Ghana, a society less firmly differentiated between élite and mass than Sri Lanka at the end of the Second World War, had had élite nationalist politicians for many decades, none of whom seemed very likely to jar the colonial rulers into conferring independence on the Gold Coast with undignified haste. The political agency of these men in the late 1940s, Dr Danquah's U.G.C.C., was pressing decorously enough for independence. But there seemed no more danger of its *compelling* the colonial power to yield to its pressures than there had been of the elected representatives of Ceylon's nationalist party, the Ceylon National Congress, having such an impact on their rulers in the two decades before the war. But while Ceylon was handed its independence very much on a platter, thanks to the nationalist vigour of its massive northern neighbour, Ghana was very much responsible for its own independence and indeed contributed handsomely to the pace of decolonisation in Africa as a whole. It contrived this feat, the apparent ease of which was severely retrospective, not by dint of displaying substantial postwar social unrest (though the unrest which it did display certainly helped) but rather by generating a successful populist political party. Just why this came about is still very hazily understood, though the outline of the story, Nkrumah's return to act as Secretary of the U.G.C.C. and his sauntering off with the nationalist movement from under the nose of his elders and social and economic betters, has been told often enough. Analysts have found it very difficult to go much beyond Dennis Austin's graphic résumé of the events themselves.[100] But although the precise causes of the C.P.P₁'s meteoric political rise remain a little obscure, what is not obscure at all is the scale of its consequences. In the perhaps rather simple dialectics of Ghanaian politics almost everything which has since followed can plausibly be seen as following more or less directly from this.

The significance of the C.P.P.'s emergence, then, can scarcely be overestimated. Moreover, while it is necessary to admit that we have little grasp of precisely which conditions proved to be sufficient to generate such a vigorous emergence, it is plain enough that one of its more obtrusive necessary conditions was the presence of the colonial regime itself. The presence of alien rulers can serve to concentrate popular disaffections wonderfully. Nothing in the subsequent history of Ghana or indeed of other colonial West African countries suggests the presence of a social and cultural base for a major national populist party like the C.P.P. in its early years in the absence of the focus furnished by colonial rule. In Sri Lanka, by contrast, the political party which presided over the process of independence was very much the party of the incumbent élite, an élite too which possessed greater social purchase and, it seems fair to add, probably enjoyed great social privilege than that of the U.G.C.C. in the Gold Coast. Yet, only a few years after independence, this élite party, in full control of the state apparatus and its patronage resources, was overwhelmed at the polls by an unmistakably populist mass party, the S.L.F.P., with a massive majority. The organisational process of assembling electoral support no doubt differed in the two countries, with the Sri Lankan élite at independence reaching much more deeply into hinterland society than their Ghanaian counterparts could and with even Bandaranaike's S.L.F.P., for example, being funded to a greater extent than any Ghanaian party could have been (at least before 1969) out of his own private acquired personal fortune.[101] But the major difference between the two countries lay not in such contrasts of organisation or economics but rather in the massive social and cultural basis for communal politics in Sri Lanka. Putting the matter a little starkly, one might say that in Sri Lanka there existed an available mass cultural and social identity, even a 'national' identity, for a political party to represent, while in Ghana any national cultural and social identity consists simply in the negation of colonial hegemony and in the preservation of a variety of local cultural *fêtes*.

This insubstantiality of Ghanaian national identity did not militate against the presence of important communal elements in Ghanaian political conflict: the efforts of some northern leaders to secure a measure of protection for their backward region in the face of the hazards of independence,[102] the explicit Ashanti nationalism of the N.L.M., the almost exclusively Ewe and Krobo popular base in southern Ghana of K.A. Gbedemah's National Alliance of Liberals, and perhaps more importantly for the considerable degree of Akan electoral solidarity which complemented this in 1969.[103] The boundaries of communal conflict groupings are not fixed historically. To a large degree indeed they may be said to be situationally determined in the process of political conflict itself. The units of political action may be units which virtually no one under any circumstances could have had occasion to use for personal cultural self-identification a decade earlier.[104] But if the American conception of ethnic arithmetic suggests the employment of rather stabler units of ethnicity than African countries do at present display, it will at least serve as a reminder that there can be crucial differences in the structural potential for communal hostility within national societies. The position of Ewes in Ghana (as in some respects the position of Ibos in pre-1966 Nigeria) does have analogies with the position of Tamils in Sri Lanka. Denizens of areas which are heavily over-populated or else unsuitable for profitable cash crop agriculture and which proved politically unable to exclude a substantial missionary presence, they were in comparison with other groups in their nation highly literate and strongly motivated, even before independence, to take up careers in the public services which put this literacy to gainful use. In the Nigerian public services, civil and military,[105] the eventual political consequences of such a recruitment pattern were notoriously catastrophic. But in Ghana no such dominant pattern has yet emerged. Ewes were over-represented statistically in 1969 not just in the teaching service or in the ranks of the police but also more importantly in crucial segments of the officer corps of the army and in the police Special

Branch. In the course of the 1969 election campaign, for a variety of reasons,[106] the main struggle came to be defined by many as a conflict between Ewes and the rather disaggregated majority cultural grouping of the Ghanaian population, the Akans. The scale of the P.P.'s electoral majority undoubtedly in part reflected this definition; and the use to which it proceeded to put its victory, sacking hundreds of largely Ewe civil servants in particular, did little to blur the definition. There can be little doubt, too, that crucial leadership for the 1972 coup came from a group of Ewe officers, notably Major Anthony Selormey, a measure of the motivation for whose participation probably came from this ethnic identification. Moreover, it is a cultural commonplace in Ghana (if not perhaps a social fact) that Ewes are rather more 'clannish', more tribally exclusive in their personal social relations, than is usual in the very open norm of inter-tribal relations in the country. There is thus a slender basis both in culture and in the popular perception of post-independence politics for seeing a communal rift as lying at the heart of Ghanaian political division (at any rate in the period from shortly after the downfall of Kwame Nkrumah to the fall of General Acheampong). But such an identification conceals on balance decidedly more than it reveals. Only a representative process as evanescent and as contingently simplified as that of 1969 could have left the Akan population of Ghana as a politically homogeneous entity whose common interests vis-à-vis the Ewe population were more salient than the multiplicity of divisions of interest within their own ranks. For most of the nineteenth century distrust and hostility between one Akan group, the Fanti, and another, the Ashanti, were considerably more urgent and evocative than any relation between Akan groups as a whole and Ewes.[107] Indeed Ewe separatist feeling had even been in some measure aligned with the Ashanti core of the United Party in the mid 1950s. Until Nkrumah's overthrow it would hardly be possible to find clear instances of politically articulated mass conflict between Akans and Ewes. Even in 1969 and in the years since, the possibility of envisaging Ghanaian politics in these terms is more an accidental consequence of ethnic representation in a number of crucial components of the apparatus of coercion than it is a reflection of any systematic structural conflict of interests between Ewes and Akans in the population at large. Certainly there was no possibility of fusing even briefly in this Ghanaian case the politics of communalism with the politics of class, as the S.L.F.P. contrived to fuse them in 1956, with the enduring consequences, both symbolic[108] and organisational, which this fusion created.

The only remaining major basis of representation which requires consideration (but an especially contentious issue) applies only in Sri Lanka and has no Ghanaian analogue. The analysis of caste has provoked continuing theoretical dispute among sociologists and ethnographers.[109] But its interaction with politics in Sri Lanka has not until recently been much discussed by scholars (unlike colonial officials) and many aspects of its political operation have yet to be described at all helpfully. It will be simplest to approach its role here by way of a more general discussion of the mechanics of patronage and clientage in the politics of both countries. Patron—client ties have been singled out by many recent writers as the distinctive organising category of the politics of peasant societies,[110] a category which unites a great many societies in the world today and which does so in a conceptually somewhat relaxed fashion. Considerable sociological and anthropological energy has been put, too, into the effort to analyse the distinctive attributes of clientage as a type of social relation.[111] But both the explanatory elasticity of these categories and the empirical understanding of the politics of the countries which they aspire to explain have become distinctly overstretched in the process: too few categories chasing too hazily described and too capriciously recorded facts. Any adequate typology of political leadership in peasant societies must be based on a more sophisticated differentiation of the immense variety of communities and sub-communities which are being led. Virtually none of the requisite information is available for either Ghana or Sri Lanka. But a few broad contrasts may be drawn. The first reflects simply the comparative strength of indigenous commercial capitalism at the time of independence. In Ghana, indigenous commercial capitalism of any scale since the late nineteenth century has, in all but a few sectors (transport, timber), been almost entirely dependent on the favours of the state. Hence in 1951 there was virtually no Ghanaian commercial capitalism of any significance (in notable contrast with the extent of indigenous dominance in the production of cocoa). By the same token such large-scale indigenous Ghanaian commercial capitalism as there is today (even in the timber and transport sectors) has depended for its viability either on the payment of protection money to those who controlled the state apparatus or on prudent investment in supporting these controllers before they had got their hands on the state apparatus. A small sector of businessmen can now afford to pay to stay out of political disfavour (and every Ghanaian government has its price); but most businessmen of any great wealth have gained this wealth by paying handsomely to enter political favour. The boundaries between commercial and political enterprise are thus hard to draw and all concerned are likely to look on both, in the terminology of Elizabethan commercial speculation, as an 'adventure'[112] in essentially the same idiom.[113]

In modern Ghana, except for a small number of large-scale cocoa farmers and a handful of professional men, lawyers, doctors and accountants, men have on the whole become wealthy by courtesy of the holders of political power. In many cases indeed they have become so by holding such power themselves. In Sri Lanka, by contrast, wealth and social influence have even at times been squandered on winning political power and not simply as a tactic of *reculer pour mieux sauter*. The important implication of this contrast does not lie, of course, in any *moral* superiority of esteeming power more than wealth; but rather in its revealing once again the relative substantiality of Sri Lankan civil society vis-à-vis the state, when set against its Ghanaian counterpart. The Sri Lankan state at independence could be seen, if a little harshly, as 'a certain conspiracy of rich men, procuring their own commodities under the name and title of the commonwealth'.[114] But in Ghana it required at least partial indigenous control over the state before the country could muster enough rich men to mount an effective conspiracy. It was not that Ghanaian civil society even in 1951 was a totally malleable medium, offering no real resistance to the political hammer; merely that even the more significant loci of power in Ghanaian society, traditional or modern, chief or entrepreneur, were far more directly and defencelessly dependent on the power of the state than large-scale landowners or well entrenched commercial or professional families in Sri Lanka. Precisely how much effective patronal power has been exercised or how much decorous cliental compliance has been elicited in the course of the electoral process in either society is a matter which can only be seriously discussed in terms of particular times and places and one about which we really know very little indeed. But what can be asserted with some confidence is that there was at least more discrete social power available for such use at independence in Sri Lanka than there was in Ghana and that — to offset this at least partially — the persistence of constitutional political conflict in Sri Lanka came to encourage aspiring patrons to avoid political overcommitment considerably earlier than this prudential lesson was brought home to comparable figures in Ghana.

How should the organisational contribution of an authority relation like that of patronage be imagined as relating in practice to such categories of social identification as communal, linguistic, religious, or even class? The two types of category, it is plain, are not alternatives to one another. Rather they represent contrasting ways of envisaging much the same relations. The leaders of trade unions or religious bodies have clients and the most obsequious of clients is likely to have some sense of his own social identity. Patron—client ties emphasise (and perhaps tend to over-emphasise) the no doubt unequal exchange of concrete benefits. Categories of social identification emphasise (and perhaps tend to over-emphasise) the social extension of an individual agent's ego. One important distinction between the two, if used at all strictly, is that the first precludes voting for any particular outcome as such and the second virtually precludes voting for any dependable *individual* advantage. In the first, a voter's behaviour is explained in terms of the direct prospective reward or penalty for his behaving in a particular way, whatever *electoral* consequences such behaviour proves to have. In the second, the voter's preparedness to act in this way at all is left substantially unexplained but his doing so is interpreted as an expression of preference for some state of affairs, possibly one which does not directly affect him as an individual, the probability of the occurrence of which is almost certain to be quite unaffected by his individual action. Too strict a conception of instrumental rationality thus makes it virtually impossible to explain most electoral commitment under any circumstances in which the ballot is believed to be secret.[115] To explain the greater part of such commitment, it is necessary to recognise the blurring of instrumental assessment by optimistic fantasy (as common a feature of vertically organised groups as it is of such horizontally organised political groupings as classes) or else to acknowledge the degree of solidarity – at least in contexts like those of electoral competition – which vertical political groupings can muster. Neither of these recognitions seems in any way factually unrealistic in relation to the politics of either Ghana[116] or Sri Lanka; nor, it may be worth adding, is there any axiomatic reason why such vertical solidarities should be any less strictly materially rational in the context of electoral competition than the less often disdained horizontal solidarities such as those of class. Indeed there is little reason to suppose, as analysts of patronal politics like James C. Scott have perhaps tended to,[117] that the distinctive impact of patronal political competition is any more steadily inflationary, any more certain to favour consumption over investment, than the more clearly class aspects of electoral competition in Sri Lanka have proved. Thus far, however, we are in no position to do much more than presume broadly that patron—client ties do indeed play a major (probably even a predominant) role in the mustering of electoral support in both Ghana and Sri Lanka, and to note the conceptual significance which this must bear in any assessment of the meaning of the process of political representation in the two countries, above all in terms of localism,[118] intracommunal faction and the personalisation of political struggle.

The only dimension of Sri Lankan social organisation which has been at all seriously studied in relation to patron—client ties is that of caste. Caste is a fundamental category of the Indic cultural world,[119] its presence an indisputable token, however residual, of contact with one of the grandest of all the Great Traditions. It is to be found in Sri Lanka among both the traditionally Hindu population of the north[120] and among the Sinhalese/Buddhist populations of the centre and south. The caste divisions among the Tamils have their idiosyncracies; but in broad terms they fall well within the range of variation in the authentically Hindu caste system of the subcontinental mainland itself. They have played a minor part on occasion in Sri Lankan representative politics but not one which demands attention here. The place of caste divisions among the Sinhalese community itself is more idiosyncratic and harder to define with any clarity. It is also decidedly more culturally surreptitious because of the ideological disharmony between Buddhist ethical universalism and the arbitrarily ascriptive obduracies of a caste system extracted from its Hindu theological matrix.[121] This mild ideological anomaly is reflected, for example, in the fact that the census statistics of Sri Lanka in the present century, unlike those of India, have never recorded caste membership[122] and in the comparative infrequency with which caste is mentioned in the full dress public rhetoric of political

192

dispute. Among the consequences of such discretion is a lack of systematic information about such basic issues as caste numbers. Most writers assume that the highest Sinhalese caste, the Goyigama, a cultivator caste (Sri Lanka in the Sinhalese areas has neither Brahmans nor Kshatriyas), are in fact not just the largest caste but form a majority of the entire Sinhalese population, though this judgement has been queried by Dr Jiggins.[123] At the other end of the caste scale, there are a number of small castes which are treated with decided aversion. But there is nothing corresponding to the very substantial numbers of 'untouchables' on the Indian mainland. This sharp compression of the caste scale at both ends plainly restricts its potential scope as a basis for political organisation. The role of caste in Indian politics as a whole has been greatly illuminated by scholars in the last two decades but most of the light which has been shed upon it has been focussed on sections of the scale or relations over the scale which can have no Sinhalese analogue. National legislation in India, trimming the permissible social definition of 'untouch-ability' to meet the criteria of citizen equality, has had major effects on political organisation,[124] while the process of 'Sanskritisation' has offered whole caste groupings at a local level opportunities for collective upward social mobility of a less drastic character.[125] The impact of national political competition on the caste-related power structure of local communities has also been striking in many cases.[126]

Public legislation restricting permissible limits on the behavioural expression of caste differences, and the intrusion of egalitarian electoral practices into highly stratified communities, offer distinct public goods to members of low castes. In due course such public goods may prove effectively convertible into private ones. Even in a caste-homogeneous community like 'Morapitiya', the echoes of electoral egalitarianism have now become ideo-logical and practical resources for the small number of caste-derogated members of the village community. Communal harmony and an unquestion-ing acceptance of caste hierarchy were intimately related there, even if in practical terms for the great majority of the community, the meaning of the relatively trivial degree of caste differentiation within the village clearly resided in the firm distance which it placed the villagers as a whole above the great majority of outsiders with whom they had any contact, practical or imaginative.[127] The ending of communal harmony within the village cer-tainly enhanced the relative power of its lowest status members. But this was a relatively adventitious consequence of 'Morapitiya's' incorporation into national politics, since even the agency of this incorporation, the local branch of the S.L.F.P., continues to consist largely of the village's high caste majority and to exhibit in their attitudes to land ownership and exploitation and to communal membership much the same attitudes as before. In general the comparative shortness of the Sinhalese caste scale has greatly restricted the possibility for politicians to isolate caste-specific public goods for offer on the electoral market and has tilted caste categories towards the more general politics of patronage, locality and governmental distributive capacity. Dr Jiggins has shown convincingly the caste homogeneity of several of the most important élite family networks which dominate the upper reaches of Sri Lankan public life;[128] and she has pointed out the consistent and almost complete exclusion from ministerial office and the steady statistical under-representation among members in the legislature of at least the two largest lower caste groups.[129] She has also put together evidence which is at least broadly convincing of the stability of caste voting in individual constituencies and of the decided preference of caste members for voting for a member of their own caste, when offered the opportunity.[130] This consistency of caste voting in its turn serves to lend greater plausibility to her claims of systematic gerrymandering to maximise the electoral effectiveness of reliable caste groupings and dissipate that of others.[131]

The lack of systematic and publicly available information and the intricate problems of political strategy arising from the presence of several caste groups in many constituencies mean that it is hard to establish clear and proven explanations in detail of patterns of electoral support. But the broad pattern, both among the élite and in the distribution of electoral allegiance seems definite enough. Within a political culture organised largely through patron–client ties, some of this caste-patterning may confidently be attributed to the distribution of purely private goods. C.P. de Silva's alleged use of S.L.F.P. colonisation schemes on behalf of Salagama caste members would be an example already cited.[132] In this case, too, the sense in which the good in question was purely private is neatly marked by one of the incidental advantages for the colonists which their move proved to offer. Being Salagama was the cause for their getting access to the new lands. But getting access to the new lands enabled them to escape from the indisputable ascriptive straitjacket of their community of origin and to 'pass' as Goyigama.[133] 'Sanskritisation' is a protracted process of collective upward social mobility, fully and explicitly identified perhaps only by sociologists or ethnographers. But acknowledged upward caste mobility for an individual is an ideological contradiction in terms. Intrinsically, caste is an existential fate, though it may of course be both experienced and manipulated by individuals simply as a status defined in the behaviour of others. The opportunity to 'pass' as belonging to a higher caste, where this depends simply on the ignorance of the audience with whom one is so passing[134] is thus a remarkably pure example of a private rather than public good.[135] But most of Dr Jiggins's evidence suggests a role for caste in the representative process of a much less strictly instrumental kind, at least outside the ranks of political entrepreneurs. Caste-membership is plainly a *signum* displayed in the politician's quest for plausible social identities to invoke. The choice of a caste member by their own caste for the task of representing it may well have elements of instrumental rationality in a patronal political system. But what serves to explain the choice of a caste member in these circumstances is not the element of instrumental rationality, independently conceived. Rather, both the choice of a representative from within the caste and the element of instrumental rationality embodied in such a choice together depend upon the prevalent social extension of the egos of both leaders and led in such vertically organised social networks. Social trust may not extend as far as the boundaries of one's caste within one's community of residence; but it seldom extends further. Caste-membership may not be enough to guarantee representative dependability; but anything less than caste-membership, at least in the rural areas, stands little chance of being thought to do so. Both the elements of instrumentality and those of projective identification come out nicely in some of Dr Jiggins's examples. Men can become too wealthy or too successful to represent their own low caste,[136] or their political alliance with a party which is itself universally seen as representing higher castes may be seen as disclosing their caste betrayal.[137] But if the capacity adequately to represent a community is judged in this way to depend on the representative plausibly remaining firmly within the bounds of the community, caste representation would have much in common with the representation of classes or localities. We need feel little surprise,[138] political and social realities being what they are, that even ascription is no very firm barrier to the perceived or actual untrustworthiness of political leaders. It would be absurd on the basis of present knowledge to presume to judge how far the U.N.P. or S.L.F.P. are defined by their leaders or by ordinary voters in purely caste terms. What can no longer be doubted though, thanks to Dr Jiggins, is the extent to which caste-identification does enter and enter consequentially into the representative process.

Obligation

The issue of allegiance arises practically within any competitive process of representation. The sentiment that it is wrong (and not simply prospectively personally disadvantageous) for a working class person to vote against the party which is the party of the working class is a judgement which links individual social station with the duties which accompany this. Class or confessional or communal loyalty is the basis of most stable electoral preference in competitive democracies. To owe allegiance to a collectivity or indeed to individuals is to have obligations towards it or them. Among all the foci of allegiance to be encountered in the world today the governments of nation states have been probably the most successful in purveying their ideological title to exact compliance from their citizenry. They have also succeeded, though less consistently and less thoroughly, in securing this compliance at the level of overt behaviour. It is a deep and singularly unwieldy question of political theory just why they have in practice proved to be so successful in establishing these entitlements and an urgent and fairly inscrutable question of political practice just how much success we may expect them to have collectively (not to say severally) in maintaining these entitlements in the future. But one simple point is not likely to be disputed. The establishment of credible ties of putatively secular obligation between individual citizens and a state power has relied on at least two factors: firstly, the existence of an effective coercive capacity at a practical level some time before anything so conceptually venturesome as a secular theory of individual obligation was essayed by any possessors of state power; and, secondly, the existence of a fair measure of cultural homogeneity and shared normative understanding (a product above all of the European Great Tradition established as a result of Constantine's vision) in the countries where the secular theory was first established. Indeed it is excessively difficult, despite the valiant efforts of Thomas Hobbes, to see how an effective secular theory of obligation can be constructed from the dispositions of resolutely egoistic individuals. In this perspective it seems a reasonable judgement that the prevailing recognition of some measure of public obligation within (and hence in part the public normative viability of) modern western democracies, such as it is, trades heavily on the extent to which the citizens of these countries feel stronger and more direct allegiances to a variety of narrower groupings which refrain from defining themselves in contraposition to the state. The example of Northern Ireland and the practical failure of Hobbesian arguments in ameliorating its condition, communal, poor, nasty and brutish as this has now become, make this point very sharply. In the same sense there can be little occasion for surprise that a sense of public obligation is thin on the ground in the plural and post-colonial societies of most of Africa and Asia, with the particularistic and clientelistic linkages between the majorities of their populations and those who man their state apparatuses,[139] and with the secular tendency in the modern world for patron—client ties to degenerate from a stable and moralised inequality towards an equally (or even more) unequal and far less stable scramble for individual advantage.[140]

Both in Ghana and in Sri Lanka obligation towards the state as such is plainly for most of the population, insofar as it has any salience at all, an ideological category manipulated for individual advantage rather than a deep existential commitment. It is perfectly clear also that this orientation (or perhaps it would be better to say this resolute normative disregard) is eminently realistic, in no way a product of false consciousness:[141] 'What's Hecuba to him, or he to Hecuba?' If this were all that could validly be said about the relevance of the concept of obligation to the politics of these countries (that there is very little of it about), then it would scarcely be worth dwelling on the concept at all. But there are at least two further points which require consideration and one of these is in fact extremely important. Firstly, as has been noted before in other contexts, categories — however ideological they may be — can only be manipulated with prospective advantage if they do have some real meaning to some persons. Since the states are there and since, particularly in the process of competitive representation, what can or cannot excusably be done within or to them is necessarily a matter of vigorous dispute, it is unlikely to remain true indefinitely that no normative significance whatever is attributed by the majority of the population to the manner in which the state conducts itself. And once reasonably clear normative significance, whether positive or negative, does become attached to the way in which states conduct themselves, then prospective obligations to incumbent state powers or to potential alternative state powers[142] will have become recognised by the subject populations of these states in the same sort of sense as they were for example by the population of France in 1940. From this viewpoint both surviving exponents of a 'modernisation theory' view of the global future and disenchanted advocates and prophets of a global revolution in effect share one common assumption: that in a literate and economically highly integrated world the protraction of institutionalised moral chaos through time will not prove a stable equilibrium. (There remains, of course, the alternative possibility that nothing will prove a stable equilibrium.) It is a reasonable perspective on many (if not all) states in the world today to envisage these in relation to most of their subjects as Frankenstein monsters running historically amok. But it does not seem so reasonable to expect them to remain in this condition indefinitely. Or at least, to put it less trustingly, there is at least more than one type of callow political optimism which would lead one to expect them to prove unable to do so. What type of genuine obligation (if any) we may conceive the prevalent, predominantly manipulative, coinage of public obligation to represent, we may leave to the conclusion. The second point (which needs to be established before considering this issue) is somewhat simpler. It is a plain enough fact that the state apparatuses of both Ghana and Sri Lanka do not depend for their viability on any sense of public obligation on the part of their subject populations.

There are three contexts in which the least morally ambitious of nation states do depend for their viability on the prevalence of recognised obligations among their members. The first of these is the upper reaches of the state bureaucracy. The tenants of these positions, even when irreproachably virtuous, are seldom poorly rewarded for their pains and, of course, many of them are less than irreproachably virtuous. But it is hard to see how a modern public bureaucracy could in fact operate for any length of time with all of its senior bureaucrats exclusively devoted to their private enrichment and the supposition that they do or might in fact choose to do so is not only contrary to casual experience but appears grossly insensitive to the non-material rewards (or, as one might put it, the pleasures) of exercising power. However evanescent in significance and inchoate in outline the state may appear when seen from the villages, it can hardly look as insubstantial from the higher echelons of the Ministry of Finance or Public Works or the Governor's chair of the National Bank. Higher civil servants are cozened into addressing themselves to the goals of the state by dint of their hourly occupational activity. Processually, if not structurally and consequentially, the state is more their state than it is the state of any other persons. Its problems and its goals are *their* problems and their goals, even if not their sole problems or their exclusive goals. This is not to suggest that this self-image is necessarily in any way morally admirable. Indeed one does not need to be a rabid democrat to find aspects of it deeply morally offensive. But however distasteful it may be as a self-image, it is a self-image the reality of which is constantly constructed and re-created by institutional process. In Ghana at least, because of the substantial interludes of non-representational politics, the continuity of public administration has been one of the most central factors in post-independence politics. The second major context of obligation on which any state whatever (not merely, in this case, a *modern* state) depends is among the specialised apparatus of coercion, the armed services and the police. *Quis custodiet ipsos custodes?* It was the armed services and the police (though not the specially created Praetorian Guard) which removed the only two men whom the Ghanaian electorate had ever, up to 1978, been permitted to choose for its rulers. It is the loyalty towards, or the desertion of, the regime by its coercive apparatus which in the first instance determines whether it can remain a regime at all. In the last decade desertion has become at least as common a response as loyalty in this relation among the states of West Africa. As President Barclay put the matter in Liberia, that prototype of West African nation states, more than seven decades ago, the militia is 'tending to become a greater danger to the loyal citizen, and his property, which it ought to protect, than to the public enemy'.[143] Certainly the militia as a corporate organisation does not appear to feel much in the way of obligation towards an incumbent civilian government, simply in virtue of the latter's incumbency. A threat to the corporate interests of the armed services and a background of regime impropriety little more acute than that which has sufficed to change the government of Sri Lanka often enough through the electoral process, has been sufficient in Ghana on two occasions already to prompt successful military rebellion. In Sri Lanka by contrast, despite (or perhaps because of?) its drastically more participatory rebelliousness, the armed services have so far remained punctiliously constitutionalist in their collective conduct.

Military dutifulness on the part of most soldiers most of the time can be adequately (if not necessarily wholly accurately) explained in prudential terms. It would plainly, for example, be unwise for even a senior Soviet military officer to attempt to foment mutiny in the Red Army on his own account. We may not possess a very intimate understanding of why this is so; but we certainly have no reason to doubt that it *is* so. Military disobedience at an individual level by the same token may be attributed stipulatively simply to imprudence, its motivation being openly recognised as heterogeneous and idiosyncratic. Many have motives, both public and private, for wishing in Ghanaian parlance 'to do a coup'. But doing a successful coup calls for a fair measure of accessible solidarism in the forces which are to secure its victory. A few may (and commonly do) initiate; but many must in due course assent. Since 1966 at least five well-known but abortive incidents in Ghana have been identified by the incumbent regime as attempted coups; and there have been two major shifts in control within the military regime itself, the last of which involved considerable violence. Only the most recent of these really raises issues of *obligation* and its recognition or repudiation. It is too early as yet to pronounce with confidence on the implications of Flight-Lieutenant Rawlings's tenure of political authority and the precise manner in which he acquired it. Issues of obligation were certainly raised, however, by the successful Ghanaian coup attempts of 1966 and 1972, as they were, revealingly, by the Sri Lankan incident which came closest to being an attempted coup, the 1962 'plot'.

The Ghanaian coup of February 1966 is not difficult to assess from this viewpoint. From the perspective of its leading executants and of their wide range of sympathisers in élite circles, civil service, universities and foreign embassies, it was a classical example of John Locke's conception of the conditions for legitimate resistance: the re-establishment of a responsible constitutional order against a group of power-holders who had dismantled a constitutional order for their own corrupt purposes. There was plainly no other way of removing the incumbent regime but by force and only the armed services possessed the requisite force. There are many ways of assessing (and hence of describing) the motives of those who acted themselves and of the groups, many of them by no means élite groups, whose enthusiastic support greeted the success of their actions, as they had confidently expected that it would. But it is not the purity of heart of the agents concerned which is significant, but, rather, the social scope over which their act was regarded as morally uncontroversial, the recapture by force of a hijacked state. To the great majority of those who saw themselves as good Ghanaian public servants, *hommes moyens sensuels*, the action of 24 February 1966 was merely the act of a good Ghanaian public servant, a felicitious discharge of the duties of their station. The coup which displaced Dr Busia, by contrast, was a less neat affair in its social appearance — and again for good Lockean reasons. For one thing, the public services were less uniform in their hostility to the Progress Party regime than they had become towards the C.P.P. by 1966. For another, it was a little early in the consolidation of the regime to presume that less drastic means of getting rid of it would not in due course become available, as the constitution prescribed that they should. Furthermore the second coup, unlike that of 1966, had distinct ethnic overtones, continuing the ethnic factionalism which was first strongly established in public life in the course of the 1969 election. The ethnic origin of the official coup leader did not suffice to blur this interpretation for very long. Whatever their respective contributions to serving the interests of the Ghanaian people (who feel on the whole a healthy detachment from the fate of those who govern them), it is clear that the 1972 coup is to be envisaged less in the idiom of (however delusory) public obligation than in those of corporate advantage (the preservation of officers' allowances) and ethnic factionalism. This is, of course, not necessarily to claim that it was in any sense a worse (or a less good) thing consequentially than its predecessor, a type of judgement which if it were to be essayed at all would require a quite different mode of assessment.

The Sri Lankan 'plot' of 1962, insofar as it has been coherently described, appears to stand somewhat closer to the second than to the first Ghanaian example, though it has some interesting overtones of the first. Those who allegedly 'plotted' a coup all came from the small public service, highly educated, anglicised inheritor group who had been permitted largely to govern the country for several decades before independence and whose representative political agency from independence up to at least 1960 had been the U.H.P.[144] Almost all of them were Christians and most of them, indeed, Roman Catholics. They epitomised the alien cultural grouping from whose haughty dominance, at least in its cultural self-presentation, Solomon Bandaranaike's S.L.F.P., had succeeded in rescuing Sri Lanka for its Sinhalese Buddhist majority. The precipitating factor for the alleged plot was the virtual expropriation of Catholic schools, following on several years of bitter conflict between the two Bandaranaikes and the Catholic Church over the control of élite educational institutions.[145] Formal norms of confessional liberty and ethnic impartiality, established by the colonial regime, had served in practice to protect a highly privileged position, politically, economically and culturally, for a communal, religious and linguistic grouping which was sharply demarcated from the majority of the population. The assault on (and eventual practical abolition of) these norms plainly looked to many of the operational custodians of the state apparatus (and past beneficiaries of these norms) like an assault on the normative state as such, on the state as it ought to be. In this sense there were evident parallels with the self-image of the 1966 coup makers and beneficiaries in Ghana. The drastic difference (whatever causal weight this may have had in determining the comparative outcomes) lay in the sheer impossibility for even the more optimistic Sri Lankan conspirators in supposing that such action on their part would be welcomed with enthusiasm by most of their fellow citizens.

Putting these three incidents together, then, we may note firstly the simple and universal, if somewhat rough and ready, truth that all regimes depend much more directly in eliciting a sense (however ambivalently motivated) of effective obligation on the part of their forces of coercion than they do on eliciting feelings warmer than the most grudging tolerance on the part of most of their subjects. Secondly, and more contentiously, we may suggest that, other things being equal, it is in practice harder to secure such a sense of obligation among the forces of coercion where electoral political competition is not tolerated than where it remains effectively institutionalised.

South Asia's formidable political matriarchs came over time to show increasingly little zest for the graceful acknowledgement of electoral defeat and they were in no danger (whilst still in office) of lacking for ingenious apologists and a ready and self-righteous rhetoric to justify such reluctance. The option of replacing competitive electoral democracy with a one-party regime has obvious charms for a government in difficulties which will have shortly to stand election. But it is a matter of power (and one which may well affect hitherto unconsidered aspects of its political control) that such a choice looks to an electorate very like a simple preference for irresponsible government over responsible government. Responsible government in this modest institutional sense provides less handsome excuses to those contemplating its overthrow (those in whom a government most needs to elicit some sense of obligation) than does a government which, if it is to be dispensed with at all, can only be so by violence. As the second Ghana coup shows clearly enough, the formal continuation of a responsible government is not a comprehensive insurance against a military putsch; and since other things are not in fact equal the establishment of 'irresponsible' government in no way guarantees a mutinous military response. But the contrast between the 1962 and the 1966 incidents serves at least as a crude reminder that incumbent regimes can lose as well as gain from abolishing the opportunity for electorates to evict them.

Keeping the janissaries in their barracks is a strenuous and costly business for most modern states. It would be naive to suppose that a recognition of civic obligations in the martial role often has much to do with the efficacy of civilian control. Most unarmed citizens most of the time have no occasion to consider extreme forms of political disobedience, however much ground they have for attempting to circumvent the laws in their private capacity. There are only two contexts in which the issue of political obligation arises with much urgency for most citizens, the threat of external aggression and the prospect of mass rebellion. Conscription for foreign war is not necessarily aptly seen (or actually experienced) as confronting a threat of external aggression, though the public cant of the modern world is likely to cause it to be so described. Modern states conscript, in their own eyes, for self-protection, not for foreign conquest. Foreign conquest is the nefarious intent of other *foreign* nation states. The threat of foreign violence is a powerful stimulus to civic solidarity. War forces many to take sides and, confronted with a choice between one's own community and a foreign invader, it is less easy to remain authentically neutral than it is among the normal routines of practical life. The synthesis of communal solidarity under alien threat is one of the most dramatic and politically consequential of twentieth-century social processes. Effective defence was the main service which states until recently claimed to offer to their subjects. Defencelessness, as Hobbes and Machiavelli and Hegel all emphasised, was a practical proof of the dependence of individuals for the very possibility of a moral life on the order of controlled violence. 'Hussars with shining sabres'[146] could teach even the morally obtuse where their true obligations lay. The Pakistan army in Bangladesh, the German army in Yugoslavia, the Portuguese army in Mozambique, the French and perhaps even the American armies in Vietnam have helped greatly to forge such nations as are now to be found within those boundaries. In Ghana at least, it is almost impossible to imagine circumstances in which nationality and the most urgent of individual obligations could become superimposed in this way by external threat. There is nothing to defend Ghana against except itself. Even in Sri Lanka it is likely that any shining sabres encountered by the citizenry in the course of their ordinary lives will belong to their own armed forces. If the Republic of India broke up and a Tamil secessionist regime established itself in South India[147] this would certainly have a major impact on Sri Lankan politics; and it would give a Sinhalese army something to defend the Sinhalese against. But, from the viewpoint of individual obligation and communal solidarity, it would have less the character of a foreign threat to a unitary Sri Lanka than of a continuation of some of the present cleavages of Sri Lankan domestic society by other and drastically intensified means. Even if civil society continues to prove viable in Ghana and Sri Lanka, these countries can hardly anticipate that foreigners will bring home to their citizens the imperious moral claims of their own states.

The second context in which the issue of political obligation may arise with urgency for an ordinary citizen is the context of rebellion or, more aspiringly, of revolution. Classically there are three main forms in which the problem of political obligation has been conceived in this context. Ought ordinary citizens (subjects) to acknowledge a political obligation to a usurping power? Can a subject have sufficient reason to rebel against a lawfully established government? Does a subject who is contemplating rebellion have sufficient grounds to recognise an obligation to the incumbent government merely because it *is* incumbent? The second of these questions, to which John Locke addressed his *Two Treatises of Government*, is relatively uncontroversial today and the first, the question to which it now seems probable that Hobbes addressed his *Leviathan*,[148] is even less likely to provoke dispute. Authentically legitimist states are increasingly few and far between. A broadly utilitarian consensus, that political obligation is owed (and only owed) to political forms towards which it is to the long term collective advantage to acknowledge it, prevails in public political discussion almost everywhere in the world — along, naturally, with abundant disagreement as to what political forms are likely to pass this experiential test in due course. The third question is less uncontroversial. Besides being a somewhat unpromising exercise in resolving the consciences of royalists over accepting oaths to the Cromwellian regime, Hobbes's *Leviathan* was (and remains) also a uniquely rigorous attempt to prove the utilitarian rationality of individual political obligation within any functioning political order. Since 1651, many regimes have sought to persuade their subject population of the desirability of sustaining them and of helping to repulse the assaults of their domestic enemies, though none of them has mustered an apologist quite as eloquent and ingenious as Hobbes. But in these stark terms the case for accepting one incumbent is necessarily much the same, both in character and in cogency, as the case for accepting any other incumbent whom history chooses to throw up. Hobbesian political obligation may seem agreeable enough to a well-entrenched regime; but it is strictly a fair weather friend. Where a regime really needs to elicit a feeling of obligation is among those of its subjects who may actually contemplate assaulting it. Prospects for mustering any great theoretical panache in this venture are at present more than a little gloomy. Even the more relaxed and unhysterical theorists of political obligation in capitalist democracies have difficulty in making much of a case to those citizens who choose to make war on the state of which they are notionally a member.[149] If a combination of utilitarian considerations and more or less tacit consent are the best that can be put together for citizens of the United Kingdom, it is hardly surprising that the Provisional I.R.A. have remained unimpressed; and it is difficult to see much sense of obligation being elicited by these theoretical methods from the Ghanaian or Sri Lankan population at large in the near future.

As yet this is a matter of little practical significance in Ghana, the citizens of which do not appear even to have contemplated assaulting the state as such. But in Sri Lanka the issue has already been rendered on one occasion as urgent as it well could be. The 1971 insurrection has not been much illuminated so far by its commentators from left or right. The demographic background and the extent of juvenile unemployment, emphasised by Professor Wriggins no doubt furnish part of the story;[150] and the caste solidarities stressed by Dr Jiggins[151] provide another part. The broad picture of a generational civil war in the areas of revolt among the Sinhalese themselves and the lack of Tamil involvement in particular seem widely agreed. But the process by which the positive solidarities of the P.L.F. came to be synthesised and the widespread collective belief that assaulting the police stations might usher in the millennium are scarcely explained in even the broadest of outlines. Only Marguerite Robinson's astonishing portrait of a village passing within a mere eight years from the millennial sleep of one of Marx's paradigm Asiatic villages to a seedbed of modernist professional revolution gives us even a fleeting glimpse into this process.[152] But that glimpse alone is enough to establish one crucial point. The state of Ceylon meant very little to the inhabitants of 'Morapitiya' in 1963. They neither loved it nor detested it. It was simply not a palpable part of their lives. Professor Robinson does not explain (and makes no claim to explain) quite how it came to play a salient enough part in her villagers' lives for it to seem worthwhile to them to attack it full-face a mere eight years later. Only an equally sensitive ethnographic record of the process of conversion would serve to explain how the state could come to mean something so definite and so negative and hence to explain the decision of so many young men and women to discount the gross imprudence of assaulting the police stations and to pay the penalty which many paid for doing so. It is not necessary to share the callow cosmopolitan political camaraderie of Mr Halliday[153] to recognise with him the startling posture in which the events of 1971 placed the Sri Lankan state, its apparatus of coercion assailed en masse in hundreds of villages by its own school leavers, but rearmed and assisted from the outside from every band of the world political spectrum. Whose state precisely was the state of Sri Lanka in April 1971 and who in consequence had obligations towards it? Put in these histrionic terms, the question invites a dusty answer. But the fact that it can without sheer absurdity be posed in these terms will serve as text for a conclusion. And, in concluding we may aptly consider obligation no longer simply as an ideological demand but rather as a moral relation which might obtain in the real world.

All civic obligation to the state apparatus of post-colonial states (and perhaps all political obligation in the world today *tout court*) must be provisional. Utilitarian political obligation is necessarily provisional. It will also for most citizens be strictly prudential in form. The states are there and discourage disobedience as best they can. But *la plus belle fille du monde ne peut donner que ce qu'elle a*. The states are only able to discourage disobedience to the extent that and for as long as they *are* able to do so. If *protectio trahit subjectionem*, *usurpatio* as promptly withdraws it; and pretenders today are ten a penny. These, perhaps, are gloomy thoughts and not only so for the holders of public office. But there is a more positive aspect to them. Utilitarian political obligation in an unrepresentative state is not much of a political resource to anyone, ruler or ruled — as Nozick says of tacit consent: 'not worth the paper it's not written on'.[154] But besides being provisional, utilitarian political obligation is also conditional — earned, not simply inherited. In its time this conditional aspect of political obligation has made a less exiguous contribution to political development. The famous coronation oaths of allegiance of the Crown of Aragon, a late sixteenth-century scholarly invention for the best of libertarian motives if on somewhat slender historical excuse, state the essence of the point: 'We who are as good as you swear to you who are no better than us allegiance as Prince and Heir to our Kingdom, on the condition that you preserve our laws and liberties; and if not, not.'[155] In their better moments neither Solomon Bandaranaike nor Kwame Nkrumah would have claimed a more obsequious allegiance. Any just claim to political obligation is necessarily heavily conditional in form. If the holders of state power in Ghana or Sri Lanka wish their subjects authentically to acknowledge an obligation to obey their commands, they should serve their subjects to the best of their abilities. This may not be enough. The remedy for disobedience may not necessarily lie within their hands: not all states are governable. But at least they will have done what they could. Fear may be a tempting cut-price surrogate for good government. But, despite Hobbes, it is not a passion to be reckoned on for any great length of time. When the governments of Ghana and Sri Lanka contrive fully to deserve their subjects' loyalty, they may be sure they will have it soon enough.

If not, not.

8

Democracy unretrieved, or the political theory of Professor Macpherson

Professor Macpherson began his well known study, *The Political Theory of Possessive Individualism*, by pointing to the persisting difficulty of finding a firm theoretical basis for the legitimacy of the liberal democratic state.[1] This difficulty has not lessened appreciably since 1962 and may indeed be thought to have shifted in some measure from the theoretical to the practical. In addition, Macpherson's diagnosis of the radical flaw in liberal democracy, its commitment to 'possessive individualism', has become in some ways more in harmony with prevalent cultural enthusiasms than it was in the complacent days of 1962. Pleasure continues to enjoy a proper utilitarian respect in western democracies but possessions, the object of *'amor sceleratus habendi'*, certainly seem to be regarded with a more jaundiced eye today than they were in 1962. Macpherson always hoped, for the most respectable of reasons, to assist in changing the world. He must have felt that the world of 1973 to which he addressed *Democratic Theory: Essays in Retrieval* was one better attuned to his persuasions than he had seen for decades. Taken together his three volumes on liberalism and its inadequacies[2] represented the most extensive and coherent critique of the continuing dependence of liberal democracy upon a capitalist economic base to be attempted by any political theorist since the Second World War. It was a critique which had the major virtue of taking the strengths of liberalism at least as seriously as its defects. At a time when the societies of advanced capitalism are facing at least a minor crisis, it seems worth inquiring how far Macpherson's views do succeed in providing a valuable guide as to how the world could appropriately be changed, how western societies could at last be rendered more genuinely democratic.

The coherence of Macpherson's critique is plainly admirable in itself. Macpherson is a faithful and a singularly diligent expositor of his own views. He does not seem to be much afflicted by second, or indeed by any subsequent thoughts.[3] But the coherence is also intimately related to some of his critique's major deficiencies. The depth of his vision is often matched by its extreme narrowness. These characteristics are both much in evidence in his first study, the very influential *The Political Theory of Possessive Individual-*

206

ism. What Macpherson attempts in this book is to demonstrate how a political theory which sanctioned capitalist economic relations and the state structures required to maintain these ever came to be created. The appearance of concepts in the thought of Hobbes and Locke, above all their view of human beings as essentially greedy and competitive, is explained by the emergence of market society. Apparent incoherences — incoherences apparent to Macpherson himself — in the thought of Harrington, the Levellers and Locke are resolved by invoking features of seventeenth-century market society to which the writers themselves had negligently failed to draw the attention of readers in future centuries. In conclusion the menace of nuclear destruction is mentioned as a possible replacement for the defective market psychology of Hobbes in closing the gap between fact and value and furnishing a rational basis for secular human community in a worldwide equality of physical insecurity.[4]

Possessive Individualism is a powerfully written work, full of striking insights, and it has been widely admired since its appearance.[5] It has, however, been received with decidedly less enthusiasm by historians of ideas who have made systematic studies of just what those seventeenth-century writers discussed by Macpherson were in fact maintaining and who have attempted to explain why the writers advanced these particular arguments.[6] The narrowness of focus of much of the book's discussion and its determined exclusion of key aspects of the writers' work in which Macpherson himself was not immediately interested lend to many of the contradictions identified and to the resolutions offered for them an air of extreme unreality, as of a somewhat arbitrary private game. The relationship, for example, between Hobbes's coruscating account of fundamental human malevolence and the market society which Macpherson painstakingly constructs as its necessary venue seems almost comically arbitrary.[7] It would certainly be hard to recover from the notably uninflected view of competitive opportunities set out in Macpherson's model of market society the fact that one of the main forms of our competitive malice mentioned by Hobbes himself is the making of jokes at one another's expense. (It is not easy to imagine a society with which Hobbes's view of human psychology would not be compatible. It may be a conception expressed in terms which reflect the impact of capitalism on seventeenth-century England. But the supposition that it could not be thought to hold good of a society without a market economy is more than optimistic.)* It is clear that Macpherson had an extensive knowledge of the writings of the authors whom he was studying, that he had read them with

* Even as a structural principle competitive malice is less tied to capitalism than the limits of Macpherson's model allow. For two examples of societies structurally organized on a principle of competitive malice which show no affection for individual consumption or greed see Marcel Mauss, trans. I. Cunnison, *The Gift* (London 1954), pp. 35—6, and J.K. Campbell, *Honour, Family and Patronage* (Oxford 1964), esp. pp. 9, 39, 181, 204—7, 211, 230, 267, 300, 312—15 (a very Hobbesian account of the social meaning of laughter), 320. There are many societies with whose *ideologies* Hobbes's account of human psychology is, of course, incompatible. See most notably Louis Dumont's account of Hindu society in *Homo Hierarchicus* (London, 1972).

great care, if very much from a particular point of view. The principles of inference which he stated at intervals in his quest for unstated assumptions may have produced some odd consequences in detail; but they were not easy to quarrel with in themselves in any general way. Yet the outcome is radically unsatisfactory as a historical study of political thinking. Why?

One obvious answer would be that Macpherson was not greatly interested in studying political thinking historically, that his interest in the seventeenth-century roots was always (and very properly) subordinated to his interest in the diseased twentieth-century tree. The precise scope of Locke's moral psychology might well in this perspective seem less important than the continued dependence of capitalist society upon the moral sanctioning of egoistic greed. But, while this might explain the historical inadvertence of such passages as those on the reasons for the unpopularity of Hobbes's theory,[8] it would hardly explain the decision to devote an entire volume concerned with contemporary political theory to a study of thinkers of the seventeenth century. The main problem which Macpherson seems to have hoped to illuminate was a genuinely historical problem: the question of how it was that such an inherently implausible belief as that in the moral adequacy of liberal capitalist democracy had ever come to be developed. The explanation offered was that the relevant moral credulity was developed in two stages. The first stage involved the creation of a belief in the possibility of valid political obligation in a liberal capitalist state of a firmly undemocratic kind. The second involved the covert (if not wholly successful) transference of belief in the validity of these obligations to the electoral democracies which developed out of the first liberal capitalist states.[9]

Even if the accounts of thinkers treated in *The Political Theory of Possessive Individualism* had been historically faithful renditions of their social and political commitments and even if the explanations of how they arrived at these commitments had been wholly convincing, it seems an error of method to suppose that such accounts would necessarily provide much help in explaining how these theories survived with such success their transition to the somewhat different ecological niche of competitive electoral democracy. It is undoubtedly an interesting historical question why anyone should ever have been convinced by the arguments of James Mill's *Essay on Government* (to take one of the few thinkers who was with some certainty both a possessive individualist and a democrat).[10] But even in the case of Mill himself the problem is not materially diminished by identifying the rather different reasons why Hobbes had earlier found the arguments of *Leviathan* so convincing. And if the explanation in both cases of their respective credulities was the hypnotic powers of the market, there seems some reason for wondering whether our own difficulties with the market, our need to elude its grasp, will be much alleviated by noting its efficacy in these instances in the past. If the intention involved is the destruction of illusion, it will surely take more than this revelation of the dual character of the market — so convincing to the hapless Hobbes, Locke and James Mill, so exquisitely unconvincing to Macpherson himself — to destroy whatever maintains its sway over us. It is, in any case, hardly self-evident that it is this sort of illusion which does serve to maintain the power of the market. The latter has had numerous power-fully disaffected observers before Macpherson. Comprehensive moral plausi-bility was never one of its stronger suits.

There are thus reasons for supposing that the more direct assault which Macpherson attempts in *Democratic Theory* may serve his purposes better than his earlier ventures into history have done. His attack on the vision of greed as the essence of human nature is certainly strengthened by being detached from a dubious presentation of the views of Locke. His account of the necessary transfer of human powers resulting from the existence of private property in the means of production — a fairly conventional Marxist argument and none the worse for that — is certainly easier to understand in this new and full presentation than it has been in earlier and less complete versions. But while there can be no doubt that his views gain greatly in clarity from this extended presentation, it cannot be said that they gain equally in plausibility. Indeed in one possibly crucial respect the passage of time itself may be thought to have weakened the argument as a whole, or at the very least to have diminished its vulgar appeal. In its assurance about the imminent transcendence of scarcity (if in few other ways) his position when it was first fully stated was very much one of the early 1960s, with their confidence in the assured persistence of industrial affluence. Anxiety over the depletion of fuel reserves, the costs of putting an end to industrial pollution and the persisting ecological deterioration of large areas of the world has made scarcity a focus of urgent concern once again. In a world of plenty a social system organised around compulsive greed does seem not merely morally ugly but also slightly absurd. But today it takes a more bracing imagination to see the world as a whole as a world of plenty than it did from the vantage point of Canada in 1965. The ending of scarcity has at times appeared in Macpherson's writings as an available condition, both necessary and sufficient, for our abandonment of the psychology of possess-ive individualism and our consequent liberation from the toils of the market. It may, however, be preferable to treat it as a (no longer quite so available) sufficient condition for our capacity to make that escape — and one with which we might at a pinch contrive to dispense. The defects of the market as a system of distributive justice, painstakingly outlined by Macpherson, do not depend in any way upon an attitude, satisfied or dissatisfied, to the total supply of goods. The persuasive effect upon capitalist societies — if it is in fact to operate at all — of the existence of contrasting social systems in other parts of the world is another component of his arguments, much insisted on in *The Real World of Democracy*,* which might serve as an alternative mechanism of release.

* In 1962 it was the menace of nuclear destruction which was at last to enable us to escape from the

It may be more illuminating to turn instead to the place given by Macpherson in his arguments to the development, the 'maximisation', of human powers. If *The Political Theory of Possessive Individualism* records the negative side of Macpherson's doctrine, with its account of how shades of the prison house began to close around the growing capitalist labour force, the treatment of the conditions for the development of human powers in the first six chapters of *Democratic Theory* gives a firm statement of his positive doctrines. The key element is the claim that any adequate theory of democracy today would have to be a theory in which all citizens had an equal right to enjoy themselves (unpossessively) and to develop their human powers to the full.[11] It is not immediately clear what an actual society in which such a theory was realised would be like nor in consequence whether the theory as sketched has any determinate meaning. Certainly Macpherson himself makes little effort to flesh out his conceptions and to render them plausible at this point. What he does attempt to do (with some success) is to show that no theory which gives all citizens an equal right to develop their human powers to the full is compatible with the institutions of a society in which labour is treated as a commodity and in which there exists any significant measure of private property in the means of production. This is neither a novel nor a surprising conclusion and it may be doubted whether it really gains particularly in force from the very extended presentation which Macpherson devotes to it. But since western democracies are still preponderantly capitalist societies with their productive systems operating on a (sometimes heavily doctored) form of market and since their populations are not universally educated in the deficiencies of the market as a system of distributive justice, the weary sense of *déjà lu* which sometimes comes over the reader may fairly be rejected as unworthy. The patience and doggedness of Macpherson's exposition ought to make it far harder for those who read him through to lose sight of these important truths.

It may still be wondered, though, just how far this argument carries Macpherson towards his destination. The idea of maximising a value which is not in any obvious sense measurable, or even linear, is a notion which wears an air of slightly bogus precision at the best of times. In relation to the development of human powers this air of precision is especially implausible. One may set aside the ambiguity over which human powers it is in fact desirable for human beings to develop, let alone to develop to the maximum,* along

---

long nightmare of capitalist greed (see p. 332 n. 4). By 1965 this formidable threat had been supplanted by peaceful coexistence and the aftermath of decolonisation, the struggle for the hearts and minds of the Third World, a struggle in which the West was seen as being prospectively crippled by its association with the moral contaminations of the market (*The Real World of Democracy*, Oxford 1962, passim, esp. pp. 65–7). This association was no longer imposed by material scarcity (*Real World*, pp. 62–4).

* The postulate of non-opposition of essentially human capacities may be too good to be true. But it is necessary to any fully democratic theory' (*Democratic Theory: Essays in Retrieval*, Oxford 1973, p. 55). For the development of this point of view see pp. 55–76. One essentially human capacity which Macpherson would plainly not wish to maximise would be the capacity deliberately to inflict

with the perhaps unintended implication that it is open to any human being to develop to the maximum all the powers which it is open to him to develop. (Few Olympic swimmers play the violin with distinction and make important contributions to the advancement of mathematics at an early age. Even if most other resources were infinitely abundant, time would remain a very scarce resource for those intent on maximising many different powers.)

Macpherson's arguments appear to rely here for such cogency as they have on a measure of conflation of two different conceptions of human power: labour power and active (or creative) ability. The idea which links them is that of access to the means of labour. Speaking very crudely, Macpherson's usage treats it as a tautologous proposition that the capitalist labour market necessarily involves transfers of labour power from labourer to capitalist. Those who are not compelled to sell their labour power thus control the development of all their own powers, whereas wage (or salaried) labourers do not control the development of all their powers. It will be clear, however, that a more realistic conception of the relation between individual labour and creativity in industrial societies would remove all the precision and perhaps much of the force from this argument. (It may well be thought, also, that there are more direct and unequivocal means of judging the inequity of the ownership of massive private wealth than a comparison between the degree to which those who do and those who do not own the means of production contrive to maximise the development of their 'essentially human capacities'.)

The idea of necessary transfers of labour power and the idea of each individual maximising the development of his own powers are indeed incompatible on Macpherson's usage. But this tells us more about Macpherson's usage than it does about the social and economic basis of individual creativity. Since many or perhaps most abilities which human beings do develop are not offered for sale — indeed are not even perceived by their possessors as being potential commodities — it is hard to believe that the relationship between the ownership of the means of production and the efflorescence of human creativity can be as simple and transparent as Macpherson argues. If one moves from the studied abstraction of labour power to the concreteness of particular human abilities, it certainly makes sense to talk of the maximisation of one human ability: a power, perhaps the power to swim fast on one's back or to carve small wooden horses. It may even make sense to discuss the relationship between the chances of maximising this power and the economic organisation of the society. (In the case of swimming, the climates and diets of Australia and California appear to be more important than the prevalent economic system.) But even if one could arrive at an agreed list of

intense pain on other humans. This is a power which may involve both intellectual or physical prowess (ability) and work (labour power). It is also one which has been known to have its price even in societies where the market is officially regarded with great moral scorn — for example, in the spheres of sport (boxing) or social control (torture).

all desirable human abilities (a list the status of which would be at best evanescent), it is hard to see in principle what it would mean to 'maximise' them as a whole. (Their sum? Their product? Their average?)

Furthermore, even if the notion of the maximisation of desirable powers is conceded to be both meaningful and coherent, it is surely fanciful to suppose that any national community in the world today organises its production in such a way as to develop *equally* all the more desirable powers of all its citizens. To write about the maximisation of human powers as though the only major impediment to its realisation is the prevalence of capitalist economic organisation, to which our addiction to competitive consumption has subjected us, is to verge on the frivolous. For all men to be able to develop their powers equally, rather more is required of a social formation than they not be affirmed officially *not* to have the right to do so. Many good consequences could rationally be expected if the productive resources of the United States of America were to become owned by its citizens as a whole, especially if this state of affairs had been produced by a reasonably peaceful progression (not an easy eventuality to imagine). But whereas collective ownership and a fairly equitable distribution of consumption benefits could in principle be established, these would scarcely go far towards producing the equal development of the human powers of all Americans. Whatever may be true in other contexts, this is one instance in which it is hard to elude a separation between ownership and control. Collective ownership would be a legal fact, collective material benefit a possible distributive policy; but collective control as it has so far been described and imagined would be little more than a verbal placebo. At no point does Macpherson give serious consideration to any obstacles to the development of human powers which arise from the social division of labour other than those produced by the control of private capital.[12] Since there are numerous countries in the world (as Macpherson frequently points out elsewhere) which do not have private ownership of the means of production, an examination of the extent to which productive labour and leisure there do in fact develop human powers more handsomely than in the blighted capitalist west is a necessary complement to the diagnosis of capitalist inequity which Macpherson advances. Within broad constraints of productive efficiency, it is probably, above all, imaginative despondency at the possibilities of a more rewarding organisation of work life which serves to maintain the more oppressive features of capitalist work organisation. To dissipate this despondency would require a far more concrete and extensively informed social imagination than that set out in Macpherson's scholastic critique of the moral defects of capitalism.

What offends Macpherson is the explicit injustice of capitalist relations of exchange. Other forms of democratic ideology, both communist and Third World, receive a more favourable treatment at his hands because such injustices as they promote in practice they have the good taste to leave unmentioned in their public self-descriptions. Macpherson is too much of a libertarian and too well-informed about the deficiencies of communist countries from the viewpoint of civil liberties for these to pass unnoticed in his account. But even here his notably sanguine disposition leads him to expectations for the future which are substantially more optimistic than those for example of Academician Sakharov or Mr Amalrik.[13] The Third World he takes unflinchingly at the value of its own moral face.[14] What he has to say about it and the prospective impact of its public disaffection with western economic values suggests neither extensive acquaintance with the realities of the nations of the Third World nor much understanding of the causation of western attitudes towards former colonial territories. It is not easy to imagine the public moral commitments of Iraq, Uganda or Burundi coming to exercise a powerful influence on the normative allegiance of western populations. Those Third World countries which undeniably exercise considerable influence of a less elevated character over the political choices of western countries, such as Libya, Saudi Arabia or Iran, could hardly be said to do so as a result of their fastidious recoil from the exercise of market power or the unique intensity of their concern for distributive social justice. The explicit moral deficiencies of capitalism no doubt hopelessly exceed the explicit moral deficiencies of many or even most non-capitalist political entities elsewhere (though the apparent supposition that capitalist economic relations do not prevail within most countries of the Third World is not easy to understand).[15] But insofar as the populations of capitalist societies are influenced in their political commitments by the pressure of normative commitments in other political communities (an extent which is perhaps rather less than Macpherson supposes), it is plausibly the balance of unstated moral deficiencies at home and abroad which weighs more heavily than does that of explicit ones. Macpherson is right to emphasise that when we proclaim our enthusiasm for liberal democracy we are in danger of forgetting or of leaving discreetly unmentioned the fact that thus far an acceptance of liberal democracy has been accomplished by an acceptance — whether cheerful or resigned — of capitalist production. What he fails to give adequate weight to is the perfectly rational basis for anxiety that a firm repudiation of the market may — in the realm of practice if not that of theory — also turn out to include a number of equally unadvertised concomitants in the package.

The extreme vagueness with which Macpherson envisages the external competitive pressure on capitalist ideology is matched by the absence of any plausible identification of the mechanisms of the transition in which western societies are to reject the market concept of the essence of man. It is also matched by a persisting obscurity as to just what audience he supposes himself to be addressing, an issue which is plainly important for a thinker intent on fostering desirable changes in the world. A crude example may help to illuminate this uncertainty. In Macpherson's writings the market, despite its repeatedly affirmed moral obsolescence, appears as virtually the sole agency

213

in social processes with the capacity to impose real structure on society. At no point does he devote serious discussion to institutions other than those connected with market exchange which might be thought to offer potential obstructions to the realisation of democracy. Especially surprising in a work preoccupied with the attempt to retrieve democratic theory is the complete absence of discussion of the institutional possibilities for the people to control the government.* This restriction of attention, as suggested earlier, seems oversanguine in itself. But if it is accepted as in any measure realistic, it also raises grave doubts about the pointfulness of Macpherson's entire undertaking. If it is right to see the market as a social agency of such unique structural potency, it is hard to imagine it softly and silently vanishing away merely because of a shift, even a unanimous shift, in the moral affections of the professional guild of political theorists. It seems apparent that the sway of the market, such as it still is, is sustained by something more robust than the moral affections of political theorists. Professor Macpherson does succeed in convicting a number of distinguished political theorists (along, less surprisingly, with Milton Friedman) of a less stringent moral hostility to the market than he feels to be proper.[16] This in itself is no doubt an enterprise of some value in eroding acceptance in cultured circles of the market concept of human essence. But it is not difficult to imagine the market — as an institution rather than an abstract term in moral thought — surviving a good many aeons of this type of weathering.

But if Macpherson's intended audience is (as seems almost certain) rather wider than this, it is necessary to enquire precisely what groups it is that are being incited to discard their possessive individualism for the more spiritual rewards of living in an unacquisitive society.[17] University teachers are already often under the optimistic impression that their choice of career reflects a stern refusal to capitulate to human greed and are thus liable to accept Macpherson's proffered values with less than an adequate sense of cultural strain. There are, furthermore, large groups of young persons in all western societies who have rejected the rationality of infinite appropriation at least as firmly as Macpherson could demand, though many of them perhaps have a more lackadaisical attitude to the maximisation of human powers than he would think quite proper. But both academics and drop-outs are somewhat peripheral to the more insistent requirements of the market. It

---

* There are a few brief comments on the possibilities of popular control in *Real World*, pp. 18, 20–1. Participatory democracy receives some support in *Democratic Theory*, p. 62, and there is a discussion of the possibilities for protecting political freedom where there exists a government monopoly of employment in *Democratic Theory*, pp. 152–4. It is possible that Macpherson's apparent lack of interest in this issue ('*The* serious difficulty about a democratic society is not how to run it but how to reach it', *Democratic Theory*, p. 74, my italics; it is better to travel hopefully than to arrive) is connected with his readiness to consider the distinction between government by and government for the people as a relatively minor one *within* democratic theory. (See *Real World*, pp. 5, 16–22 etc. and especially p. 19 with the explicit parallels between Plato and Lenin.) For a corrective to the view that democracy in the ancient world meant indifferently government by or government for the *demos* see M.I. Finley, *Democracy Ancient and Modern* (London 1973).

is in relation to these more central structural needs that one must ask precisely what is meant, and for whom, by the proposal to discard these tawdry values. What for instance would it mean for an owner of private capital contemplating an investment programme or for an academic whose pension is secured by an equity-based insurance fund to do so? What would it mean for a trade union leader in a wage negotiation confronted by governmental wage controls to do so?

Relaxing the scarcity assumption in any of these contexts is likely to seem to the agents concerned to be at best premature. To abandon appropriative strategies while a market of sorts is still in operation is simply to put oneself at a competitive disadvantage. In practical terms it is at least as likely to strengthen the power of the market as to impair it. President Carter and Mrs Thatcher might reasonably urge trade union leaders to restrain their greed; but it is clearly no part of Macpherson's intentions to throw his weight onto that particular side of the social scale. It is certainly true that the incidence of market forces has been altered often in the past as a result of moral revulsion from their effects. This is a process which we can no doubt expect to continue and perhaps to intensify into the future. But it is not because most western citizens are rapt devotees of the morality of the market that the rather doctored markets, internal and foreign, which we experience still persist. It is not a wholly discretionary matter for any non-autarkic economy at a particular point in time how far it is subjected to market forces prevailing outside its borders. Even within a particular society the market serves other functions besides that of maintaining a conspicuously unjust distribution.[18] It can, for example, continue to perform services in factor allocation even in countries in which ideologies favoured by Macpherson prevail. Most important of all, it is not a discretionary matter at all for an individual in an existing market, however doctored, how far he is subject to market forces — though it is of course open to him to decide at whatever cost the market then imposes (if necessary, starvation) that refusing to offer his labour on it is the spiritually most enriching (i.e. developing) purchase.

The rationality of operating markets, however rigged, cannot be eluded merely by looking down one's moral nose at them. What keeps markets operating is not on the whole moral credulity. What stops them operating at the level of a whole society has never been — and is never likely to be — merely a shift in moral tastes. Both the world trading system and the highly doctored markets of advanced capitalist societies today have many grave difficulties in functioning effectively. It is their difficulties in functioning effectively which are likely to imperil their continuation,[19] not the crass character of their moral self-description. If and when the living standards of the Russian populace become clearly superior to those of the American populace, we may certainly expect this to have an impact on American attitudes to capitalist production. What is not obvious is why the effect which we may expect it to have is one of making them less greedy.[20] All this is

215

extremely simple-minded and more than a little airy. But if one is to engage with Macpherson's thought as a whole one must engage with it at the level at which it possesses coherence. What Macpherson invokes, to put it crudely, is the prospect of a peaceful transition to libertarian socialism for the mechanics of which he fails to give any plausible characterisation whatever. As a scholar Macpherson is one of the most agreeable, the most civilised and the most learned of theorists working in the Marxist tradition who concern themselves with the future of western capitalism. But for anyone who wishes to attend to what really requires consideration for the future of western capitalism from those working in the Marxist tradition it will be necessary to engage with the works of those who are less civilised, less agreeable and — except in their knowledge of the writings of Marx and Lenin — for the most part appreciably less learned.

9

The success and failure of modern revolutions

Success for whom? Failure of what?

Ever since there have been polities, there have been political upheavals. As soon as systematic reflection about politics began in the Western world, it was recognised that political upheavals could mean not merely an alteration in the ruling personnel of a particular polity but also a change in the form of its political regime. The core of modern ideas of revolution remains the conception of transforming political regimes by means of or as a result of political upheaval. The main difference between ancient and modern ideas of the connection between political upheaval and regime transformation lies in the directional character of modern conceptions of regime transformation. Such ancient theories of regime transformation as were directional in character at all were explicitly cyclical.[1] Modern analysis of regime transformation need not accept a directional view of historical process; but if it accepts any view of historical process at all[2] it can hardly, except at the most abstract level, suppose its direction to be circular. Elites may circulate, individual rulers or groups of rulers may come and go; but regimes themselves can hardly now be supposed to follow a cyclical path. Modern revolutionaries are historical actors who aspire to transform political regimes in an intended direction by promoting political upheaval. The promotion of political upheaval is a regrettable necessity for (or an invigorating prelude to) regime transformation. It is an instrument which some clearly cherish more tenderly than others; but few revolutionaries would be prepared to admit, were it in some case to prove dispensable, to loving it for its own sake.

The role of revolutionary is central to modern revolutionary processes. It is also unique to modern revolutionary processes. The birth of the role can be fixed with some precision as lying between 1789 and 1796: between the first meeting of the Estates General and the abortive *Conjuration des Égaux* of 'Gracchus' Babeuf, as mythically transmitted to the revolutionaries of the nineteenth century by Filippo Buonarroti.[3] At the beginning of 1789, as George Taylor neatly indicates,[4] no significant political force in France expected or advocated a revolution, partly at least because no one in France

217

knew that a revolution was a possible type of historical occurrence.* Before 1789 there were classical utopians who set themselves to imagine a better moral world — Rousseau, for example, or Morelly.[5] But classical utopians were above all else men who knew that there was *nothing* to be *done*. As Morelly himself put it: 'It is, sadly, only too true that it would be impossible in our day to form any such Republic . . . I do not have the temerity to claim to be able to reform the human race — only the courage to tell the truth, without troubling myself over the bleating of those who fear it.'[6] Since 1789 temerity has increased greatly (partly no doubt at the expense of veracity and the courage this demands) and professional revolutionaries have come to display this temerity in action. Until the French revolution, revolutionary practice was linked to overtly sacred theories. There were religious prophets before 1789 who had taken or aspired to take state power: Müntzer, possibly Savonarola, certainly the Fifth Monarchists.[7] There were agitators, too, who had struggled more or less self-consciously to alter government and society by direct political action, most notably among the Levellers of the Great Rebellion, like John Lilburne.[8] But there were no examples of men who saw their life in strictly secular terms and devoted the whole of it to the project of transforming the political and social order of their country by an attempt to seize power within it. Since shortly after the fall of Robespierre in Thermidor of the Year II there have always been such men, living in closed or open conspiracy or in the solitude of their own fantasies,[9] in the hope and with the purpose of changing the political and social world by their acts.

To look at political upheavals through the eyes of these men is to see at once not just a single definition but two very different definitions of success and failure. If their aspiration is to use political upheaval to take state power, they fail if they do not contrive to take state power. There is very much more to revolutionary success than the taking and keeping of state power, but there certainly cannot well be *less*. Revolutionaries, like any other rebels, risk military defeat by incumbent state power, and they also risk defeat by other contenders for the state power which they seek. But even if they contrive to take state power they do not necessarily succeed in realising their ambitions. Post-revolutionary regimes are seldom wholly unmodified by the political vicissitudes which precede their inception; but they are also seldom or never modified solely in the directions intended or proclaimed by the victorious revolutionaries.

It is not difficult, if one takes the more inflated statements of revolutionary intention *au pied de la lettre*, to mount a strong case for the view that no revolutionaries *ever* succeed. At the other extreme, where political upheaval

---

* It was well understood even in the highest circles that the heads of kings could be cut off, and a number of conservative truths about the meaning of revolutionary processes were grasped by some. See, for example, Laurence L. Bongie, *David Hume: Prophet of the Counterrevolution* (Oxford 1965), pp. xv, 59, 66, 77, 123–4, and 126. What was not anticipated by pre-revolutionary thinkers or actors was the momentum and the directional political dynamic of the revolution.

is perceived by at least some participants or bystanders as purely reactive violence, without clearly conceived goals or even hopes of desired consequences, the issue of success or failure scarcely arises. Most participants in revolutionary processes in practice fall somewhere in between those who have literally no hopes at all and those for whom a more or less coherently conceived utopia is not merely the limit of their ambitions but actually no great distance from their expectations. Insofar as revolutions are constituted by mass processes of social change with ill-defined chronological,[10] geographical, and demographic boundaries, it is apparent that the concepts of success and failure fit them poorly indeed. Social process, one might be tempted to say, does not succeed or fail. It merely occurs. It is men who succeed or fail[11] — or perhaps, more reductively still, it is particular human actions or projects that do so. It only makes sense to speak of success or failure in relation to intended actions or assemblages of actions. To the question of precisely what it is or who it is that succeeds or fails in modern revolutions, the natural answer is that professional revolutionaries and their careers as a whole or particular actions they undertake are the subjects of success and failure. Such a judgement is likely to be common ground between those who sympathise with modern revolutionary enterprises and those who abhor them. The breadth of audience to which it appeals, however, is not a trustworthy measure of its analytical merit. Its crucial weakness is the status which it gives within the revolutionary process to the beliefs of professional revolutionaries themselves. Acceptance of this status suggests that revolutionaries are obliged, if they wish to vindicate the rationality·of the revolutionary process, to establish the logical coherence and the grounding in social reality of their whole system of beliefs. It also suggests, conversely, that anyone who can expose major incoherences within the belief systems of revolutionaries, or gross disparities between their beliefs and social or political fact, has established the substantive irrationality of the revolutionary process, at least in this instance. To establish the logical coherence and the grounding in social reality of one's whole system of beliefs may possibly be thought to be an obligation incumbent on all who occupy the professional role of a social scientist. But it is not a light endeavour, and there is some doubt whether it is a task at which it is in principle possible to succeed.[12] If the criterion for historically rational action is made as strong as this, the effect may well be to denude the historical process of rationality altogether. And, whether we appreciate the historical opportunities for doing so or not (and whether or not we grasp the fact that we *are* doing so), act we must.

It may help at this stage to distinguish the rationality of action from the rationality of belief. What is rational for an agent to do in a particular context depends logically upon what the agent believes. His beliefs may turn out to be factually false; but although that may make it more likely that his action will prove unsuccessful, it does not suffice to make his action any less rational. But, if the rationality of action is tied directly to an agent's belief,

219

what is rational for an agent to believe does not rest, unfortunately, in any such neat logical niche. If act-rationality is taken on its own, the individual acts of revolutionaries considered seriatim are probably as rational as the acts of any other miscellaneously sampled group of social actors. There would certainly be no reason, for example, to suppose that the acts of revolutionaries are any less simply related to their clearly identified beliefs than are those of policemen, a grouping seldom selected by social scientists for axiomatic epistemological disdain. Edmund Burke, searching, as counterrevolutionaries will, for a firm epistemological put-down for the French enthusiasts, took his stand on the axiomatic sanity of the British House of Commons: 'Madmen are not our lawgivers.'[13] As social scientists have been badgered into acknowledging the large measure of not merely act-rationality but even rational belief which subsists among those who have lapsed or been forced into the moral career of the insane, such epistemological put-downs have become far harder to maintain.[14]

To note that it has become much harder to challenge the belief-rationality of revolutionary practice is not, however, necessarily to admit that it has become impossible to do so. It may be tempting, for example, to suspect that the lives of revolutionaries taken as wholes are in some way less rational than the lives of most other men; but to suppose this is probably to adopt a rather credulous view of the coherence of the lives of the majority of human beings. The more important point is to grasp the extent to which the lives of revolutionaries demand to be taken as wholes. Professional revolutionaries, as Macintyre argues,[15] are obliged (along perhaps with some sorts of social scientists) to claim to transcend that agitated precariousness which he identifies as the epistemological situation of the ordinary agent and which, rethought in tranquillity, he commends as the proper self-image for those engaged in intellectual practice in the human sciences. It is an easy matter to defend the act-rationality of revolutionaries against the external charge that they in fact know worse than other men what they are doing, act by act. What is far more difficult and may well be quite impossible is to defend professional revolutionaries against the charge that they are obliged to *claim* to know what they are doing better than it can in fact be *known*. The most distinctive feature of professional revolutionaries is the degree to which their beliefs put them permanently epistemologically on the line. The lives of professional revolutionaries are necessarily teleological to a degree that ordinary agents have no ground for emulating; and, even if the telos can be tacitly or explicitly reconsidered in the light of experience, there is always a real possibility that such a modification will imperil its essential identity as a goal. More even than most political careers, the careers of professional revolutionaries are an exercise less in learning how to get what they want than in learning to like what they can get. The teleological logic of the career and its adaptive content are necessarily very much at odds. In the doctrine of the unity of theory and practice, theory usually proves easier to adjust than does practice. Even if one fails to change the world quite as one intended, one can always hit upon a more attractive redescription for the consequences which one's actions prove to have. The limiting case of the unity of theory and practice is complete capitulation to *la force des choses*.

Revolutionaries can certainly fail: when Robespierre lay in the former Hotel de Ville as the troops of the Convention entered on the tenth of Thermidor, his jaw smashed by a pistol shot in an ineffective attempt at suicide, or later stretched out in agony on a table in the antechamber of the Committee of Public Safety, taunted by curious passers-by, he was fully justified in supposing that success had eluded him.[16] But it is a very nice question indeed whether any professional revolutionaries can ever really succeed — not because there are no projects in which any of them ever really succeed (a clearly preposterous claim), but because what they do succeed in bringing about may be always very different from what they had hoped. The greatest dead revolutionary of the twentieth century is by common consent Lenin. Even sympathetic analysts have wondered just in what sense Lenin had succeeded at the end of his life, and there is good reason to believe that Lenin himself was at least ambivalent about the question.[17] Revolutionaries who never take state power fail. But even those who do take state power and keep it as long as they live do not necessarily succeed. No man can keep state power forever. Lenin, it is widely agreed, should have died hereafter. But if his death was Russia's tragedy, it may well have been (as Trotsky's political defeat almost certainly was for Trotsky himself) his own moral salvation. One revolutionary who cannot very aptly be said simply to have failed is Josef Stalin; but then few professional revolutionaries would be happy in prospect to adopt such a drastic interpretation of what the unity of theory and practice requires as emerged from Stalin's later years. It would hardly be an apter judgement from the perspective of 1980 to claim that Stalin had in fact succeeded. Succeeded in what precisely?

The careers of professional revolutionaries, like the careers of all professional politicians, stand in a somewhat uncomfortable relation to the beliefs which they (at least publicly) hold. But some beliefs are much less embarrassing to discard for instrumental reasons than are others. It may be no more unlikely for a professional revolutionary to be a careerist than it is for any other professional politician; but it is more damaging for him to be identified as such in the course of his career. The logic of revolutionary belief systems requires that the career of the revolutionary be taken, as good radicals were supposed to take the French revolution, en bloc. Considered en bloc, their careers and the consequences of their careers have always been in uncomfortable tension with aspects of their belief systems, and there are strong (if in the end inconclusive) reasons for expecting them to continue to be in such tension in the future.

But all this holds good, if it holds good at all, only of professional revolutionaries. It does not hold good of the vast preponderance of their followers or colleagues in the wars which they judge just. Amateur revolutionaries, those whose actions *give* power to professional revolutionaries, do not have revolutionary careers. Rather, they take part in revolutionary episodes. They neither live *for* nor *off* revolution, as their professional prompters often must. Consequently they cannot properly be said to undertake revolutionary careers which require to be assessed en bloc though they certainly perform revolutionary acts; and the sense in which they succeed or fail is more contextual and less teleological than the sense in which professional revolutionaries do so. The Paris artisans who made the great revolutionary *journées* of the first five years of the revolution, or even the peasant infantry whose gun barrels carried Mao to power, may not have known quite what they were bringing about; but they undeniably achieved something. On balance it requires an excess of scepticism to believe that they were unhappy with their handiwork in retrospect: the breaking of the *ancien régime*, the founding of the People's Republic. Both as particular acts and as completed episodes, there is no reason to suppose these performances any less well adjusted to beliefs, or adjusted to less well justified beliefs, about their situation than any other segments of their lives. Amateur revolutionaries need not make (and in practice seldom would wish to make) the least pretence to transcend the epistemological situation of ordinary agents. Robespierre and Babeuf, Lenin and Mao, may all have been epistemologically hopelessly overcommitted. But the great majority of actors in revolution are amateurs and not professionals. They do not make revolutions because they suppose themselves to know better than men can in principle know. Rather, they act as they do because these actions seem preferable in each instance to any identified alternative. They make revolutions *faute de mieux*.

In considering the careers of professional revolutionaries it makes good sense to begin by conceiving the making of revolutions as the performance of bounded rational acts, since the making of revolutions is the goal to which revolutionaries address themselves. Revolutionaries who do not contrive to make a revolution fail both in their own understanding and in ours. The positive judgements, however, define themselves much less deftly. Do revolutionaries who contrive to make a revolution necessarily succeed either in their own understanding or in ours; and if they are thought to succeed, what exactly is it that they are thought to have succeeded in doing? The doctrine of the unity of theory and practice readily celebrates accommodation to the practicable, to what it turns out to be possible to do. Revolutionaries who have made a revolution in this understanding have succeeded in doing what could be done, and this in itself constitutes the theoretical sanction for their practice: a providentialist theory of the divine right of post-revolutionary state power.[18] A less bleakly tautologous version of this line of thought would be the ascriptive classification of post-revolutionary state power as socialist by virtue (and solely by virtue) of its having shifted a territorial area from the perimeter of the capitalist mode of production to that of its historically designated, if blearily described, successor.[19]

But if success is not permitted in this fashion to be wholly self-defining, the question of what criteria ought to be employed in defining it presents severe difficulties. The unity of theory and practice does offer a formidable resource for moral evasive action; but it does so precisely because of the real force of its emphasis on the conceptual instability of the revolutionary process. It seems worth insisting on three valid aspects of this emphasis in particular.

1. Revolution is a learning process, both social and individual, not simply an exploration of technically efficient means for moving towards precisely specified ends. Conservative interpreters of the revolutionary process were very quick to stress that what revolutionaries learn is rational despondency in place of moral wilfulness, by virtue of their complete practical subordination to the logic of the revolutionary situation.* More sympathetic accounts would stress the extent to which what is learned in the revolutionary process is not the fact of moral impotence nor the attitude of moral passivity, but a deep moral realism which grasps at last how it is indeed possible to transpose the values of utopia into values which are no longer too good for this world: the education of the educators. A more detached view would underline the extreme heterogeneity of what is learned both individually and collectively in revolutions, its discomfitingly wide moral scatter and necessary unpredictability. It would also, since what is learned may always be learned by counterrevolutionaries as well as by revolutionaries, stress the symmetry in this perspective between the success or failure of revolutions and that of other national political ventures. What succeeded in the Russian revolution may well have been the certainty or at least the probability of Stalinism. What succeeded in the failure of the German revolution was perhaps the probability and certainly the possibility of nazism. In considering precisely what succeeded in the Russian or North Vietnamese revolutions it is essential to bear in mind what succeeded in the partition of Ireland or in the prolongation of the life of the government of South Vietnam or in the establishment of the present government of Chile. Much of what is learned in revolutions stands in a most disagreeable relationship to the proclaimed values of revolutionaries (or, for that matter, of their opponents): electric drills through the kneecap as a disciplinary expedient in the oldest war of national liberation in Western Europe, the application of electrodes to the

---

* See Joseph de Maistre: 'The revolutionary current has taken successively different courses; and the most prominent revolutionary leaders have acquired the kind of power and renown appropriate to them only by following the demands of the moment. Once they attempted to oppose it or even to turn it from its predestined course, by isolating themselves and following their own bent, they disappeared from the scene ... In short, the more one examines the apparently more active personalities of the Revolution, the more one finds something passive and mechanical about them. It cannot be too often repeated that men do not at all guide the Revolution; it is the Revolution that uses men. It is well said that it has its own impetus' (quoted from Jack Lively, ed. and trans., *The Works of Joseph de Maistre*, New York 1964, pp. 49–50).

genitals in defence of the *mission civilisatrice* in Vietnam and Algeria. Such increments of practical learning have a way of turning out to be more permanent possessions than many of the more edifying novelties of social organisation. If initially unintended desirable consequences can be counted to the credit of revolutionaries, they cannot expect wholly to escape blame for initially unintended consequences of a less inviting character. Modern revolutionary history begins with the storming of a prison, but in the subsequent century and three quarters it has given ample and evenhanded sustenance to the jailing trades.

2. A consistently consequentialist assessment of revolutions establishes some definite dimensions of success (not always of a very attractive kind) and some dimensions of claimed success which are more contested either factually or conceptually. If the minimal condition for revolutionary success is the taking and keeping of state power, the least factually disputed attainments of revolutionaries are likely to be those most nearly related to the proven capacity to retain state power. The most enticing political hypotheses can get slain by the ugly little fact of defencelessness.[20] Military power is the best demonstrated idiom of revolutionary success precisely because it is a (causal) necessary condition for any such success. Stalin may not have left a country culturally ripe for the transition to communism; but he did (with assistance) win the Great Fatherland Patriotic War. A comparison between the economic base and social organisation of the United States and that of Russia late in 1917 and of their comparative military power today, even ignoring the German invasion of Russia during World War II, establishes an astonishing measure of success in generating military power. Whether or not it is true that capitalist societies need to spend a large proportion of their national income on armaments, it seems most unlikely that those societies which remain democracies have proved (or will prove in the future) politically capable of devoting such a large proportion of their wealth to increasing their military capability as has the Soviet regime. However prudent an investment it may be, this mode of achievement is not the most ingratiating of revolutionary performances, but a success it undoubtedly is — and so, *mutatis mutandis*, for China and North Vietnam and perhaps also for Yugoslavia.

A second idiom of achievement, more dependably ingratiating and hence more factually disputed, is that of economic development. Sympathetic assessments of the performance of the Soviet economy would emphasise its rate of expansion over decades in heavy industrial production, the rapidity of its educational, scientific, and technological development from the appallingly low level at the end of the civil war, and perhaps, once again, the formidable military apparatus which it has contrived to sustain. Less sympathetic assessments would concentrate on the problems of agricultural organisation and output, the inefficient utilisation of factors of production, the unimpressive volume and quality of products offered to individual consumers, and the distortions of official statistics as a basis for comparison with the economies of predominantly capitalist countries.[21] Similar but more acute difficulties of assessment arise in the case of the Chinese economy. Travellers' tales and sympathetic rapportage stress the striking improvements in urban diet and rural economic comfort and security since the early 1950s. They tend to contrast a picture of rural China as a society which has fundamentally solved the problem of how to improve steadily the economic welfare of its population with a picture, in particular, of rural India as a society moving relentlessly towards famine and ruin (the *terminus ad quem* of the capitalist road). But, as in the case of Russia, other analysts think differently.[22]

Far more complex and puzzling to assess than the sowing of dragon's teeth or the production of economic goods are questions of social organisation and cultural change. Here what is learned in revolution may quite often be not simply how to do something which others have already discovered ways to do, but how to do something which no one had previously envisaged doing at all. Yugoslavia, for example, more by ideological impulsion than by good judgement and not at all by initial intention, stumbled upon a form of productive organisation which is unique in the modern world.[23] There is ample doubt as to its merits or durability; but there are also grounds for viewing it as the sole vital reflection of a whole moral tradition or even, in extremis, as the sole embodiment of that tradition.[24] In the case of China, more formidably, there have been extraordinarily elaborate and persistent attempts to establish novel and much more egalitarian styles of organisation within the units in which men and women reside and work.[25] Furthermore, the development of these organisational novelties has been genuinely a product of (among other factors) collective social learning, not simply a matter of brushing in the initially imagined characters onto blank paper, as Mao incautiously suggested. But to say that it has been a product of social learning is not to imply that it has necessarily been at all a pleasant trip. One people's labour discipline is another people's brainwashing, and it is hard to tell for sure (at least without personal comparative experience) whether working for the east wind to prevail is really more consistently agreeable than working for Ford.[26] From the outside, the way other cultures learn readily seems like collective religious trance — to cite an old English adage, subjects for social anthropology begin at Calais. If we were they, we probably would not wish to learn that. But the proof of the learning is in the experience; and, while the Cuban New Man no doubt has elements of risibility, it requires great assurance to be certain that the Chinese are not learning something to their own advantage. Nor is the ritual expression of egalitarian social values by any means the only field in which the Chinese revolutionary experience has generated the learning of novel social strategies which, if they do in fact work, might represent major world historical achievements. In particular, the Chinese response in practice to the problems of relating city and countryside in a largely preindustrial society in ways which promote the benefit of both is something of a tonic in the face of the spreading panic at the economic parasitism and culturally blighting impact of the Third World city upon its rural hinterland. Mao's orientation towards industrial society has, as Maurice Meisner has well insisted, more in common with the utopian socialist phase of European political thought than it has with Marx's own bracing commitment in the medium-term future to the 'urbanisation of the countryside'.[27] But there is no reason in principle to believe that utopian socialists with state power at their disposal (a facility denied to Fourier or Cabet) might not hit upon some new advantages of backwardness[28] — at least in comparison with those whose conception of the demands of progress is more rigid. Even though their performance may as yet be more clearly delineated as ideological project than as concrete achievement, there seems good reason to believe that what the Chinese are now attempting in the relationship between their countryside and their cities, in economic complementarity, in education and in health provision, is a major advance on what other comparably poor countries have had the social insight or the political capacity to essay.[29]

3. The third point can be made with merciful brevity. Professional revolutionaries may be necessarily in some degree utopians. They may set themselves to achieve what cannot in practice (or perhaps even in principle[30]) be brought about. But this does not license those who are not themselves revolutionaries to adopt utopian standards of assessment when considering the achievements of revolutionaries. Those who are not utopians must deploy nonutopian standards, and for them the criterion of revolutionary success is not some form of social transcendence but simply doing better: a plain improvement on how matters would otherwise have been.* Yugoslavia has national problems and persisting regional economic inequalities (as has Great Britain). It bullies its intellectuals. A large section of its labour force

---

* Assessment of any such counterfactuals notoriously raises severe epistemological difficulties. Begging all the philosophical questions, the position assumed here is that politics consists in the choice between real historical possibilities. Very strong determinist assumptions would deny the conceptual reality (though not the experiential salience) of any choice at all: the history that has occurred was the sole and exclusive real historical possibility. Rejecting strong determinist assumptions does not involve denying that political choice is always choice between (probably not very clearly understood) limits; but it is likely to be based on the belief, as here, that in politics there are important choices to be made and that it is morally and intellectually desirable to recognise this. The technical problems of establishing the correctness of counterfactual arguments are severe. But assessing the correctness of counterfactual arguments is precisely what political judgement consists in. As historical actors we have no alternative but to attempt it as best we may.

The notion of one possible social state of affairs as superior to another possible social state of affairs could hardly exclude altogether considerations of utility. But it is intended here to be formally indeterminate as between evaluative theories which permit the comparison of possible social states of affairs. Any evaluative theory which precludes the possibility of such comparisons seems intellectually, morally, and practically reckless to a degree. In the practical judgment of historical possibilities intellectual sophistication has no privileged status before the facts. An elegant example would be Hu Shih's epistemologically sophisticated pragmatist arguments for the gradualist path in China under the Kuomintang. See Jerome B. Grieder, *Hu Shih and the Chinese Renaissance: Liberalism in the Chinese Revolution, 1917–37* (Cambridge, Mass. 1970), especially pp. 123–8. To be rigorously pragmatic, Hu Shih ended up on Taiwan.

works as migrants abroad and its domestic economy is heavily penetrated by foreign capital. Even the rate of growth of its economy is becoming a little sluggish. But even when all due allowance has been made for the frailties of real social history, a comparison between Yugoslavia in 1942 or 1930 and Yugoslavia today does *not* suggest failure in the interim. Even if its more distinctive social innovations prove to be something of a historical dead end (which is as yet far from self-evident), there are ample ways in which its title to have done better than could reasonably be expected has already been established. As the Cuba of the Soviet periphery, it has made friends along with its initial enemies. But in the end both the credit and the blame for its social balance sheet rest with the leadership of the country itself, and the net balance is clearly positive. In the same sense, there is much about modern China which is not endearing to most inhabitants of the West: its grim Puritanism, its sometimes demented political simplicity of mind. But what it was readily open for China to become in 1911 or 1919 or 1945 was not the United States of America or Sweden or Switzerland. In the end professional revolutionaries, like amateurs, make such history as they can, make revolution *faute de mieux*. In the universe of real possibilities, if not in the universe of fantasy which they have at times invoked, the Chinese revolutionaries too have to their credit towering achievements of social betterment. It is not a somehow logically or scientifically guaranteed truth that revolutionaries who can take and keep state power learn how to improve on the objective consequences of their predecessors' rule. But it does seem to be a fairly frequent conjunction.

When is state power likely to founder?

Whatever else they may constitute, all revolutions necessarily represent the debacle of existing state power within a more or less distinct territorial perimeter. But while the debacle of existing state power is plainly a necessary condition (and one of evident causal significance) for revolutionary success, it is some way from being a sufficient condition. A plausible minimum criterion for revolutionary success would be the destruction of existing state power and the effective establishment and maintenance of a new state power. Such a criterion has the advantage of providing a reasonably firm set of boundaries for the concept which it specifies and of edging the set of cases considered away from simple changes in governing personnel or transfers between different segments of the state apparatus, particularly from barracks to presidential palace. Any specification of the concept must be in some measure arbitrary and politically tendentious. This criterion for success at least avoids violence to ordinary linguistic usage, and such broad *tendance* as it does clearly imply can, on the whole, be deserted only at the cost of abandoning historical reality. Criteria of greater moral stringency do offer firmer obstacles to the temptations of euphemism. But the time to consider them more seriously in the context of practice will be after men have shown that the social world *can* be changed to that attractive a degree by revolutionary action. If we define revolutionary success in these terms — as the historical experiences of very many real men and women, living and dead — two points are immediately apparent. The first and probably the more important is that, even in the twentieth century, the century of revolutionary *success* par excellence, not very many states have in fact succumbed to the assaults of revolutionaries. The second is that even when revolutionaries have succeeded in destroying incumbent state power they have often not contrived to build a stable alternative with which to replace it, and even where revolutionaries have succeeded in establishing a new state power they have not always been substantially responsible for the demise of its predecessor. The lexical paradigm for revolution is a political analogue of domestic murder by overt assault. But, as they occur, revolutions are seldom purely domestic in their causation, and in many cases the destruction of the regimes which they eventually replace is in fact a service performed by other historical actors with little intrinsic interest in their domestic animosities.

The great bulk of revolutionary success in the twentieth century has been very intimately related to one or the other of two very undomestic processes: world war and decolonisation. The most striking anomalies in this pattern — the Mexican revolution (the most domestic of twentieth-century revolutions) and the Cuban revolution — serve on closer inspection to strengthen rather than to weaken the force of this observation. The Mexican revolution eludes the pattern by having commenced before the pattern was set. But after October 1917 the most domestic of revolutions will hardly escape international entanglements. After October 1917 residual revolutionary features of Mexican history on the whole have been contributions of the state power itself.[31] The Cuban revolution breaks the pattern more recklessly by delaying the making of its major external enemy and its indispensable external friend until it was too late for the former to act effectively against it without immediately encountering the latter. This is scarcely a tightrope which one could expect to see walked to the end twice. Even in retrospect the completion of the transition retains a distinct air of fluke; and it may be doubted whether it could have been walked to the end even once by an agent who was clear throughout what he was doing. It is not wholly inappropriate that the strategic lesson learned from the Cuban experience has been a form of ultravoluntarism.[32] If the damnedest things *can* happen, reasons for not trying to make them happen can hardly be presented as conclusive.

It is not obscure how involvement in a major war (and above all crushing military defeat), let alone effective foreign military occupation, could wreck the control of an incumbent government. The connection between the revolutions of 1917—19 in Central and Eastern Europe and in Russia and the impact of the First World War scarcely requires emphasis. The disproportion between the damage inflicted by foreign armies on the effective political

228

standing and repressive capacity of incumbent governments and the additional harm which the revolutionaries themselves were able to (or needed to) inflict can be left to speak for itself.[33] The survival of the Soviet revolution and the dramatic military recovery of the Red Army in the face of the Nazi invasion meant that revolutionary energies in the aftermath of the Second World War in Europe had to work themselves out in a considerably more effectively interventionist environment than that of 1918—21. But as in 1917—19, the closing years of the Second World War and the period which immediately followed saw a clear revolutionary advance: the successful establishment of one new revolutionary power in Yugoslavia, the attempt to establish at least one other (Greece), and levels of revolutionary mobilisation in two of the Western European nations (France and Italy) which had not been attained before in the present century and have not recurred since. The same years, also, of course, saw massive territorial conquest by the armies of the Soviet Union. Whatever the scope of its social and economic consequences, it does not serve the cause of either conceptual clarity or political honesty to consider the Russian occupation of Eastern Europe as any sort of revolution. But it is perhaps worth indicating one continuity between the Soviet-established governments in Eastern Europe and the self-established government of Yugoslavia: in both cases they owed the effective destruction of incumbent state power in the countries which they came to rule largely to the military efforts of others. The Yugoslavs managed, for the most part, to dispose of the instruments of this destruction (the German invaders) for themselves, while the other East European successor regimes did little but gratefully accept the gift of their foreign friends. But even in the Yugoslav case it is hard to imagine how they could have succeeded without the intervention of these initially unwelcome external aids.[34]

The drastic weakening of incumbent state power through heavy military defeat, and still more through foreign military occupation, is naturally a far more frequent occurrence during world wars than at any other time. But the insight that world wars provide ecologically favourable conditions for revolutionary mobilisation (precisely because they provide ecologically threatening conditions for the survival of even the less unfit powers) does less to illuminate the future than it does to summarise the past. A third world war, if it occurs, will undoubtedly be unpropitious for many incumbent state powers. But, despite Chairman Mao, it seems not only in lamentable taste but also arithmetically baffling to attempt to calculate how far it is likely to be propitious for any revolutionary triumph. To turn instead to the second major geopolitical process which has plainly favoured revolution in this century is certainly less depressing and may well also prove more instructive.

The largest single ebb of incumbent state power in the twentieth century has been the rolling back of the map of European empire in the last three decades. The beginnings of this process (except perhaps in the case of the

Indian subcontinent) are plainly very much involved with the Second World War, the collapse of the French Third Republic, the German conquests in North Africa, and the Japanese triumph in the Far East. Even in noncolonial territories in the Far East this aspect of the Second World War was clearly of great importance in the changing balance between revolutionary and counter-revolutionary power, though the precise significance of the relationship is still in some dispute.[35] In colonial territories, Vietnam, Indonesia, even Burma and Malaysia, the meaning of the impact is more unequivocal. Despite its impressive global scope the maintenance of colonial empire always depended upon a narrow balance of cost and advantage, repressive force and military liability. The Second World War tipped the balance decisively. Since 1947 the map of Western empire has rolled back apace, leaving only a last few feet, the imperial status of which is for the most part worse than ambiguous — colonies which lack an imperial overlord or colonists who no longer possess a metropolis to which they can, even resentfully, return: South Africa, Ulster, perhaps Israel. The only nineteenth-century empires which have lasted are either themselves now post-revolutionary states like the Soviet Union (the only European dynastic empire to survive the aftermath of the First World War with its territorial limits more or less intact), or else they belong to a distinctive set of white colonies of settlement, like the United States, Canada, and Australia. Both of these categories teach a lesson of sorts about the viability of empire, in neither case a wholly agreeable one. Both, of course, emphasise the advantage of a single territorial unit. But both also hint broadly that if you are an imperial power and you wish to avoid revolution within your own territory the best course is to pick a thinly peopled territory in the first place, one with its indigenes at a very low level of technology, and to kill off substantial numbers of them as you go along. The paradigm of imperial counterrevolutionary insurance is, in short, the commonwealth of Australia (most spectacularly the state of Tasmania); and the distinguished nineteenth-century American performance in continental clearance has been marred in retrospect solely by the fecklessness of its eighteenth- and early nineteenth-century importation of what was to become at least in part a domestic racial enemy. In the politics of empire comprehensive massacre is the only dependably final solution.

These somewhat strident considerations serve to make plain that what is precarious in imperial rule is not a relation between alien rulers and indigene ruled, but essentially a demographic ratio of very few rulers to very many ruled, where these groups are differentiated along essentially ethnic lines. In the immediate aftermath of the Second World War, it was easy for British or French colonial authorities to confuse the suddenly apparent frailty in imperial authority with the disagreeable conjunctures of the war itself — above all the Japanese invasions. The Fourth Republic subjected this conjunctural theory to the most rigorous practical tests, first in Vietnam and then in Algeria, and in due course paid for the privilege of doing so with its own life. The British, the French, the Belgian, and now the Portuguese empires have all been duly liquidated, though not because the Vietnamese experiment proved that colonial rebels in the postwar geopolitical context could thrash the armies of their colonial masters (an incorrect report of the result of the experiment in even the Vietnamese case). The empires have certainly been liquidated because they were structurally unviable; but the unviability was more political and economic than it was purely military. What Vietnam did show up to 1954 (and what all subsequent repeats of the experiment have essentially served to confirm) was that almost any colony, Guinea-Bissau as much as Algeria and Kenya, could be made to cost its masters, in the blood and domestic disaffiliation of conscript armies and in strictly economic terms as well, exorbitantly more than it could possibly be worth to them to retain it. The shift in the geopolitical context of colonial power was plainly important at the margin. Foreign arms and training and treasure and indeed political friendship were of some importance in Vietnam even at the beginning, and they certainly retained their importance there as well as in later cases like Algeria or Mozambique. But it is important to insist that the differences have come at the margin and that what they reveal is how narrow the balance of repressive capacity had always been. Just as success proved incremental in colonial expansion, so failure naturally proved to be incremental in colonial contraction, until in the end colonial rule came to seem even to the imperial powers to be an *economically* superannuated mode of promoting the foreign economic relations of the metropolis. The collaborative equation, as Robinson and Gallagher like to put it,[36] evidently required reworking. The shift in the external ecological context of colonial rule may have been crucial, but what it showed was that the frailty in colonial authority was not superficial but fundamental.

The changing international context and the restrictions on inductive generalisation

Revolution is far from being the only or even the most frequent manner in which the practical commitments of the state apparatus within a given territory can alter drastically and rapidly. More sharp and politically significant change probably occurs in the twentieth century as a result of shifts in the loyalty of the apparatus of coercion than as a direct consequence of any other political factor. Egypt, Libya, Ethiopia, Indonesia, Brazil, Iraq, Chile, Greece, Argentina, Peru, France, Portugal, and very many other countries have had their political history changed drastically in the last third of a century by the desertion of their incumbent regimes by the armed forces. The social consequences of such regime changes have been extremely varied, as have their immediate precipitants. In one or two cases it still seems possible that the longer-term consequences of the regime change may be aptly describable as revolutionary. But even in these cases it would be the

231

process of constituting the new political order which could be reasonably thought to merit the epithet 'revolutionary', while to apply this epithet in the majority of cases would be to debase the language of political analysis and to deplete its meaning. To insist that there have been few modern revolutions, even at the minimal criterion of revolutionary success, is not to deny that in recent years as in the more distant past many regimes have foundered. But to widen the scope for the analysis of revolution to take in all cases in recent years in which the janissaries have turned on the palace would mean taking in such historical heterogeneity as to preclude any but the most bleary analytical definition of the conditions for success or failure. By definition revolution implies the debacle of existing state power and the constitution of a new state power. In 1789 the symbolic homogeneity and historical depth of the European *ancien régime* was such that its demise at the hands of its own armies might have coined the modern conception of revolution even if no popular assault had taken place. But after 14 July 1789, the medium of the dynasty's fall had become part of its message, and the popular *journée* came to be considered as essential to the revolutionary process as the debacle of the dynasty itself. The forms of popular action in the twentieth century in most cases do not much resemble those of the Sansculottes' *foules révolution-naires*.[37] The long march has perforce a less hasty rhythm than the *journée*, and organisation through time is well understood as an instrumental precondition for its success. Modern revolution is a professional venture, and its professional exponents are very clear that it is better to arrive than to travel hopefully.

Very many regimes, then, may have foundered in the twentieth century, but rather few of them have foundered as a result of revolutionary action by significant sections of their civilian populations. Military coups have been successful by the score, but very few revolutionary attempts have attained even the minimal success of displacing the incumbent regime and replacing it with what proved to be a viable successor. Even among these, much the greater part have depended on two very drastic geopolitical processes, one of which (the collapse of colonial rule) appears to have very nearly run its course and the other of which (world war) although it may not be nearly improbable enough, is excessively difficult to assess clearly in the form in which it may occur in the future. Looking inductively at the twentieth-century record, it is thus tempting initially to conclude either that future revolutions closely resembling those of the first three quarters of the twentieth century are most unlikely to occur, or that if revolutions do occur in the future they are likely to follow the path of the Cuban revolution — a model the main theoretical property of which is thus in effect identified as its merciful improbability[38] and the ultra-voluntarism to which this improbability lends a slender licence. For a number of reasons, however, thinking inductively about revolutions is a very poor basis for predicting the probability of their future occurrence and the forms which they are most likely

232

to take.[39] Whatever it is likely to be like, the revolutionary future is least likely to be an exact replica of the past. In studies of voting, the fallacy of induction may be more often a philosophical error than an instance of empirical misguidance. In the study of revolution it is almost certain to prove to be both. Under the revolutionary sun new things happen almost all the time. The Cuban revolution may have had elements of a fluke; but it did, after all, occur.

Improving our understanding of revolutions and what we might hope to learn from doing so

There is good reason to believe that we cannot *know* about the prospects for future revolutionary success. We may certainly, however, attempt to tune up our sensibilities. It seems worth attempting to do so in at least two ways, first by examining briefly such augmentation of theoretical understanding as has come out of recent analysis of the revolutionary process,* and second by considering in an even more ad hoc fashion what sorts of regimes appear especially prone to revolutionary accident or what sorts of social relations seem to nurture the most vigorous and socially persuasive revolutionary entrepreneurship.

The most striking theoretical shift in the analysis of the revolutionary process has been the progressive abandonment of strictly reductionist ambitions by both sociologists and political scientists. The incessant oscillation between determinism and voluntarism characteristic of the theory of revolutionary action ever since the mid nineteenth century, and perhaps even logically implied by the union of theory and practice, has been transposed into the academic analysis of revolution. Even such a dogged reductionist as Chalmers Johnson has come to believe that the role of conscious action in revolutions needs greater emphasis.[40] In some measure we are all, it seems, voluntarists now. The awesome spectacle of the collapse of the French and later of the European *ancien régime* served to shape the imaginative responses of both revolutionaries and counterrevolutionaries and to impose upon their understandings of revolution an image of ineluctable process, an image which was to be of enormous practical importance in subsequent historical action.[41] Recently these hypnotic effects have begun to wear off, leaving a less providential and far more dangerously contingent world for revolutionaries and counterrevolutionaries alike. An understanding of revolution in terms of profound systemic crisis can only appear adequate where observers are reasonably confident of their ability to discriminate prospectively societies which exhibit profound systemic crisis from those which do not. In retrospect any post-revolutionary society exhibits the symptoms of pre-

* This brief discussion is not an attempt to do justice to a literature which has plainly had many heterogeneous intellectual purposes: it is simply a report on what appears to illuminate some possibly idiosyncratic but personally troubling questions.

revolutionary systemic crisis, even to the most casual historical analyst. But the ready identifiability of the symptoms, and the possibility of discriminating them with assurance from the superficial difficulties to which all regimes are liable, have come with the privilege of hindsight. If it had been clear that Cuba was in a state of so much profounder systemic crisis than the rest of Latin America, if foresight had been so easy, it is not improbable that the Cuban revolution would not have been permitted to occur at all, and it is virtually certain that the process of its occurrence would have been markedly different. The category of stable polity, once so prevalent in American political science, and so intelligibly extracted from American domestic political experience, never had much theoretical merit.[42] Exposing its practical limitations has enabled revolutionaries to provide not merely an index of how much more voluntarist real revolutionary political history has been in recent decades than it used to be in the bad old nineteenth century, but also an incentive to make it distinctly more voluntarist still. The Napoleonic zest for engaging and seeing what happens is highly infectious when something does happen, though it frequently ebbs fast in the face of effective repression.* In retrospect the objective probabilities for the success of any revolutionary enterprise are always low when evaluated in the context of all other revolutionary enterprises contemporary with it: revolutionaries lose far more battles than they win.[43] But sometimes revolutionary enterprises do succeed; and because it is as hard (if not harder) for revolutionaries as it is for political scientists to discriminate a stable polity from an unstable one when they confront it, it is not irrational for them to commit their forces if they attach a high enough value to their (highly improbable) success. The revolutionary wager may have more in common with that commended by Pascal than with most of those placed at Las Vegas. But, unlike Pascal's, it does sometimes pay off in this world.

The central focus of any analysis of the modern revolutionary process must be on the rising net reproduction rate and spreading geographical scatter of professional or semiprofessional revolutionaries in the modern world (seen essentially as rational actors, at least in their contention for state power), and on the environmental conditions which appear to militate for or against their accumulating committed popular support in this quest.[44] Analytical explanations of revolutionary allegiance have for the most part centred on the consciousness of individuals, seen as rational actors whose conduct is determined by perceived balances of prospective reward and risk, resentment and protection. Such accounts, whether cast in terms of relative deprivation[45] or of more explicit individual calculation,[46] can in principle have great explanatory power, but they require inordinate quantities of

* Much insight might perhaps be drawn from a sensitively conducted comparative inquiry into the varying success of the Comintern's initiatives in different settings and at different times: comparative views from the Comintern periphery. The extensive and valuable body of writing on the Comintern has tended, for understandable reasons of academic division of labour, to be either rather central in its perspective or else somewhat regionally parochial.

information if they are to be at all illuminating prospectively. Moreover, they require *types* of information which, although they may well be available to the intelligence services of a few major nations, political scientists in their private capacity are unlikely to be able to accumulate in time. A historian considering such theoretical explanations is apt to be struck by their descriptive viscosity, and to suspect that they have much in common with the retrospectively imputed rationality which any plausible and careful storyteller can always fictively impose upon known past behaviour.[47] A more promising line of thought is that sketched out by Charles Tilly in a series of interesting papers. Tilly's inquiries began with an examination of the changing nature of collective violence in mid-nineteenth-century France from an idiom of localist and communally defensive behaviour to an idiom predicated upon the expected responses of the central state apparatus.[48] From this, Tilly proceeded to consider, *inter alia*, the relationship between economic and social modernisation and the tendency of alternative polities to begin to build themselves within the territorial authority of legally sovereign states and to compete with their incumbent governments for dominion.[49] It is certainly helpful to think of the voluntarist contribution of professional revolutionaries at least since 1917 (and in some measure in the creation of secret societies and putatively revolutionary political parties for a century beforehand[50]) in terms of the attempt to create competing polities within sovereign states. The shift from legally recognised political organisation to illegal and armed political organisation may have depended more on the intolerance of incumbent power than on the initiative of revolutionaries themselves. But even conditions in which legitimate political activity was precluded from leading towards socialism — or indeed wholly forbidden — by no means always furnished environments in which such competing polities were successfully created *ex nihilo* or sustained at all handsomely. Both instrumental political calculation, and structural change in the society at large which permits the creation of novel competing polities, plainly require emphasis. But it is most helpful to concentrate rather more attention on a middle term: the capacity of a distinctive type of social organisation, the potentially revolutionary party or the party already in arms, to build itself in varying social, political, and geographical environments.[51] This focus escapes from nineteenth-century conceptions of revolutionary process without committing the analyst to any facile reductionist credo of more recent vintage. It cannot well hinder us and may well assist us to move from a fetishism of geography, tenurial relations, communal animosities, foreign sustenance, or counterinsurgent striking power towards the development of a more inflected sociological sensibility as to just what sorts of regimes and social relations are most likely to generate revolution. The predictive contribution of such a sensibility would be much less than that of an effective predicting machine, an invention which in this case there are good reasons neither to anticipate nor much to welcome. But we may reasonably expect our sensibilities to contribute to other ends than that of increasing our predictive skills; and we might at least hope in this instance that they might edify our social purposes and improve our taste in which polities we choose to succour and which we attempt to erase.

Guessing and refusing to guess the future

At this point prudence probably requires an analyst to throw in his hand. The more sensitive the analytical touch developed in the analysis of the revolutionary process, the more acute the feeling for all political order as an intricate balance of multifarious forces which are almost as difficult to identify with assurance as they are to calibrate with any accuracy, the stronger the grounds for supposing that an adequate discussion of the potentiality for revolution must inevitably be a discussion of the concrete particularity of individual societies at particular points in time. To offer cheap wisdom in this context is almost necessarily asinine. The appeal of a global strategic vantage point from which it would be possible to inspect the susceptibility of entire societies to revolution in terms of an essentially external ecology is plain enough for academic analysts, as it is for professional revolutionaries themselves. Virtually the only body of writing which seriously undertakes to attempt such a treatment arises out of Marxist analysis of the operations of capitalism as an integrated system functioning on a world scale: the law of uneven development (*plus c'est la même chose, plus ça change*), or more generally the theory of imperialism.[52] This body of writing has been of practical importance ever since 1917[53] because of its impact on the political strategies of the governments of the Soviet Union and later of China. But its theoretical importance lies rather in its attempt to take account of the geopolitical context of domestic politics,[54] one of the two aspects of the revolutionary process (the other being the dynamics of state power[55]) for which classical Marxism's focus on revolution as a product of endogenous socioeconomic struggle[56] has proved singularly ill equipped. Unfortunately, the merits of Marxist understanding of imperialism as a metaphysical gloss on the character of international power relations fail more or less completely to extend to an ability to generate particular concrete implications for the prospective experience of particular societies. Marxist analysts of imperialism proclaim the potential significance of the world market and the geopolitical context for revolutionary prospects in all societies with resonance and plausibility. But they scarcely contribute much as yet to telling us just where to look next and when. That geopolitical factors are of crucial importance to revolutionary prospects is evident enough; and there is no a priori reason why geopolitical factors should prove less predictable than the course of domestic social development. But the amateur eye is likely to be caught by how often geopolitical developments which in retrospect were so glaringly predictable as to seem almost inevitable come as a great surprise to those

236

most deeply concerned. Macintyre's insistence on the epistemological significance of the fact that we are all being surprised a great deal of the time[57] has obvious applications in international relations. What could have been more totally predictable in international affairs than the eventual formation of the OPEC cartel?[58] It is hard to imagine that there is often as much conjunctural necessity in major shifts in the world context of revolution as there was in the OPEC case; and the less the conjunctural necessity the less real the prospect for warding off surprises merely by more sustained study and reflection.

Further generalities are likely to be worth stating here only in the very crudest of terms. In the revolutions of the twentieth century there have been essentially two very different models: revolutions, as Tilly puts it,[59] from the centre outwards and revolutions from the periphery inwards. The classical nineteenth-century model of revolution moved politically from upheaval in the metropolis to political reconstruction throughout the society. Even in the case of the great exemplar, from 1789 onwards, the role of the metropolis as political cynosure does not adequately disclose where exactly the regime was broken;[60] and, in its pettier recapitulations, three glorious Parisian days might have very little provincial impact by the time their ripples had reached out into the more distant *départements*.[61] But the political image of the capital imposing its will on the countryside epitomised a type of political project which stretched from the Terror and its bedraggled *armées révolutionnaires*[62] through the careers of Buonarroti and Blanqui and the experience of the Commune to the reconsolidation of political control over Russia by the militarised working classes of Petrograd and Moscow (with their more or less reluctant allies), working their way out down the railway lines with firearms in their hands.[63] Even Engels judged that military technology and urban planning had rendered the tactics of mass urban uprising anachronistic in Western Europe by the late nineteenth century.[64] History has yet to prove him wrong. But, even if the experience of May 1968 was more of a cultural fête than a real threat to the viability of the French state (a contentious verdict in itself),[65] the capacity of such a fête to present itself even evanescently as a real political menace is plainly a reflection on the enduring strength of a particular cultural tradition. If in the future there are going to be any centrally engendered political revolutions in industrialised capitalist societies, it will be considerably less surprising if they prove to take place in societies where large sections of the industrial work force are ritually instructed in the merits of revolutionary practice than if they do so in, for example, the United States of America.[66]

The alternative paradigm for revolutionary process (pioneered in China — or perhaps even in Mexico), encircling the cities from the rural periphery, has been more widely emulated in recent decades. Countries plainly vary greatly in their susceptibility to this type of assault. Among the more susceptible groups of countries might be the few surviving colonial societies or societies perceived as colonies by a large proportion (not necessarily a majority) of

237

their indigenes or current inhabitants: South Africa, Israel. In the case of Ulster, even urban guerrilla tactics[67] have proved sufficient to pose a serious threat to the continuity of a regime in a war of national liberation which has not merely lasted intermittently for three centuries but which is now confined to a periphery in which the self-identified indigenes are in a demographic minority. The potential for ethnic mobilisation in any society which is seen to be governed by a group drawn from a minority is plain enough. But more careful consideration tends to emphasise the distinction between the now almost wholly abandoned colonial systems of the Western European countries or the United States, and these rumps of the colonial process. Mass popular challenge to the state power is more likely in a territorially extended Israel, in South Africa, or in Ulster over decades than in perhaps the commonwealth of Australia; but such popular challenge is not only sustained by assistance from outside the units in question, it is also plainly largely dependent for its prospects of success on the possibility of external pressure on the existing state power. The political situation of long-lasting immigrant communities which for a variety of reasons no longer perceive themselves as having a metropolis to return to is decisively different from the situation of those colonies from which France, Britain, Belgium, Holland, and now Portugal have elected to withdraw in such haste. The rhythms of decolonisation proved so hasty in substantial measure because colonies turned out to be economically such ready targets for revolutionary pressure. It was the colonial metropolis which would be politically priced out of the market. 'Colonial' societies which no longer possess a metropolis are less accessible targets, and the rhythms in which they could become 'decolonised' should prove rather less hasty — if indeed it turns out to be possible for them to be 'decolonised' at all. In these societies mass ethnic mobilisation will not be enough: some means of rendering the repressive purpose or capacity of the incumbent state infirm is also required.

A further group of societies in which peripherally initiated revolutionary efforts might prove effective in due course are those which combine a potentially sympathetic neighbouring power with a substantial section of their own peasant population trapped in distinctive tenurial relations (outlined by Donald Zagoria[68]) in family-size tenancy systems in areas with high literacy rates. Much has been written recently about the relationship between the degree and type of economic discontent and the capacity for political initiative among peasant populations.[69] Where endogenous peasant discontent is high and the social preconditions for peasant political initiative are widely satisfied, and where geographical circumstances facilitate external military and economic assistance, there are likely to be at least some prospects of building a revolutionary polity from the ground up. But even then the prospects for that policy to succeed in wresting state power from an incumbent regime will continue to depend to a great extent on the political and military capabilities of the regime itself. In the revolutionary process nothing succeeds nearly as well as success and nothing fails like failure.

One final point requires underlining. Unexpected major upheavals in the world economic,* political, and perhaps even military environment will continue to occur. The role of professional revolutionary will continue to draw more than ample recruits in many places because there will continue to be many regimes which invite enmity more intensely and more dependably than they are capable of punishing its expression. Armies will continue to shift their allegiance from the regimes which have created and nurtured them, sometimes with consequences far more drastic than their generals or colonels intend. It may be impossible (and it is certainly excessively difficult) to predict with assurance exactly where and when future revolutions will take place. But it is child's play to predict that *some* revolutions are going to take place at some time somewhere. And which revolutions *do* take place will subsequently have very sharp effects on which further revolutions take place after them. A revolution which was permitted to survive in Italy or France would change the politics of Western Europe. Even a revolutionary outcome in Portugal or Spain (perhaps a less improbable eventuality) would have its consequences. A revolution in Brazil or even Argentina would change the politics of Latin America. Nor is it self-evident that there will never be successful revolutionary enterprises within what is now the Soviet bloc. The collaborative equation in the present American 'empire' (the imperialism of semi-open economies) or the present Russian 'empire' (a neater geographical perimeter) is not a wholly stable balance; and even if it were wholly stable now, there could be no guarantee that it would still be so in ten years' time. We cannot tell which revolutions will happen: only that *some* undesignated revolutions are very likely indeed to occur and that some designated places are less likely to experience them than others. The close ties between geopolitical factors and internal revolutionary processes within a society, and the extent to which revolutionary practice involves mimesis and conceptual invention, taken together, imply one very clear conclusion. What we may be *certain* lies ahead for us in future decades of revolutionary experience is surprises.

---

* The cessation of growth in almost all capitalist economies, however temporary on this occasion in most cases, makes it natural for analysts to emphasise the causal weight of economic failure in revolutionary genesis, perhaps even to reassert its status as a putative necessary condition. A priori it seems plausible enough that revolution is less likely at the peak of an economic boom and more likely at the bottom of an economic trough. But since the middle of the nineteenth century, when Marx prophesied that the next revolution was as certain as the next trade cycle slump (Karl Marx, 'The Class Struggle in France: 1848–1850', in David Fernbach, ed., *Political Writings*, vol. 2, *Surveys from Exile*, pb. ed., 1973, p. 131), it is difficult to point to a single revolution which appears to have been largely generated by cyclical economic crisis. Thus far the renewal of capitalist economic crisis has served more effectively to resuscitate the plausibility of one major tradition of revolutionary theory to those already strongly inclined to credit it than it has to show that we can in any sense *know* there to be a strong connection between purely economic crisis and revolution. The fact that the meaning of revolutionary conflict and change (like the meaning of most political conflict, actual or potential) must be analysed largely in terms of class power does not imply that the genesis of revolutions can be at all adequately explained (let alone foreseen) by concentrating largely on economic factors.

Conclusion

10

Political obligations and political possibilities

Things goeing soe easy soe smooth and soe right in your house, I know you will excuse me that I went into the country to enjoy there an uninterrupted satisfaction and quiet in the contemplation of them. I hope they continue in the same course since my comeing away, and the zeale and forwardnesse of you your selves makes it needlesse for us without dores soe much as to thinke of the publique which is the happyest state a country can be in, when those whose businesse it is, take such care of affairs that all others quietly and with resignation acquisce and thinke it superfluous and impertinent to medle or beat their heads about them.

> John Locke to Edward Clarke (a Member of the House of Commons), 17 October 1690 (E.S. de Beer (ed.), *The Correspondence of John Locke*, Vol. IV, Oxford 1979, p. 148)

1. Do all human beings (or any human beings) have rational political obligations? Are political commitments, commitments either to sustain holders of political authority or to further socially extended shared human purposes, a necessary component of any rationally conceived human life? Or is it more appropriate to think of the moral acceptance of existing political institutions or the disposition to attempt to create what are presumed to be superior political institutions simply as an ideological condition, a state of belief and sentiment which we might (for example) be sure to have been causally generated but in relation to which no question of truth or falsehood, intrinsic validity or contingent error can coherently arise? These alternatives are certainly not exhaustive; but we may conveniently take them as a crude initial index of the *range* of disagreement about this issue which obtains at present.

Plainly they are extremely intricate questions, questions which raise with disconcerting simultaneity a considerable variety of issues and which can scarcely be resolved decisively except by the deployment of strong and perspicuous theories as to the nature of rationality, the character and epistemic status of human values and the causal possibilities of human social existence. Such theories are hard to come by. Indeed few are now confident that *all* of them are available even in principle. An intellectually prudent (if mildly ignominious) answer to the initial question would thus be simply:

243

'Who knows?' But even if no one today can cogently claim to *know*, perhaps it may be possible to shed a little light on the question of what it now makes sense to believe.

2. The question whether human beings do always or ever have rational political obligations can be read in many different ways. Is it in the first instance a question about the theory of *rational action* for historically constituted agents (men as they at any particular time are) — of what acts it is rational for them to perform or irrational for them to eschew? Or is it better conceived as primarily a question about the place of *obligations* within the moral life, our obligations being distinguished from the more extensive array of what we ought to do (what it would be morally becoming to do or morally ignoble to refrain from doing) by, perhaps, the superior precision or decisiveness of their incidence? Or is it perhaps better judged to see the core of the issue (an issue of practical reason) as a question of the relation between a conceptually given shape of individual existence and a problematic social and political context, or a (historically? morally?) given social and political context and a conceptually problematic individual existence?

How, precisely, should we see the relations between individual existence, the substance of society, the status of morality and the demands of reason?

For a political theorist to advance, offhandedly and incompetently, a purported *answer* to this last question would be merely ludicrous. But it is at least equally ludicrous for such a theorist to presume that the central issues of political theory can be seriously addressed without considering the truth or falsity of possible answers to this question. What I attempt in the present paper is to sketch from a number of angles the conceptual space within which the issue of the rationality and moral status of political duties arises. I attempt this with three ends in view: firstly to indicate some of the limits on what might *possibly* prove to be valid theories of political obligation; secondly, to bring home to political theorists the centrality of a range of epistemic issues the significance of which they have come increasingly to ignore; thirdly and more presumptuously to suggest that some of the implications within *political* theory of positions which philosophers have found attractive in the theory of ethics or individual practical reason are sufficiently startling to make it wholly implausible that they rest on an epistemically sound way of seeing the relations between individual existence, the status of morality and the demands of reason.

3. We may begin by considering the theory of rational action.

There are, very broadly, two ways of conceiving the relation between reason, individual human existence and social reality. One of these treats human rationality as essentially the guide of human *action*. It treats individual human agents as historically given, one by one, endowed with a set of existent purposes, dispositions etc. and with causal and factual beliefs

244

broadly instrumental to the realisation of these purposes and, insofar as they are so instrumental, epistemically corrigible in principle. Men as they historically are have their own reasons for acting and, whatever the rationality of their personal ordering of these reasons, it is not irrational for them to refrain from acting on the basis of reasons which *they* happen not to have. Rational action is action accurately calculated on the basis of materials, cognitive in part but more importantly motivational, which are indisputably historically *given*. The content of rationality is constrained tightly by historical contingency and by the immediacy of the context of action. On this view even the *fact* (if there can properly be said to be facts about the future) that he or she will regret an action does not necessarily now give an agent a reason for not performing it, where the regret is conceptually predicated upon his or her in the future incorporating into their 'subjective motivational set'[1] a component which is now absent from this. On some readings of the concept of personal identity this might be a paradox since the consideration (if he or she were in principle in a position to believe it true — and nothing in this case precludes this) that he or she will come to regret an action is not one which could be *absent* from anyone's subjective motivational set. An alternative reading of the concept of personal identity, that of Parfit,[2] makes the latter a far more serial concept and by doing so removes the air of paradox.

The second of these two ways of conceiving human rationality considers individual human beings from a more external point of view and focusses in the first instance on society as this exists and can (or could) be caused to become. What is rational for individual human agents is determined by what it is, over time and under comparatively ideal circumstances, rational for them to believe about social actuality and possibility. Epistemic rationality treats reason as intrinsically heuristic and, at least in some respects, teleological and resists in consequence seeing it as intrinsically and appropriately constrained by the immediate contingencies of historical visibility. It thus resists, also, imaginative encapsulation in the immediate importunities of agency. If taking a longer view improves visual judgement, epistemic rationality will insist on taking the longer view. In the context of action, deliberation must be relatively brisk. In the context of a human life as a whole (one of the natural units, though not of course the only natural unit, in which to seek to specify epistemic rationality) deliberation is less temporally constricted. A person who comes to see the human world and their own place within it differently is likely to feel differently about each and to have formed a correspondingly different subjective motivational set. Incorporating over time fresh epistemic elements may well result in seeing the human world and one's own place within it differently. Deliberation over an extended timespan may in fact be a process of *becoming* in some respects a different person.[3] In the light of epistemic rationality (its more ambitious theoretical exponents such as Williams's 'external reasons theorists' might

245

presume) historically given individual agents are trapped within an essentially myopic style of rationality and it is the task of reason to seek, insofar as the historical future will permit, to release them from this bondage by extending their powers of vision.

Exponents of each of these conceptions are inclined to regard exponents of the other as wildly superstitious. Exponents of the second see the first as implying an abject, if perhaps often inadvertent, sociological fideism or fatalism. They see its prevalence in capitalist societies as a compulsive product of the immanent logic of these societies, in the flattest of senses an *ideology*, within which the denizens of capitalist society are imaginatively imprisoned. Capitalist society constricts the social imaginations of its members and has come, over time, to articulate with immense theoretical power an entire conception of what it is to know or to have good reasons which renders this constriction of their social imaginations with chilling fidelity. They become the persons who they become because, increasingly, they cannot perceive what it is to be a member of a *society* of other persons. And because they cannot perceive themselves to be such they fashion themselves (and refashion their society) to make it less and less the case that members of a society is what they now truly are.

Exponents of the first by contrast, revelling in the theoretical power of the conceptions of the nature of knowledge and rationality to which they are heirs, see the second as superstitious in an altogether more literal sense, as a shadowy conceptual after-image of an irretrievably *past* style of thought or a confused echo of long-discarded false beliefs. What seems clearest at present — at least in historical perspective — is that each of these conceptions, whether or not it could in broad terms be epistemically vindicated in principle, is in the form in which it is believed today by most of those who do believe it, believed *as* a superstition, a surviving complex of belief, amply endowed, to be sure, with its own capacities for eliciting and sustaining credal loyalty or habit but lacking the (identified) power to vindicate its epistemic authority out of its own resources.

4. For an agent to have a rational obligation to X, it must be true both that it is rational for him or her to X and that it is obligatory for him or her to do so. (And so, *mutatis mutandis*, with rational moral duties, acts which they rationally ought to perform, etc.) It remains an important question in ethical epistemology how far all valid obligations or all acts which an agent ought to perform necessarily fall within the class of acts which it would be rational for him or her to perform (or even of those which it would be irrational for them not to perform).

There are grounds for doubting whether moral judgements can be validly represented as hypothetical imperatives.[4] But it remains importantly obscure what other forms of epistemic weight can be given to them[5] and implausible that *no* other form of epistemic weight can be given to them. If it simply is the case that all moral judgements are hypothetical imperatives, then the theory of rational political obligation can have no content apart from the theory of rational action for historical agents. If, on the other hand, judgements that an agent ought to act in a particular way are not correctly read logically either as hypothetical imperatives or simply as individual prescriptions without intrinsic epistemic weight, then it is still an open question how they relate to the theory of rational action. We have at present no firm reason for denying the possibility of a large measure of disjunction between the theory of rational action and the theory of what agents ought to do. There is evident conceptual space between the two theories (at the very least, whatever irretrievable moral damage is done to agents by biological mishap or defective socialisation).

The only way in which presumed moral obligations might be conclusively whipped in under the aegis of rational action is by constructing and vindicating a comprehensive theory of what, theoretically, ethically, factually etc., it is rational for men to believe. (Epistemic rationality does have authority over practical rationality, even though there is insufficient reason to presume *all* elements of epistemic rationality to possess authority over every element of practical rationality.*) Such projects certainly have a distinguished past; but it requires considerable optimism to expect them to have much of a future. And in relation to *political* obligations, it is unclear that there would be much point in pursuing them, even if they were realisable in principle. If the goal of a theory of rational political obligations is to clarify the content of pressing moral duties in relation to the political realm, in the hope that such clarification will give agents firmer reasons for honouring these duties, it is likely to be more profitable to proceed on the basis of the theory of rational action. If historical agents are to be provided with reasons for acting, they must be furnished with reasons which are reasons for *them*. How far the 'subjective motivational set' of a historical agent can be stretched is an explicitly historically contingent matter. What is certain is that it cannot be stretched further than it *can* be stretched. Rational political duty cannot prescribe any form of historical impossibility. (All theories of action must take men not so much as they are but as it is still causally *true* that they can or could be.) If political edification is to be a theoretically coherent activity, it must work upon (as well as with) the materials furnished by history.

5. There is a sharp bifurcation in theories of the nature of rational action between those which treat all reasons for an agent to act as what Bernard Williams has termed 'internal reasons'† and those which allow in addition for

---

* See e.g. S.I. Benn & G.W. Mortimore 'Introduction', p. 5 in Benn & Mortimore (eds.), *Rationality and the Social Sciences*, London 1976. It is not possible, simply by so deciding, instantaneously to change one's beliefs. But, given a little time, most human beings have (and on occasion exercise) the power to alter their beliefs in what they expect to prove an agreeable direction.

† Williams, 'Internal and External Reasons', in Ross Harrison (ed.), *Rational Action*, Cambridge 1979,

the theoretical admissibility of what he calls 'external reasons'. 'Internal reasons' theories treat it as a criterion for an agent to be validly said to have a reason to X that Xing be connectable by rational deliberation to what Williams terms the agent's 'subjective motivational set'. 'External reasons' theories, seeing rationality as essentially *self*-justifying and *self*-explanatory[6] elect instead to treat the issue of reasons for acting independently of an analysis of the agent's historically contingent beliefs and sentiments. Williams's dismissal of the capacity of 'external reasons' to figure in the theory of rational action is convincing. But he has no occasion for attempting to illuminate the persisting appeal of 'external reasons' theories in the analysis of practical reason. For our purposes the grounds for this persisting appeal are of considerable importance.

One way of seeing the difference of opinion between exponents of the two types of theory is as a slightly confused disagreement as to how best to represent or model the process of deliberation. Internal reasons theorists insist (very cogently) that nothing can be a reason for an agent to act but what has at the time of acting *become* one of his or her reasons. (Williams gives an extremely clear account of the sense in which this must be true.) External reasons theorists by contrast stress the key importance in human practical reason of future contingencies of deliberative energy and patience, experiential learning and external advice or persuasion. They treat the goal of practical reason as the identification of conduct which one could under optimal conditions rationally be led to adopt and they resist with great tenacity a conception of rational agency as essentially given by beliefs and sentiments which are already fully present at the commencement of the agent's deliberation. Rational action is action which lies at the full limit of an agent's rational grasp, not action the merits of which are all but compulsively present to the agent as soon as he or she begins to deliberate. On the basis of an internal reasons theory, rational agency is conceived of as a matter of judging accurately on the basis of historically given materials and by the (relatively speedy) application of historically available powers. On the basis of an external reasons theory rational agency is conceived, rather, as a matter of judging in terms of what is in principle historically *accessible* to the agent, taking advantage of *all* the aid which can be derived from the advice of others, from individual learning and from the passage of time. (Deliberation is a heuristic process* and is best undertaken in a patient and not in a hasty manner.) Internal reasons theories treat coming to espouse a reason as an index of already incipiently possessing it. (Their key conception is that of an agent's motivational susceptibility.) External reasons

---

p. 17. In what follows I have deliberately abused Williams's terminology to point up what seems to me the theoretical *motivation* of at least some external reasons theorists.

* Williams himself emphasises the importance of this point (op. cit., esp. pp. 20, 25). The generous role which he allots to the imagination and the emphasis which he lays upon the intrinsically indeterminate and heuristic character of rational deliberation gives the 'external reasons theorist' all the licence that he or she could reasonably require.

theorists, because they see that good reasons can be (and often are) brought from the outside presume that what makes them good reasons is not the initial motivational susceptibility of the agent or the intrinsic potentialities embodied in this susceptibility (which are, presumably, very varied indeed) but rather the eventual motivational susceptibility attained, as thus actualised, perhaps largely as a result of the persuasions of others. Their key disagreement is over how far good reasons for acting emerge from within a self and how far they are conferred upon the self by the more or less benign assistance of others.

Internal reasons theories thus model deliberation as operating essentially *from* given motivations. External reasons theories by contrast model it essentially as operating *towards* accessible conclusions. Exponents of internal reasons theories may or may not be concerned to improve the cognitive prowess of human agents. But exponents of external reasons theories will in almost every case prove to be eager to enhance the *visual* capacities of historical agents. Characteristically, the role allotted to imagination in the two types of theories will differ accordingly. In internal reasons theories it will be in essence a device for efficient instrumental calculation of the implications of existing sentiment and belief. In external reasons theories it will be closer to a heuristic device for the construction through time of a more acceptable self, a device for *forming* sager sentiments and beliefs. Williams's discussion makes it clear that an internal reasons theory need not (and should not) deny such an extensive role within deliberation to the imagination, to moral experience or even to the advice of others. But it is perhaps worth underlining the connection between the readiness to allow such wide licence to the imagination within the theory of rational action and the holding of a strong conception of personal identity, one which sets much store by the integrity of the personality and sees its site firmly as the human life cycle as a whole. A more serial or conceptually weak conception of personal identity,[7] a more restrictive attitude to the place of the imagination *within* rational deliberation, a more drastically sceptical attitude to incorporating the advice or persuasions of others, even heuristically, into the content of what it is rational for a historically given agent to do, a commitment to conceive all motivation as substantively egoist in character, any or all of these, set in apposition to an internal reasons theory will open up a large gap between the conception of rational action which they sanction and those which virtually any exponent of an external reasons theory would wish to defend. Williams's charge that exponents of external reasons theories, however unwittingly, are taking their stand on an essentially unintelligible philosophical psychology is convincing. But, however infelicitous their theoretical strategy, there is no reason to suppose them to have misjudged the force, direction or prevalence of the wind into which they are seeking to steer.

It is apparent that these differences of view are crucial for any conception of rational political duty. If, in order to prove an act to be a rational duty, it is necessary to prove that this act is one for which an agent *must now* be in full possession of a reason to perform it, the chances of vindicating the rationality of most political duty seem very slight indeed. (The *point* of vindicating its rationality also becomes somewhat obscure. Human beings either will be in full possession of it or they won't: and, either way, that will be that.) If, however, in order to prove an act to be a rational political duty it is merely necessary to establish that the act in question is one which an agent *could*, under relatively favourable heuristic conditions, come to grasp that he or she possessed a reason for regarding as a duty, the venture looks less forlorn. If the rational deliberation which specifies what (if any) rational political duties historical agents possess is conceived as extended over protracted periods of time and as involving the persuasions of other persons as well as the calculations of the agent in question, motivational susceptibility becomes decidedly more elastic. It is still true that the ledge along which such benign 'advisers' have to make their way is the motivational susceptibility through time of the agent concerned. No doubt the going will sometimes be distressingly slow and the distances attained often derisorily short. But at least the enterprise itself is not evidently incoherent. It might well be true that there could be no *rational* duties for agents which are wholly beyond their motivational susceptibilities. (If so, there would be an important gap between the theory of rational action and the theory of what ought to be the case.) What is evident is that at any point in history many or even most such rational duties may well lie some distance beyond the existing tastes of agents.

6. In the tradition of western political thought what has distinguished political obligation from other human obligations has not been its immediacy and practical salience in everyday life. Rather, it has been a certain primacy of entitlement on the part of holders of political authority, a primacy which empowers them legitimately to constrain human liberty and even to take human life on behalf of the interests entrusted to their charge,* and which enjoins those who are subject to such authorities to commit not simply their propensity to social submission or to the living of an orderly and decent life but all purely *personal* capacities and concerns† to sustain these authorities

---

* Radical individualist theories of political authority (such as that, in some interpretations, of Rousseau), which deny the possibility of political adults alienating their political wills, institutionally locate political authority at the level of a participatory and democratic assembly. (See e.g. Carole Pateman, *Participation and Democratic Theory*, Cambridge 1970 and *The Problem of Political Obligation*, London 1979). In these cases the holders of political authority are all political adults, acting through their own sovereign institutions.

† Political duties, whether or not they are owed to specific holders of political authority, do not necessarily override all other obligations. (Cf. recently, Richard K. Dagger, 'What is Political Obligation?', *American Political Science Review*, LXXI, 1, March 1977, 86–94; Burton Zwiebach, *Civility and Disobedience*, Cambridge 1975. John Locke's *Two Treatises of Government* is one classic account which explicitly takes this view.) Other duties, to God or to other human beings, may well have prior claims. The distinctive primacy of entitlement of political authority can be reconciled with such an admission (if at all) only by treating any other type of claim which is accorded priority over it as a concern which is *not* purely personal in character.

in the face of challenge. Not only is the right to take life one of the marks of sovereignty;[8] but the duty to *give* life, should it be necessary to do so, in order to sustain or generate a political order is one of the central duties of citizenship. It has never been easy conceptually to reconcile this primacy of entitlement with the impoverished theoretical idiom of egoistic rationality which dominates modern capitalist political theory, in lineal descent from the political theory of Hobbes. The ideological dominance of explicitly or implicitly contractarian individualism has always given, as David Gauthier has recently insisted,[9] a misleading account of the motivational basis of the solidarity which renders capitalist society politically and socially viable. But, of course, the psychic materials which render a society ideologically viable do not necessarily furnish a rational theory of obligation. (A theory of obligation in which ideological conviction in itself necessarily constitutes a sufficient basis for the *rational* acceptance of obligation must rigorously relativise both rationality and human value to the beliefs and sentiments prevailing amongst a particular population and thus deny the meaningfulness of any standard of intrinsic human value.)

7. If political obligation is conceived as a logical correlate of legitimate state authority, it is easy to see why it should be thought to accord the latter a primacy of entitlement. (This is what states now require.) It is also easy to see why political obligation might seem a paradigm example of an *obligation* and not simply a mere instance of what morally ought to be done. A perspicuous distinction would still need to be drawn between legitimate and illegitimate state authorities. A legitimate state authority would be a state authority the content of whose public commands constituted the political obligations of its subjects. (*All* such commands entailed that subjects were obliged to execute them.) Anarchists presume the very idea of such a state authority to be incoherent;[10] but it is perhaps sufficiently despondent simply to note how unlikely one is to encounter such an authority in practice.

Exactly what the commands of a political authority (legitimate or otherwise) in fact *are* is not always clear. But political theorists have not erred in supposing that what commands require of an agent to whom they apply is on the whole clearer than what (if anything) moral considerations require of such an agent. The traditional problem of political obligation, at least since the seventeenth century, has been conceived essentially as a problem about the relation between the demands of reason and the obligatory force of the legitimate commands of a legitimate public authority. With increasingly individualist conceptions of rationality and a corresponding scepticism about the specification of value at the level of society or polity as a whole, this problem has come more and more to seem one which can be 'solved' only by fiat or myopia. Anarchism may often be a silly and pernicious political mood; but if political theorists were correct in judging that this is the central problem which requires a solution, anarchism, in presuming it insoluble,

251

might well be the most realistic political *theory* extant. But the matter of political mood is important; and the silliness and perniciousness of anarchism as a political mood gives a sound clue that this way of conceiving the problem is mistaken.

Obligation is an overbearing word and irrationality is a wounding charge. It does not require much theoretical ingenuity, in the face of the chaos of contemporary ethical theory, to repudiate the view that all individuals, irrespective of their contingent sentiments and values, have particularly conclusive and determinate duties in relation to the political realm, duties so clear and conclusive that it would necessarily be irrational for them to deny these. What is more likely to be true is that most men do have better reasons than they register for recognising the existence of pressing moral duties on their part towards or within the political realm. (To recognise the existence of a duty in this sense entails the agent having *a* reason for executing it. Agents may also, of course, have other overriding or countervailing reasons of an immense variety of different sorts for not executing it.)

It might also be true (if some clear sense can be given to such claims) that even men who do not themselves possess reasons for recognising such duties (because *they* are so heartless or so obtuse) nevertheless *ought* to act in accordance with them — because what ought to be done is *not* relativised to the contingent psychological properties of individual agents.

Of these two instances it is certainly the first which is of immediate practical importance. (Human beings simply are the way they are; and we — and they — must make the best we can of their being so.) Such duties are certainly not 'obligations' because their scope is especially easy to assess or their content impossible rationally to dispute. On the contrary, they are often (perhaps usually) more than a little elusive in their demands and it seldom requires much prevaricatory skill to question whether they really do *require* exactly one action rather than another (or indeed any *action* at all). If they are to be termed obligations at all in many instances they can only be so in the vestigial sense in which everything which we ought to do is an obligation;[11] and if they are to be termed rational obligations in any sense they can be so only insofar as they are connected with reasons which are potentially such for men as they are and which are not, when so connected, *effortlessly* overridden by other countervailing reasons.

It seems best, accordingly, to leave the term 'obligation' simply as a part of the name of the problem to be addressed and to employ elsewhere the term 'duty'. A political duty is a manner of acting in relation to the political realm of which it is true that an agent *ought*, *ceteris paribus*, to implement it if he or she can do so. A rational political duty for an individual agent is one which that agent has good reason to believe that he or she ought, *ceteris paribus*, to perform. (The *ceteris paribus* clauses are, obviously, important.)

What is crucial about political duties is not what we call them. (We can perfectly well, for the purposes of the present argument, term them political drudgeries or political rituals, if we prefer to do so.) It is certainly, however, preferable *not* to call them by a name which has misleading implications. What is crucial about them is whether or not there are pressing moral grounds for performing them. If there *are* such grounds, it will also of course be important how exactly 'pressing moral grounds' stand, psychically and epistemically, in relation to the other sorts of reasons for acting which human beings possess. It will also be important, if there are such grounds, to inquire how far there are conceptually determinate procedures for identifying the *content* of political duties.

I argue below that there neither are nor could be conceptually very determinate procedures for identifying the content of such duties a priori (though there is a certain range of considerations which is always relevant to the assessment of their content). Whether this is a surprising claim will depend on one's conception of the character of practical reason.[12] (What we ought politically to do is a question in practical reason.) But even if it were unconvincing as a claim about individual practical reason in general, I argue that the systematically contingent character of the political realm makes it plainly valid in relation to politics.

8. Whether men as they historically are do have rational political obligations depends on how rationality is appropriately to be construed and on what history has done to the men in question.

Possible constructions for the scope of rationality extend over the full range from those reasons of which men at a time have full present possession (casting them as passive prisoners of their experiences) to those reasons to which men as they are have historical access under optimal future conditions. The distance between the two poles of this range is a product of the time allotted for and the degree of external 'assistance' permitted within the process of deliberation, as well, no doubt, as of the personal optimism or pessimism of the theorist. (See 5 above.)

For our purposes the key difference may be seen as lying between a conception of duties which it *must* be irrational for historical agents exactly as they are at any particular time to deny (rationality as compulsion) and a conception of duties which it could be rational for them to acknowledge (rationality as permission).

Duties which it *must* be irrational for an agent to deny are few and far between in politics. (It is a stimulating exercise for the historical imagination to recapture how and why it should ever have been possible to see (and perhaps even *feel*) them to be so prevalent.)

Duties which it *could* be rational for such an agent to acknowledge may well be as extensive as anyone could wish; but at first sight they appear alarmingly subjective in character. Duties of the first kind show impressive epistemic solidity; but unfortunately history has been sparing in their distribution. Duties of the second kind have certainly been more promiscuously distributed; but they appear distressingly devoid of epistemic weight.

Inquiry into the existence and character of rational political duties must be largely inquiry into the question of how much epistemic weight can in principle be accorded to duties of the second kind — how far they can be epistemically bulked up. Characteristically it will take the form of inquiry into what men could have good reason politically to do (and could justifiably come to believe that they have good reason to do) — not an inquiry into what it *must* be irrational for them to deny that *they* have good reason to do.

One hope which has been much held out in relation to political duties (not least by holders of political authority) is that these should possess particular determinacy of content (you *owe* exactly what you owe and not anything else) and perspicuousness of incidence (it would always be clear what you owed and when and to whom you owed it). It is impossible to see how this conception can rationally be sustained today.

At the very least what men have a rational duty politically to do must depend on what for better or worse can be caused to occur by their actions. The intrinsic vagueness of social causality and the exceedingly poor visual opportunities from which human agents must seek to assess the relevant causal context of political actions together mean that no human political agent ever knows himself or herself to have all the relevant causal characteristics of a political action thrust upon them.

A second hope which has been entertained is that political duties should display a certain priority of public entitlement over purely personal interests and that they perhaps should be identifiable in comparative detachment from the personal sentiments of individuals. The force of the first of these considerations is obvious enough. It is not a good defence for having chosen to become a Quisling that one sets a high regard on the values of the purely private life. Even in the light of less explicitly *political* conduct, setting a high regard on the values of the purely private life is not in all (or perhaps even in *any*) historical circumstances evidently a self-justifying moral choice. It is not an accident that belligerently individualist moral theories should be hard to reconcile with any such priority of public over private entitlement. Such theories can be set out with great philosophical panache and it would be most imprudent to presume that all of them must be irrational (tacitly self-contradictory). What seems a comparatively safe bet is that any such theory will prove on close examination to be either damagingly discreet about some of its premises or theoretically excessively high-handed. (A striking example of the second would be Robert Nozick's conception of individuals as the bearers of rights without explicitly social responsibilities — though with the general duty, of course, not to violate the rights of other individuals.[13]) A suitable slogan for the present essay would be 'no *individual* rights without *social* responsibilities'.

I argue, then, that we must reject:

1. A conception of the *type* of theory that a theory of political duty must or can be as one which presents political duties as uniting simplicity, conclusiveness and practical directiveness.

2. A conception of the *scope* of a theory of political duty which sees it as centred on the commands of states and as divided up centrally between a theory of why it is appropriate to obey the legitimate commands of legitimate states and a theory of when (and perhaps how) it is appropriate to seek to displace illegitimate holders of authority in legitimate states or, more ambitiously, illegitimate states in their entirety.

1. must be rejected because valid theories of such a kind are necessarily unavailable. No such theory could be constructed.

2. must be rejected because we now stand at too great a distance from the historical trajectory which first made it seem a valid way of conceiving the issue[14] and have discarded too much of the credal background to this experience to make our retention of this conventional assumption any more than a superstition. States and individuals remain important conceptual units within this domain of practical reason, but it is a purely contingent matter just how heavily states should weigh in relation for example to kin groups or ethnic groups or communities or classes or ideological groupings or state alliances or even the species as a whole, present or future. It is not difficult to see why one should often be proffered utilitarianism today in lieu of a theory of political duty. Not only is it, at least on initial inspection, a magnificently *strong* theory, it is also splendidly simple in outline, marvellously uncluttered by superstitious commitment to historically inappropriate social or political foci. As a moral theory it might well be false; but at least it will scarcely be simply *historically* out of date.

9. If what has rendered capitalist society ideologically viable in recent centuries has been (as Gauthier — and before him Hegel — have insisted) love and patriotism rather than the rational pursuit of individual economic utility, there is every reason to wonder whether we do today possess any coherent theory of rational political duty. States in practice today succeed in enforcing a level and scope of citizen compliance greater than ever before in world history.[15] It is virtually a truism of modern international law that any human being now alive and legally adult owes political obligations to some state authority, in most cases in virtue of citizenship but in the uncomfortable remainder simply as a consequence of residence or even temporary location. All modern states, whatever their official ideological affiliations, hold extremely strong and confident doctrines of their primacy of entitlement to the obedience of their citizens or subjects. Yet it may well also be true that we are today in a position to recognise clearly the blatantly intellectually inconsequential character of all the theories of the rational status of these claims to authority. Never before, over the world as a whole, have political duties (duties to comply with the dictates of state authority or

duties to sustain, even at great personal cost, an alternative set of contenders for the exercise of state power) been so widely and so effectively touted. Yet never before has it been so easy to discern (so much within common intellectual view) how intellectually perfunctory are the grounds offered for crediting the force of these duties. Can it really be the case that this overwhelming tide of sheer political power — capacity to cause men to act as instructed — lacks any morally or rationally coherent theoretical basis? (It is clear that it could be — and very plausibly is — the case that such morally and rationally coherent basis as it has is very much more substantial in some sites than it is in others).

10. In considering the possibility that political duty might *in general* lack such a basis it is important not to be too ready to take as a paradigm instance of political duty the duty to obey a legally valid (and not intrinsically pernicious) law within one's own society: for example the duty to eschew shoplifting from Marks and Spencers. There may be many sound reasons (prudence, fairness, immediate utility, etc.) for obeying such a law (as, *in extremis*, there might also well be overriding reasons for flouting it) which are wholly unconnected with *political* duty, and which leave the rational agent (however tightly constrained rationally to eschew the offence in question) radically uncommitted on the issue (for example) of the incumbent state's claimed primacy of entitlement. Mild counterfactual reflection on how life would now be if Marks and Spencers were unable to rely on the enforced property law of modern Britain will not necessarily succeed in engaging with the issue of *political* duty at all. In the sixteenth and seventeenth centuries, the heyday of theories of political obligation, such theories were primarily addressed conceptually to agents who were engaged in considering whether to sustain or to desert or to assail the holders of state authority in circumstances in which their decisions might be expected to have some effect upon the prospective fate of these authorities. To attempt to link such practical choices to a universal conception of what it is rational for human beings to do is to seek for (though not necessarily of course to run much risk of *attaining*) very great imaginative breadth and penetration. At the least it is to attempt to take seriously Sheldon Wolin's insistence that it is a defining characteristic of political theory that within it the separate roles of human beings (and the discrete rationalities in terms of which these roles are likely in large measure to be specified) be 'surveyed from a more general point of view'.[16]

11. Rational political duties, if such there be, are answers to the question what politically is to be done, political actions which individuals have reason to perform (though not necessarily actions which it would be *irrational* for them not to perform) and which they ought to perform. What rational political duties (if any) men have is a prior question to the question of what

orders they have good reason to obey. It is necessary to set aside at the start the superannuated view that, politically speaking, what was to be done was for most people what they were told. (The theoretical problem of political obligation was, then, the problem of explaining *why* for the most part this was what was so.) The problem of political obligation (as here conceived) is the problem of how to see the relations between three types of consideration: the nature of rationality, the character and epistemic status of human values and the causal possibilities of human social existence. It is the problem of how to see the intellectual *shape* constituted by the intersection of these three dimensions of conceptual constraint and analytical jeopardy. Political obligation is the central issue in political theory (what do *we* owe states or political agencies and how should their actual or potential properties affect our actions?). However far from the encouragement of activism a political theory may be, it is irretrievably a part of the theory of practical reason, the theory of what men in practice have good reason to *do*. Even if the theory of value espoused is one which sets *otium* firmly above *negotium*,[17] the political theory which it implies is still a theory about what to do with a man's life: for instance that the way for a man to live is (in part) to keep as far away from 'politics' as possible.

12. It may help to consider the treatment of political obligation within one of the most carefully developed recent accounts of the theory of practical reason. In his article, 'Political Obligation', Professor R.M. Hare identifies political obligation not as a species of the genus 'obligation', but as a sub-species of moral obligation,[18] comprising those moral obligations which lie upon us because we are citizens of a state with laws.[19] (No very explicit account is offered of what difference it may make for the state of which one happens to be a citizen to be one of dubious legitimacy. If Hare still holds to the account of the nature of legitimacy which he gave in 'The Lawful Govern-ment',[20] it is hard to see how this omission could be rectified within the bounds of the theory as presented.) The moral obligations in question are those of (in general) obeying the laws of one's polity, taking part in its political processes in order to improve these laws (should they need improve-ment) and defending them where they need no improvement.[21] In addition Hare makes it clear that such obligations can be expected to extend to defending the society itself, should this be attacked,[22] and, on occasion, to disobeying the law in the special circumstances 'in which there is a moral justification for crimes or acts of rebellion'.[23] The central example of such an obligation, to which Hare devotes much of his paper, is the general prin-ciple that we ought to obey the law,[24] political obligation amounting essen-tially to those obligations which 'arise only because there is a state with laws'.[25] On the basis of a simple model of 'the political situation',[26] Hare demonstrates that the existence of an enforced law[27] alters the conditions within which an individual considers the moral eligibility of a discrete action

by altering the consequences which this action is likely to bring about. In accordance with his general theory of morality, Hare treats political obligations as universal prescriptions, mitigated in their prospective arbitrariness by an egalitarian regard for consequence. His view is developed with exemplary lucidity and is especially illuminating for the close and perspicuous connection which it displays between the conception of political duty advanced and the general metaethical theory on which it is presumed to rest.

13. The main positive conclusion which Hare draws is the breadth of the range of moral responsibilities which falls upon citizens in virtue of the existence of an enforced set of laws (a consideration underlined, from a very different standpoint, for example, by Thomas Nagel in his criticism of Nozick's equation of taxes with forced labour).[28] Setting aside the status of the moral theory itself, what is least convincing in Hare's treatment is the very simple conception of citizenship, polity and legality which it employs and the heavy emphasis on the horrors of anarchy as the counterfactual alternative to a particular existent set of laws, duly observed. It is an admittedly preliminary conceptual analysis of political duty of a singularly law-abiding and politically unimaginative character. The public laws enforcing hygiene as a prophylactic against especially deadly and infectious illnesses (the main example explored) are certainly, as Hare's editor noted to him,[29] more plausible candidates for objective specifications of the public good than the property laws (and the historical allocations which derive from these) of any society in the world today. The additional considerations which Hare musters as to the consequential demerits of theft are cogent enough in themselves. But they are also remarkably restricted in scope and fall discernibly short of vindicating the moral authority of any set of laws allocating property. Taken with the conception of citizenship as participation in a public life which may well in practice have the consequence of improving the public laws of the society, they suggest that Hare's tacit model of 'the political situation' is both more elaborate and historically more specific than he contrives to express.

14. In a society in which there are indeed laws (however erratically these may be enforced) but in which in addition most members are plainly subjects rather than citizens, persons whose participation in defending state authority is certainly welcomed (and may indeed be exacted) but who are decidedly discouraged from seeking to emend the laws or to modify the manner of their enforcement in a direction less inimical to their own interests, it is difficult to identify a theoretically or humanly attractive content for political duty in Hare's terms. (Such societies have been extremely frequent in the past and they remain common enough today.)

There are many actions which one ought to perform and in relation to which, if one were to perform them, it would be true to say that one was 'obeying the law'. But in some polities there might be singularly few such actions which one ought to perform *because* to do so was to obey the law. It is difficult to disentangle such issues very successfully without at least covertly invoking a distinction between more legitimate and less legitimate polities. Given the properties of many states, now as throughout recorded history, there is no plausibility whatever in the recently canvassed view[30] that an understanding of the concept of social obligation in itself entails an acceptance that citizens or subjects have a prima facie duty to obey all incumbent state authorities.

15. If political duty is conceived in the first instance as the sustaining and improvement of the public institutions of a historically given society, *because* of the consequences of these institutions for fellow human beings, a theory of political duty could be as individualist and as consequentialist as Hare's* without being so imaginatively constricted in its sense of alternative social possibilities and so narrowly focussed on obedience to public law and the dictates of state authority. Our moral duties are certainly duties to our fellow human beings (as well perhaps as to ourselves). Precisely what role state authority or public law (as these actually exist) should play in specifying their content is a highly contingent matter, history having been as it has and human society today being as it now is. However ample such a role might be within a liberal democratic polity of whose social and economic structure there were unequivocal grounds for approval, it would still be true that in many other places and at many other times the role might be very narrow indeed — might even be comprehensively absent. Hare's conception of political obligation seems over-informed by (a tolerably complacent view of) the experience of this island in recent decades.

Yet is there in fact any conceptually reliable method of eluding such imaginative constriction and developing a conception of political duty which is temporally and geographically more cosmopolitan? More pointedly, can an *imaginative* exploration of alternative social possibilities escape the danger of proving simply whimsical and credulous? Hare's view may be imaginatively parochial. But it might well be thought by many to be based upon a relevantly firm sense of the properties of the parish in which he happens to reside. Being determinedly consequentialist in orientation, it also takes very seriously the intractably historically *given* character of political duty, its heavy causal embedding in a real society at a particular time. How can we hope to explore imaginatively the range of accessible political possibilities with due respect for history and causality and without succumbing to self-deception?†

---

* It is not necessarily a merit for a political theory to be either as individualist or as consequentialist as Hare's theory is. But a theory which unites both characteristics does avoid some of the demerits implicit in espousing either characteristic on its own.

† Self-deception is not a *prerogative* of the morally aspiring. Moral indolence and a supine political passivity are both compatible with very large measures of self-deception.

16. Political duty is contingent on political possibility. This consideration is likely to present an important difficulty to the more moralistic theories of the scope of political duty. Agents who by their actions had the power to contribute decisively to the realisation of a politically superior order (and who knew that they possessed this power) would, perhaps, according to such theories, have a prima facie duty to make such a contribution and not to sustain, through lassitude or moral indifference, the inferior order which at present obtains. Perhaps, however, no human being has ever possessed such *knowledge*. The conception of prima facie duty might more readily be sustained if the proviso were weakened to read 'had good reason to believe that they possessed the power so to do and were aware that they had good reason to believe this — correctly judged that they possessed it'. But what, then, of those who had good reason to believe this but were *unaware* that they had good reason to do so? The shadow of a conception of *cognitive* duty begins to fall here. The key issue lies in the *explanation* of why they were unaware. Was it, for example, because of cultural misfortune? Was it because of a distinctive personal indifference to the condition of all other sentient creatures? And so on. (If deep and valid social understanding were epistemically impossible in principle, or if it were always effortless in practice, or if it were always a simple function of the degree of effort exerted by an individual, it would be far easier to see how to consider this issue. It is because of the conceptual intricacy of the relations between individual will, cognitive capacity and the transparency of social reality that it is so difficult in general to assess how far social myopia is morally blameworthy. This difficulty relates intimately to the very general theoretical problem posed by the relation of morality to the contingencies of agency.[31])

What it makes sense to believe to be politically *possible* is a fundamental consideration in the analysis of political duty, while what is the legally valid law of an incumbent state, by contrast, cannot be a *fundamental* consideration in the analysis of political duty.

17. But what is in fact politically possible is not easy to ascertain. Nor is it easy even to see how to construe political possibility as a conception. What is politically possible depends in part on what men believe. Indeed it is arguable that one of the more important factors in determining it is often the set of beliefs which men entertain on the issue of what they politically have a duty to do. It is, for example, easier to conquer and to hold a country which none of its inhabitants feels under any obligation to defend than it is to conquer one which all of its inhabitants feel obliged to defend. In the course of the Nazi occupation of Europe it proved decidedly easier for the invaders to round up Jews in some countries than it did in others. If what men ought politically to do depends inter alia upon what can politically be brought about and what can politically be brought about depends inter alia upon what men *suppose* that they ought to do, there is apparent theoretical

indeterminacy to both concepts. The indeterminacy is admittedly narrowest when the human audience addressed is confined to a single person (an intrinsically unpromising characterisation of the apt audience for a political argument outside an absolute monarchy). I shall not (or, at any rate, not *rapidly*) alter what is politically possible to any great degree simply by changing my beliefs. (The same, however, would not have held good for Hitler or Stalin, Mao or Napoleon, over quite long periods of time.[32] Nor would it even hold true of more custodial denizens of political posts as lofty as the Presidency of the United States or the Secretaryship of the C.P.S.U., even when these incumbents do for long periods of time appear to be little more than the *träger* of bureaucratic politics.)[33] But theorising about the character of political duty, although it must address persons one by one, within the 'terrible algebra' of their own lives, must also address them firmly as members of categories who may reasonably be expected to act, if not unanimously in the same direction, at least predominantly so. The reason for taking classes, for example, as rational action units (as opposed to the totality of the human race) is that classes, it is presumed, can plausibly be expected to *act* as such in practice, whereas the totality of the human race cannot. (What, concretely, would it be rational for the totality of the human race as such to *do*?) But if classes flout this expectation in practice, their eligibility for categorical privilege in the theory of practical reason is virtually extinguished. Power — what can or cannot be brought about — is a fundamental consideration in political theory: hence the moral force of the claim to realism in political theory. To presume on eliciting a level of mutual charity and energy higher than will in practice be available and to issue injunctions, on the basis of the presumption, which will impose, if they are followed, real costs on those so enjoined is an error in practical reason. (It is an error the character of which could be represented in a number of different ways; but there is no way in which it could be *validly* represented in which it would not come out as an error in practical reason.) The propensity regularly to issue such injunctions, to overestimate the resources of mutual human concern and commitment and to subject others to the painful consequences of such consistent misjudgement is a moral defect in a political theorist, as in a political actor. But it is not, of course, the only moral disability from which political theorists can suffer. There is a corruption of low expectations[34] — a regular propensity to underestimate the resources of mutual concern and commitment which are or would be accessible — which is at least as likely, where it does obtain, to impose heavy costs on the targets of injunctions. No political theorist, when speaking sincerely, *intends* to take human beings other than as they are and (causally) could be — to misjudge human properties and potentialities. But there are no simple and stable and trustworthy recipes for how to judge human properties and potentialities correctly.[35]

18. What men rationally ought to do depends very broadly on what they

believe and value. How strongly and how exclusively does it depend on what they believe and value at a particular time? Does it depend on *all* that they then believe or value or only on what, among their beliefs and values, *they* then have good reason to believe and value? If rational duties were to be conceived, at the limit, as contingent on literally *all* that men believe or value, it is hard to see what such duties might mean. To apply the epithet 'rational' to them would be perverse. Practical rationality is certainly compatible with an agent's holding false beliefs about relevant matters of fact or relevant causal considerations. (If it were not so, human life would come nervously to a halt.) But however externally permissive from an epistemic point of view the status allotted to the beliefs of an agent might be in the theory of practical reason, even weak ideas of practical rationality require that these beliefs be reduced to some degree of internal order. The idea of epistemic rationality (which might be made a criterion for a very *strong* idea of practical rationality) makes, of course, considerably more imperious demands. Quite how strong these demands can become whilst still retaining authority within practical reason is an extremely intricate question.[36] It is important not to overestimate their force within the theory of rational action. It is possible, for example, that there are contradictory duties in human historical *reality*, moral contexts so impervious to moral acceptance that all conduct which they causally permit is plainly a violation of a profound moral imperative, where, even if one course of conduct is preferable to another, any course of conduct is in itself morally insupportable.[37] We may also be confident that it could not conceivably be the case that men's rational duties are largely or wholly unaffected by what they contingently happen to believe or value. The very fact that I believe or value something gives *me* good reason to act in ways in which someone who did not believe it or value it would lack at least *that* good reason to act. But both rationality and duty are incipiently absolutist conceptions; and their conjunct, rational duty, can scarcely be relativised to such comfortable incoherence. The very conception of rational duty raises directly the issue of the internal consistency and the external validity of an agent's beliefs and values, forces us at least to *consider* practical rationality in the more demanding context of epistemic rationality.

19. If it did not do so, the question of whether men do have rational political obligations could have little intellectual substance. Men everywhere always would have broadly the political duties which they supposed themselves to have. This somewhat blank view would extricate political duties as such from the category of epistemically problematic beliefs, even if it did not consign them comprehensively to the realm of pure and unsullied subjectivity.

Could such a decisive allocation be correct? If it were in any sense correct, within what cognitive idiom could it be coherently appraised as such? One simple strategy for establishing it as correct would be the vindication of a radically non-cognitivist theory of value, a theory which in practice relativised value to individual sentiment. This could scarcely prove as effective in the case of political duties as it might hope to be in some other dimensions of ethical judgement simply because of the obtrusive presence within the former of judgements as to what in political and social terms is factually the case, as well as of judgements of what is or is not politically or socially possible. A less individualistic form of ethical subjectivism would relativise political value to a socially more extended system of ethical beliefs, that of a community or class or society or even civilisation. As the units concerned become demographically more extensive the supposition that the cognitive relativisation of value to particular systems of belief will dispose of the question of the rationality of duty would become steadily less plausible. Even individuals find themselves on occasion in some disarray as to what they have good reason to value, find themselves in intermittent disagreement with themselves (at the very least, in the vein of Parfit,[38] they find themselves in disagreement over time with others of their selves). But if a credally and evaluatively stable and integrated individual is distressingly (or mercifully) infrequent, a real community or society, let alone a civilisation, wholly evaluatively in agreement with itself is scarcely even conceivable.

It is not easy to imagine how we would live with each other if we were indeed for the most part (or in every instance) cognitively and evaluatively assured solipsists. The idea of rational political duties, both problematic and possible, arises from the extreme discomfort, psychic as much as practical, which we suffer from the experience of such credal isolation. More profoundly it arises from the fact that one of the most acute and urgent components of this discomfort is a specifically *credal* discomfort.

20. If we take the beliefs, factual, theoretical and evaluative of all historical agents broadly as given, submitting them merely to a degree of internal rationalisation, we may certainly presume that history has been full of (and is, even now, far from denuded of) 'rational' political duties. The normative acceptance of political duty and social hierarchy is certainly in some societies today appreciably less unhesitating than even the secular moralists of eighteenth-century Scotland presumed that it would remain.[39] But there have been many societies in history (and even today perhaps remain a few) in which theories of political duty as simple as those advanced by Sir Robert Filmer have been believed at least by *some*. We do not really know how many people in England in the 1640s or 1680s believed that they ought to do whatever the King or his duly instructed subordinates ordered them to do, because he was (within England) the lawful heir to the comprehensive authority over mankind which God himself had bestowed on Adam. But it is plain enough that Filmer himself held such a belief.[40] The scope and precision of such beliefs amongst human beings have varied very widely with history and geography.[41] But it would be hard to find a community persisting for any length of time in which no such beliefs obtained. Nor can there have

been many societies so morally deplorable or cognitively incoherent that an individual who happened to grow up and live within them had literally *no* rational duties which were contingent on the beliefs which did obtain within them. To be *wholly* unprejudiced by historical location could scarcely be quite sane. For historical location must determine at the very least what one has *personally* good reason to value and believe true and what one is able by one's own actions to affect.[42] (What one has personally good reason to value, in its turn, could scarcely be wholly independent of what one is able by one's own actions to affect.)

21. Whether a particular person on a particular occasion has any rational political duties and what, if so, such duties consist in depends on:
(a) what that person then values and then believes true about how the human world, politically, socially and economically, is and could be caused to become. (The human world being taken as what he or she conceives to be the human social environment relevant to his or her existence.)
(b) what that person then has *good reason* to value and believe true about how the human world is (politically, socially, economically) and can be caused to become.
(c) how the human world in fact then is.
(d) how the human world *can* be caused to become.

22. Of these considerations, (d) may well be the most difficult to analyse. Even (c) leaves ample room for interpretative licence, whilst the most extreme relativist would have difficulty in refusing to attach *any* meaning to (a). But it is probably differing views about (b) which divide theories of the rational content of political (or other) duties with the greatest sharpness. One form of relativism, perhaps of limited appeal to philosophers but rather often unwittingly espoused by social scientists, implicitly denies any clear sense to the idea of having good reason to value. In so doing, it treats the present tense as the exhaustive locus of human value, restricting to vanishing point such concepts as the self, and implicitly espousing an epistemological conception of the nature of human value which entails that 'only the fact that a person has goals is reason for him' and that 'moral and other derivative considerations are reasons only if adopted by the agent' and that 'his adoption or non-adoption of moral considerations is not necessitated by reason or nature'.[43] If this view of 'the fundamental question of moral epistemology' were valid it would certainly greatly simplify the issue of whether or not there are rational political duties, enabling us to take human values as they in fact obtain — as externally historically given, much as the descriptive historical properties and causal properties of human society at a particular time are historically given; not necessarily as causally inelastic in the face of changing human beliefs but at least as determinately causally elastic in the face of determinate distributions of such beliefs. If, on the other hand, this

view of the fundamental question of moral epistemology is *not* correct there is no theoretical reason why the existing distribution of human sentiments need be accorded any very commanding authority in this branch of practical reason. It will, of course, continue to be of the greatest practical importance to the judging agent because of its salience in constituting human society as this now is and as it can be caused to become.[44] But, simply as sentiment, what it will require is to be taken causally into account in his judgement and to be practically negotiated, not necessarily in any sense to be morally *deferred* to by him.

23. Purely egoist theories of human value (theories, for example, which instal self-regarding prudence at the acme of practical reason) face severe difficulties in distinguishing the issue of what a man has good reason to value at a particular time from the question of what it can truly be said that he *does* in fact value at that time (see 5 above). Within this last question both the term for the personal identity of agency or judgement and the temporal extension of the judgement may raise difficulties. It is clear that there are links between the theory of value and the account of the nature of the human agent given in philosophical psychology.[45] The narrower the time-slices of an agent's values which are considered to be relevant and the more commanding the evaluative authority which is accorded to these, the less appeal can be made to other times and to at present disregarded interests in specifying what he or she can be truly said to value. (The briefer he or she, the more feckless when judged by less recherché criteria of personal identity.) At the limit even a minimum of egoist prudence is beyond the agent's rational reach. At this point the coherence of the conception of agency itself begins to be imperilled. In order to decide how it is rational for him to weight his present concerns against his future concerns an agent must have some conception of the extent and character of the relations between his present self and 'his' future selves. The idea of being temporally impartial within one's own life, of refusing to weight the present more heavily than the future, could only be rational (insofar as it could be rational at all) to the degree to which the judging self can rationally see itself as continuous with 'its' future states.

The motive for privileging the present as against all other times need not be a non-cognitivist theory of value (though there may well be connections between radically non-cognitivist theories of value and drastic difficulties in relating the categories of rational agency and personal identity to those of time). Parfit's account of personal identity has the implication that prudence over excessively long time spans is, even for the most serene egoist, a symptom of ideological confusion. Rationally self-conceived, he contends, human beings are decidedly more serial creatures than they used to suppose themselves (or indeed in many cases *still* suppose themselves to be). In Parfit's own thought, serial personal identity remains subject to rather fierce moral assessment from the outside in terms of a decisively cognitivist ethical theory, utilitarianism. To be impartial qua agent between different times of the 'same' self is a form of superstition within individual practical reason. But in his general theory of value Parfit is at pains to display intertemporal and interpersonal impartiality towards all states of feeling in the universe. It is an error to take one's own future too personally since it is in part a mistake to regard it as fully belonging to one's present self. But the extremes of inter-temporal personal irresponsibility are restrained (the constant dominance of the violent over the calm passions averted) by the utilitarian requirement not to inflict gratuitous suffering on any sentient creatures at all. Within its own terms this is an impressively unsuperstitious view of the character of human existence, even if it displays a number of residual theoretical difficulties.*

24. A cognitivist theory of value which specifies its content in largely altruist terms (such as being unprejudiced — or merely weakly prejudiced — in favour of a given unit of happiness or pleasure simply on the grounds that it is one's own) will address the problem of the rationality of political duty from very different angles, depending on whether it allots a preponderant conceptual role to agency or a well-nigh exclusive role (as most versions of utilitarianism do) to causal possibilities. A strict utilitarianism would pre-sumably entail the judgement that every human agent has good reason to conceive him- or her-self as having one (and only one) political duty — namely the duty to attempt to bring about through his or her acts that state of affairs, amongst all possible states of affairs which he or she has the power to bring about, which will generate the largest surplus of happiness over misery for all sentient creatures. Such an agent would certainly have a paren-thetic obligation to act cost-effectively and to act prudently (in the manner most likely to generate the intended effects and least likely to generate un-intended effects of a regrettable kind). But to say that they would be obliged to act prudently is certainly not to imply that their political duties would be exhausted by adopting a disposition of altruistic risk-aversiveness. A key part of their political duties would fall within the domain of the ethics of belief.[46] Indeed it would not be fanciful to say that a central aspect of their duties would be to attempt to construe political and social possibilities with *imagin-ation* as well as with realism. A consistent consequentialism cannot, other things being equal, rate sins of commission as more important than sins of omission;[47] and it cannot consistently attach greater theoretical opprobrium to the performance of what are at a given time in a particular setting con-ventionally regarded as sins of omission than it does to the non-performance of possible acts which, if performed, would avert greater disutilities.

* It is, for example, unclear what implications agent-relative permissions would carry for a conception of univocally better or worse outcomes or how they could be reconciled with interpersonal im-partiality within the theory of value. Cf. Derek Parfit, 'Innumerate Ethics', *Philosophy and Public Affairs*, VII, 2, Winter 1978, 285–301, at 289–91. For more general doubts see Williams, 'Persons, Character and Morality' in Rorty (ed.), *The Identities of Persons*.

25. 'Rational' political duties could be rendered co-extensive with the duties which persons presume themselves to have only by relativising them completely to the factual, causal and evaluative beliefs which they hold. On this interpretation the theoretical problem of the rationality of political duty would be swallowed up in a morass of comprehensive scepticism about the validity of all human belief; and rationality (whatever content it may be presumed to retain) would be effectively deprived of all critical potential.

At the opposite extreme rational political duties might be construed wholly independently of the actual beliefs (factual, causal or evaluative) of particular human beings — as theoretical implications of extremely strong and determinate theories of value and of the epistemically objective causal properties of human society and its historically constituted individual members. (A consistent utilitarian theory aspires to this condition. Within it the actual beliefs or values of agents need enter solely as causally relevant parts of the data, not in any sense as criteria of judgement.) Most of the confident analyses of the character and scope of political duty, in the present as in the past, in Rawls as in Plato, derive their confidence from the weight and decisiveness of the theories of value which they presuppose. At least in recent decades political theory has drawn from ethics such strength as it has succeeded in mustering and has concentrated its defensive energies in rather narrowly ethical dispute. This was less a battleground which political theorists themselves sought out than it was one which they found thrust upon them in the brash heyday of ethical non-cognitivism. Ethical relativism in one form or another has been widely credited in recent decades, particularly by social scientists, whilst more generalised versions of relativism took longer to win favour even amongst social scientists, perhaps understandably reluctant in the first instance to conclude that human society, for example, was devoid of epistemically objective properties. But whatever the theoretical merit or demerit of more generalised cognitive relativisms, what is quite certain is that it must be a central concern for a political theorist just how it is epistemically appropriate to conceive of and to judge political and social actuality and possibility.

26. A strongly objectivist conception of the character of political and social actuality and possibility would allot to the presumed objective properties of human society a decisive status in practical reason. Rational political duties would be linked to actual agents by strengthening to the limit a conception of what these agents have good reason to believe true about social actuality and possibility. What constitutes this limit would be the implicit adoption of a cognitive vantage point in which *perfect* reason to believe true an intelligible proposition about social actuality and its conditional possibilities would be the proposition's simply being true, or being realised if the conditions on which it was claimed to depend were realised (that is: on the way society is or will be, or, under specified conditions, would be). To consider

appropriate beliefs for human beings in this way, independently of any beliefs which they may already happen to possess is utterly implausible (if indeed it can even be said to be wholly intelligible as a conception). But whether or not such a vantage point (an extreme realist conception) can be coherently described, it would certainly, if successfully described, prove too 'objective' to be directly relevant to the issue in hand.

We may be confident that there are historically determinate limits to the causal powers of any individual or set of individuals and that all human beings hold theories (of very varying elaboration) of the scope and limits of these powers. But we may also be confident, whether or not determinism is in any sense true, that human beings are (and perhaps even that they will always remain) poorly placed to assess the extent of these powers with any great accuracy. If determinism does hold, *and* if it also has any implications at all for the theory of practical reason, the implications which it is likeliest to have are ones which would obliterate the rationality of agency (and, most brusquely, of *moral* agency)* in its entirety. (From the viewpoint of practical rationality, accordingly, this might well be one component of epistemic rationality which we would have good reason practically to choose to dispense with within our own beliefs.)

From the viewpoint of human practical reason what determines what the future will be is the present, together with the laws of nature, together with what human beings will decide to do. The idea of a suprahuman cognitive vantage point which could subsume what human beings will decide to do, without residue, under the laws of nature is an idea which can scarcely without absurdity be included *within* the viewpoint of human practical reason.

27. Between a relativism so untrammelled as to abandon practical reason in effect to the flow of impulse, and an objectivism so decisive as to reify human social relations in their entirety and thus to reduce human practical reason to absurdity, what is needed is some altogether more promising middle ground. Somewhere between a sub-bestial experiential inconsequence and a supra-human perspective on the destiny of human performance which holds the futility of future failure in its entirety against the rationality of present effort, there must lie an appropriately human vantage point which neither denies to human beings in the exercise of their practical reason a degree of self-control and moral insight of which they are capable, nor requires of them a depth of vision into the causal circumstances of their social existence which is necessarily beyond their natural capacities. In this middle ground men must be taken as they historically are, situated in their own historical locations and endowed with all of (but only with all of) the ethical and cognitive susceptibilities with which history has furnished them.

---

* Nagel, *Mortal Questions*, Cambridge 1979, ch. 3. There can certainly be no rational duties unless it is possible in principle to give a coherent account of the 'internal conception of agency' (see ibid., p. 38).

The business of human practical reason is making the best of history; and history enters into the determination of the materials (individual or collective) through which it must work as much as it does into those of the materials upon which it must work.

28. An extreme relativism would take the uncorrected serial subjective consciousness of the agent, his or her momentary conscious beliefs and preferences, as furnishing him or her with incorrigible reasons for acting. There could not be sound grounds for espousing a version of relativism as abrasive as this. The view that human values are intrinsically *rationally* incorrigible is more plausibly focussed on entire ways of life, whole cultures,* than it is on even the relatively stable preferences of single individuals. If fools are to be met within all societies, it can scarcely be the case that the beliefs of all individuals are incorrigible within any society. Nor is it significantly more probable, since knaves and hypocrites are also to be found within most societies, that even the stable preferences of *all* individuals are evaluatively incorrigible. In the light of these considerations a more chastened individualistic theory of value might well prefer to take as the criterion of what an agent has *good* reason to value his or her subjective consciousness internally rationalised and assessed over a fairly lengthy span of time. Even if it is presumed epistemologically that an individual *can* only have good reason to value what they do or will value, the consistency (if not the practical compatibility[48] between the components) of what they value and the stability of this over time will serve to distinguish what amongst their values they, as continuing agents, have good reason to allow to determine their actions from the disorder of what they, as discontinuous patients, must submit to in the way of evaluative experience. A less individualist theory of value would certainly refuse to regard the normative preferences of an *individual* as incorrigible merely in virtue of the fact that they happened to be *his* or *hers*,

---

* If practical reason were to sunder desires (as original existences) completely from perceptions and beliefs, then it would follow that forms of life are in some respects incorrigible, except in terms of their internal coherence and their relation to natural causality, since desires are extensively predicated on forms of life and forms of life extensively causally dependent on the distribution of desires. If moral epistemology does split desire definitively from vision, one form of life cannot be normatively corrigible from the outside, though it may well be open to internal learning (the lessons of experience) or to external causal modification (cultural imperialism). Yet even in these terms it is difficult, once the possibility of *learning* from experience entirely within the terms of the culture itself is conceded, to see how the *general* possibility of learning rationally from the experience of another culture can be precluded. Since all individuals learn to value much of what they value in the course of their own individual experiences and since in most, if not all, societies there are very extensive disagreements between individuals as a result of these individual experiences as to just what it is normatively and epistemically appropriate to value, it is hard to see how *rational* susceptibility over time can be denied a role in the analysis of the status of human values. And, once the idea of rational susceptibility within the life of the most sheltered individual or the most parochial society is incorporated into the analysis of values, it is hard to see why men or societies should be denied to be (what history has abundantly shown them to be) rationally susceptible to moral conceptions deriving from somewhere completely different. Once any cognitive element is admitted into the status of human values it is hard to set limits to the distance to which moral argument, persuasion or experience may *rationally* carry someone.

more particularly if they happened to conflict sharply with the normative preferences of their fellow members of society (family, village, class, nation state, religion, etc.). On a non-cognitivist theory of value,* tacit moral authority will in practice be accorded either to a radical moral individualism (all will be fated and entitled to value for themselves) or to an equally radical moral collectivism (with the key theoretical choice being the choice of the appropriately authoritative collectivity).† But the theoretical motivation of less individualist theories seldom inclines their proponents to opt for a rigorously non-cognitivist moral epistemology. Once the status of values rests upon the judgements of others and not solely on the intractable ontological integrity (and the resulting moral solipsism) of individual experience, the view that good reasons for valuing are *wholly* unlike the grounds for rational belief about how the world is becomes considerably less attractive. (Because human practical reason is connected with the project of making the world match our beliefs and not simply to that of making our beliefs match the world[49] there is no chance that good reason for valuing could be *wholly* like (simply be part of or be correctly equated with) the grounds for rational belief about how the world is.)

29. Strongly cognitivist evaluative theories, theories of what all human beings in all societies and at all times have good reason to value (at the limit – Plato, Hobbes, Kant perhaps – what they have conclusively good reason to permit to determine all their actions) offer the most attractive foundation for a crisply directive theory of political duty. Radically non-cognitivist evaluative theories in effect preclude there being a rationally directive theory of political duty at all. But with the single exception of utilitarianism (which has on the whole been comparatively discreet in sponsoring theories of the character of political duty) such theories of political duty as have been founded on strongly cognitivist conceptions of the nature of human values have been implausibly simplistic in their conclusions and at best perfunctorily consequentialist in their approach. As a result none of them has succeeded in taking fully into account the systematically contingent character of the political realm (more particularly the extent to which this realm is consti-

* This implicitly presumes that metaethical positions have theoretical implications *within* substantive ethics. This is sometimes denied (see, e.g. Geoffrey Harrison, 'Relativism and Tolerance', in Laslett & Fishkin (eds.), *Philosophy, Politics and Society, Fifth Series*, Oxford 1979, pp. 273–90). It may well be difficult in any instance to identify just what the valid implications are (though, as Harrison insists, it certainly is unlikely that one valid implication of relativism in metaethics is a general duty of tolerance: a likelier candidate would be a general licence for intolerance, mitigated merely by the dictates of egoistic prudence). But the view that there *are* no such implications is unconvincing. Moral viewpoints are not in general conceived by those whose viewpoints they are simply as floating in thin air. If they were so conceived, it is not at all clear that they could continue to be held. (Cf. also, proceeding from the opposite direction, Alasdair Macintyre, *Against the Self-Images of the Age*, London 1971, pp. 277–9).

† It is not in fact clear that the choice of any particular collectivity as authoritative is in itself any *more* arbitrary than the choice of the individual as such. (Like individuals, collectivities are there.) But individualist theorists have little difficulty in noting the essential arbitrariness of the choice of one particular collectivity as against another as the locus of authority.

tuted by men's real but historically limited powers and the intrinsic obstacles which their possessors face in identifying the scope and limits of these powers).

30. Rational political duties, if there are any such duties, must subsist fully within *practical* reason, the theory of what actual agents, situated as they are situated, have good reason actually to *do*. They cannot be located merely within the general theory of consummations devoutly to be wished. This is not because the rational political duties of, for example, saints and heroes cannot exceed in force and scope the rational political duties of the selfish, cowardly and myopic. Within the theory of practical reason even saints and heroes,[50] whilst they may well be undeterred from fulfilling their duties at whatever costs to themselves, must submit to the discipline of other-regarding consequences. In form, political duties are always duties assessed as fully as they can be in the light of causality. They can never take the form of simple obligations, obligations which hold irrespective of the consequences to all concerned. Causality, of course, is very difficult to assess in political contexts; but the requirement of assessing it (a condition of rationality in political action) puts severe epistemic limits on the extent to which a theory of rational *political* duty can be relativised to the actual beliefs of agents.

31. Some insight into the question of how relativist a theory of political duty could be without simply relapsing into incoherence can be obtained from considering Gilbert Harman's article, 'Relativistic Ethics: Morality as Politics'.[51] Harman treats it as a criterion for a valid theory of morality that, under it, agents should have good reason to *do* what it prescribes and he insists that both act-utilitarianism and rule-utilitarianism are by this criterion obviously false theories, whatever their felicity as theories of what states of affairs would be intrinsically desirable.[52] In Harman's conception (which explicitly regards morality as a form of politics) 'the principles that give you moral reasons to do things are the moral principles that you actually accept'.[53] Morality 'is basically a group affair, depending on moral demands jointly accepted by several people after a certain amount of tacit bargaining', though at the limit there also could be purely personal moralities in which individuals placed demands solely upon themselves. Conceptually this seems an almost whimsically individualist account. Moral reasons are reasons for an agent precisely insofar as (and only insofar as) he or she espouses them as such. But, contingently, most persons under the importunities of social existence to *some* measure of mutual understanding on what it will be best collaboratively to espouse. A Humean naturalism of this kind is perhaps necessarily morally rather lowering, encouraging, as it does, moral agents (more particularly those who require little encouragement) to bargain hard for whatever restraints on the fulfilment of their own desires they are persuaded to acknowledge[54] and displaying a morality of aspiration as little

more than individual or collective caprice. A theory of value in which agents can only appropriately be seen as evaluatively committed explicitly by their own personal beliefs, and never as committed implicitly even by the social relations in which they find themselves placed,* makes the contingent attitudes of *individual* agents towards the norms which they encounter remarkably authoritative. Only the morally very complacent are likely to find this a plausible account of the cognitive status of their own moral beliefs (and if not of their own, how much less so of those of most others).† The view that much actual human evaluation is a product of some variety or other of *moral* incomprehension (not the view that this is so when seen in the light of one's own moral conceptions or in the light of the conceptions of some distinct group of persons, but the view that it simply *is* so) is not theoretically compatible with Harman's position; and those who are inclined to believe this true will be correspondingly disinclined to accept either Harman's views of moral epistemology or his radical separation between the theory of what agents have good reason to do and the theory of what ought to be the case. Yet even those who see more substance to moral inquiry than Harman allows must concede the validity of one implication of his conception. Whatever might be true of moral duties in general, there can be no doubt that *political* duties must be conceived as duties to perform actions which those who are subject to them have good reason in practice to *perform*. (Whatever may be true of moral actions in general, it is certainly part of the *point* of political actions to come off.)

32. Because political duties are duties which obtain, if they obtain at all, within history, in the circumstances in which men find themselves historically placed, they cannot readily be rendered dependent solely on even an exceptionally strong theory of what men have good reason to value. Such theories may proffer commanding regulative ideals: the form of the good, the categorical duty under no circumstances to alienate one's own moral autonomy to a political authority,[55] a comprehensive conception of a just society,[56] a conception of a participatory political order procedurally centred on a practice of self-incurred obligation.[57] Within their own terms each of these theories is in some respects edifying. But, quite apart from the essentially disputable status of these terms themselves, and even if the theories are regarded as authoritatively edifying, it is quite unclear what implications

---

* It is not *wholly* clear that Harman intends his position to be as radically individualist as this. The 'universality' of moral demands is relativised to sets of persons, all of whom 'accept *or have reason to accept*' ('Relativistic Ethics', *Midwest Studies in Philosophy*, III, 1978, 113, 114) certain basic moral demands (my italics).

† Harman's theory is an *explanatory* theory of the character of the moral reasons which persons actually suppose themselves to have. But by its explicit separation of the evaluative *ought to be* from the moral *ought to do*, it makes it obscure how to conceive the issue of whether men in general may not be radically in error as to the moral reasons which it is cognitively appropriate for them to see themselves as having. (Cf. Harman's implicit criterion of acceptability for the prospective surrogate for the universal view: 'Relativistic Ethics', 113—14.)

they rationally carry for the concrete political duties of actual historical agents. How is a historical agent rationally to distinguish a commanding regulative ideal from pie in the sky? To be told, as for example by Dr Pateman, that an agent would be politically obliged within a co-operative and open practice of public self-commitment may in itself be persuasive enough. But it is not immediately obvious that it implies anything at all about what a given person's duties are in the historical setting in which he or she happens to find themselves. Good reasons for an individual or set of individuals to favour or value institutions of a particular kind are not necessarily in any way directive as to precisely what to *do* in a context in which such institutions do not as yet exist and in which they will certainly not be inaugurated simply by the individual or set of individuals espousing their claims. (It is for example clear that participatory democracy on a smallish demographic scale can (or certainly *could*) be coherently described. But could it rationally be expected causally to persist (to be capable of reproducing itself within any political ecology which the world organised as it is today might in fact come to accord it)? Or, still more pressingly, is there any good reason to believe that such a self-subsistent political universe could be causally *generated* — brought into existence — from our present historical location?)

33. Vigorously corrective moral theories (theories of what agents have good reason to value, whether or not particular agents *do* value these things in practice) might generate (synthesise?) universalist conclusions about what men have good reason to value. If such a theory were presumed valid — and even if it could not in itself suffice to tell us exactly or even approximately how to conduct ourselves in the context in which history has set us — one form of political duty which it can be presumed to impose is a duty, within some limit of egoist and altruist prudence, to affirm and foster the values in question. In the case, for example, of someone who accepted the validity and the relevance of Dr Pateman's arguments and who happened to inhabit Great Britain or Australia or some country within which the frank and vigorous expression of most political opinions is not for most of the time prohibitively dangerous, it might well be judged to impose the duty of arguing for the merits of (and even perhaps of campaigning politically for the establishment of) such institutions. Even on Harman's account of the status of morality (let alone on one which is less individually morally permissive) anyone who *accepted* the validity and the pragmatic relevance of Pateman's arguments would have good reason to put themselves out in such a setting to proselytise for the merits of appropriate institutions. Vigorously corrective moral theories need not necessarily imply a breaking down of the boundaries between politics and purely private life — they may, for instance prize the moral claims of *otium* decidedly above those of *negotium*.[58] But such theories certainly place in jeopardy the status of socially conventional lines of division between those states of affairs for which a person is presumed to

273

be responsible and those for which he or she is not so presumed. Nor are such disruptive modifications confined to the more morally histrionic theories of value. A relatively relaxed version of utilitarianism readily yields the result that so reorganising the political world that in practice fewer millions starve in it is a project of sufficient urgency to legitimate a considerable measure of political violence[59] or that a very large redistribution of income from the individual inhabitants of industrial to those of pre-industrial societies and a redistribution conducted by the deliberate choices of the individuals concerned is morally mandatory.[60]

34. Vigorously corrective theories of value, by underlining the discrepancies between what agents do value and what they have good reason to value, serve to identify many possible actions which agents ought to perform and which the agents themselves do not at the moment in question recognise any corresponding duty to perform. Even without a vigorously corrective theory of value, the internal disorder of many agents' conceptions of value, and the discontinuous and careless grasp which most agents possess even of such conceptions of value as may properly be said to be theirs, will guarantee there being many actions which agents ought to perform and which they fail at a given moment to recognise that they ought to perform, while the prevalence of *akrasia* will guarantee there being, in addition to all these, a numerous set of actions the obligatoriness of which the agents (in some sense, *fully*) recognise and yet which they fail in the event to execute.

35. To say of an agent that he or she has a duty to act in a particular manner may be to express a cognitive judgement about their interests or about human interests more generally or to offer an appraisal of the moral rationality of their present or future conduct. Vigorously corrective theories of value aspire to bridge any possible gulf between these two types of claim, in effect, by replacing the values which historical agents happen to have (and perhaps some of the causal judgements which they happen to make) with ones which are presumed to be superior. From an acceptance of the superior values it follows that the agents do have good reason to act as enjoined and that if they do not in fact do so, they are appropriately subject to moral criticism for their failure. The presumption of moral authority which lies behind the cognitive judgement of their interests is a necessary presupposition for making the judgement. Whether it is valid depends upon whether or not the theory of value can be epistemically vindicated. It does not depend at all on what the historical agents in question happen to value or believe. (In Harman's terms such judgements are judgements about what should be the case, a class of judgements on the epistemic status of which he is understandably discreet.)[61] It is less evident that this independence can hold good for moral injunctions to particular agents to act in particular ways on particular occasions. At the limit, we may at least be certain that no one can have a

duty to (or can have good reason to) hold comprehensively different beliefs or to value comprehensively different values from those which he or she does hold or value. In relation to particular historical agents at particular points in time the authority of even the most vigorously corrective theory of value, at the point at which an individual agent is morally enjoined to act, depends upon the (causal?) power of the theory of value, when clearly articulated, to convince the agent of its validity. A theory of value in relation to which it was a causal truth that a given agent *could* not believe it could not be one which furnished the agent with rational duties. Creatures that *cannot* value the good cannot be *rationally* constrained by it. They may well represent a practical hazard. But it is absurd to accuse them on this ground alone of miscalculation or credal incoherence.

Less drastically, it must also be appropriate to recognise within the practice of moral appraisal of a particular agent's conduct a large measure of relativisation to the actual values and beliefs of the agent concerned (or at least, less individualistically, to the actual values and beliefs widely shared within his or her social milieu, class or society as a whole).

36. The general problem which lies behind these difficulties is the issue of the coherence or incoherence of an ethics of belief.[62] Vigorously corrective theories of value presume at least that their espousal by a historical agent, social group or society is not causally precluded. Insofar as they imply moral injunctions they imply these in a decidedly unindividuated manner and make little pretence to appraise the conduct of historical agents within the intricacies of their own values and beliefs. At the level of individual moral appraisal, there is an element of absurdity in bringing to bear upon the conduct of a single agent an entire apparatus of historically external evaluations and beliefs. The appropriate *unit* on which to bring such an apparatus to bear is a whole society or at the least an entire social class. It is a perfectly coherent (and important) type of judgement within the theory of value that the moral vision and many of the causal beliefs about society prevalent in some social groups (perhaps American plantation slave-owners or Gestapo officers or English barons of the mid twelfth century) have been or are objectively morally odious and that they constitute systems of belief which it is utterly inappropriate for human beings ever to have held. (It is a matter of *moral* luck not to be born into some social roles; and in the case of the morally infirm, it may even be a matter of moral luck not to encounter certain social opportunities.) Such judgements do not depend upon the view that the prevalence of these beliefs was in any way causally *surprising* or (necessarily) that there was any historically real possibility of *most* of those who held them avoiding so doing. All they depend upon is the presumption that the beliefs are not epistemically justified. It is not helpful to regard judgements of this character as implying an ethics of belief.

At the level of appraising individual conduct *within* a particular historical

275

setting, however (or of offering individual moral injunctions within such a setting), the idea of an ethics of belief is more attractive. No one can be rationally obliged to transcend their visual capabilities. But perhaps anyone can be morally obliged somewhat beyond their visual *habits*. A habit of moral indolence or of self-indulgence in the exercise of the social imagination, an over-susceptibility to the psychic mechanism of denial, are all dispositions which will certainly have a considerable impact over time on an agent's consciousness of society, both moral and causal. It is not morally over-fastidious to insist that political responsibililities cannot be restricted by (trimmed to) the measure of each agent's moral and cognitive limitations, more particularly where these limitations are ones for which the agent is clearly quite largely responsible.* Whether or not particular schemes of social organisation (for example, plantation slavery) are morally defensible can be appraised with some confidence from the outside. But what the rational political duties of an individual plantation slave-holder amounted to can hardly be appraised as confidently without in some measure entering imaginatively into the sorry frame of social practices in question. That a social role should not exist at all is not necessarily a clearly directive rational consideration for someone who happens to occupy it. An ethics of belief within which every holder of an evaluatively odious social role was judged to have a conclusive duty to quit it, irrespective of what beliefs he or she held (or had even encountered in the course of their entire lives) shows too little awareness of the causal ecology of human belief to be ethically cogent. On the other hand, a theoretical view of the evaluative authority of human beliefs which sanctioned a wholly blithe conception of the social actuality of plantation slavery or of the political and social order of Nazi Germany, simply because an individual historical agent happened not to feel a trace of queasiness at these, replaces ethical concern with a servile submission to the worst in human nature. Conduct despicable even for a Georgia plantation owner or political complaisance striking even in a German bourgeois of the late 1930s is conduct which can be presumed to fall short of the rational political duties of the agents concerned, irrespective of their acknowledged beliefs.

37. Vigorously corrective theories of value (whether intended, as with Plato or Rousseau or Kant, to elevate the moral aspirations of agents, or merely to simplify the issue of what agents have good reason to value by replacing many of their existing beliefs, as with Hobbes or Bentham or perhaps Marx) serve to alter an agent's estimate of his or her rational political duties by altering their normative attitudes. Vigorously corrective theories of value

* The extent of such responsibility is certainly hard to assess in principle (Nagel, *Mortal Questions*, ch. 3); but the *existence* of such responsibility is difficult to deny, unless men simply have no responsibility for their actions. (See Harry Frankfurt, 'Identification and Externality' and Charles Taylor, 'Responsibility for Self', in Rorty (ed.), *The Identities of Persons*, Berkeley, Calif. 1976, pp. 239–51, 281–99).

imply, in the abstract, clear cognitive duties. Those who are adequately appraised of their content are thereby furnished with rational grounds for *seeing* themselves as appropriately constrained. The importance of such theories in the analysis of political duty is obvious enough, where they are to be found. Where they are in practice perhaps most likely to figure is in the identification of intrinsically deplorable types of social institution or social relationships (slavery, the subjection of females to males, the capitalist mode of production or the dictatorship of the proletariat as thus far institutionalised). The duty to recognise the moral odiousness of such institutions, where it is clearly articulated, might be a cognitive *duty* because it might be within the natural capacity of any human being to whom it was clearly articulated to recognise and it might be the case that the only cause, under these circumstances, of any human beings failing to recognise it would be their choosing not to recognise it because they were benefited by (and knew that they were benefited by) its continued existence and preferred to avert their eyes from the (even to them incipiently evident) moral demerits of arrangements which suited their convenience.

38. It seems probable, however, that the most important and difficult dimension of the ethics of belief in relation to political duty concerns not evaluation as such but rather beliefs about what is and what could be socially and politically the case. A studied preference for ignoring the morally objectionable aspects of convenient social arrangements is neither difficult to identify nor particularly puzzling to appraise. But the conception of politics which directs an agent as to his or her political duties cannot be exhausted by a list of offences to avoid or institutions to deplore or avert. The most important component of such a conception is the causal theory held, more or less consciously, by the agent as to what is at stake in politics. This is one major reason why considering rational political duty in terms of single individual agents at particular points in time is conceptually so misleading. What is at stake in politics at a particular point in time is seldom (though not never) very much and what will turn at that time on the personal contribution of a single individual is in the vast majority of cases necessarily nugatory. (This point has been worked through with some rigour in the application of economic theory to politics, with the unsurprising conclusion that rigorously egoistic and rational agents will seldom have good grounds for performing personal or co-operative political acts (voting, joining a union, etc., finding out what is politically going on) unless they contrive to subject each other to dependable collective constraints.)[63] A conviction of the probable marginal insignificance of *each* person's individual political contribution is an important ground for the prevalence of political inactivity in a culture in which the rationality of politics is considered as both essentially consequentialist and fairly narrowly egoist.[64] To infer, however, from the premise that no individual agent, thinking and acting restrictedly for himself or herself, has good

reason politically to do a hand's turn to the conclusion that all individual agents, thinking restrictedly for themselves have no reason politically to do a hand's turn, while in itself a valid inference, brings out an important and unobvious limitation within the conception of egoistic rationality. The consequences for all agents of acting independently and in terms of the egoistic rationality institutionally nurtured within such a society would be to obliterate the society.[65] If egoistic rationality was an ineluctable component of the human conditions, the best that could be done would be to seek to alter the rules for social co-operation to those of a less hazardous game.[66] But it is in any case unclear that egoistic rationality is entitled to enjoy any such monopoly status. What the findings of the economic theory of politics imply is not that no historical agents have good reason to see themselves as having any rational political duties, but simply that historical agents have good reason to envisage both their own selves and the context in which they act politically in a rather less narrow (and collectively imprudent) light than the economic theory of politics (or the culture of capitalist society, increasingly) encourages them to. In particular, these 'findings' imply that historical agents, however obsessively egoistic in the first instance, have good reason to form a less callow type of *causal* theory as to what is at stake in politics and in consequence, in due course and after due deliberation, a less socially myopic conception of what individual human beings have good reason to value and to permit to determine their actions. If a human self-conception is rationally appropriate to conduct on the market but rationally self-destructive when transposed into the context of the polity, the grounds for judging it in general an epistemically rational self-conception are drastically weakened. Surveying the rational consequences of egoistic rationality from Wolin's 'more general point of view', it is not hard to discern elements of contradiction within its conjunct terms. In *political* theory it cannot be a valid result that what is collectively suicidal is individually rational. (The lemming does not offer a suitable model for human practical reason.) Political theory, accordingly, will resist with some tenacity being defined as the theory of what individuals seriatim can do about history (in each instance, virtually nothing) and focus instead on the question of what they might contrive to do about it together, partly at least in the hope that such considerations may in time exert some (epistemically respectable) pressure on their self-conceptions, on how they imagine themselves and their societies and on what they conceive to be of value to themselves. 'For the limits of social imagination are what determine what men in the last instance can place their trust in. Men, as Locke said, *live* upon trust. And there is simply no conceptual truth in political theory more fundamental than the truth that men trust in what they *can*.'[67]

39. Virtually all adult agents must have beliefs of some kind as to how the world politically and socially is (at least in their immediate vicinity) at a

particular time (at the very least that they are or are not under the immediate threat of violence from outside the domestic frame). What is here important about these beliefs is not the extent of their coverage of what is or is not factually the case at the time of inquiry (not the sheer volume of information which they comprise) but rather the more or less articulated causal theory which they imply as to what at present is and what in the relevant future is at all likely to become at stake in politics. Most of an agent's causal theory of what is at stake in politics consists of beliefs about conditional future possibilities or of counterfactual beliefs about the *recent* past. (Few British citizens' beliefs about the perils and opportunities of British foreign and defence policy today turn on the menace of a French invasion.) In any actual society the causal theories of what is at stake in politics which are held will vary drastically in scope and density between individuals. Rational political obligations, where the theories which individuals hold about relevant political causality vary from the exceedingly thick and elaborate to the dismally thin and simple (it will be deplorable if the Russians take over but splendid if the Tories win the next election) will, if relativised to the actual beliefs of agents, vary correspondingly. It is thus an important issue in the theory of rational political duty how far the ethics of belief have an appropriate role in relation to agents' causal theories of what is at stake in politics. In a small-scale participatory democracy a high level of political education was, perhaps, incumbent on every member of the demos. If not sufficiently educated to understand very deeply for himself, at the very least he had the responsibility of learning how to recognise with confidence and to allot his trust to those who truly were his betters (a difficult political feat in itself and one which could hardly even be seriously attempted without a tacit theory of what is and has been and will be causally at stake in politics). If the purpose for which a theory of rational political duty has been devised is largely the moral reprobation or encouragement of individuals, it can hardly apply very severe standards of cognitive duty in advance of entering into dialogue with them. Ideas of cognitive duty or even cognitive responsibility will figure not in its moral appraisal of existing agents, as they exist or have existed in the past, but in its efforts to form politically more edifying agents for the future. Such a theory is likely to be above all a theory of the significance of political education. (The commonest form for such theories to take is that of a theory of rational political socialisation. But a theory of rational political socialisation is perhaps overconfident in *form* on the prospective educational needs of the educators themselves. A more democratic conception might centre on a conception of a duty of *mutual* political education: not of promiscuous political didacticism but of the effort to foster, in ourselves as well as others, a clearer understanding of what is politically at risk and what is politically of value (a matter of learning to listen better and more patiently as much as of learning to speak persuasively or electing to spend more of one's own — and hence of others' — time on so doing).)

40. But within a conception of rational political duty the idea of cognitive duty or cognitive responsibility has a more urgent implication for some political agents than it does for others. It has the most urgent implications of all for those who take on or *seek* to take on the responsibilities of political leadership. Political leadership is a sensitive topic today because it suggests the need for a cognitive division of labour, causally and perhaps even ethically, amongst the inhabitants of a polity and because it is difficult to reconcile any such division of responsibilities with the egalitarianism of democratic theory. Radical moral egalitarians can scarcely acknowledge the admissibility of any such division; and the most consistent of them, the anarchists, accordingly deny the ethical legitimacy of any coercive political institutions whatever. This denial lends their views an appealing purity of outline; but since it necessarily reposes on a blank denial of the significance of the causal complexity and the intractably hazardous reality of the political realm, it achieves purity at the cost of being practically inconsequential and morally evasive. Since human practical reason is in essence an attempt to fit the world to human conceptions, it is a severe criticism of a political theory that it should seek to impose its moral will upon history by little more than pure wish-fulfilment. Egalitarian democrats, if prepared to consider the causal complexity and reality of the political realm at all, lay heavy emphasis on the social and political necessity for all citizens to have access to (and, in more moralistic versions, to be compelled to incur) extensive political education. Particularly in its less moralistic versions, this preoccupation is admirable. But it offers no immediate remedy for the existing inequalities in human moral insight and practical understanding of the political domain, and it is difficult to see why it should be expected to prevent such inequalities of understanding being reproduced at a more educated level, even after it has been institutionally realised for an indefinite period.

Within the practice of leadership, the continuing necessity and importance of such cognitive divisions of labour is difficult to deny. (Societies which do not need political leadership are societies which have made a complete escape from history and which need not expect at any later point to face practical problems of re-entry. Perhaps there once were such societies. But certainly there are none of them remaining in the world today; and there is little reason to expect them to reappear in any numbers in the future.) Political professionals have very different cognitive responsibilities from the remainder of the population;[68] and they do so (though, naturally, in varying degrees), whatever the constitutional form of the political regime. Because political leadership involves taking on responsibility for the political cognition of others, the ethics of belief is a central consideration in the role of leader.* Like other human agents, leaders have their own motives and reasons for

---

* This is one reason, though not the only reason, why the behavioural approach to the analysis of political leadership is so inept. (Dunn, 'The Eligible and the Elect', in W.H. Morris-Jones (ed.), *The Making of Politicians*, London 1976, 49–65.)

acting as they do. But unlike most human agents, the degree of their responsibility to others for how they choose to act is always very great because of the extent and the importance of the consequences for others which their actions or inaction will help to bring about. It is incumbent upon political leaders (political entrepreneurs as much as holders of existing state authority) at the very least to hold beliefs which are neither feckless nor unconcerned with the interests of their fellow human beings. It may well be true that most human beings who feel casually sanguine about the prospective political risks and opportunities which face their society, are living politically in a fool's paradise. But, for most citizens, to live politically in a fool's paradise is at worst unwise. If the beliefs which they hold about political actuality and political possibility gratuitously expose them to disagreeable surprises, the most perhaps that can be said is that they hold imprudently foolish beliefs. It is hard to see how they could intelligibly be said to have a *duty* to hold other and less imprudent beliefs. It cannot be the rational political duty of all adult human beings to waste their entire lives in endlessly scanning the political horizon for signs of approaching squalls. But for political leaders the case is very different. The Platonic metaphor of the leader as navigator is notoriously tendentious in its equation of technical skill with entitlement to political authority. But the metaphor is perhaps valid, if its implications are simply reversed. The responsibilities of a ship's captain are not exhausted by human decency and calmness of demeanour. A large proportion of them consist of irretrievably *cognitive* duties.

41. Where a theory of rational political duty is devised principally for the appraisal of the performance of actual historical agents, there will be good reason to include within it not merely a vigorously corrective moral theory (to amend the moral damage which history has done to us all), but also a fairly vigorously corrective cognitive theory in terms of which to assess in the present and the past, and to seek to rectify in the future, the infirmities of judgement of political leaders. It is not difficult to see how a vigorously corrective moral theory, if valid, might have direct implications for the duties of historical agents. But doubts have been expressed as to whether vigorously corrective cognitive theories could relate to the *duties* of historical agents at all.[69]

Can there *be* an ethics of belief? Certainly cognitive duties, if there are any such duties, cannot be duties to believe at a particular time something other than what an agent does believe at that time. There may be — indeed there *is* — a considerable measure of past choice embodied in the broad array of what a person at any time believes. But no one can at a particular time simply decide what to believe. Cognitive duties have thus to be conceived not in terms of the discretionary holding of a belief at a single particular moment of time but rather of the deliberate adoption and implementation of vigorous policies of inquiry and reflection, policies, above all, which seek to elude the self-protective or complacent myopia of the adaptive culture of political professionals. No one can have cognitively good reason to believe anything which his or her experience (very sophisticatedly construed) does not *give* them good reason to believe true. Theories of cognitive duty demand an axiom of cognitive accessibility and some measure of choice over the application of cognitive attention.[70] At least since the demise in most areas of hereditary absolute monarchy, those who compete for and, still more, those who attain political authority may be seen as essentially free agents in so doing. There is no sound reason why they may not also be presumed to be in quite a large measure free agents in determining how they apply their cognitive attention and thus to have incurred, in undertaking their political roles, cognitive duties corresponding to the responsibilities of these roles. What is somewhat less clear in assessing the nature of these duties, however, is how far the axiom of cognitive accessibility is satisfied.

Plainly some political leaders, in historical practice, inflict more damage than others. Some of the damage which they do is accurately foreseen, occasionally by themselves and more frequently by others. Much of it which is not in fact foreseen appears in retrospect to have been fairly readily foreseeable.* Human beings plainly do have expectations about the future and these expectations are realised or disappointed in experience. Ideally prudent policies of inquiry and reflection would, it might be hoped, separate expectations which were always realised and never disappointed. A creature which, on the strength of its beliefs, anticipated the future correctly in all aspects which it regarded as relevant and which never had experiential occasion to revise its canons of relevance would hardly be accused of holding imprudent beliefs. Whatever cognitive duties in this dimension of expectation were truly incumbent upon it, it would more than satisfy. There are, however, no such creatures; and the cognitive condition of human beings resembles that of such creatures very distantly indeed.[71] Surprise is intrinsic to human history. For a political actor to hold prudent beliefs is certainly not for him or her to be beyond the reach of surprise, an unnervingly jaded state. Beliefs prudent for a political agent to hold are beliefs which articulate adequately the rational interests of relevant human beings and which assess accurately the context of political and social possibilities on which he or she is in a position to act in the attempt to promote these interests. The central component of an individual's set of such beliefs is a more or less elaborated theory of what is causally at stake in politics in the context, very broadly conceived, in which he or she is acting. Precisely what is the appropriate criterion for assessing the validity of such a theory is a deeply puzzling question.

42. What would it mean, for example, to predicate political duty on political

---

* A striking example of an unanticipated but foreseeable outcome in recent world politics is provided by the formation of the OPEC oil cartel (see Peter Odell, *Oil and World Power*, 3rd ed., pb., Harmondsworth 1974).

possibility — on how the human world *can* in practice be caused to become? Rational political duties in this reading would be contingent on the relation of political accessibility. (To conceive political duties in this way is to apply what is epistemically an extremely strong criterion to the content of what rationally ought to be done — very possibly a criterion which will prove too strong for identifying the rational duties of mere human beings, a criterion which implies the adoption of a conceptually inappropriate God's eye view of the human political predicament.)

The most serious attempt to analyse the relation of political accessibility has been made by Jon Elster.[72] He treats the relation as ontologically unique but epistemologically potentially plural, presuming determinism but acknowledging the underdetermination of the future by any possible finite description of the present. The direction in which he seeks to develop a theory of political possibility impels him to opt for one which is not merely actor-oriented (it is a theory for agents of what can be brought about), but also confined in scope to 'routine politics',[73] since drastic political transformation raises such formidable difficulties for the insulation of theory from praxis. Because revolutionary practitioners discount understanding in favour of efficacy,[74] their misunderstandings can[75] (and perhaps often do) have very substantial desired consequences (they also, of course, often have even more substantial *undesired* consequences). Because the possibility of some political outcomes being realised may depend upon the espousal by agents of the *theory* that such outcomes *can* indeed be realised, there is no sense in which what can or cannot come about can be identified independently of the beliefs and actions of agents. 'Between what is unambiguously possible and what is unambiguously impossible there is a limbo where only action can decide.'[76]

Rational political duties are, of course, likely to be most theoretically contentious *and* of greatest practical significance in contexts outside 'routine politics'. Rational political duties are (*ceteris paribus*) sufficient reasons for agents to implement chosen interventions in the course of nature. Sufficient reasons, here, must be tightly linked to causality — have a heavy consequentialist component. (Either the particular chosen intervention in question must be reasonably presumed to have beneficent consequences — an act-utilitarian criterion — or the prevalence of a propensity to choose to intervene in this fashion must have beneficent consequences — a rule-utilitarian view.)[77] The view that men have political duties which hold *whatever* the consequences of observing them is not plausible, though it is perhaps prototypical of political duties that they may be judged to hold whatever the cost *to the agent* whose duties they are. Certainly the chosen interventions in question, to be morally binding, need not show or be expected to show a purely personal net profit. But they must be chosen on the basis of the belief that their net causal impact will benefit those whom they affect. (The virtue of integrity[78] and the more aesthetically fastidious conceptions of agency such as those which emphasise one version or another of the doctrine of double effect may properly and perhaps profitably serve in public life to inhibit the performance of some political actions.* But it is easy to over-emphasise their directive merits when transposed from private into fully public life. The secular critique of the role of Christianity in public life, a critique which reaches back to Machiavelli and Rousseau, is entirely correct to stress the very limited part which moral self-absorption can play in politi-cal virtue.) It is a key aspect of the political realm that it is a field of insti-tutionalised (and therefore to some degree predictable) mutual benefit (as well as harm), a complex nexus of practices.[79] Where no such realm exists — however restricted in demographic scope — the appropriate axiom for chosen human interventions in the order of nature may well be (over whatever human scope the agent feels himself or herself to be personally committed): 'sauve qui peut'.

43. What is the epistemic criterion for whether a political state of affairs in the past or in the future *is* truly possible? In the past there is a unique cri-terion for political possibility, open to counterfactual modification through explicitly counterfactual theorising. Thinking causally about past political possibilities, on the basis of whatever theoretical analysis of the epistemic status of counterfactuals it is judged appropriate to adopt, is a relatively coherent enterprise.[80] Assessing the rational political duties of past persons, however practically futile an exercise, can at least proceed within a con-ceptually determinate frame. Thinking causally about the future (a pre-condition for assessing what can or cannot politically be caused to occur) lacks any such epistemically *given* frame. What makes factual claims about the past true or false is the way the world actually was. But about the future there are perhaps no *facts*[81] in virtue of which statements are rendered true or false. What is of importance here, however, is not whether it is possible to give a valid 'realist' analysis of the truth status of statements about the future nor whether determinism is true, but simply whether there is any fundamental epistemic coherence to the human practice of predicting and acting upon the basis of predictions. Even if it were in any sense true that the way the future will be is already fully determined, there would still be no way of bringing this truth theoretically to bear upon human practical

---

* See e.g. Nagel, 'Ruthlessness in Public Life. (note 28, p. 340); Michael Walzer, *Just and Unjust Wars*, London 1978; Stuart Hampshire, in Hampshire (ed.), *Public and Private Morality*, Cambridge 1978, chs. 1 & 2; and cf. Honderich, *Three Essays on Political Violence*, Oxford 1976, pp. 22—9; R.M. Hare, 'Rules of War and Moral Reasoning', in Marshall Cohen, Thomas Nagel & Thomas Scanlon (eds.), *War and Moral Responsibility*, pb. ed. Princeton 1974, pp. 46—61. Utilitarians seldom find it difficult to construct individual examples of horrendous acts which they see it as morally appropri-ate on balance to perform. What is difficult for them to do is to link the propensity to *perform* such acts, even in extremis and after careful deliberation, to any coherent general conception of the character of agency. Utilitarianism offers an abstract standard for what it is for an action to be right or wrong which is radically disconnected from any concrete conception of what it is to lead a moral life.

reason. By contrast the excessively many ways in which it is certain that the future will *not* be are of central significance in practical reason. What can or cannot be brought about by political action, the extent and limits of the causal powers of political agents, forms one of the main considerations in the theory of political duty. Simply possessing good intentions is a very small part of political virtue.

Objectivity sets the scope within which good intentions can be implemented. A radically objectified context of political choice treats the single agent addressed as exercising choice and takes everything else* as the context of choice (hence the extreme instability of such theories in application, whatever the theoretical intentions of their authors).[82] An individualist political theory, set within a radically objectified theory of practical reason, treats the issue of what to do severely in the idiom of net consequence. It can add aesthetic or ethically expressive considerations to this — not simply the venting of political emotions because their venting brings psychic relief[83] but also the expression in action of judgements which are taken to be true. But it can scarcely allow any great weight to such considerations. By imposing such a fierce criterion of cost-effectiveness and by highlighting the probable inconsequence of strictly individual action, its main tendency is to shrivel the rationality of political agency. Because the theory of political obligation is an attempt to direct individuals on what it is rational for them to *do*, it cannot be coherently conceived in terms of addressing single individuals strictly in private. But neither can it be coherently conceived as an attempt to edify at a more collective level, whilst studiedly ignoring the consideration that many amongst those addressed will not succumb to edification.[84] Men have (broadly) good reason politically to strive to bring about the best that they (if they strove) *could*, at an acceptable collective cost, bring about. But this lofty political plateau (the summit of rational political ambitions) is not the highest *logically* possible human political achievement — the best that human beings outside history could be coherently conceived as realising. Rather, it is the highest historically attainable political plateau; and its attainability depends on the causal consideration of what proportion of persons concerned will commit themselves to striving towards it. There is no guaranteed method for assessing such matters; but great variation in the soundness and sobriety of individual judgement. The Napoleonic maxim, 'On s'engage et puis on voit', may reflect a temperament which it is in some ways appropriate for a political leader to possess; but it certainly does not offer a sound criterion for the exercise of political judgement.

44. The relations between individualism, public values and rationality are thus both complicated and of central significance. Any theory in which it is presumed appropriate to consider the political agent merely as an individual

---

* Including the present choices of other agents and the future choices of other agents except insofar as these are contingent on the choice taken by the agent concerned.

contributing consequences at a given margin is irretrievably sub-political. It need not necessarily be (and in the case of such a theory as Hare's will not in fact be) explicitly morally irresponsible. But if it is both individualist in reference and instrumental in character, a very large proportion of politics is conceived as being over before it can start to be applied. If in addition it is also aggressively egoist in its view of human motivation, the destructive implications are still further accentuated.

Political theories are in essence theories of the attainable scope of constructive human co-operation. The actions which they prescribe for a valued group of human beings must be actions which a causally sufficient proportion of the group addressed will, if appropriately instructed (if, that is, they are enabled to grasp clearly what is at stake), in practice *perform*. A pragmatically adequate political theory for a particular group must identify the causal ecology within which that group's social ambience is located and by which it is sustained, with sufficient precision to enable its members to judge, individually and collectively, sound strategies for implementing their values within this ecology. The beliefs of all human groups (like the beliefs of all individuals) are permanently at risk in both the dimension of moral care and that of natural skill. Rational political duties will be duties to act in a manner which avoids not merely moral depravity but also political stupidity.

Because the sense in which the political future is *knowable* even in principle is so restricted, it is impossible to make the criterion of sound political judgement as strong as predictive success — a consideration of great importance if rational political duties are to be predicated upon political *judgement* (assessment of future possibilities and probabilities). Being rationally sanguine requires no apology even in the face of subsequent disappointment. But to be irrationally sanguine or to be simply eupeptic cannot plausibly be excused even by the contingency of subsequent success. (Or rather they could only be so excused in the case of *purely* individual action — action which is, ex hypothesi, *politically* inconsequential.)

The attainable scope of human social co-operation depends quite largely on what each of the human beings concerned conceives that scope to be.

45. There are at least two distinct ways in which it is possible to conceive rational political duties. The existing consciousness of agents may be taken blankly as given — as fate — however incoherent or myopic, both practically and morally, this may be when viewed firmly from the outside. Whatever duties this consciousness rationally furnishes an agent with are his positively rational duties. (Positively rational duty is simply a matter of the *internal* coherence of beliefs about public and private goods and the means to attain these goods in practice.) Alternatively this consciousness may be revised not simply by internal re-arrangement but by whatever external rational pressures are compatible with the proviso that the consciousness in question should remain that of the agent concerned. Whatever duties

this revised consciousness endows an agent with are his critically rational duties.

The dangers of either of these approaches are evident enough. The first lends an unwarranted moral and cognitive authority to the obtuseness of actual historical agents. The second quite readily replaces historical agents (the creatures whose *rational* duties are supposedly in question) with abstract artefacts of the moral taste of the theorist. Positively rational duties are excessively deferential to history, critically rational duties, if perhaps appropriately supra-historical in the epistemic ambition of their assessors, are suspiciously heedless of the historicity of human agents.

Inquiry into the content of rational duty may be conceived as a dialogue between an agent and an interlocutor. In this dialogue even those who believe that positively rational duties are the most by which agents could rationally see themselves as morally constrained will admit the appropriateness of some criticism of an agent's existing consciousness: 'Given *all* your beliefs and all *your* values, would it not be better not to act as you now feel inclined or at this instant judge to be best, but rather in some different fashion?' What is disputed is whether (and if so, exactly how) it makes sense to inquire of an agent: 'Would it not be better in relation to future issues of practical reason to *alter* your beliefs or values in some distinct fashion, and thus in due course see yourself to have good reasons for acting quite differently in future?' The view that it does not make sense to ask this question is most likely to be motivated by the presumption that the change suggested will constitute a change in the values of the agent and that, evaluation not being a cognitive matter, no possibility of *rational* abandonment of present values or espousal of fresh values can arise. But it is at least equally puzzling how far (and exactly how) it makes sense to propose to an agent that he or she changes at all drastically their causal beliefs. ('Holding the false beliefs that you do, it is rational for you to regard yourself as having those and also those duties. But if you held only true beliefs and all practically relevant true beliefs it would be rational for you to regard yourself as morally constrained in these (surely *very*) other ways.') Critically rational duty is duty construed under some humanly appropriate etiolation of omniscience. Modern individualists are much struck by the absurdity of the idea of it even making sense to claim that anyone else morally knows better than they do themselves. But even the most modern of individualists could hardly deny that it makes sense to presume that others can hold cognitively better judged factual or causal beliefs than they do themselves.

46. There are three main ways in which an assessment of the critically rational duties of a historical agent is fundamentally in jeopardy. Firstly it may weaken the conceptual relation between the personal identity of the agent and the duty suggested to such a degree that it becomes quite unclear that the agent in question does *have* good reason to discharge it. Secondly

it may revise the consciousness of the agent addressed quite drastically but fail to take accurate account of the causal context within which the agent will have to act, holding out illusory (because historically irrelevant) prospects of benefit from the action or propensity to act enjoined, and substituting moral fairy stories for practically sound directives. Thirdly it may select as appropriate components of the agent's practical reasoning considerations which the agents themselves *could* not have good reason to believe. The second of these possibilities is relatively distinct from the others. Usually a product either of absolutist moral theories or of carelessness in counterfactual reflection, the central error which it commits is the political vice of imprudence. Whilst not necessarily in any way misdirecting historical agents as to what they have good reason to value, it severely misdirects them on the politically crucial issue of what they have good reason to do.

Between the first and the third possibilities there are important links. No one can have rational duties which require their holding *comprehensively* different beliefs and valuing comprehensively different values from those which they do. Even the most intrepidly critical and the most drastically revisionary dialogue between interlocutor and agent must generate changes *within* the agent's system of beliefs. No agent can have duties which are situated beyond what are in principle their visual *capabilities*. Supra-historical duties are duties conceived in abstraction from the natural skills, as well as from the moral attentiveness, of historical agents. They represent a God's-eye-view of human duties. The dialogue in which they are derived is conceived as a dialogue between a historical agent and trans-temporal omniscience, aware, as in the imaginary museum of Dummett's caricature,[85] of all the properties of the future. ('Would it not be better to hold wholly different (and all true) beliefs and to value wholly different (and all valid) values and therefore to act in a wholly different fashion?') This proposal is in effect a proposal to the agent to become someone else, to change his or her personal identity, epistemically to escape from history. It is not, of course, or at least not avowedly, a proposal to escape existentially from history. The agent remains where and when he or she is, remains himself or herself. There can scarcely be a serious alternative to this aspect of the offer in political theory. Agents can leave their society (emigrate); but they cannot leave their selves. Even emigration could hardly have in modern political theory the somewhat exaggerated role which it was allocated by some in the seventeenth century. The choice for an emigre between affiliating him- or her-self to the U.S.A. or U.S.S.R. or Switzerland or Israel does not resemble the choice to undertake the errand into the wilderness in more or less select company.[86] There is also some danger of educational overkill on the interlocutor's part, of leaving the agent too removed cognitively from the political assumptions of his or her fellows to exercise the slightest intended political influence. *Mildly* idiosyncratic beliefs and values may be a source of potential influence and significance in politics. But beliefs and values wholly discontinuous from those of all other contemporaries, if not perhaps a proof of insanity, are certainly a sound recipe for political inconsequence.

From these considerations it is possible to draw two main clear conclusions. Comprehensively critical evaluative rationality may or may not be accessible in principle to historical agents. But if it *is* accessible to them, it cannot suffice to direct them in political theory, where the central question is always what they have good reason to do.

What historical agents have good reason to do depends, inter alia, on what, within a scheme of beliefs which is truly theirs, they have good reason to judge efficacious. Endowing them with comprehensively different values as an outcome of an imaginary dialogue is likely (though not perhaps quite certain*) to constitute not so much an intrusion into their moral privacy as a denial of their historical identity. Correcting their judgement of what will be efficacious by comparing it with what in due course occurs (and thereby endowing them with better-judged beliefs about future contingencies) enhances their cognitive prowess. But it does so by removing them entirely from the context of practical reason. To invoke the future in all its conclusiveness and definition as a standard for the cognitive efforts of the present is to transcend the condition of temporal finitude within which human beings have any duties at all. Beliefs based upon *knowledge* of the future are beliefs which human beings could not have good reason to hold. Even on the severest of criteria, the rational duties of human beings must depend upon beliefs which *they* could historically have good reason to hold.

47. And *do* human beings have any rational political duties? It is perhaps a peculiarity of late capitalist society that this question can be regarded by many well-educated, sophisticated and secularly-minded persons as one which might quite generally lack an affirmative answer. Not, of course, that such a view is the most commonly-held in a society like Great Britain today. The most common perhaps is simply that rational political duties consist essentially in the duty, more or less punctiliously, to obey at least in serious matters the law wherever a person happens to find himself or herself or, more fastidiously, in view of the felicity of living here in such a blatantly legitimate polity, simply that *we* should obey the laws here. Perhaps the commonest form of theoretical dissent from this view amounts, more or less sparely, to espousing a varyingly transcendent alternative political locus for moral authority and treating all efforts on behalf of this as axiomatically sanctioned.[87] Each of these views is both confused in its assumptions and imprudent in its implications. But there is at present no seriously character-

---

* Whether or not it does so depends partly on the causal elasticity (within the rational deliberation presupposed) of the initial 'subjective motivational set', in the face of the passage of time and the bringing to bear of the persuasions of others. Even if the imputed eloquence, imaginative force and insight of the interlocutor were superlative (moralistic theorists tend to cast themselves as the interlocutor in question) and the agent were thus under ideal instruction, large changes in belief would presumably take a considerable amount of time.

ised contending conception with which to replace them. (To offer utilitarianism, unglossed, in lieu of a theory of rational duty is simply to take the fifth amendment.)

To attempt to set out such a contending conception would be an awesome task. But two rather simple points seem worth making even on the strength of the present inquiry.

The first is a point about the essential heterogeneity and contextual dependence of political duties. At different times and in different places and for persons of different abilities and temperaments and in different social roles political duties will differ very drastically indeed in urgency and in character. In some contexts they will stretch over very wide social spaces. In others they may shrink very narrowly indeed. In content, they will be duties to commit time and patience and energy at least as often as they are duties to incur great risks or make supreme sacrifices; and only seldom (very, very seldom) will they be exhausted by the punctilious observance of laws. The merits of obedience and legality are as much overestimated by political theorists as the virtues of disobedience and self-righteous illegality are overestimated by disgruntled adolescents. Social life does depend upon a large measure of order, predictability and routine; and it *would* be dreadful if we could never trust each other. But it would also be necessary to live under a government of remarkably good laws or remarkably good men for an agent's political duties to be exhausted by even the most active programme of obedience. Because of the irreducible heterogeneity of context, political duties can only be trimmed to a Procrustean uniformity by the application of an overweening theory of value, a theory which obliterates the diversity of historical social circumstances in which men live, either (as with Hobbes) by grossly overstressing their biological uniformity and absurdly exaggerating the clarity of its implications for what it is rational for them to do, or by vindicating the authority of some values for a human agent, whatever the actual consequences of her or his seeking to implement them. If we make a due regard for consequence a constraint on any valid political theory, such a theory will necessarily consist quite largely in a theory of prudence, a theory of how to act in order to improve the quality of social existence and, still more urgently, to prevent this quality from degenerating drastically. A sound theory of men's rational political duties will be a theory which relativises these not crudely to men's existing beliefs and values in all their cognitive and moral disorder, but as delicately as it can contrive, to men's actual political situations. It will be a theory of how to make the best and avoid the worst of historically provided political possibilities. (It will also recognise that one of the main forces which determines what possibilities history at any time has provided is the beliefs and values of the human agents then living.)

The second (and perhaps more interesting and contentious) point is that such a theory, in the teeth of modern egalitarianism, will recognise the heterogeneity of men's historical responsibilities and the central role in political reason of a cognitive and moral division of labour. It will do this not because those who fashion it wish to felicitate the deity on designing (or permitting) the human history which has actually occurred or because they find the actuality of human inequalities of understanding and concern to be morally attractive, but simply because, like Mount Everest, these inequalities are there; and because political theory is the theory of what to do about what is there, not the theory of what, were we God, we would have brought about or merely of what we, while not being God, would greatly prefer. In any historical society the political responsibilities of its members will differ very greatly because their powers (what they are capable of bringing about) and their understanding of what is politically at stake will differ very greatly. Those who understand more and who can exercise greater power will have greater responsibilities. In an aristocratic form of society nobility obliges; but in any form of society comprehension obliges. The better an agent understands, the more they will be prepared in principle to ask of themselves and the more that others can reasonably ask of them. Because political duty is necessarily mediated through the level of an agent's understanding of what is politically at stake, one key aspect of political duty falls within the domain of an ethics of belief. What level of incomprehension in a political agent may be judged discreditable; how far a pattern of political conduct reflects the psychological mechanism of denial; what constitutes, in the context of action, courage and devotion, cowardice, betrayal and irresponsibility, these are the modalities of observing or neglecting political duty.

48. What type of duty, then, is political duty?

The theory of value which a theorist adopts will determine precisely how 'duty' or 'obligation' or 'responsibility' are conceived in relation to politics. Thomist theories of the character of a political duty will differ sharply from those held by positivist utilitarians. Nuer theories will differ from both. Clear and precisely demarcated duties will be easiest to locate at the least exacting end of the cognitive and moral division of labour. To feed the starving, when well and safely able to do so, not lightly and selfishly to betray one's fellows, these are certainly political *duties*, 'rock-bottom duties' in Urmson's phrase,[88] items of conduct which 'we can expect and demand from others', not ones which 'we can merely hope for and receive with gratitude when we get' them.[89] Any theory of value in which abstention from such acts fails to appear as intrinsically discreditable is an unsound theory of what is of value for human beings. At the opposite end of the cognitive and moral division of labour, appropriate political conduct has more in common with the performance of saints and heroes. It is a disturbing commonplace of political theory, at least since Machiavelli, that those who understand best seldom retain the best of intentions, whilst those whose intentions are persistently excellent seldom grasp political causality with any great finesse. But power and political understanding are both morally exigent (though what they demand is intricate and variegated and seldom has the clarity of outline of political obligations as these have usually been conceived in the past and as states have always been anxious to define them). Moral exigency in relation to politics certainly demands the effort to understand clearly and judge soberly what is politically at stake, whether or not (one of the oldest questions in political theory) it also demands the attempt to secure power.

The scope and limits of political duty are never securely given by conventional categories of law and public authority. They stretch elusively across a much wider stratum of human conduct than these categories can specify, at times overwhelming in their force and centrality, at others mercifully peripheral to the living of a full and decent life. Their content and character is always changing; and, in so changing, it mirrors the historical contingency of human existence. The hope that political duty can be rendered cut-and-dried, simple, dominant and perspicuous is in essence the hope that historical contingency can be conclusively eluded and human social existence be rendered as simply willed and committing as an exchange of private promises.[90]

It is easy to see the charm of such a conception. The fact that one has promised to do something does in most circumstances give one a firmer and a more definite *obligation* to *do* it than is provided by most of the types of good reason which one has to act in a particular manner. The view that political life would be altogether more crisply and perspicuously *obligatory* in its demands if only it could all be reduced to the execution of promises is thus, in its own terms, convincing enough. But it is hard to see that this offers any very helpful instruction on the political duties of actual historical agents — on what they should in fact do in the sorry circumstances in which they happen to find themselves.

49. The broadest contrast between plausible conceptions of the place of duty within politically rational action lies today between those which favour strong interpretations of the character of rationality and those which favour strong conceptions of the character of duty. (The slightly forlorn charm which the theories of Plato and Kant retain for the moralistic lies in the decisiveness of the synthesis which they attempt between these two.) Strong criteria for the rationality of action yield an account of political duties as acts the claims of which it *must* be irrational for an agent to deny. Human beings have only such duties as those which states or cultures contrive (causally) to inflict credally upon them; and these duties are relativised in their entirety to the history of human power and belief. In the egoistic cultural climate of late capitalist society this conception is morally regressive. Political *duties* as such arise only by conjunctural accident. Rational political agency consists predominantly in the enjoyment of intrinsic political pleasures and the placing of instrumentally efficacious political investments.

Looser criteria for the rationality of action (criteria which leave more room for optimism within the practice of rational deliberation) and more moralistic accounts of the claims of moral duty focus instead on the rationality of belief, on more holistic conceptions of the nature of the human agent and on the exercise of imagination. They yield an account of political duties which acknowledges the causal refractoriness of the context of political action and the historicity of human agency but which relativises the scope of political duty not to the existing tastes and preferences of such agents in their entirety, but instead to the *limits* of their imagination and concern, as well as of their causal powers. The moralism of such a theory is evident enough. (That is its point.) It is a moralism which runs the standing risk of inadvertently eluding the theory of rational action altogether. But it is explicitly conceived as a *part* of that theory, a form of 'optimistic internal reasons theory', focussed epistemically on the rationality of hope and pragmatically on the project of making the best of history. Insofar as the theory is overoptimistic and historical persons are wholly without reasons for making (what could otherwise be) the best of history, there is simply a gap between the duties men have a reason to acknowledge and what is desirable or what ought to be the case.

50. What sorts of claims does the existence of the political realm (a causal product of the history of the species) rationally impose upon human beings? Do human beings as such have rational political *duties*? Political duties are acts in relation to the political realm which an agent has a good reason to perform (the reason that she or he ought to perform them) but which are not in themselves necessarily either political pleasures or political acts expected to yield an essentially personal profit. (One may enjoy or profit by performing one's political duties. But one cannot *expect* always to do so.)

There are many possible types of theory of the claims which the existence of the political realm rationally imposes on human beings. Some theories seek to derive the content of such claims from considering the nature of the political realm itself. There is for example the theory that the nature of this realm necessarily rationally imposes upon men the duty to obey the commands of their rulers (broadly, the theory of Hobbes). There is also the theory that it morally imposes upon them the moral duty to obey the commands of their rulers and morally forbids them in all cases to resist their lawful rulers (broadly, the theory of Kant).[91] There is the theory that in a democratic (or in some sense *procedurally* legitimate) polity it requires them to observe the laws of that polity.* In each of these cases there is some force to the theory; but in none is the theory itself appropriate in *shape* to address

* Pateman, *Problem of Political Obligation*. It is, of course, true that different types of polity have different moral merits (see e.g. Rawls: Nozick: Pateman, op. cit. etc.; and Peter Singer, *Democracy and Disobedience*, pb. ed. Oxford 1973; Brian Barry, 'Is Democracy Special?', Laslett & Fishkin (eds.), *Philosophy, Politics and Society, 5th Series*, pp. 155–96). But in the world of action, where what we need to be able to decide is always what is to be *done*, it is unclear what follows from this.

the central question of what, given the historical reality of the political realm, men at any point have good reason to do.

51. A second possible approach is to seek to answer the question by developing a conception of the nature of rational action or a general theory of value. Theories of egoistic rationality have a lengthy ancestry in political theory. But they have always depended upon an impoverished or implausible philosophical psychology, and the idiom of single-act instrumental calculation with which they have now become deeply associated has more the air, when generalised to society at large, of an index of cultural self-destruction than it does of an epistemically cogent theory of the character of human practical reason. Little effort has as yet been made to construct a less culturally blighted conception of the relations between the political realm and rational action as such. A possible position would be that, as with any other part of their environment, the existence of the political realm *simply* imposes on men the rational imperative of acting (as far as their cognitive powers permit) cost-effectively in the light of its causal presence. In itself this has an important implication and one which requires underlining. (It is hard to see how any *less* consequentialist conception of the implications of the causal refractoriness and pragmatic importance of the political realm for individual life could be defensible.) But it is disagreeably discreet on the issue of how even to begin to conceive of the appropriate *goals* for human action.

Vigorously corrective theories of value are strikingly less discreet. But they are also on the whole notably insensitive to the historicity of the context which they aspire to edify and (perhaps and *therefore*?) very vaguely related to the theory of rational action. Utilitarianism is as well equipped as any general moral theory can be to take account of the causal refractoriness and pragmatic indeterminacy of the political realm. But its being theoretically open to such considerations does not mean that most of its exponents display the imaginative depth, the degree of counterfactual insight into the properties of human society or indeed the extent of informed understanding of contemporary societies which would be necessary to realise this theoretical promise in intellectual practice. (It is, for example, interesting that Hare's anti-descriptivist account of his own substantive ethical views[92] should yield such a feeble conception of the relation between ethics and politics.)[93] Both act-utilitarianism and ideal rule-utilitarianism are highly implausible as theories of the rational implications for action of 'the moral reasons people actually have'. Act-utilitarianism requires that one consider rational action with utter disregard for all aspects of the life of the agent. Ideal rule-utilitarianism requires that one consider what ought to be done in utter disregard of what the consequences of so doing will be in the real world.[94] Whatever their merits as theories of what is intrinsically desirable (of the character of an ideal world in which they might well prove extensionally equivalent), each of these theories can be incorporated into the theory of rational action only by stipulative fiat. It is wholly implausible that either could be validly *derived* from the theory of rational action and consequently wholly implausible that they can in principle specify what men as they historically are have good reason to do or, more particularly, what they have good reason politically to do.

52. The simplest conception of the content of rational political duty relativises this at an individual level to the values which individuals happen to possess* and, by composition, at a social level to the values which social groupings happen to possess.† Depending on the values prevailing in particular social groupings at particular times and on how forensic a conception of rationality and obligation a theorist adopts, this conception might yield no rational political duties at all (making rational political action coextensive with political pleasures and egoistically rational political investments) or, with less rigid egoism and more theoretical play for the imagination – perhaps even the moral imagination – it might yield a decidedly richer harvest, extending prudence outwards from a mean egoism to a concern for family, descendants, friends, neighbours, fellow citizens, the human species at large and even (perhaps a trifle indiscriminately) the class of all sentient creatures.

The main contrast can be drawn between a conception which combines two modes of pessimism and a conception which combines two modes of optimism. The first conception, now often developed in a narrowly egoist form but in no sense necessarily requiring such a form, defines the class of rational acts in a rigorously instrumental and cost-effective spirit. It conceives rationality as essentially compulsive, taking as the criterion of rationality what it is irrational to deny. It is averse to risk, treats the expenditure of effort as inherently costly, is in general insensitive to the addictive properties (internal rewards) of moral agency, and thus tends to conflate the rationality of hope with the rationality of investment. Its account of the nature of reasons for action is a pessimistic 'internal reasons theory', sceptical, though not dogmatically dismissive, of the truth status of claims that agents have reasons (and more particularly *moral* reasons) for acting at a particular time of which they are blithely unaware. It seems a natural concomitant of such a view (though not one for which all exponents of the view possess the least sympathy)* to conceive the ego in the theory of rational action as temporally rather thin.[95] In more specifically political terms the substantively egoist forms of such theories correctly (on their own assumptions) interpret virtually all political action as pure waste. In less egoist forms they may take a more delicately ecological view of the contribution (positive and negative)

---

* Williams, 'Internal and External Reasons'. It is precisely the point of 'internal reasons theories' to guarantee this.
† Harman, 'Relativistic Ethics'. There are, of course, very important theoretical differences of opinion as to how to interpret this relativisation and in particular how to interpret, within it, the epistemic status (if any) of the moral *ought* of agency.
* Williams in particular is strongly opposed to any such inference.

which political action makes to the reproduction of acceptable social life. But they remain, in either version, more sensitive to the rationality of purely personal life (the view from within one's own life and from the present)[96] than to the rationality of social reproduction.[97]

53. Personal lives, however, require societies in which they may be lived. From a firmly subjective viewpoint the rational status of morality depends upon the degree to which it contrives to insinuate itself into the motivation of persons.[98] From a firmly objective viewpoint, whatever the *rational status* of morality may be, it is evident that the capacity of morality to insinuate itself into the motivation of persons is strongly linked to the requirements of social reproduction. The tendency of vigorously corrective ethical theories in confrontation with the historical reality of politics is to mutate from theories of rational action into theories of the desirable content and consequences of political education. But there is a less fanciful and altogether more robustly rational social practice, the practice of socialisation, which indicates a certain theoretical disingenuousness to the more individualist relativisations of rationality. Seen from the inside, it just happens to be the case that what human agents come to value is affected by their socialisation and it just happens to be the case that they seek to socialise their successors. It is, it is true, because of these happy eventualities that human society as a continuing entity is possible. But except insofar as their own earlier socialisation happens to have insinuated the continuation of human society as a goal into their affections, no particular human being necessarily has any reason to conceive it as such. *Après nous le déluge*. At this point the claims for the relative priority of an external (and rather more comprehensive) point of view become insistent.[99]

The inherently fragmented character of human value[100] and in particular the profound and ineradicable split between the subjective and objective viewpoints on human existence precludes a simple and permanent victory of the objective over the subjective. Even optimally desirable states of affairs do not necessarily present human agents as these actually are with strong reasons (let alone sufficient reasons) for implementing them. Moral rationality cannot be made by any conceivable sleight of hand *motivationally* compulsive. But, by the same token, there is no way in which the epistemic status of purely internal conceptions of what is of value for men can be comprehensively vindicated. It is not plausible that the rational way for any man (let alone all men) to live is to turn themselves 'as far as possible into an instrument for the realization of what is best *sub specie aeternitatis*'.[101] But neither is it plausible that good reasons for anyone are exhausted by the set of reasons of which she or he is undeniably in full possession.

54. The alternative conception of the fundamental rationality of political duty leans rather heavily on the more external point of view. It treats the

rationality of acts in a more generous and open-minded (a more profligate) mood, casting its bread upon the waters, partly because it is less ready to regard effort as pure cost, partly because it has a more elaborate conception of social causality and fears the ecological consequences of an excessively instrumental and cost-effective idiom of agency. It takes the egos in the theory of action as temporally extended over the whole of their lives (and correspondingly prudent) and conceives them not simply as the bearers of experiences but also as self-producers[102] and as producers of society. The theory of rational action for agents so considered will necessarily include a theory of rational socialisation for the *self* as well as for others, and it will also necessarily include a theory of rational social reproduction. It will treat the avoidance of foreseeable consequences of an undesirable kind as an important constraint on what can count as rational action. Within this broad conception it models the character of rational deliberation for human agents with resolute optimism, seeing the telos of such deliberation for an individual as the project of making the best of oneself and for groups, societies and the species as a whole, as the project of making the best of history as they find this. It will, accordingly, allot an extended role within deliberation to the exercise of imagination, construe deliberation as a protracted (perhaps even life-long, if not species-long, process) and allow a generous role within the process of deliberation to the contributions of other persons besides the agent, whether simply as bearers of relevant information or as moral theorists. In these ways it will be profoundly sceptical of the epistemic and evaluative adequacy of the agent's self-conception as directly encountered. It will be so in essence because it doubts that the 'objective viewpoint', however far it may be (and is likely to be) from being motivationally *compelling*, *could* be epistemically irrelevant for human beings.

But it will still be, on Williams' account,[103] an internal reasons theory, though one of an exceedingly moralistic as well as optimistic kind. It will be such *because* its theoretical point is to specify what, at the most optimistic, we can presume that men have reason politically to do *for one another*. Where men's self-conception sets what they could have good reason to do for one another irreducibly in opposition to what they have good reason to do for themselves, political duties are *defined* as part of what they do not have reason to do for themselves. If human beings as they are truly have no reason to do anything except for themselves, then that is simply a fact about what human beings have now become. (Whatever is true about human beings now is a fact about what human beings have become.) If it were the full truth about the human present, it would promise a bleak political future. But perhaps it is still simply false.

55. The types of theory of political obligation which have been constructed in the past can only be credited today (at least as theories about obligations which real persons may today *possess*) by an exercise in superstition. No

very robust theory of the relations between political duty and the theory of rational action is at present extant. But we may reasonably presume at least that there must *be* theoretical relations between these two (even if, at the limit, these were relations of simple disjunction). Neither of the two broad conceptions of the nature of rationality which are more or less superstitiously credited at present is *necessarily* superstitious in character. Indeed each is theoretically so elastic that there may well be a large measure of extensional overlap between the two. Whether either of them can be articulated without superstition in a form which relates the rationality of acceptable individual existence to the causal prerequisites for desirable social reproduction is not yet clear. But what we may be confident of is that there is very little danger of their being so, unless some effort is put into the attempt to make them so.

56. State power (the governmental capacity to act effectively for good or ill) and social co-operation and trust are all being built and destroyed all the time in every country in the world today. It is reasonable to expect all of these processes to persist over any human future which we can coherently imagine. The circumstances in which it is open to us to live the rest of our lives and the circumstances in which it will be open to our descendants to live the whole of their lives will be overwhelmingly affected by the course of these processes. To say that all human life is politics is merely to remove the meaning from an important word. But to insist that most of what is truly important in human life depends profoundly upon politics, however little this consideration may have intruded into the lives of most inhabitants of wealthy capitalist democracies since 1945, is no more than realistic. If human beings rationally owe each other any duties at all (or any which they do not create by arbitrary personal whim), if they are not all islands entire unto themselves, then there can be no doubt that each and every one of them has the most urgent of duties (within the limits set by their powers) to sustain the better potentialities and to seek to avert the worse potentialities of this hugely important domain. Only the deepest historical and social myopia or the crassest and most reductively egoist ideologies of arbitrary entitlement to historical privilege can offer sufficient grounds for denying this.

In a (temporarily) ideal polity under an ideally wise and virtuous political leadership, an individual's political duties might amount simply to a punctilious observance of the laws of his polity and the commands of its leaders, together with a vigorous commitment to sustain these in the face of challenge from others inside or outside the society. (Even under these propitious circumstances, the individual concerned would need to judge that the circumstances were indeed *very* broadly as described.) Under historically more normal circumstances the broad distribution (the character and direction) of an individual's political duties would be appreciably different. Since political duties are duties to sustain the viability of decent and humanly concerned values within the society of which one is a member, they imply a measure of allegiance to leaders (whether governmental or private) who act effectively on behalf of these values. To perceive and to acknowledge political duties in this sense is thus to repudiate or escape from political alienation — to escape not from the self-righteous *ressentiment* or psychic malaise of disgruntled adolescents, but from a state of not understanding causally how the conditions of one's life depend upon the political properties of the society of which one is a member and of not grasping morally what this dependence implies for one's responsibilities to other human beings. To accept our political duties in this sense is certainly to set ourselves against the cultural field of gravity of late capitalist society. But it is to do so, not by waiting complacently for the auto-destruction of capitalism to work itself through but by recognising the need within capitalist society at this stage of its history for political invention and cultural creation and by seeking to generate within its bleak ecology a politics of mutual understanding and human solidarity rather than one of placid greed or self-righteous malice.

57. I conclude, therefore, that the prospects for a theory of rational political obligation as this has generally been conceived are beyond hope, not because (as has sometimes been supposed) there is nothing for such a theory to be about, but because there is so much that such a theory *has* to be about (so much to which it *has* to do justice), if it is to stand a chance of proving valid.

But, while the prospects for inventing theories which unite power with validity in this area are so uninviting, the need for attaining greater insight into the theoretical problems which it presents has never been more urgent.

Notes

1 Introduction

1 R.G. Collingwood, *An Autobiography*, pb. ed. London 1970, p. 62.
2 See particularly Quentin Skinner, *The Foundations of Modern Political Thought*, 2 vols., Cambridge 1979 and the lengthy series of methodological articles there cited at Vol. I, pp. 285—6. See also J.G.A. Pocock, *Politics, Language and Time*, London 1972, esp. ch. 1.
3 For a representative critique see Charles D. Tarlton, 'Historicity, Meaning and Revisionism in the Study of Political Thought', *History and Theory*, XII, 3, 1973, 307—28. For an extension of the argument into the more challenging field of philosophy proper see Michael Ayers, 'Analytical Philosophy and the History of Philosophy', in Jonathan Rée et al., *Philosophy and its Past*, Hassocks, Sussex 1978, 41—66. For examples of works explicitly conceived in this idiom see Geoffrey Hawthorn, *Enlightenment and Despair: A History of Sociology*, Cambridge 1976; Donald Winch, *Adam Smith's Politics; an Essay in Historiographic Revision*, Cambridge 1978.
4 See especially Hans-Georg Gadamer, *Truth and Method*, London 1975; *Philosophical Hermeneutics*, tr. & ed. David E. Linge, pb. ed. Berkeley 1977. (Cf. Jane Austen's verdict: History 'is very tiresome; and yet I often think it odd that it should be so dull, for a great deal of it must be invention' (*Northanger Abbey*, Everyman ed. London 1906, p. 87).
5 *Philosophy*, XLIII, 164, p. 96.
6 W.V.O. Quine, *Word and Object*, Cambridge, Mass., 1960; *Ontological Relativity and other Essays*, New York 1969; Paul Feyerabend, *Against Method*, London 1975; T.S. Kuhn, *The Structure of Scientific Revolutions*, Chicago 1962; Imré Lakatos & Alan Musgrave (eds.), *Criticism and the Growth of Knowledge*, pb. Cambridge 1970; Richard Rorty, 'The World Well Lost', *Journal of Philosophy*, LXIX, 19, 26 Oct. 1972, 649—65; 'Realism and Reference', *The Monist*, LIX, 3, July 1976, 321—40; Hilary Putnam, *Philosophical Papers*, 2 vols. Cambridge 1975; *Meaning and the Moral Sciences*, London 1978; Donald Davidson, 'The Very Idea of a Conceptual Scheme', *Proceedings of the American Philosophical Association*, XLVII, 1973—74, 5—20.
7 *Philosophy*, XLIII, 164, p. 86.
8 For attempts to apply this conception in historical analysis see John Dunn, *The Political Thought of John Locke*, Cambridge 1969 and 'Individuality and Clientage in the Formation of Locke's Social Imagination', in Reinhard Brandt (ed.), *Locke Symposium*, Berlin and New York 1980.
9 For valuable subsequent discussions of Locke's arguments on this issue see: Frank Snare, 'Consent and Conventional Acts in John Locke', *Journal of the History of Philosophy*, XIII, 1, January 1975, 27—36; A. John Simmons, 'Tacit Consent and Political Obligation', *Philosophy and Public Affairs*, V, 3, Spring 1976, 274—91; Iain W. Hampsher-Monk, 'Tacit Consent in Locke's *Two Treatises*', *Journal of the History of Ideas*, XL, 1, Jan.—March 1979, 135—9.

10 For a more schematic treatment of the contextual rationality of Locke's web of beliefs as a whole see Dunn, *Political Thought of John Locke*.

11 See especially Martyn P. Thompson, 'The Reception of Locke's *Two Treatises of Government* 1690–1705', *Political Studies*, XXIV, 2, June 1976, 184–91; 'Hume's Critique of Locke and the "Original Contract" ', *Il pensiero Politico*, X, 2, 1977, 189–201; Jeffrey M. Nelson, 'Unlocking Locke's Legacy: A Comment', *Political Studies*, XXVI, 1, March, 1978, 101–8; Nicholas Jolley, 'Leibniz on Hobbes, Locke's *Two Treatises* and Sherlock's *Case of Allegiance*', *Historical Journal*, XVIII, 1, March 1975, 21–35; 'Leibniz on Locke and Socinianism', *Journal of the History of Ideas*, XXXIX, 2, April 1978, 233–50. Bernard Bailyn (ed.), Thomas Hutchinson, 'A Dialogue between an American and a European Englishman (1768)', *Perspectives on American History*, IX, 1975, 343–410.

12 Major works include John Kenyon, *Revolution Principles: The Politics of Party 1689–1720*, Cambridge 1977; Isaac Kramnick, *Bolingbroke and his Circle*, Cambridge, Mass. 1968; Duncan Forbes, *Hume's Philosophical Politics*, Cambridge 1975; H.T. Dickinson, *Liberty and Property: Political Ideology in Eighteenth-Century Britain*, London 1977; J.G.A. Pocock, *The Machiavellian Moment*, Princeton, N.J. 1975; Gordon S. Wood, *The Creation of the American Republic 1776–1787*, Chapel Hill, 1969; Bernard Bailyn, *The Ordeal of Thomas Hutchinson*, London 1975; Robert M. Calhoon, *The Loyalists in Revolutionary America 1760–1781*, New York 1973.

13 For the importance of this tradition see now James Tully's admirable *A Discourse of Property*, Cambridge 1980 and a forthcoming article by James Moore, 'John Locke and the Scottish Jurists'.

14 See e.g. Alasdair Macintyre, *Against the Self-Images of the Age*, London 1971, esp. ch. 22; 'Ideology, Social Science and Revolution', *Comparative Politics*, V, 3, April 1973, 321–42; Charles Taylor, 'Interpretation and the Sciences of Man', *Review of Metaphysics*, XXV, September 1971, 3–51; Richard J. Bernstein, *The Restructuring of Social and Political Theory*, Oxford 1976; H.G. Gadamer, *Truth and Method: Philosophical Hermeneutics*; Jürgen Habermas, *Knowledge and Human Interests*, tr. J.J. Shapiro, London 1972; *Theory and Practice*, tr. J. Viertel, London 1974.

15 For a recent attempt to start firmly at the opposite end of the theoretical spectrum see David Wiggins, *Truth, Invention and the Meaning of Life*, Henriette Hertz Philosophical Lecture, British Academy 1976.

2 The identity of the history of ideas

1 This claim is clearly more plausible when made about the history of political theory than it is, for instance, about the history of philosophy. But it seems to me to be quite unmet by even such a helpful series of treatments as those edited by Professor Passmore in Beiheft 5, 'The Historiography of the History of Philosophy', of the journal *History and Theory*. For examples of the two different perspectives in the history of political theory in work of some distinction see on the one hand Alan Ryan, 'Locke and the Dictatorship of the Bourgeoisie', *Political Studies*, vol. VIII, no. 2 (June 1965), p. 219 and, on the other, Quentin Skinner, 'Hobbes's *Leviathan*' (review article on F.C. Hood, *The Divine Politics of Thomas Hobbes*), *The Historical Journal*, vol. VII, no. 2 (1964), p. 333. For an example of the sort of difference which is likely to appear in full-length treatments from these different perspectives cf. Howard Warrender, *The Political Philosophy of Hobbes* (Oxford 1957) with the treatment of Hobbes in C.B. Macpherson, *The Political Theory of Possessive Individualism* (Oxford 1962).

2 It seems to be the case that the interpretation of the famous passage in David Hume's *Treatise of Human Nature* on deducing 'ought' statements from 'is' statements has been distorted in just this way. Cf. *Treatise*, bk. III, 1, i, with, e.g. R.M. Hare, *The Language of Morals* (Oxford 1952), p. 29. But this is controversial. Cf. A.C. Macintyre, 'Hume on "Is" and "Ought" ', *Philosophical Review*, vol. LXVIII (October 1959) with R.F. Atkinson, 'Hume on "Is" and "Ought". A reply to Mr

Macintyre', *Philosophical Review*, vol. LXX (April 1961); M.J. Scott-Taggart, 'Macintyre's Hume', *Philosophical Review*, vol. LXX (April 1961). Later, Geoffrey Hunter, 'Hume on "Is" and "Ought" ', *Philosophy*, vol. XXXVII (April 1961). Antony Flew, 'On the Interpretation of Hume', *Philosophy*, vol. XXXVIII (April 1963) and Geoffrey Hunter, 'A Reply to Professor Flew', *Philosophy*, vol. XXXVIII (April 1963).

3 I have learnt most from the following, without fully agreeing with any of them: R.G. Collingwood, *The Idea of History* (Oxford, pb. ed. 1961); Patrick Gardiner, *The Nature of Historical Explanation* (Oxford 1952); William Dray, *Laws and Explanation in History* (Oxford 1957); W.B. Gallie, *Philosophy and the Historical Understanding* (London 1964); A. Donagan, *The Later Philosophy of R.G. Collingwood* (Oxford 1962); A. Danto, *Analytical Philosophy of History* (Cambridge 1965); various of the articles cited by Patrick Gardiner in *Theories of History* (Glencoe, Ill. 1959) and the journal, *History and Theory* (ed. George Nadel); also from two striking works by practising historians, T.S. Kuhn, *The Structure of Scientific Revolutions* (Chicago 1962) and E.H. Gombrich, *Art and Illusion* (London 1959).

4 Arthur C. Danto, *Analytical Philosophy of History* (Cambridge 1965). The whole book is devoted to expounding the importance of the difference between contemporary-specific and future-specific descriptions of events, say, for example, ours and theirs, to the understanding of historical analysis. The Yeats poem is very deftly quoted at page 151. To rephrase Danto's point, the data-language of history changes throughout history. The future constantly changes the set of true descriptive statements which could in principle be made about the past. No contemporary description of an event can take this particular sort of account of the future which it 'engenders'.

5 *Op. cit.* (p. 302, n. 1), p. 219. Such an account (namely, an analysis of Locke's concept of property, taken from the *Second Treatise* alone) 'may perhaps be in danger of refutation by the historian as an account of *what Locke intended*. It is in less, even no, danger of contradiction from such a quarter as an account of *what Locke said*. And in case this is thought too small a claim, let me point out that we usually hold people to what they say, rather than to what they suppose to follow from what they meant to say.' I should like to emphasise that the very able article in question does not in practice suffer at all from ill consequences deriving from this, to me, misconceived methodological doctrine.

6 Cf. Emile Durkheim, *Socialism and Saint-Simon* (New York, pb. ed. 1958), p. 41.

7 See J.L. Austin, *How to do things with words* (Oxford 1962), *passim*.

8 For an example of the acute interpretative difficulties which this fact raises, see the remarkable reconstruction by Professor Ryle, *Plato's Progress* (Cambridge 1966).

9 Cf. Eugene Kamenka, 'Marxism and the History of Philosophy', in Beiheft 5, *History and Theory*, pp. 83—104.

10 John Passmore, 'The Idea of a History of Philosophy', in Beiheft 5, *History and Theory*, p. 13.

11 See, briefly, W.G. Runciman, *Social Science and Political Theory* (Cambridge 1963), ch. 6. For a penetrating account of the sources and deficiencies of the notion as employed by Malinowski see E.R. Leach, 'The Epistemological Background to Malinowski's Empiricism', in *Man and Culture: An Evaluation of the Work of Bronislaw Malinowski* (ed. Raymond Firth, London 1957).

12 Anthony Kenny, *Action, Emotion and Will* (London 1963), pp. 28—51.

13 Peter Winch, *The Idea of a Social Science* (London 1958), *passim*.

14 As part of the causal story, this can be very considerable indeed. Cf. on Plato, Arthur W.H. Adkins, *Merit and Responsibility* (Oxford 1960).

15 See Peter Laslett (ed.), John Locke, *Two Treatises of Government* (Cambridge 1960), pp. 67—76.

16 *Proc. Aris. Soc. supplementary vol.* XXII, 'Things and Persons', (quoted by John Passmore, 'The Dreariness of Aesthetics', in William Elton (ed.), *Aesthetics and Language* (Oxford 1959), p. 40.

3 Consent in the political theory of John Locke

1 I am using this notion very vulgarly. For two perceptive examples of the use to which it can be put in historical investigation see E.H. Gombrich, *Art and Illusion* (London 1960), and T.S. Kuhn, *The Structure of Scientific Revolutions* (Chicago 1962).

2 Or, alternatively, some form of it is importantly not the proper mode of government — cf. Leo Strauss, *Natural Right and History* (Chicago 1953), pp. 202—51 and C.B. Macpherson, *The Political Theory of Possessive Individualism* (Oxford 1962). Perhaps also the brilliant, if wayward, work of Willmoore Kendall, *John Locke and the Doctrine of Majority-Rule* (Urbana, Illinois 1941. Reprinted 1959).

3 John Locke, *Two Tracts on Government*, ed. P. Abrams (Cambridge 1967), pp. 172, 201 (231—2). (Cited hereafter as Abrams (ed.) op. cit.)

4 John Locke, *Essays on the Law of Nature*, ed. W. Von Leyden (Oxford 1954), esp. pp. 181—9. (Hereafter cited as Von Leyden (ed.) op. cit.)

5 John Locke, *Two Treatises of Government*, ed. Peter Laslett (Cambridge 1964). See esp. 2nd Treatise, para. 77, ll. 1—5 (pp. 336—7). 'God having made Man such a Creature, that, in his own Judgment, it was not good for him to be alone, put him under strong Obligations of Necessity, Convenience, and Inclination to drive him into *Society*, as well as fitted him with Understanding and Language to continue and enjoy it.' The Abrams, Von Leyden, and Laslett editions cited in this and the two previous notes are all outstanding pieces of editorial work and their introductions contain major contributions to the analysis of Locke's thought. I should like to acknowledge a heavy debt to all three, most particularly to Mr Laslett. This work is cited hereafter as Laslett (ed.), op. cit.

6 Bodleian Library, MSS. Locke, c. 28, fo. 113 v (Homo ante et post lapsum), and fo. 139, 'Morality'. The Bodleian collection of Locke manuscripts are hereafter cited simply as 'MSS. Locke'.

7 MSS. Locke f. 3, fos. 201—2. Lex nāā. 'God having given man *above other creatures of this habitable part of the universe* a knowledge of himself which the beasts have not, he is thereby under obligations which the beasts are not, for knowing God to be a wise agent he cannot but conclude that he has that knowledge and those faculties which he finds in himself above the other creatures given him for some use and end. If therefore he comprehend the relation between father and son and find it reasonable that his son whom he hath begot (only in pursuance of his pleasure without thinking of his son) and nourished should obey love and reverence him and be grateful to him, he cannot but find it much more reasonable that he and every other man should obey and revere [?] love and thank the author of their being to whom they owe all that they are. If he finds it reasonable to punish one of his children that injures another, he cannot but expect the same from God the father of all men when any one injures another, if he finds it reasonable that his children should assist and help one another and expects it from them as their duty will he not also by the same reason conclude that God expects the same of all men one to another. If he finds . . . etc.' (Spelling modernised and contractions restored as elsewhere in transcribed passages. Emphases as in original as elsewhere in quotations.)

8 Laslett (ed.), op. cit. 2nd Treatise, para. 6, ll. 10—14 (p. 289).

9 Ibid. 19—22 (p. 289). 'Every one as he is *bound to preserve himself*, and not quit his station wilfully; so by the like reason when his own Preservation comes not in competition, ought he, as much as he can, *to preserve the rest of Mankind.*'

10 Laslett (ed.), op. cit. 2nd Treatise, para. 23, ll. 4—9 (p. 302). 'For a Man, not having the Power of his own Life, *cannot*, by Compact, or his own Consent, *enslave himself* to any one, nor put himself under the Absolute, Arbitrary Power of another, to take away his Life, when he pleases. No body can give more Power than he has himself; and he that cannot take away his own Life, cannot give another power over it.'

11 Laslett (ed.), op. cit. 2nd Treatise, para. 6, ll. 15—19 (p. 289): 'being furnished with like Faculties, sharing all in one Community of Nature, there cannot be supposed any such *Subordination* among us, that may Authorize us to destroy one

another, as if we were made for one anothers uses, as the inferior ranks of Creatures are for ours'.

12 Laslett (ed.), op. cit. 2nd Treatise, paras. 6, 23, 56, 135, 137, 149, 168, 172. Also 197—243, etc.

13 J. Plamenatz, *Man and Society* (London 1963), I, 227.

14 Plamenatz, *Man and Society*, I, 209—52; esp. pp. 277—8 (see also Plamenatz, *Consent, Freedom, and Political Obligation*, pp. 6—8). These criticisms seem precisely to be met by a consideration of those broader features of Locke's argument here emphasised.

15 For the important historical basis of these observations see Laslett (ed.), op. cit. Introduction, esp. pp. 44—91. Most clearly and crudely, this point is put in the very important letter which Locke wrote to his friend Edward Clarke on 8 February 1689 on the meetings of the Convention Parliament, the most illuminating document that we have available for gauging Locke's attitude to the particular form of the Revolution Settlement. (The importance of this document seems to have escaped previous interpreters of Locke's politics.) '. . . the settlement of the nation upon the sure grounds of peace and security is put into their hands, which can no way so well be done as by restoring our ancient government; the best possible that ever was, if taken and put together all of a piece in its original constitution. If this has not been invaded men have done very ill to complain, and if it has men must certainly be so wise by feeling as to know where the frame has been put out of order, or is amiss; and for that now they have an opportunity offered to find remedies, and set up a constitution, that may be lasting, for the security of civil rights and the liberty and property of all the subjects of the nation.' *Locke and Clarke* (ed. Benjamin Rand) (Oxford 1927), p. 289.

16 Laslett (ed.), op. cit. 2nd Treatise, para. 4, ll. 2—6 (p. 287). See also para. 114, ll. 5—11 (pp. 362—3) and para. 119, ll. 1—3 (p. 365) etc.

17 Laslett (ed.), op. cit. 2nd Treatise para. 116, ll. 14—19 (p. 364), para 118, ll. 11—21, (p. 365); para. 193, ll. 1—8 (p. 413), etc.

18 *Reasonableness. Works*, III, 3, 5. etc, for the interpretation of Adam's original sin and the insistence that it could not simply be said to *cause* the sins of his descendants (a necessary condition, here, distinguished from a sufficient condition); esp. p. 5, 'every one's sin is charged upon himself only'.

19 It is perhaps necessary to emphasise that the problems had been raised already interminably by Robert Filmer. (See *Patriarcha and other Political Works of Sir Robert Filmer*, ed. P. Laslett, Oxford, 1949, pp. 81, 82, 189, 217, 218, 224—6, 243, 244, 273, 274. etc.)

20 Laslett (ed.), op. cit. 2nd Treatise, para. 117, ll. 8—13; 'thus *the Consent of Freemen, born under Government*, which only *makes them Members of it*, being given separately in their turns, as each comes to be of Age, and not in a multitude together; People take no notice of it, and thinking it not done at all, or not necessary, conclude they are naturally Subjects as they are Men', and see para. 114, ll. 5—11 (pp. 362—3). Locke himself seems sometimes to condone such an empirically plausible error; cf. his taking 'countrymen', 'those who were born in the same country or tract of ground' as an example of a 'natural relation'. *Hum. Und.* I, 294, (Bk. 2 C. 28 S. 2).

21 Laslett (ed.) op. cit. 2nd Treatise, para. 120, l. 13 (p. 366).

22 Laslett (ed.), op. cit. 2nd Treatise, para. 119, ll. 9—22 (pp. 365—6). 'The difficulty is, what ought to be look'd upon as a *tacit Consent*, and how far it binds, i.e. how far any one shall be looked on to have consented, and thereby to have submitted to any Government, where he has made no Expressions of it at all. And to this I say, that every Man, that hath any Possession, or Enjoyment, of any part of the Dominions of any Government, doth thereby give his *tacit Consent*, and is as far forth obliged to Obedience to the Laws of that Government, during such Enjoyment, as any one under it; whether this his Possession be of Land, to him and his Heirs for ever, or a Lodging only for a Week; or whether it be barely travelling freely on the Highway; and in Effect, it reaches as far as the very being of any one

within the Territories of that Government.' *N.B.* What is in question is 'how far any one shall be looked on to have consented . . . where he has made no Expressions of it at all' (ll. 11—13).

23 For the elements of this account see Laslett (ed.), op. cit. 2nd Treatise, paras. 95—101 (pp. 348—52); para. 108, ll. 1—10 (pp. 357—8); para. 111, ll. 1—17, esp. ll. 4—5 (pp. 360—1); and esp. paras. 123—7 (pp. 368—70); also, paras. 128—31 (pp. 370—1).

24 Plamenatz, *Man and Society*, I, 226—7. C.B. Macpherson, *The Political Theory of Possessive Individualism* (Oxford 1962), pp. 247—51 (and cf. Alan Ryan, 'Locke and the Dictatorship of the Bourgeoisie', *Political Studies*, XIII, no. 2 (June 1965), 219—30; esp. 226—7).

25 See especially Laslett (ed.), op. cit. 2nd Treatise, para. 120, ll. 1—21 (p. 366).

26 See Laslett (ed.), op. cit. 2nd Treatise, para. 99, ll. 1—5 (p. 351).

27 Macpherson, op. cit. pp. 194—271, esp. pp. 247—51.

28 Ibid. pp. 249—50.

29 Ibid. p. 249.

30 Laslett (ed.), op. cit. 2nd Treatise, para. 120, ll. 2—11 (p. 366). (Cited by Macpherson, op. cit. pp. 249—50.) ' . . . every Man, when he, at first, incorporates himself into any Commonwealth, by his uniting himself thereunto, annexed also, and submits to the Community those Possessions, which he has, or shall acquire, that do not already belong to any other Government. For it would be a direct Contradiction, for any one, to enter into Society with others for the securing and regulating of Property; and yet to suppose his Land, whose Property is to be regulated by the Laws of the Society, should be exempt from the Jurisdiction of that Government, to which he himself the Proprietor of the Land, is a Subject.'

31 Macpherson, op. cit. p. 250.

32 Laslett (ed.), op. cit. 2nd Treatise, para. 122, ll. 17—18 (p. 367). For Locke's relationship with Shaftesbury see Laslett (ed.), op. cit. Introduction, *passim*. For a convenient brief account of the politics of the Whigs during the Exclusion crisis see J.R. Jones, *The First Whigs* (London 1961).

33 For some of the occasions on which such an oath was administered and some idea of the sorts of persons to whom it would be administered, see e.g. K. Feiling, *A History of the Tory Party 1640—1714* (Oxford 1924), pp. 262—6, 284—5, 319—21 and J.R. Western, *The English Militia in the Eighteenth Century* (London 1965), pp. 33—4, 83.

34 See e.g. Feiling, op. cit. pp. 284—5 and Western, op. cit. pp. 33—4.

35 Cf. the example of 'countrymen' as a 'natural relation' in the *Essay concerning Human Understanding* (cited in n. 2 (p. 305) and Laslett (ed.), op. cit. 2nd Treatise, para. 117, ll. 1—8 (p. 364).

36 Western, op. cit. pp. 33—4.

37 Laslett (ed.), op. cit. 2nd Treatise, para. 121, ll. 11—18 (p. 367): 'he, that has once, by actual Agreement, and any *express* Declaration, given his *Consent* to be of any Commonweal, is perpetually and indispensably obliged to be and remain unalterably a Subject to it, and can never be again in the liberty of the state of Nature; unless by any Calamity, the Government, he was under, comes to be dissolved; or else by some publick Act cuts him off from being any longer a member of it'. See also para. 122, ll. 6—10 (p. 367).

38 Laslett (ed.), op. cit. 2nd Treatise, para. 25, ll. 16—19 (p. 304). 'I shall endeavour to shew, how Men might come to have a *property* in several parts of that which God gave to Mankind in common, and that without any express Compact of all the Commoners.' See also para. 28, ll. 11—24 (pp. 306—7); para. 29, ll. 1—5 (p. 307); para. 32, ll. 4—10 (pp. 308—9).

39 Filmer, op. cit. pp. 203—4, 266, 273—4.

40 Laslett (ed.), op. cit. 2nd Treatise, para. 192, l. 9 (p. 413); and see para. 138, ll. 1—17 (pp. 378—9); para. 139, ll. 3—8 (p. 379); para. 140, ll. 6—11 (p. 380); and para. 192, ll. 23—7 (p. 412): 'their due property, which is so to be Proprietors of what they have, that no body can take away any part of it without their own con-

sent, without which, Men under any Government are not in the state of Free-men, but are direct Slaves under the Force of War'.

41 Laslett (ed.), op. cit. 2nd Treatise, para. 190, ll. 1—4 (pp. 411—12).

42 Laslett (ed.), op. cit. 2nd Treatise, para. 116, ll. 14—24 (p. 364): esp. 'any *act of the Father can no more give away the liberty of the Son*, than it can of any body else: He may indeed annex such Conditions to the Land, he enjoyed as a Subject of any Commonwealth, as may oblige his Son to be of that Community, if he will enjoy those Possessions which were his Fathers; because that Estate being his Fathers Property, he may dispose or settle it as he pleases'.

43 Laslett (ed.), op. cit. 2nd Treatise, para. 138, ll. 1—17 (pp. 378—9): esp. 'it is a mistake to think, that the Supream or *Legislative Power* of any Commonwealth, can do what it will, and dispose of the Estates of the Subjects *arbitrarily*, or take any part of them at pleasure.' *N.B. any* part of them; see also para. 139, ll. 3—8 (p. 379).

44 Laslett (ed.), op. cit. 2nd Treatise, para. 155, ll. 1—17 (pp. 388—9); para. 216, ll. 1—7 (p. 427); para. 222, ll. 1—62 (pp. 430—2).

45 See p. 38, n. *. Laslett (ed.), op. cit. 2nd Treatise, paras. 96—9 (pp. 349—51).

46 See Laslett (ed.), op. cit. 2nd Treatise, para. 88, ll. 8—18 (pp. 342—3 and below). Indeed the status of representative is contingent on the due exercise of its functions; see para. 151, ll. 15—26 (p. 386).

47 Laslett (ed.), op. cit. 2nd Treatise, para. 138, ll. 21—31 (p. 379); para. 143, ll. 7—15 (p. 382).

48 Laslett (ed.), op. cit. 2nd Treatise, para. 138, ll. 17—21 (p. 379) see also para. 143, ll. 15—23 (p. 382); para. 142, ll. 10—15 (p. 381).

49 Laslett (ed.), op. cit. 2nd Treatise, para. 131, ll. 8—10 (p. 371).

50 Laslett (ed.), op. cit. 2nd Treatise, para. 131, ll. 6—8 (p. 371) ('For no rational Creature can be supposed to change his condition with an intention to be worse') and para. 164, ll. 1—2 (p. 395) etc.

51 Laslett (ed.), op. cit. 2nd Treatise, para. 15, ll. 13—16 (p. 296); para. 22, ll. 1—8 (p. 301); para. 95, ll. 1—14 (pp. 348—9); para. 171, ll. 12—25 (p. 400); para. 175, ll. 1—13 (pp. 402—3); para. 176, ll. 28—31 (p. 404); para. 198, ll. 1—19 (pp. 415—16); para. 212, ll. 16—22 (pp. 425—6); para. 192, ll. 1—27 (p. 412); and references cited in note 12 (p. 305).

52 See footnote *, p. 32 above.

53 Laslett (ed.), op. cit. 2nd Treatise, para. 14, ll. 12—17 (p. 295).

54 Laslett (ed.), op. cit. 2nd Treatise, para. 75, ll. 1—5 (p. 335); para. 76, ll. 1—2 (p. 336); paras. 105—12 (pp. 354—62); and 1st Treatise, paras. 130—2 (pp. 254—6); para. 153 (p. 272). Also *A Second Letter concerning Toleration, Works*, II, 423; and *A Third Letter for Toleration, Works*, II, 488. MSS. Locke, c. 33, fo. 11^r miscited by Laslett (ed.), op. cit. p. 356 n.

55 Laslett (ed.), op. cit. 2nd Treatise, para. 105, ll. 1—3 (p. 354); para. 106, ll. 1—8 (p. 355).

56 Laslett (ed.), op. cit. 2nd Treatise, para. 107 (pp. 356—7); paras. 110—11 (pp. 359—61); para. 162 (p. 394); and for its application to the history of England, paras. 165—6 (pp. 395—6).

57 Laslett (ed.), op. cit. 2nd Treatise, para. 175, ll. 9—13 (p. 403); '*Conquest* is as far from setting up any Government, as demolishing an House is from building a new one in the place. Indeed it often makes way for a new Frame of a Common-wealth, by destroying the former; but, without the Consent of the people, can never erect a new one.'

58 Laslett (ed.), op. cit. 2nd Treatise, para. 192, ll. 17—25 (p. 412): 'no Government can have a right to obedience from a people who have not freely consented to it; which they can never be supposed to do, till either they are put in a full state of Liberty to chuse their Government and Governors, or at least till they have such standing Laws, to which they have by themselves or their Representatives, given their free consent, and also till they are allowed their due property, which is so to be Proprietors of what they have, that nobody can take away any part of it with-

out their own consent', and see para. 176, ll. 26—31 (p. 404); para. 198, ll. 11—19 (p. 416).

59 See John Pocock, *The Ancient Constitution and the Feudal Law* (Cambridge 1957); also J.W. Gough, *Fundamental Law in English Constitutional History* (Oxford 1955); David Douglas, *English Scholars 1660—1740* (London 1951); Christopher Hill, *Puritanism and Revolution* (ch. 3 'The Norman Yoke') (London 1958); S. Kliger, *The Goths in England* (Cambridge, Mass. 1952) and an important article by Quentin Skinner, 'History and Ideology in the English Revolution,' *Historical Journal*, VIII, no. 2 (1965), 151—78, for the nature of the disputes about the historicity of the 'Ancient Constitution'. Locke himself seems always to have shown a judicious lack of interest in the details of the dispute — unless, that is, the missing portion of the *Two Treatises* contained such material, a hypothesis for which there is really no evidence; but his letter to Edward Clarke (cited in note 15, p. 305) suggests that it is the authentic 'ancient constitution' that he has in mind.

60 Sherlock notes, MSS. Locke, c. 28, fos. 83—96 (see note *, p. 34). No very searching treatment of Sherlock exists but see Gerald M. Straka, 'The Final Phase of Divine Right Theory in England, 1688—1702', *English Historical Review* (1962), pp. 638—58; and more extendedly in his *The Anglican Reaction to the Revolution of 1688* (Madison, Wisconsin 1962).

61 Sherlock, op. cit. p. 43.

62 Sherlock notes, MSS. Locke, c. 28, fo. 92^{v}. 'If rebels be the minority they may be fought against, if the majority they are our country and must not be fought against.' Cf. the discussion on the status of majority-consent above, footnotes † (p. 38) and * (p. 44) esp.

63 Sherlock notes, MSS. Locke, c. 28, fos. 83—96 *passim* and esp. the comment on Sherlock's claim that the 'settlement' of a government gave it political authority (fo. 96^{r}). 'How long a month a year. — or an hundred & by what rule what law of God. Long and short in such cases unless defined have no meaning people submit where they do not resist so that where there is no resistance there is a general submission, but there may be a general submission without a general consent which is an other thing.' Cf. Plamenatz, *Consent, Freedom, and Political Obligation*, p. 7, etc.

64 See Sherlock notes, MSS. Locke, c. 28 fo. 96^{r} cited in the previous note.

65 Laslett (ed.), op. cit. 2nd Treatise, para. 189, ll. 5—12 (p. 411): 'the Absolute Power of the *Conqueror* reaches no farther than the Persons of the Men, that were subdued by him, and dies with them; and should he govern them as slaves, subjected to his Absolute, Arbitrary Power, he *has no* such *Right of Dominion over their Children*. He can have no Power over them, but by their own consent, whatever he may drive them to say, or do; and he has no lawful Authority, whilst Force, and not Choice, compels them to submission.' And see para. 186, ll. 1—22 (pp. 410—11).

66 Laslett (ed.), op. cit. 2nd Treatise, para. 179, ll. 1—8 (p. 406); para. 186, ll. 1—22 (pp. 410—11); para. 189, ll. 2—12 (p. 411); para. 192, ll. 1—27 (p. 412); para. 176, ll. 26—31 (p. 404).

67 Laslett (ed.), op. cit. 2nd Treatise, para. 189, ll. 11—12 (p. 411); para. 186, ll. 1—22 (pp. 410—11); para. 192, ll. 1—14, and ll. 19—22 (p. 412).

68 Laslett (ed.), op. cit. para. 175, ll. 1—13, pp. 402—3.

69 Abrams (ed.), op. cit. pp. 124, 125, 126, 128, 129, 130, 138, 150, 172, 200—1 (230—1). These references seem all to be hypothetical, though cf. Abrams (ed.), op. cit. pp. 25—7, 75, 76, 78 (and esp. deleted passage at p. 172), for the claim that the hypothesis is essential to the form of Locke's argument. *Toleration (1667)*, Fox Bourne, op. cit. I, 175, 177. Notes on Parker, MSS. Locke, c. 29, fo. 7 (Cranston, op. cit. pp. 132—3). *Excommunicàcon*, in King, op. cit. II, 109, Toleratio, MSS. Locke, d. I, fo. 125. Stillingfleet, MSS. Locke, c. 34, fos. 113, 114, 115, 116, 118, 121. *A Letter concerning Toleration* (ed. Montuori), pp. 17, 23, 25. *Two Treatises*, Sherlock notes. Additional *Letters on Toleration*, etc. Apart from the first three works cited, consent as the origin of government is not argued for in these references but simply assumed.

70 Laslett (ed.), op. cit. 2nd Treatise, para. 97, ll. 8—14 (p. 350): 'For what appearance would there be of any Compact? What new Engagement if he were no farther tied by any Decrees of the Society, than he himself thought fit, and did actually consent to? This would be still as great a liberty as he himself had before his Compact, or any one else in the State of Nature hath, who may submit himself and consent to any acts of it if he thinks fit.'

71 See notes 9 and 12 (pp. 304—5).

72 Laslett (ed.), op. cit. 2nd Treatise, para. 222, ll. 40—6 (p. 431): 'For the People having reserved to themselves the Choice of their *Representation*, as the Fence to their Properties, could do it for no other end, but that they might always be freely chosen and so chosen, freely act and advise, as the necessity of the Commonwealth, and the publick Good should, upon examination, and mature debate, be judged to require.' See also para. 17, ll. 4—16 (p. 297); para. 139, ll. 9—11 (p. 379): 'even *absolute Power*, where it is necessary, is *not Arbitrary* by being absolute, but is limited by that reason, and confined to those ends, which required it in some Cases to be absolute', and more generally para. 104, ll. 1—7 (p. 354); para. 118, ll. 11—13 (p. 365) and the form of the argument in para. 120, ll. 1—21 (esp. l. 6) (p. 366).

73 Laslett (ed.), op. cit. 2nd Treatise, para. 164, ll. 1—19 (esp. ll. 1—9), (p. 395). 'But since a Rational Creature cannot be supposed when free, to put himself into Subjection to another, for his own harm: (Though where he finds a good and wise Ruler, he may not perhaps think it either necessary, or useful to set precise Bounds to his Power in all things) *Prerogative* can be nothing, but the Peoples permitting their Rulers, to do several things of their own free choice, where the law was silent, and sometimes too against the direct Letter of the Law, for the publick good; and their acquiescence in it when so done.'

74 Laslett (ed.), op. cit. 2nd Treatise, para. 179, ll. 1—12 (p. 406): 'the *Conqueror* gets no Power but only over those, who have actually assisted, concurr'd, or consented to that unjust force, that is used against him. For the People having given to their Governours no Power to do an unjust thing, such as to make an unjust War, (for they never had such a Power in themselves:) They ought not to be charged, as guilty of the Violence and Unjustice that is committed in an Unjust War, any farther, than they actually abet it; no more, than they are to be thought guilty of any Violence or Oppression their Governours should use upon the People themselves, or any part of their Fellow Subjects, they having impowered them no more to the one, than to the other.'

75 Laslett (ed.), op. cit. 2nd Treatise, para. 158, ll. 1—39 (pp. 391—2) (esp. ll. 12—16): 'it being the interest, as well as the intention of the People, to have a fair and *equal* Representative; whoever brings it nearest to that, is an undoubted Friend, to, and Establisher of the Government, and cannot miss the Consent and Approbation of the Community.' See also ch. XIV, 'Of Prerogative', pp. 392—8, *passim*.

76 Laslett (ed.), op. cit. 2nd Treatise, para. 192, ll. 1—27 (p. 412) and see note 58 (p. 307).

77 Cf. R.M. Hare, 'The Lawful Government' (in Peter Laslett and W.G. Runciman, *Philosophy, Politics and Society*, 3rd Series, Oxford 1972, pp. 157—72).

78 See Laslett (ed.), op. cit. 2nd Treatise, paras. 208, 209, 223, 225, 230 etc. and cf. Locke, *Some Considerations of the Consequences of the Lowering of Interest . . . Works*, II, 46. It is only in conditions of acute scarcity, and normally only as a result of maladministration that members of the working classes attempt to act as an economic pressure group; but it seems to be also only at such a time that Locke expects them to 'forget respect'.

79 Laslett (ed.), op. cit. 2nd Treatise, chs. XIV and VIII, esp. para. 105, ll. 8—16, 24—9 (pp. 354—5); para. 112, ll. 1—8 (p. 361); para. 74, ll. 10—37 (pp. 334—5); para. 75, ll. 1—5 (p. 335) ('Thus 'twas easie, and almost natural for Children by a tacit, and scarce avoidable consent to make way for the *Father's* Authority and Government. They had been accustomed in their Childhood to follow his Direction, and to refer their little differences to him, and when they were Men, who fitter to rule them?'); para. 76, ll. 1—2 (p. 336) ('by an insensible change'). Besides above on

patriarchal origins see, on prerogative, esp. para. 94, ll. 10—17 (p. 347); para. 158, ll. 12—16 (p. 391); para. 161, 162 (pp. 383—4).

80 See notes 78 and 79 above; e.g. Locke, *Some Thoughts concerning Education ... Works*, IV, Preface, side 2 (not paginated): 'that most to be taken care of, is the gentleman's calling. For if those of that rank are by their education once set right, they will quickly bring all the rest into order'.

81 See *Hum. Und. passim* (e.g. 1, 6, 10, 12, 14, 15, 16, 22, 39, etc.) and see Draft A of the *Essay* (ed. Aaron and Gibb); Draft B (ed. Rand), etc.

82 Cf. the development of the suicide taboo argument in more radical eighteenth-century writers into the specific *duty* to resist arbitrary power — e.g. Jonathan Mayhew, *A Discourse concerning Unlimited Submission and Non-resistance to the Higher Powers* (Boston 1750), conveniently in Bernard Bailyn (and Jane N. Garrett), *Pamphlets of the American Revolution: 1750—1776* (Cambridge, Mass. 1965) (with excellent introduction), I, 203—47.

83 See *Hum. Und.* I, 219: 'He that has his chains knocked off and the prison doors set open to him is perfectly at *liberty*, because he may either go or stay as he best likes, though his preference be determined to stay by the darkness of the night or illness of the weather or want of other lodging. He ceases not to be free, though the desire of some convenience to be had there absolutely determines his preference and makes him stay in his prison.' This passage seems closely to parallel the implications of his discussion of the right of emigration, a notion which plays an essential role in his theory.

84 See the discussion in ch. V of the *Two Treatises* of the origins of large differentials in property-holdings through the (necessarily consensual) development of a money economy. Cf. for a clear statement, John Rawls, 'Justice as Fairness', in Peter Laslett and W.G. Runciman, *Philosophy, Politics, and Society*, 2nd Series (Oxford 1962) — though it seems important to point out that in the world as it is some people always `do` have less deft senses of their probable future situation within a 'practice' than others — and that these differences in predictive skills seem highly correlated with class differentials.

4 The politics of Locke in England and America in the eighteenth century

1 See classically Carl L. Becker, *The Declaration of Independence: A Study in the History of Political Ideas* (paperback, New York 1959), p. 27: 'Most Americans had absorbed Locke's works as a kind of political gospel; ... ', etc. See also Merle Curti, 'The Great Mr. Locke, America's Philosopher, 1783—1861', *Huntington Library Bulletin* (1937), pp. 107—51, esp. pp. 107—8; Clinton Rossiter, *Seedtime of the Republic* (New York 1953), p. 141 (see esp. n. 111, p. 491); *Pamphlets of the American Revolution 1750—1776*, ed. Bernard Bailyn (Cambridge, Mass. 1965), I, 25—7.

2 See Rossiter, *Seedtime of the Republic*, pp. 139—47; Bernard Bailyn, *The Ideological Origins of the American Revolution* (Cambridge, Mass. 1967), esp. pp. 22—54 for a particularly well-articulated documentation. And see in general for the growing assurance of this reading the works noted below (p. 319, n. 81). The problem of relating intellectual history to political and social development is faced boldly by Gordon S. Wood, 'Rhetoric and Reality in the American Revolution', *William and Mary Quarterly*, 3rd series, XXIII, 4 (October 1966), 3—32.

3 See esp. Daniel J. Boorstin, *The Genius of American Politics* (paperback ed. Chicago 1959), pp. 66—98 and, for his blisteringly effective assault on the methodology of the influence model applied to eighteenth-century America, see Daniel J. Boorstin, *America and the Image of Europe* (New York 1960), pp. 65—78, 'The Myth of an American Enlightenment'.

4 A convenient summary of the politics of the Exclusion controversy with adequate references to past literature is J.R. Jones, *The First Whigs: The Politics of the Exclusion Crisis 1678—1683* (London 1961); and the events are effectively placed in the development of English politics in J.H. Plumb, *The Growth of Political Stability in England 1675—1725* (London 1966).

5 There is a useful discussion of pamphlet literature produced on Shaftesbury's behalf in O.W. Furley, 'The Whig Exclusionists: Pamphlet literature in the Exclusion Campaign, 1679—81', *Cambridge Historical Journal*, XIII, I (1957), 19—36.

6 Sir Robert Filmer, *Patriarcha, passim*, in *Patriarcha and Other Political Works of Sir Robert Filmer*, ed. P. Laslett (Oxford 1949). I have discussed the structure of Filmer's arguments at length in the study referred to in n. 7 below.

7 See J. Dunn, *The Political Thought of John Locke* (Cambridge 1969) for a more extended presentation.

8 Cf. Laslett's introductions to *Patriarcha* (Oxford 1949), pp. 39—42, and *John Locke: Two Treatises of Government* (Cambridge 1960), p. 69.

9 John Locke, *Some Considerations of the Consequences of the Lowering of Interest . . . , The Works of John Locke*, 7th ed. (London 1768), II, 46.

10 I have stressed the importance of this in chapter 3 above.

11 John Locke, *An Essay concerning Human Understanding*, ed. J.W. Yolton (London 1961), I, I, § 5.

12 *Two Treatises*, II, § § 20, 21, etc.

13 See [William Atwood,] *The Fundamental Constitution of the English Government . . .* (London 1690), pp. 97 (= p. 101), 102, appendix, p. 19 (I owe this reference to Professor Gordon Schochet) (p. 97: 'The Author of the best Treatises of Civil Polity which I have met with in the *English* Tongue'); Walter Moyle, *Essay on the Lacedaemonian Government* (1698), *The Whole Works of Walter Moyle . . .* (London 1727), p. 58; [Simon Clement,] *An Answer to Mr. Molyneux, his Case of Ireland's being bound by Acts of Parliament in England . . .* (London 1698), p. 30.

14 Cf. Le Clerc, *The Life and Character of Mr. John Locke . . .* (London 1706), pp. 16—17 with the length at which the *Essay concerning Human Understanding* is discussed there. See also Pierre Coste's letter in *Nouvelles de la République des Lettres* (February 1705), pp. 154—77. *A Complete History of Europe: or, A View of the Affairs thereof, Civil and Military, for The Year 1704 . . .* (London 1705), pp. 589—92, 'Mr. Locke's Death'.

15 The 1691 Amsterdam printing and the 1724 Geneva printing were both anonymous. The Brussels *Du Gouvernement Civil de Mr. Locke* of 1749 was the first French edition to bear Locke's name. The first French edition of other works of Locke to bear his name include *Thoughts on Education* (Amsterdam 1695), *An Essay concerning Human Understanding* (Amsterdam 1700), *Œuvres Diverses* (Rotterdam 1710), *Reasonableness of Christianity* (Amsterdam 1715). For French editions of *Two Treatises* see conveniently Laslett's list in *Two Treatises*, p. 216. For other works see British Museum and Bibliothèque Nationale holdings and John Hampton, 'Les Traductions françaises de Locke au XVIIIe siècle', *Revue de Littérature Comparée*, XXIX (1955), 240—51.

16 William Molyneux, *The Case of Ireland's Being Bound by Acts of Parliament in England Stated* (Dublin 1725) (first published Dublin, 1698), pp. 18 (pp. 12—18 are simply a summary of the treatment of conquest in the *Two Treatises*), 101, 104, etc. Walter Moyle, *Works*, p. 58. Richard Price, *Observations on the Nature of Civil Liberty, the Principles of Government and the Justice and Policy of the War with America* (London 1776), pp. 16, 93, 100; *Additional Observations on the Nature and Value of Civil Liberty*, 2nd ed. (London 1777), pp. xvi, 25, 45—6. Richard Watson, *Anecdotes of the Life of Richard Watson, Bishop of Llandaff . . .* (London 1817), pp. 57, 96. James Burgh, *Political Disquisitions: Or, An Enquiry into public Errors, Defects and Abuses*, 3 vols. (London 1774—5), I, vii, 72—5, 116, 279. John Cary, *A Vindication of the Parliament of England in Answer to a Book Written by W. Molyneux . . .* (London 1698), p. 103. [Clement,] *An Answer to Mr. Molyneux*, p. 30. *The Letters of Philip Dormer Stanhope* ([London] 1932), ed. B. Dobrée, IV, 1307. For the appearance of Locke as a paradigm of intellectual virtue see *ibid*. III, 784, 1130; IV, 1260, 1269, 1358, 1717, etc. Sir William Blackstone, *Commentaries on the Laws of England*, 21st ed. (London 1844), 1, 51, 126, 178, 243, 251 (but for distinct reservations on several points see I, 161, 213; II, 8—9). Hawkins, *Life of Samuel Johnson*, p. 503. Thomas Elrington (ed.), *An Essay*

concerning the True Original Extent and End of Civil Government, by John Locke (Dublin 1798), notes *passim*. (For the circumstances surrounding the preparation of this edition see R.B. McDowell, *Irish Public Opinion 1750—1800*, London 1944, chapter VIII, esp. p. 164.)

17 *Letters Written by the Late Earl of Chatham to his Nephew Thomas Pitt, Esq. (Afterwards Lord Camelford) Then at Cambridge*, 3rd ed. (London 1804), pp. 15, 42—3, 50.

18 Richard Watson, *Anecdotes of the Life of Richard Watson, Bishop of Llandaff . . .* (London 1817), pp. 49 (Lord Granby to Watson, 'I can never thank you too much for making me study Locke; while I exist, those tenets, which are so attentive to the natural rights of mankind, shall ever be the guide and direction of my actions'), 51—2.

19 Anthony Ashley Cooper, Third Earl of Shaftesbury, *Characteristicks of Men, Manners, Opinions, Times*, 5th ed. (Birmingham 1773). For the details of what Shaftesbury saw as the implications of Locke's philosophy see I, 97—8, 107—8, 109—11, 116—17, 125, 127; II, 67—9, 308—9, 312, 319—20; III, 143—6. The evidence for taking these attacks as attacks applying to Locke's philosophy as well as to that of Hobbes is to be found in two letters in *The Life, Unpublished Letters, and Philosophical Regimen of Anthony, Earl of Shaftesbury*, ed. B. Rand (London 1900), pp. 403—4, 414—16. There is a discussion of Shaftesbury's critique of Locke by Jason Aaronson, 'Shaftesbury on Locke', *American Political Science Review*, LIII, 4 (December 1959), 1101—4, but it does not bring out the central theme of Shaftesbury's hostility to Locke, their disagreement over the existence of innate ideas. See esp. Shaftesbury, *Second Characters or The Language of Forms*, ed. B. Rand (Cambridge 1914), pp. 173—8. Bolingbroke, *The Works of Lord Bolingbroke . . .* (Philadelphia 1841), IV, *Fragments or Minutes of Essays*, pp. 194—9. The main thrust of Bolingbroke's arguments is directed against Hobbes (*ibid*. 145—51, 156—60, 168, 183, 188), though Filmer comes in for passing abuse (*ibid*. 183, 187, 193—4, 199). It is not Locke's substantive political doctrine (with which in fact Bolingbroke agreed) but his philosophical exposition of it which is criticised (on Bolingbroke, see Isaac Kramnick's *Bolingbroke and his Circle*, Cambridge, Mass. 1968). David Hume, 'Of the Original Contract' (1748), *Essays Moral, Political and Literary* (London 1903), pp. 452—73 and see p. 313, n. 25, below, William Paley, *The Principles of Moral and Political Philosophy* (London 1785), pp. xviii—xix, cf. pp. 99—105, 414—24. Jeremy Bentham in Elie Halévy, *La Formation du Radicalisme Philosophique* (Paris 1901), I, appendix, pp. 416—23. Cf. e.g. Bertrand de Jouvenel, *The Pure Theory of Politics* (Cambridge 1963), p. 45: ' "Social contract" theories are the views of childless men who must have forgotten their childhood'; and for evidence that de Jouvenel would see this as applying to Locke see B. de Jouvenel, *Sovereignty* (Cambridge 1957), p. 232.

20 Charles Leslie, *The New Association of Those Called Moderate-Church-Men with the Modern Whigs and Fanatics to Undermine and Blow Up the Present Church and Government* (London 1703), part II, appendix, 'A Short account of the Original of Government'.

21 George Horne, *Discourses of the Right Reverend George Horne, D.D., Late Lord Bishop of Norwich* (London 1812), II, 18—33; III, 121—34, 'Submission to Government'. Cf. William Jones, *The Life and Writings of Dr. Horne etc., Works of the Rev. William Jones* (London 1801), XII, 73—5. William Jones, *A Letter to the Church of England Pointing Out Some Popular Errors of Bad Consequence, Works*, XII, cf: pp. 315 and 325—6. Jonathan Boucher, 'On Civil Liberty, Passive Obedience, and Non-resistance', in *A View of the Causes and Consequences of the American Revolution* (London 1797), pp. 495—560, esp. pp. 516—19 (against Locke), 522, 527—33, 551—2 (pro-Filmer *v.* Locke), 525 (Overall), 548 (Sherlock), 551 (Berkeley) and 332, 361, 543 (Hobbes); 257—9, 408 (Locke); and see also Jonathan Boucher, *Reminiscences of an American Loyalist* (Boston 1925). [Sir James Allan Park,] *Memoirs of William Stevens, Esq., Treasurer of Queen Anne's Bounty*, 2nd ed. (London 1814), pp. 169—78. John Whitaker, *The Real Origin of Government*

(London 1795), esp. pp. 17–20, 22–4, and cf. (anon.), *Divine Institutes of True Religion and Civil Government* (London 1788), esp. pp. 27–30 for acknowledgements to Horne.

22 William Sherlock, *The Case of the Allegiance due to Soveraign Powers, Stated and Resolved According to Scripture and Reason* . . . (London 1691). For Sherlock and other Anglican passive obedience theorists contemporary with him see conveniently Gerald M. Straka, *Anglican Reaction to the Revolution of 1688* (Madison, Wisconsin 1962). Offspring Blackall, *The Subject's Duty. A Sermon* . . . (London 1705); *The Divine Institution of Magistracy, and the Gracious Design of its Institution* . . . *a Sermon* . . . (London 1708). George Berkeley, *Passive Obedience* (1712), in *The Works of George Berkeley, Bishop of Cloyne*, ed. A.A. Luce and T.E. Jessop (London 1953), VI, 15–46 (esp. p. 15). And for the important disjunction between the measure of the subject's obedience and the bounds of the ruler's power noted in his letter to Percival on 21 October 1709, see *Works*, VIII, *Letters* (1956), p. 23. Stock appears to claim that it was the *Two Treatises* which directed Berkeley's attention to the subject in 1712 (J. Stock, *An Account of the Life of George Berkeley, D.D.*, London 1776, pp. 3–4). But this is hard to reconcile with the evidence of the 1709 letter. Josiah Tucker, *A Letter to Edmund Burke, Esq.* . . . (Glocester 1775), Advertisement, pp. 11–13; *Tract V. The Respective Pleas and Arguments of the Mother Country and of the Colonies, distinctly set forth;* . . . (Glocester 1775), see esp. p. v (the key question posed by the American Revolution: 'Permit me therefore to ask, Why are not the poor Negroes, and the poor Indians entitled to the like Rights and Benefits?') and pp. 12, 13, 13 n.; *The Notions of Mr Locke and his Followers* . . . ([Glocester] 1778), *passim*; *A Treatise concerning Civil Government in Three Parts* (London 1781), parts I and II *passim*; *A Series of Answers to Certain Popular Objections against Separating from the Rebellious Colonies* . . . (Glocester 1776), pp. 102–6 (further attack on Locke's treatment of slavery in *Two Treatises* and *Fundamental Constitutions of Carolina*); *Four Letters on Important National Subjects. Addressed to the Right Honourable Earl of Shelburne* . . . (Glocester 1783), pp. 20, 50–1, 53–4, 55–8, 67, 89–113.

23 S. Puffendorfii, *De Officio Hominis et Civis* . . . ed. Gerschomus Carmichael (Edinburgh 1724), pp. 12 n., 122–4 n., 216 (but cf. 224), 316, 327–8, 330–1, 338, 357, 366, 379, 386–7, 405, 409, 423, 453, 482, 497.

24 Francis Hutcheson, *Philosophiae Moralis Institutio Compendiaria* (Glasgow 1724), pp. i–ii and *passim* (cf. English translation, *A Short Introduction to Moral Philosophy*, 2nd ed. Glasgow, 1753, p. viii). For Hume, Paley and Bentham see note 20 above.

25 David Hume, *A Treatise of Human Nature*, 2 vols. (London 1911), II, book III, 191–202, 233–55. For an indication that this criticism should be taken as bearing upon Locke's work see Hume's letter to Francis Hutcheson of 10 January 1743, 'P. 266. L. 18. & quae seq: You imply a Condemnation of Locke's Opinion, which being the receiv'd one, I cou'd have wisht the Condemnation had been more express', *The Letters of David Hume*, ed. J.Y.T. Greig (Oxford 1932), I, 48. (Cf. in Hutcheson's *Philosophiae Moralis Institutio Compendiaria*, p. 266, l. 18.) For the continuity of Hume's impatience see his 'Of the Original Contract', *Essays*, pp. 452–73; the letter to Lord Elibank of 8 January 1748 in E.C. Mossner, 'New Hume Letters to Lord Elibank', *Texas Studies in Language and Literature*, IV, 3 (1962), 437 (Professor J.H. Plumb kindly called these letters to my attention); and the splendid footnote identifying the authors of 'Compositions the most despicable both for style and matter' which Hume added to later editions of the *History* (cf. *The History of Great Britain* . . . 2nd ed. London, 1759, II, 443 with a posthumous edition). All the direct attacks subsequent to the *Treatise* imply that Hume thought Locke's political theory practically dangerous as well as theoretically incoherent.

26 See works cited in p. 312, n. 19, and esp. Shaftesbury, *Life, Letters*, p. 415: 'Locke, whose *State of Nature* he supposes to be chimerical, and less serviceable to Mr Locke's own system than to Mr Hobbes's that is more of a piece as I believe.'

27 Benjamin Hoadly, *An Humble Reply to the Right Reverend the Lord Bishop of*

Exeter's Answer in which the Considerations Lately Offered to his Lordship are Vindicated ... (London 1709), p. 48: 'the ablest Hand that ever yet managed "the Patriarchal Scheme" '.

28 Charles Leslie, *The Finishing Stroke. Being a Vindication of the Patriarchal Scheme of Government* ... (London 1711), p. 87.

29 Soame Jenyns, *Disquisitions on Several Subjects* (London 1782); Disquisition I, 'On the Chain of Universal Being'; Disquisition VII, 'On Government and Civil Liberty' (cf. the tactics used earlier in his *The Objections to the Taxation of our American Colonies by the Legislative of Great Britain Briefly Consider'd*, London 1765, pp. 7–8). The latter disquisition was taken as an attack on Locke (B.N. Turner, *Candid Suggestions in Eight Letters to Soame Jenyns, Esq.* ... London, 1782, pp. 126–7, 130–3, 135–8, 141–4 and [?R. Watson,] *An Answer to the Disquisition on Government and Civil Liberty* ... , London 1782, pp. 22, 27–30, 35).

30 Soame Jenyns, *A Free Inquiry into the Nature and Origin of Evil* (London 1757), p. 40.

31 Charles Leslie, *The New Association* ... (London 1703), part II, appendix, pp. 6–7.

32 *Ibid*. pp. 4–5, 10, 14.

33 *Ibid*. p. 10.

34 The political background is described helpfully in H.F. Kearney, 'The Political Background to English Mercantilism: 1695–1700', *Economic History Review*, 2nd series, XI, 3 (April 1959), 484–96. The personal relationship can be investigated in *Some Familiar Letters between Mr. Locke and his Friends, Works of John Locke*, 7th ed. (London 1768), IV, 267–391. There is one important piece of additional information in what remains of the original file of these letters in the Carl H. Pforzheimer Library, New York. (Information by courtesy of Dr E.S. De Beer.)

35 See Molyneux, *The Case of Ireland*, p. 18 and cf. *Some Familiar Letters, Works of John Locke*, IV, 269, 306–9, 377 ('How justly they can bind us without our consent and representatives, I leave the author of the *Two Treatises of Government* to consider'), and Locke's reply, pp. 378–9.

36 *Journals of the House of Commons* (London 1742), XII, 281, 321, 324, 331. Kearney's account of this episode, *loc. cit.* n. 34 above, should be compared with these texts.

37 [Clement,] *An Answer to Mr. Molyneux* (London 1698), Epistle Dedicatory (not numbered, = pp. 5–7, 10–12).

38 See the responses of Bishop William King (Kearney, 'Political Background', *Economic History Review*, XI, 491), to whom Molyneux had presented a specially bound copy of the work (C.S. King, *A Great Archbishop of Dublin*, London 1906, p. 175 n.), and of Sir Richard Cox, *Historical Manuscripts Commission, Manuscripts of the Duke of Portland*, III, 609–10.

39 See the letters in *Some Familiar Letters, Works of John Locke*, subsequent to Molyneux's admission of his authorship of *The Case of Ireland*, IV, 380.

40 Jonathan Swift, *The Drapier's Letters and other Works 1724–1725* (Oxford 1941), pp. 62, 86. Charles Lucas, *The Political Constitutions of Great Britain and Ireland Asserted and Vindicated* ... 2 vols. (London 1751), I, xxviii, xxxiii, 113. There is a valuable recent discussion of Lucas's role in the development of a radical press in Dublin in Robert Munter, *The History of the Irish Newspaper 1685–1760* (Cambridge 1967), esp. pp. 170–85. Speeches of the *Rt. Hon. Henry Grattan* in *The Irish Parliament in 1780 and 1782* ... (London 1821), p. 45 ('Spirit of Swift! Spirit of Molyneux! Your genius has prevailed!'); see also pp. 36, 53, 54, etc.; but cf. *Hibernian Magazine* (May 1782), pp. 277–9 and (July 1783), pp. 380–2. For the problems of authenticity in the texts of Grattan's speeches see Richard Koebner, 'The Early Speeches of Henry Grattan', *Bulletin of the Institute for Historical Research*, XXX (1957), 102–14. [J. Pollock,] *The Letters of Owen Roe O'Niall* (printed with Molyneux's *Case of Ireland*) (Dublin 1782), p. 73. *Memoirs of Theobald Wolfe Tone. Written by himself* ... , 2 vols. (London 1827), I, 34, 263.

41 John Cary, *A Vindication of the Parliament of England* ... (London 1698), p. 96: 'If this be allowed to the Gentlemen of Ireland, why should it be denied to those

who are settled in our Plantations in America . . . ?' Molyneux himself was eager to repudiate the aspersion that Ireland was a colony, *Case of Ireland*, pp. 100—1.

42 See *The Trial of Thomas Hardy for High Treason . . . taken down in shorthand . . .* , 4 vols. (London 1794—5). For the presentment and prosecution case see vols. I—III, 381. For Richmond's appearance in court see IV, 3—21. For Erskine's references to Pitt, Burke and Richmond's sympathy for ideas ostensibly espoused by Hardy see III, 228—33, 235—40. And for references to Richmond in the second defence speech see IV, 144—54. See also Erskine's emphasis that one of the most 'incendiary' documents in question, Henry Yorke's speech in Sheffield, derived entirely from Locke, III, 241: 'It is proved that Mr Yorke held in his hand Mr. Locke upon Government, when he delivered his speech on the Castle Hill at Sheffield.' Cf. *The Spirit of John Locke Revived . . .* (Sheffield 1794).

43 On Richmond's career see Alison Gilbert Olson, *The Radical Duke: Career and Correspondence of Charles Lennox, third Duke of Richmond* (Oxford 1961).

44 *Trial of Thomas Hardy*, III, 243—5.

45 Thomas Spence, *The Rights of Man as Exhibited in a Lecture . . . to which is now added, An Interesting Conversation . . .* , 4th ed. (London 1793), p. 23 (after quoting Leviticus XXV): 'Well, we have heard what God has said on the subject, let us next hear what man says. Locke in his Treatise of Government writes thus: ' "Whether we consider natural reason [cf. *Two Treatises*, II, § 25, ll. 1—8) . . ." ' See also p. 24: 'Here we find this great man concurring in these same fundamental principles as we shall likewise.' *The Case of Thomas Spence, Bookseller . . .* (London 1792), p. 5: 'two runners, at the instance of a Mr. Reeves, came to T. Spence's stall, and bought by mistake, Spence's Rights of Man, instead of Paine's Rights of Man. Immediately on which they took him . . . before the civil magistrate . . . Mr Spence told him in his defence, that he might as well commit every one who sold Gulliver's Travels, More's Eutropia, Lock on Government, Puffendorff on the Law of Nature, &c, &c. all of which treated the subject of Government in a manner vastly opposite to the British system.' *Ibid.* p. 6. *The Important Trial of Thomas Spence . . .* (London 1803), pp. 59—60: 'Locke's Essay on Government and many other eminent works as well as the Bible have contributed to strengthen my confidence in this my Millennial Form of Government, and therefore such Books ought in Justice to stand or fall with mine' [quotes *Two Treatises*, II, § 25, ll. 1—8]. 'This Gentlemen is the Rights of Man! And upon this Rock of Nature have I built my Commonwealth, and the Gates of Hell shall not prevail against it.'

46 Thomas Hodgskin, *The Natural and Artificial Right of Property Contrasted . . .* (London 1832), esp. pp. 25—6 (esp. 26 n.: 'It is not a little extraordinary that every writer of any authority, since the days of Mr Locke, has theoretically adopted this view of the origin of the right of property, and has, at the same time, in defending the present right of property in practice, continually denied it') and pp. 12, 16—17, 21, 22, 24, 28, 34—6, 41—2, 53, 55, 61—2, 68, 106, 115.

47 'Inventory of Ralph Wormeley, II', *William and Mary College Quarterly*, 1st series, II, 3 (January 1894), 172.

48 Cf. Harvard Catalogue, *Catalogus Librorum Bibliothecae Collegii Harvardini . . .* (Boston 1723), containing over 2,800 titles including, e.g., Pufendorf, Grotius, Machiavelli, *Vindiciae contra Tyrannos*, Lawson on Hobbes, Harrington, Clarendon, Bodin, etc., with the Catalogue supplement of 1725 in which the arrival of the *Complete Works* is recorded in the 3-volume London 1722 edition.

49 Louis Shores, *Origins of the American College Library* (New York 1935), p. 261.

50 *Ibid.* p. 263.

51 Sereno E. Dwight, *The Life of President Edwards*, in *Works of Jonathan Edwards* (New York 1829—30), I, 30. Jonathan Edwards's manuscript 'Catalogue of Books' which he proposed to read, 1723—57, is in the Beinecke Library at Yale, MS. Vault. Sect. 4, Dr. 4, Folder IX. It lists as independent items Locke on *Human Understanding*, Locke on *Education*, Locke on *Toleration*, and Locke on the *Reasonableness of Christianity*, then the *Complete Works* in 3 vols. This hardly argues a consuming interest in the *Two Treatises*.

52   *The Autobiography of Benjamin Franklin*, ed. L.W. Labaree *et al.* (New Haven 1964), p. 64 and n.

53   There is a convenient summary of information on this point in Anna Haddow, *Political Science in American Colleges and Universities, 1636–1900* (New York 1939). I have confirmed this by comparing it with the standard histories of all the colonial colleges and with surviving manuscript materials from the pre-revolutionary period which remain in their libraries.

54   T.H. Montgomery, *A History of the University of Pennsylvania. From its Foundation to AD 1770* (Philadelphia 1900), pp. 239, 273.

55   'Letters from William and Mary College 1798–1801', *The Virginia Magazine of History and Biography*, XXIX, 2 (April 1921), 160: 'Another great fault in Locke is, that he is so exceptionally diffuse, and beats the same track continually over again, that he almost exhausts the patience of the reader.'

56   Edmund F. Slafter, *John Checkley: or the Evolution of Religious Tolerance in Massachusetts Bay . . .* , 2 vols. (for the Prince Society, Boston 1897), prints most of the surviving documentation for the Checkley affair. The publication which led to his prosecution was *A Discourse Concerning Episcopacy* (added to Charles Leslie, *A Short and Easie Method with the Deists . . .*) (London 1723). See esp. pp. 107–8 and 45, 53, 62–3, 98, 105, 118–19. There is a fine presentation of the significance of the episode in New England history in Perry Miller, *The New England Mind: From Colony to Province* (paperback ed., Boston 1961), pp. 466–74.

57   *The Speech of Mr. John Checkley upon his Tryal at Boston in New-England . . .* (London 1730), pp. 11–18, esp. p. 15: 'That great Man Mr. Locke expressly says, that the free Vote of every individual is absolutely necessary to the erecting of Government, and, at the same time, says *that it is impossible to be had.* And nothing is more certain than this, that no Country or Nation can be produced, where *every one of the People* hath a free Vote in the choice of their Rulers.'

58   Miller, *The New England Mind*, p. 473. For the legal history of Checkley's battle, see C.A. Duniway, *The Development of the Freedom of the Press in Massachusetts* (New York 1906), pp. 84–6, 107–10.

59   John Bulkley, in Roger Wolcott, *Poetical Meditations, Being the Improvement of some Vacant Hours . . .* (New London 1725), pp. xii-lvi, *passim.* For the background to Bulkley's concern over the basis of land titles see Richard L. Bushman, *From Puritan to Yankee: Character and the Social Order in Connecticut, 1690–1765* (Cambridge, Mass. 1967), chapter 3, esp. pp. 50, 52–3, 84–9, 93–5, 97, 99, 102. And for the continuity of Wolcott's attitudes in these disputes see *ibid.* p. 102.

60   Bulkley, *Poetical Meditations*, pp. xxiv–xxix, xxvi–xli, esp. p. xxxviii: 'Living almost entirely on what *Nature* prepared to their Hands, and so disproportioned in number to the quantity of their Provisions that after their Consumption of what was needful for them, there remained enough for perhaps *Ten Times the Number*, and at the same time nothing in the *Island* either because of its *Commonness* or *Perishableness* fit to supply the place of *Money*; what Inducement could such Societies have by *any Compact* either with one another, or among themselves respectively, to fix a *Property in Lands*, beyond what was done in the way before mentioned by *the Law of Nature*, for my own part I can't Excogitate any.'

61   Jared Eliot, *Give Cesar his Due. Or, The Obligation that Subjects are under to their Civil Rulers . . .* (New London 1738). Cf. the work as a whole with the statement on p. 27.

62   John Wise, *A Vindication of the Government of the New England Churches* (Boston 1717). There was a time when scholars detected 'the influence of Locke' in this work (but then there was a time when one of the most distinguished of American historians detected the possible influence of Locke's *Essay* on the Harvard curriculum before the book had been printed in any form). For an astute placing of the work see Miller, *The New England Mind*, pp. 289–302.

63   [Elisha Williams,] *The essential Rights and Liberties of Protestants. A seasonable Plea for the Liberty of Conscience and the Right of private Judgement . . .* (Boston 1744), pp. 2–8, 12, and esp. p. 6: 'I cannot forbear taking notice of *one Point of*

Liberty which all Members of a free State and particularly *Englishmen* think belonging to them, and are fond of; and that is the *Right* that *everyone* has *to speak his Sentiments openly* concerning *such Matters as affect the good of the whole*. Every Member of a Community ought to be concerned for the *whole*.' On Williams see the biography by Clifford K. Shipton in *Sibley's Harvard Graduates*, V, 588—97, and Francis Parsons, 'Elisha Williams: Minister, Soldier, President of Yale', *Papers of the New Haven Colony Historical Society*, VII (1908), 188—217. For the impact of the Great Awakening on Connecticut see Edwin S. Gaustad, *The Great Awakening in New England* (New York 1957), and Bushman, *From Puritan to Yankee*, esp. pp. 195, 230.

64 For Backus's use of Locke see esp. his *Seasonable Plea for Liberty of Conscience* ... (Boston 1770) and *A Letter to a Gentleman in the Massachusetts General Assembly* ... (n.p. 1771). His major interest in Locke was always as an exponent of the right of toleration, and he does not seem to have acquired a copy of Locke on *Government* until the appearance of the Boston 1773 printing (see T.B. Maston, *Isaac Backus: Pioneer of Religious Liberty*, London, 1962, p. 75 n.). He seems to have developed his main ideas before there is any reason to suppose that he had read Locke (see Maston, op. cit. pp. 105—6). The major biographical source is Alvah Hovey, *A Memoir of the Life and Times of the Rev. Isaac Backus, A.M.* (Boston 1858).

65 Louis L. Tucker, *Puritan Protagonist: President Thomas Clap of Yale College* (Chapel Hill, N.C. 1962), p. 146.

66 *Jasper Mauduit, Agent in London for the province of Massachusetts-Bay, 1762—65, Massachusetts Historical Society Collections*, LXXIV (1918), 39—40, 12 June 1762.

67 James Otis, *A Vindication of the Conduct of the House of Representatives of the Province of the Massachusetts-Bay* ... (Boston 1762), pp. 17—20.

68 Jack P. Greene, *The Quest for Power; the Lower Houses of Assembly in the Southern Royal Colonies 1689—1776* (Chapel Hill, N.C. 1963). See also more extendedly J.R. Pole, *Political Representation in England and the Origins of the American Republic* (London 1966).

69 Sir John Hawkins, *The Life of Samuel Johnson, LL.D.* (London 1787), p. 503.

70 *The Writings of Samuel Adams*, ed. H.A. Cushing (New York 1906), II, 22 (House of Representatives to Lieutenant-Governor Hutchinson, 3 August 1770): 'We beg Leave to recite to your Honor what the Great Mr. Locke has advanced in his Treatise of civil Government, upon the like Prerogative of the Crown.' See also p. 23: 'We would however, by no means be understood to suggest that this People have Occasion at present to proceed to such Extremity.'

71 Thomas Hutchinson, *History of the Colony and Province of Massachusetts-Bay*, ed. Lawrence Shaw Mayo, 3 vols. (Cambridge, Mass. 1936), III, 395: 'Your quotation from Mr. Locke, detached as it is from the rest of the treatise, cannot be applied to your case. I know of no attempt to enslave or destroy you, and as you, very prudently, would not be understood to suggest that this people have occasion at present to proceed to such extremity as to appeal to heaven, I am at a loss to conceive for what good purpose you adduce it.'

72 Cf. *ibid.* with [John Cary,] *A Vindication of the Parliament of England* ... (London 1698), p. 103: 'Pray what means all the Clamour you have made against our late Kings and the Parliaments of England, for infringing your Liberties and breaking through the very design of settling Communities, and putting you in a worse Condition than you were in the state of Nature. You are very much beholding to the ingenious Mr Lock for the fineness of your Argument about the State of Conquest Etc in the former part of your Book, which I do not at all blame you for, because I think no Man can handle a Subject smoothly, whereon he hath treated, that doth not follow his Copy; but I blame you for not applying those excellent Arguments more fitly.' Hutchinson himself extended his exposition of the very different implications of Locke's political theory in his unpublished writings, see e.g. *Massachusetts Archives*, XXV, 121—35 etc. (My attention was called to these by Professor R. Calhoon of the University of North Carolina, Greensboro.)

73 Boucher, *Causes and Consequences of the American Revolution*, see esp. pp. 486–7, on continuity of the Church of England's doctrine of non-resistance, and pp. 495–560 *passim*. It is not certain that the text of the sermon as published in 1797 was the same as that of 1775. The heavy footnote documentation seems to assimilate the polemic against Locke to the more systematic critique of Locke developed by the group of High Anglicans to which Boucher belonged in the early 1790s. See p. 312, n. 21.

74 Henry C. Van Schaack, *The Life of Peter Van Schaack, LL.D. . . .* (New York 1842), pp. 16–47 (leading role in early resistance of New York). pp. 54–8 (conscientious doubts and casuistry of the right of resistance, January 1776).

75 *Ibid.* pp. 56–7: 'In short, I think those acts may have been passed without a preconcerted plan of enslaving us, and it appears to me that the more favourable interpretation ought ever to be put on the conduct of our rulers. I cannot therefore think the government *dissolved*; and as long as the society lasts, the power that every individual gave the society when he entered into it, can never revert to the individuals again, but will always remain in the community (Locke).' See also p. 57: 'I am fully convinced, that men of the greatest abilities, and the soundest integrity, have taken parts in this war with America, and their measures should have a fair trial. But this is too serious a matter, implicitly to yield to the authority of any characters, however respectable. Every man must exercise his own reason, and judge for himself; "for he that appeals to Heaven, must be sure that he has right on his side", according to Mr. Locke.' And see p. 58, for his systematic consultation of authorities in the effort to 'enlighten his mind'.

76 *The Works of John Adams . . .* , ed. Charles Francis Adams, 10 vols. (Boston 1850–6), IV, 216: 'There never was an example of such precautions as are taken by this wise and jealous people in the formation of their government. None was ever made so perfectly upon the principle of the people's rights and equality. It is Locke, Sidney, and Rousseau and De Mably reduced to practice, in the first instance.' For the relative interest manifested by Adams in Locke as a philosopher and Locke as a political writer before the heights of the revolutionary struggle cf. *Diary & Autobiography of John Adams*, ed. L.H. Butterfield et al. (paperback ed. New York 1964), I, 177, III, 272, etc. with III, 358–9: 'I had read Harrington, Sydney, Hobbs, Nedham and Lock, but with very little Application to any particular Views: till these Debates in Congress . . . ' (November–December 1775).

77 Benjamin Rush, *Observations on the Government of Pennsylvania*, in *Selected Writings of Benjamin Rush* (New York 1947), p. 78: 'It is one thing to understand the *principles*, and another thing to understand the *forms* of government. The former are simple; the latter are difficult and complicated . . . Who understood the principles of mechanics and optics better than Sir Isaac Newton? and yet Sir Isaac could not for his life have made a watch or a microscope. Mr. Locke is an oracle as to the *principles*, Harrington and Montesquieu are oracles as to the *forms* of government.'

78 Jefferson to Thomas Mann Randolph, Jr., 30 May 1790, *The Papers of Thomas Jefferson*, ed. J.P. Boyd (Princeton 1961), XVI, 449: 'Locke's little book on Government is perfect as far as it goes. Descending from theory to practice there is no better book than the Federalist.'

79 Francis Lieber, *Manual of Political Ethics . . .* (Boston 1838), p. 356. MS. note in Lieber's own copy, now in library of Johns Hopkins University: 'All this I will present clearer, and mention how the English mind left the theory of politics and turned to political economy entirely. Pol. theory ended with Locke, and pol. econ. began with Adam Smith.'

80 George Fitzhugh, *Cannibals All . . .* , ed. C. Vann Woodward (Cambridge, Mass. 1960), pp. 12–15; p. 71: 'Modern social reformers, except Mr. Carlyle, proceeding upon the theory of Locke, which is the opposite of Aristotle, propose to dissolve and disintegrate society, falsely supposing that they thereby follow nature. There is not a human tie that binds man to man that they do not propose to cut "sheer asunder".' See also George Fitzhugh, *Sociology for the South . . .* (Richmond,

Virginia 1854), pp. 187, 209. See also the letter of Fitzhugh to George Frederick Holmes, quoted in Harvey Wish, *George Fitzhugh, Propagandist of the Old South* (Baton Rouge 1943), pp. 118—19. For Fitzhugh's championship of Filmer against Locke see esp. Vann Woodward's introduction to *Cannibals All* and cf. for Holmes's views of Locke, the MS. notes on *Two Treatises* in his edition of the *Collected Works* in the Alderman Library, University of Virginia.

81 Caroline Robbins, *The Eighteenth Century Commonwealthman* (Cambridge, Mass. 1959), presents exhaustive documentation of the more radical exponents of this theme, and J.G.A. Pocock, 'Machiavelli, Harrington and English Political Ideologies in the Eighteenth Century', *William and Mary Quarterly*, 3rd series, XXII, 4 (October 1965), 549—83 provides a brilliant interpretation of the character of its development. The history of its reception in America has been illuminated by many American scholars, notably Professor Douglass Adair. The most effective recent treatments at length are H. Trevor Colbourn, *The Lamp of Experience. Whig History and the Intellectual Origins of the American Revolution* (Chapel Hill, N.C. 1965) (on historical writing), and Bailyn, *Ideological Origins of the American Revolution* (on the whole range of ideas).

82 The most memorable expression of this point of view is perhaps Judge Mellen Chamberlain's interview in 1842 with a ninety-one-year old veteran of Concord: 'Then I suppose you had been reading Harington or Sidney and Locke about the eternal principles of liberty?' 'Never heard of 'em. We read only the Bible, the Catechism, Watts' Psalms and Hymns, and the Almanac.' Quoted from Samuel Eliot Morison, *The Oxford History of the American People* (London 1965), p. 212.

5 Practising history and social science on 'realist' assumptions

1 W.G. Runciman, 'Describing', *Mind*, n.s., 81 (July 1972), 372—88.

2 See e.g. Donald Davidson, 'Mental Events', in Lawrence Foster and J.W. Swanson (eds.), *Experience and Theory* (London 1970), pp. 79—101; an alternative possibility would be to adopt Hilary Putnam's less committal defence of the autonomy of the mental in his 'Philosophy and Our Mental Life', in *Philosophical Papers*, vol. 2: *Mind, Language and Reality* (Cambridge 1975), pp. 291—303.

3 See e.g. Crispin Wright, 'Language-Mastery and the Sorites Paradox', in Gareth Evans and John McDowell (eds.), *Truth and Meaning: Essays in Semantics* (Oxford 1976), pp. 223—47.

4 Cf. Donald Davidson, 'How Is Weakness of the Will Possible?', in Joel Feinberg (ed.), *Moral Concepts* (London 1969), pp. 93—113.

5 Runciman, op. cit.

6 Carl G. Hempel, 'The Function of General Laws in History' (*Journal of Philosophy*, 1942), in Patrick Gardiner (ed.), *Theories of History* (New York 1959), pp. 344—56. Patrick Gardiner, *The Nature of Historical Explanation* (London 1952). Cf. William Dray, *Laws and Explanation in History* (London 1957). W.B. Gallie, *Philosophy and the Historical Understanding* (London 1964).

7 Charles Taylor, 'Interpretation and the Sciences of Man', *Review of Metaphysics*, 25 (September 1971), 3—51. Alasdair MacIntyre, 'Ideology, Social Science and Revolution', *Comparative Politics*, 5, 3 (April 1973), 321—42.

8 See Bernard Williams, 'Deciding to Believe', in his *Problems of the Self* (Cambridge 1973), p. 140.

9 See especially H.G. Gadamer, *Truth and Method* (London 1975). Weber's views are not discussed here because of the formidable exegetic difficulties which they raise. For a helpful discussion see W.G. Runciman, *A Critique of Max Weber's Philosophy of Social Science* (Cambridge 1972). It should be emphasised that the account offered here, even if it is properly titled hermeneutic, does not resemble that of Gadamer, particularly in its epistemological conclusions.

10 See the extended series of articles by Quentin Skinner: 'Meaning and Understanding in the History of Ideas', *History and Theory*, 8, 1 (1969), 3—53: 'Conventions and the Understanding of Speech Acts', *Philosophical Quarterly*, 20:79 (April 1970),

113—38; 'On Performing and Explaining Linguistic Actions', *Philosophical Quarterly*, 21, 82 (January 1971), 1—21; ' "Social Meaning" and the Explanation of Social Action', in Peter Laslett, W.G. Runciman and Quentin Skinner (eds.), *Philosophy, Politics and Society*, 4th ser. (Oxford 1972), pp. 136—57; 'Some Problems in the Analysis of Political Thought and Action', *Political Theory*, 2, 3 (August 1974), 277—303; ' Hermeneutics and the Role of History', *New Literary History*, 7 (1975—6), 209—32.

11 MacIntyre, 'Ideology, Social Science and Revolution', 332.

12 Alasdair MacIntyre, *Against the Self-Images of the Age*, London 1971, 263.

13 Hilary Putnam, 'What is "Realism"?', *Proceedings of the Aristotelian Society*, New Series, LXXVI, 1975—6, 177—94.

14 Cf. Ted Gurr, *Why Men Rebel*, Princeton, N.J. 1970 and the articles by Zagorin, Hermassi & Skocpol in *Comparative Studies in Society and History*, XVIII, 2, April 1976, with J. Dunn, *Modern Revolutions*, Cambridge 1972, Introduction and Conclusion; Michael Freeman, 'Theories of Revolution', *British Journal of Political Science*, II, 1972, 339—59 and the articles by MacIntyre and Tilly in *Comparative Politics*, V, 2, April 1973.

15 See J.M. Roberts, *The Mythology of the Secret Societies*, London 1972; Jack P. Lively, ed. & trans., *The Works of Joseph de Maistre*, New York 1964; and below ch. 9.

16 'Was there ever in history an example of a great revolution occurring by itself, not tied to war? Of course not' (Lenin, 1916). Quoted in Roger Pethybridge, *The Social Prelude to Stalinism*, London 1974, 77. For an attempt to analyse the causation of revolution more firmly within its geopolitical context see now Theda Skocpol, *States and Social Revolutions*, Cambridge 1979.

17 See Hilary Putnam, 'What is "Realism"?', and Nick Jardine, ' "Realistic" Realism and the Progress of Science', in C. Hookway and P. Pettit (eds.), *Action and Interpretation*, Cambridge 1978, 107—26.

18 Runciman, 'Describing'.

19 R. Hilferding, quoted in Lucio Colletti, *From Rousseau to Lenin* (London 1972), p. 34.

20 W.V.O. Quine, *Ontological Relativity and Other Essays* (New York 1969). 'On deeper reflection, radical translation begins at home.'

21 W.V.O. Quine, *Word and Object* (Cambridge, Mass. 1960), p. 27.

22 Martin Hollis, 'Reason and Ritual', in Alan Ryan (ed.), *The Philosophy of Social Explanation* (London 1973), pp. 33—49, at pp. 39—42.

23 For a variety of attempts to show either that indeterminacy does not obtain or that its implications are no more anti-realist in the case of meaning than in the general underdetermination of theory by evidence see: Jonathan Bennett, *Linguistic Behaviour* (Cambridge 1976), pp. 261, 263; David F. Graybeal, 'The In- and Underdeterminacy of Translation', *Dialectica*, 30, 1 (1976), 9—15; Hilary Putnam, 'The Refutation of Conventionalism', *Noûs*, 8 (1974), 25—40; Michael Dummett, *Frege: Philosophy of Language* (London 1973), pp. 589—627; Richard Rorty, 'Indeterminacy of Translation and of Truth', *Synthèse*, 23 (1972), 443—62; Donald Davidson, 'Radical Interpretation', *Dialectica*, 27 (1973), 313—28; Donald Davidson, 'Belief and the Basis of Meaning', *Synthèse*, 27 (1974), 309—23, and 'Replies to David Lewis and W.V. Quine', *ibid.*, 345—9; David Lewis, 'Radical Interpretation', *Synthèse*, 27 (1974), 331—44. For powerful criticism of these, on which I have depended heavily, see the paper by Hookway, 'Indeterminacy and Interpretation', in C. Hookway & P. Pettit (eds.), *Action and Interpretation*, 17—42.

24 For a helpful brief discussion of the intelligibility of desires, see A.J. Watt, 'The Intelligibility of Wants', *Mind*, n.s., 81 (July 1972), 372—88.

25 Alfred Schutz, 'Problems of Interpretive Sociology', quoted from Ryan (ed.), *Philosophy of Social Explanation*, 211.

26 Evan Fales, 'Truth, Tradition and Rationality', *Philosophy of the Social Sciences*, 6:2 (June 1976), 97—113.

27 J.W.N. Watkins, 'Imperfect Rationality', in Robert Borger and Frank Cioffi

(eds.), *Explanation in the Behavioural Sciences* (Cambridge 1970), pp. 167–217.

28 On trying to believe and choosing to believe, see Bernard Williams, 'Deciding to Believe', in *Problems of the Self*, pp. 136–51.

29 See the articles by Skinner cited in note 10 (p. 319).

30 MacIntyre, 'Ideology, Social Science and Revolution'.

31 Arthur C. Danto, *Analytical Philosophy of History* (Cambridge 1965), esp. pp. 149–81.

32 Cf. Ludwig Wittgenstein, *Lectures and Conversations on Aesthetics, Psychology and Religious Belief*, ed. Cyril Barrett (Oxford 1966), pp. 41–52, esp. 51–2.

33 Richard E. Grandy, 'Reference, Meaning and Belief', *Journal of Philosophy*, 70, 14 (16 August 1973), 439–52, 451–2.

34 See e.g. P.F. Strawson, 'Intention and Convention in Speech Acts', and H.P. Grice, 'Utterer's Meaning, Sentence-Meaning, and Word-Meaning', both in J.R. Searle (ed.), *The Philosophy of Language* (London 1971), pp. 23–38, 54–70; Stephen Schiffer, *Meaning* (Oxford 1972); etc.

35 John McDowell, 'Truth Conditions, Bivalence, and Verificationism', in Evans and McDowell (eds.), *Truth and Meaning*, pp. 42–66, at pp. 64–6.

36 See especially the paper by McDowell, 'On "The Reality of the Past" ', in C. Hookway and P. Pettit (eds.), *Action and Interpretation*, pp. 127–44, and the article cited in note 35 above.

37 See especially the work of Michael Dummett, and the articles by Dummett and Wright in Evans and McDowell (eds.), op. cit., pp. 67–137 and 223–47.

38 See e.g. Davidson, 'Radical Interpretation'.

39 Grandy, 'Reference, Meaning and Belief'.

40 Putnam, 'What is "Realism"?'.

41 Lewis, 'Radical Interpretation', 338–9.

6 From democracy to representation: an interpretation of a Ghanaian election

1 Jean-Jacques Rousseau, *Du Contrat Social*, Bk 111, ch. XV, *Political Writings*, ed. C.E. Vaughan, Oxford 1962, II, p. 96.

2 This picture emerges equally clearly from the studies conducted in the tradition of Paul Lazarsfeld and Bernard Berelson, *The People's Choice* (New York 1944) and *Voting* (Chicago 1954), and from the work of the Survey Research Centre, Michigan. A. Campbell et al., *The American Voter*, 1960 and P. Converse, 'The Nature of Belief Systems in Mass Publics', in D. Apter (ed.), *Ideology and Discontent* (Glencoe 1964).

3 Brief accounts of the changing structures within which the Ahafo division was administered up to the 1939–45 war can be found in W. Tordoff, *Ashanti under the Prempehs*, Oxford 1965, and K.A. Busia, *The Position of the Chief in the Modern Political System of Ashanti*, 2nd ed. London 1968. There are extensive records of the conduct of British administration in the Ahafo division in the Ghana National Archives in Accra, Kumasi and Sunyani.

4 The main road from the administrative capital of Ahafo, Goaso, to the north is the lifeline along which the vast bulk of the area's production of timber and cocoa passes. It was one of the two major roads which the British administration decided to build to Goaso at the time at which the main Ashanti road system was designed. The surviving records of the execution of this plan make it clear that it was a consequence more of administrative accident than of economic or geographical calculation that this road was in fact built and the other road which would have connected Goaso directly with Kumasi was never completed.

5 For the economics of this process see especially R. Szereszewski, *Structural Changes in the Economy of Ghana, 1891–1911*, London 1965.

6 The 1960 population census records the population of the Brong-Ahafo South Local Council Area as 81,590. Of these only 9,030 are recorded as Ahafos. It is plausible that, of the 36,150 recorded as Ashanti, some have been resident for more

than two generations. But there are good reasons to believe that the proportion of long-term resident families suggested by these figures is of the right order of magnitude. See *1960 Population Census of Ghana. Special Report E. Tribes in Ghana,* Table S 1.

7　One of the largest landholders in Ahafo, for example, is Bafuor Osei Akoto, a major organiser of the N.L.M. in 1954.

8　B. Fitch and M. Oppenheimer, *Ghana: End of an Illusion,* New York 1966, pp. 38—40, 129—30.

9　F.R. Bray, *Cocoa Development in Ahafo, West Ashanti,* Achimota 1959 has a useful discussion of the process by which land rights (the basis of local citizenship) are acquired, see pp. 17—23. Slightly under a seventh of the recorded population of the Brong-Ahafo South Local Council area was born outside Ghana. (*1960 Population Census,* Vol. 11.)

10　The classic treatment of the development of tenurial systems in cocoa production is in Polly Hill's, *The Gold Coast Cocoa Farmer,* Oxford 1956 and *Migrant Cocoa Farmers of Southern Ghana,* Cambridge 1963.

11　The slow progress of both missions and government schools is recorded in the Ahafo District Record Book, Vols. I and II, *Ghana National Archives,* Kumasi. The *1960 Census* (Vol. II) recorded roughly the same percentage of male children in the 6—14 age group as currently enjoying education as was deprived of it (whereas among those over the age of 15 nearly four times as many males had never had access to education as had enjoyed the opportunity). Today the percentage of children attending school appears to be substantially higher than in 1960.

12　Christian religious affiliation is almost as strongly connected with achieved social status in Ahafo among those over the age of thirty as is educational experience. Before the Nkrumah government's expansion of education, the link between organised Christianity and educational provision was a very close one.

13　When questioned as to which of three roles they would prefer their children to attain, the majority of those interviewed in Goaso preferred an office in the state bureaucracy (District Commissioner) to that of politician or chief on the grounds that the first enjoyed comparable pickings and far greater security of tenure.

14　He felt it necessary to testify at length (and in essentially the same terms) to his devotion to the ideals of multi-party democracy in his speech in Goaso in August as he had in a speech to the Legon students some months earlier. The similarity of the pronouncements may have testified to the sincerity of his commitment. In Goaso at any rate they certainly did not testify to his political sensitivity. Few had any idea of what he was talking about.

15　The theme was repeated at length in Busia's speech at the party's inauguration rally at Sunyani and again at a speech at Techimentia which the Asunafo party dignitaries contrived to attend. It was also emphasised by R.R. Amponsah on his visit to Akrodie. In a more rough and ready way it featured in many local rallies. The behaviour of the party's organisers in the immediate aftermath of victory provided clear testimony of the sincerity of the commitment of most of them.

16　'We have got two kinds of people, United Party people and C.P.P. people.' (Interview with N.A.L. constituency official, explaining the basis of political allegiance in the election.)

17　Senkyire 5,400. Osei 1,744. Addai 579.

18　Osei 7,248. Senkyire 2,854.

19　See the remarkable speech on the expediency of maintaining diplomatic relationships with South Africa made by Osei on 15 February 1965 (*Hansard* cols. 1062—63) and the scornful comment of a C.P.P. member 'A short man with a small sense.' Whatever may be thought of the rationality of Osei's argument it required considerable courage to put it forward in the Ghanaian legislature in 1965.

20　The main road north of Goaso is frequently impassable in the rainy season because it has not been tarred. There was alleged to be a confidential file on this road in the Regional Office with a minute from one of the C.P.P. Regional Commissioners instructing that the road not be tarred any further south because the area to the south was solidly United Party in political allegiance.

21 When asked what individual had done most for the town of Goaso in the last few years virtually all of those whom I interviewed in Goaso named the then District Administrative Officer.

22 He took pains to see that his wife did not make friends among the local Goaso community and his social life was largely confined to the official community resident in Goaso. He did not himself speak to the local populace in Twi, although he understood Twi perfectly and could speak it quite well.

23 Both A.W. Osei and Badu Nkansah in their capacity as members of the Ahafo Youth Society claimed responsibility for its arrival in several speeches.

24 Cf. Busia's speech at Techimentia in July (translated from the Twi) 'This is the meaning of our name, the Progress ... Everyone likes Progress. If you have one cloth and we help you to get one more, will you not like it? If you have no house and you are provided with a house to buy by instalments, will you not like it? As we are short of drinking water, if a pipe is brought into your town to save you going four or five miles to fetch water, will you not like it? Everyone needs progress.'

25 It was not clear until the day of nomination itself how many parties would in fact contest the seat. On the day in question, the Progress Party District Secretary took the trouble to accumulate a new set of signatures on the nomination form because of the rumour that one of the nominators had been nominated himself at the last minute to stand as a candidate for the U.N.P.

26 For a full account of the origin and working of this body see Austin & Luckham (eds.), *Politicians and Soldiers*, ch. 4.

27 His initial statement in the Constituent Assembly included a strong attack on the abuses of chieftaincy and an allegation that the Constitution was biased in favour of the chiefs (*Proceedings of the Constituent Assembly*, 23 January 1969, pp. 143–5.) Later his attitude upon this point became considerably less urgent.

28 He was celebrating his acquittal before the High Court in Sunyani of a State Prosecution for not carrying out the summons of his lawful traditional overlord, the Asantehene, to go to pay his allegiance. The political significance of this prosecution and the verdict are discussed below.

29 The campaign outside the major centres of population was a sporadic affair. The voting figures are in general (for reasons discussed below) more favourable to the P.P. outside the major centres of population.

30 They were both, for example, members in 1952 of the Ahafo Information Service Panel (*Ghana National Archives, Sunyani*, Sunyani District Files, 515).

31 The contrast between this speech and the eloquence of Busia's speech at Techimentia was noted even by N.A.L. supporters who had listened to both. This comparative linguistic advantage would, of course, have been reversed in the Ewe areas.

32 It should be noted that the strains of the campaigning tour meant that Busia's frequently announced (and genuinely expected) visit to Ahafo never materialised at all.

33 In the last C.P.P. election, that of 1965, there was only one box because there was only one party permitted to contest the election. Earlier there had been separate boxes for the different parties, the choice between the two boxes being at times made simpler by the fact that the poll was directly supervised by representatives of the ruling party.

34 Stein Rokkan, 'Mass Suffrage, Secret Voting and Political Participation', in L. Coser (ed.), *Political Sociology*, New York 1967, especially pp. 114–19.

35 It is unlikely that he wasted his time insisting on this point in the Ewe areas.

36 Anthony Downs, *An Economic Theory of Democracy*, New York 1957, chapter 14. M. Olson, *The Logic of Collective Action*, Cambridge, Mass. 1965. See the comments of Brian Barry, *Political Argument*, London 1965, pp. 281, 328–30 and *Sociologists, Economists and Democracy*, London 1970.

37 If the number of voters was very small (as at the Oseikrom polling station, 17 voters, or the Mintumi No. 1 Cocoa Shed polling station, also 17) the chances of punitive

action against the disobedient being directed against the right individual or set of individuals is clearly much higher than at a polling station (e.g. the Mim Roman Catholic Primary School) at which more than 400 cast their vote. The sense of security which is the presumable psychological point of the secrecy of the ballot can hardly be maintained when voting is conducted on the scale of these few isolated polling stations and when the results are made public polling station by polling station.

38 It is possible that the personalised, televisual and consensual politics of western democracies are reverting to a condition in which this is the basis of rational choice in their elections also.

39 These two adjoining villages have a tradition of intermittently violent conflict which reaches back to their initial separation.

40 The present Regional and District administrations appear to devote as substantial a proportion of their efforts to the management of traditional affairs as their colonial predecessors. The fact that they do so is an accurate articulation of the real political values of most Ghanaians as well as a technically necessary response to concrete problems of social control. It is the latter *because* it is the former.

41 The post-electoral massacre in September 1969 in which the Yendi skin dispute came to its climax recorded a death toll which modernist social conflict in Ghana in the form of industrial disputes are unlikely to match within the near future.

42 They fall at any one time into two broad constitutional traditions, localist or Ashanti. But since they are expounded on given occasions usually in order to sanction particular political positions it cannot be assumed that the history of any particular settlement will always be found in the same constitutional tradition on different occasions. My understanding of the political basis of Ahafo historiography derives largely from the extensive series of interviews with the chiefs of Ahafo which Dr Robertson carried out.

43 Cf. John Pocock, *The Ancient Constitution and the Feudal Law*, Cambridge 1957.

44 Cf. in addition to Pocock's brilliant book, Q. Skinner, 'History and Ideology in the English Revolution', *The Historical Journal*, VIII, 1965. F. Neumann, *The Democratic and the Authoritarian State*, Glencoe 1957, ch. IV., F.L. Ford, *Sword and Robe*, Cambridge, Mass. 1963, ch. XII.

45 W. Tordoff, *Ashanti under the Prempehs*, Oxford 1965 gives the clearest account available of the impact of British pressures on the Ashanti political order in this period.

46 The late Asantehene affirmed in an interview with Dr Robertson that no such person as Asibi Entwi had ever existed.

47 Tordoff, *Ashanti under the Prempehs*, pp. 409–10.

48 Busia, *Position of the Chief*, pp. 189–93 especially.

49 The Circuit Judge in his judgement on 9 June 1969 stated that it was undisputed that no Kukuomhene had *ever* taken the oath of allegiance to the Asantehene or the Akroponghene. (Transcript p. 19.)

50 Personal communication from J.A. Braimah, formerly member of the Chieftaincy Secretariat.

51 The legal specification of the judgement is quite complicated. The key premise, however, is explicitly the historical reality of Asibi Entwi and of either the preservation or the establishment of Ahafo independence which his defeat represented. (Transcript, passim.)

52 It was claimed by one former C.P.P. official that the plans for the coming of the water preceded the coup of February 1966. It is, however, clear from the administrative files dealing with the project and from personal communication with the former head of the Ghana Water and Sewerage Corporation, M.K. Apaloo, that local political initiative would probably not have been enough ever to get it beyond the planning stage.

53 Cf. at the regional level Dr Busia's promise in his inauguration speech in Sunyani not to dismantle the Brong-Ahafo region and the more local effort to cement the unity of Ahafo as a geographical community.

54 The point was made by several of the less sophisticated party speakers in local rallies in Goaso in terms of the difference between the sheer distances to be traversed if one wished to go to approach one of the two men about some issue. The degree of personalisation in Ghanaian political perception (not to say conduct) makes geographical inaccessibility a natural symbol for political inaccessibility.

55 Cf. *Logic of Collective Action*, ch. VI, D., pp. 141—8.

56 Cf. Staniland's observation that we have at the moment no basis for predicting 'how long it will take before ordinary Ivoiriens want to and can make politics more than a growth industry of élites and political scientists, more something they participate in and less something they have done for them' (Martin Staniland, 'Single-Party Regimes and Political Change: The P.D.C.I. and Ivory Coast Politics', in Colin Leys (ed.), *Politics and Change in Developing Countries*, Cambridge 1969).

57 If action is analysed, as by Erving Goffman, *Where the Action Is*, London 1969, in terms of the enactment of socially specified roles, this was the role most persistently identifiable in the actual behaviour of the agents. The deficiencies of such an analysis on philosophical grounds do not affect the point at issue.

58 Either in terms of direct cash payments or of the potentially remunerative consequences of holding power in a ruling party. ('I think we will get something out of it', was a formulation produced impartially by one leading N.A.L. organiser to inquiries about the reasons for and about the causes of the party's political support.)

59 Cf. G.W.F. Hegel, *Philosophy of Right*, (trans. T.M. Knox), Oxford 1942, paras. 324, 325, p. 210 and *Political Writings*, (trans. Knox and ed. Pelczynski), Oxford 1964, pp. 143—4.

60 Cf. 'Ce n'est rien de bien partir si l'on ne fournit la carrière: le prix est au bout de la lice, et la fin regle toujours le commencement' (Gabriel Naudé, *Considerations Politiques sur les Coups d'Estat*, n.p. 1667).

61 The repetitive and resonant affirmation, 'We are going to *win*' was the keynote of all large N.A.L. rallies and the main theme, for instance, of the editorials in the party newspaper, the *Evening Standard*.

62 Cf. Busia speech cited in note 24 above.

63 See note 58 above.

64 Cf. Edward C. Banfield, *The Moral Basis of a Backward Society*, Glencoe 1958, a study of a South Italian village in which the value system is described by the author as one of 'amoral familism', in that the *interesse* of any family is regarded by all as totally unrestrained by moral responsibility to any larger social collectivity.

65 The rewards may take the form of direct cash payments or they may (in more politically specific clientages) create fairly stable structures of dependence in which the client provides extensive services, rather than cash. For their character in Mexico see Eric R. Wolf, 'Aspects of Group Relations in a Complex Society: Mexico', *American Anthropologist*, LVIII, No. 6, December 1956, pp. 1065—78.

66 This formulation was one of the commonest responses to the question in interviews in Goaso about what was the point of education.

67 There are close kinship links in Ahafo as elsewhere in Ghana between traditional and modern élites. The relationship between initial wealth, traditional power and inequality of educational access, although intricate in detail, is extremely strong. The key position of educational achievement in Ghanaian status perception is firmly based on the economic returns on educational investment (P. Foster, *Education and Social Change in Ghana*, London 1965, and for a clear account of an area of Nigeria in which this connection is resulting in the formation of a distinct social class see E. Krapf-Askari, *Yoruba Towns and Cities*, Oxford 1969, ch. VI, 'Social Stratification').

68 The Weberian notion of status as a conceptually irreducible dimension of social stratification — as argued by W.G. Runciman, 'Class, Status and Power', in J.A. Jackson (ed.), *Social Stratification*, Cambridge 1968.

69 Ralf Dahrendorf, *Society and Democracy in Germany*, London 1968, p. 230.

70 This moral image did not, of course, correspond to fact. Disunion had always been extremely prevalent in Ahafo.

71 An M.P. has to be able to speak English, most adult Ghanaians cannot.
72 This chapter was completed in May 1970. I have altered a number of tenses where subsequent events have made this necessary. A fuller account of the historical and sociological background of Ahafo is now available in John Dunn and A.F. Robertson, *Dependence and Opportunity: Political Change in Ahafo*, Cambridge 1973.

7 'Hoc signo victor eris': representation, allegiance and obligation in the politics of Ghana and Sri Lanka

1 Andrew Alföldi, *The Conversion of Constantine and Pagan Rome*, Oxford 1969 edition, ch. 11. A.H.M. Jones, *Constantine and the Conversion of Europe*, London 1948, ch. VI. The version of the legend given in the title to the present piece differs from the common *In Hoc Signo Vinces*. But the latter is less authentic, according to Alföldi, being a translation from the Greek version of Eusebius, *Vita Constantini*, in place of a direct quotation from the best authority Lactantius, *De Mortibus Persecutorum*. (See Alföldi, op. cit., pp. 16—18).
2 Perry Anderson, *Passages from Antiquity To Feudalism*, New Left Books, London 1974, pp. 131—7. And for a comparable judgement from the greatest and most level-headed of the empire's modern historians, see Jones, op. cit., p. 258.
3 See A. Jeyaratnam Wilson, *Politics in Sri Lanka 1947—1973*, London 1974, pp. 128 & 142. I have drawn heavily for my treatment of Sri Lankan politics throughout on this book, together with Wilson's study of the 1970 election, *Electoral Politics in an Emergent State*, Cambridge 1975; Robert N. Kearney, *Communalism and Language in the Politics of Ceylon*, Durham, North Carolina 1967 and *Trade Unions and Politics in Ceylon*, Berkeley 1971; Calvin A. Woodward, *The Growth of a Party System in Ceylon*, Providence 1969; and Donald E. Smith (ed.), *South Asian Politics and Religion*, Princeton, N.J. 1966. I have not thought it worthwhile to cite them specifically on most points which are unlikely to be controversial.
4 E.H. Gombrich, *Art and Illusion*, Pantheon Books, New York 1960, p. 5.
5 See Anthony Giddens, ' "Power" in the Recent Writings of Talcott Parsons', *Sociology*, 11, 3, September 1968, 257—72. John Dunn, 'The Eligible and the Elect: Arminian Thoughts on the Social Determination of Ahafo Leaders', in W.H. Morris-Jones (ed.), *The Making of Politicians*, London 1976, pp. 49—65.
6 David Hume, *Treatise of Human Nature*, Book III, Part II, Section II (1740). Adam Smith, *The Theory of Moral Sentiments* (1759).
7 See e.g. Quentin Skinner, 'The Principles and Practice of Opposition: The Case of Bolingbroke versus Walpole', in Neil McKendrick (ed.), *Historical Perspectives: Studies in English Thought and Society in honour of J.H. Plumb*, London 1974, pp. 93—128; and John Dunn, 'But How Will They Eat?': review article, *Transactions of the Historical Society of Ghana*, XIII, 1, June 1972, 113—24.
8 Mancur Olson Jr, *The Logic of Collective Action*, Cambridge, Mass. 1965.
9 The most helpful general study of the concept of representation is Hanna F. Pitkin, *The Concept of Representation*, Berkeley, pb. ed. 1972.
10 The best overall study of the Ghanaian economy remains Walter Birmingham, I. Neustadt & E.N. Omaboe (eds.), *A Study of Contemporary Ghana*, 2 vols., London 1966—7. For Sri Lanka see Donald R. Snodgrass, *Ceylon: An Export Economy in Transition*, Homewood, Illinois 1966. I have also been able to make use of two unpublished papers by Snodgrass on developments up to 1973.
11 Andrzej Krassowski, *Development and the Debt Trap: Economic Planning and External Borrowing in Ghana*, London 1974 and the unpublished papers by Snodgrass cited in note 10 above.
12 For the background to the Indian Tamils' presence in Ceylon see Hugh Tinker, *A New System of Slavery. The export of Indian Labour Overseas 1830—1920*, London 1974. For some details on their present predicament see Walter Schwartz, *The Tamils of Sri Lanka*, Minority Rights Group Report no. 25, London 1975.
13 Professor Robinson recorded this myth during her first spell of fieldwork from 1962 to 1963 (Marguerite S. Robinson, ' "The House of the Mighty Hero" or "The

House of Enough Paddy"? Some Implications of a Sinhalese Myth', in Edmund Leach (ed.), *Dialectic in Practical Religion*, Cambridge 1968, pp. 128–32. For the changes in the community's attitudes to party politics between 1963 and 1967 see Marguerite S. Robinson, *Political Structure in a Changing Sinhalese Village*, Cambridge 1975, pts II & III.

14 Robinson, *Political Structure*, p. 284. *Dialectic*, p. 129.

15 Richard F. Gombrich, *Precept and Practice. Traditional Buddhism in the Rural Highlands of Ceylon*, Oxford 1971, p. 29.

16 Robert Redfield, *Peasant Society and Culture*, Chicago 1960.

17 See e.g. Smith (ed.), *South Asian Politics and Religion*, chs. 21 & 23, and Richard F. Gombrich, 'Le clergé bouddhiste d'une circonscription kandienne et les élections générales de 1965', *Social Compass*, XX, 2, 1973, 257–66, esp. 261–3. Cf. also the anti-Muslim riots in Colombo earlier in the century.

18 Cf. Maxwell Owusu, *Uses and Abuses of Political Power*, Chicago 1970.

19 Robinson, *Political Structure*, passim.

20 Gombrich, *Precept and Practice*, pp. 208–9, 215–16, 257–8.

21 Gananath Obeyesekere, 'Theodicy, Sin and Salvation in a Sociology of Buddhism', in Leach (ed.), *Dialectic in Practical Religion*, pp. 7–40, at p. 30. Gombrich, *Precept and Practice*, ch. 6, esp. p. 261.

22 Cf. J.D.Y. Peel, 'Cultural Factors in the Contemporary Theory of Development', *Archives Européennes de Sociologie*, XIV, 1973, 283–303.

23 Smith (ed.), *South Asian Religion and Politics*, p. 456.

24 Woodward, *Party System*, p. 97.

25 Wilson, *Electoral Politics*, passim.

26 Wilson, *Electoral Politics*, pp. 35, 92, 115, 117–19.

27 Wilson, *Electoral Politics*, pp. 118–19.

28 Richard Rathbone, 'Businessmen in Politics: Party Struggle in Ghana 1949–57', *Journal of Development Studies*, IX, 3, April 1973, 391–401. Since no one in Ghana is too haughty to be in trade, *all* political parties there, as Rathbone indicates, have their entrepreneurial element. The novelty in the C.P.P. case was their success in using the state of which they had got hold as an implement for rapid private capital formation. For an exceptionally illuminating study of class relations between the C.P.P. political apparat and Ghanaian cocoa producers see now: Björn Beckman, *Organising the Farmers: Cocoa Politics and National Development in Ghana*, Uppsala 1976.

29 Samuel G. Ikoku, *Le Ghana de Nkrumah*, trad. Y. Bénot, Paris 1971.

30 This point is emphasised in Yaw Saffu's Oxford D.Phil. thesis on the N.L.C. government (1973).

31 J. Adomako-Sarfoh, 'The Effects of the Expulsion of Migrant Workers on Ghana's Economy, with special reference to the cocoa industry', in Samir Amin (ed.), *Modern Migrations in Western Africa*, London 1974, pp. 138–52.

32 Krassowski, *Development and Debt Trap*. Elliot J. Berg, 'Structural Transformation versus Gradualism: Recent Economic Development in Ghana and the Ivory Coast', in Philip Foster & Aristide R. Zolberg (eds.), *Ghana and the Ivory Coast: Perspectives on Modernization*, Chicago 1971, pp. 187–230 (and cf. chapter by Green, ibid., pp. 231–64).

33 See e.g. Roger Genoud, *Nationalism and Economic Development in Ghana*, New York 1969. But cf. Berg article cited in note 32 above.

34 See e.g. Dennis Austin, *Politics in Ghana 1946–1960*, Oxford University Press, London 1964, pp. 272–3, 341–3. John Dunn & A.F. Robertson, *Dependence and Opportunity: Political Change in Ahafo*, Cambridge University Press, Cambridge 1973, pp. 321, 324–5, 336, 338.

35 Anthony Downs, *An Economic Theory of Democracy*, Harper & Row, New York 1957, pp. 115–17.

36 The most valuable study of the L.S.S.P. is Yodage Ranjith Amarasinghe, *Trotskyism in Ceylon: A Study of the Development, Ideology and Political Role of the Lanka Sama Samaja Party, 1935–1964*, London University Ph.D. (Institute of

Commonwealth Studies) (1974). For a study in print which covers the earlier period of the movement see George Jan Lerski, *Origins of Trotskyism in Ceylon. A Documentary History of the Lanka Sama Samaja Party, 1935–1942*, Stanford 1968.

37   *The Times*, 25 July 1975, p. 12.

38   See Baron Holmes III, *Some Economic and Social Organizations in Gold Coast Politics, 1920–45*, Ph.D., Department of Political Science, University of Chicago 1972, and see Leo Spitzer and Laray Denzer, 'I.T.A. Wallace-Johnson and the West African Youth League', *International Journal of African Historical Studies*, VI, 3, 1973, 413–52.

39   Amarasinghe, op. cit., gives the best account.

40   For some more specific doubts on the universalism of the left vote see the University of Ceylon, Peradeniya, Ph.D. by Janice Jiggins (1973), pp. 189 & 266–70.

41   Karl Marx & Frederick Engels, *The German Ideology*, New York 1963, pp. 57–8, 67–9.

42   Amarasinghe, op. cit., pp. 412–31; & Jiggins, loc. cit., note 40 above.

43   *The Times*, 25 July 1975 & 3 September 1975.

44   *The Times*, 25 July 1975; & Saul Rose, 'Sri Lanka at the Turning Point. The Future of Parliamentary Democracy', *The Round Table*, 256, October 1974, 411–22.

45   The only published general study on the role of trade unions in Ghanaian politics is unfortunately worthless (Ukandi G. Damachi, *The Role of Trade Unions in the Development Process; With a Case Study of Ghana*, New York 1974). However, much valuable material, especially on the railway workers union, is now available in Richard Jeffries, *Class, Power and Ideology in Ghana: the Railwaymen of Sekondi*, Cambridge 1978.

46   See Jeffries, op. cit.; & St Clair Drake & Leslie Alexander Lacy, 'Government Versus the Unions: The Sekondi-Takoradi Strike, 1961', in Gwendolen M. Carter (ed.), *Politics in Africa. 7 Cases*, New York 1966, ch. 3.

47   Kearney, *Trade Unions and Politics*; & for much useful background on the early history see Visakha Kumari Jayawardena, *The Rise of the Labor Movement in Ceylon*, Durham, North Carolina 1972.

48   Kearney, *Trade Unions and Politics*, p. 43.

49   Kearney, *Trade Unions and Politics*, pp. 51–2.

50   Kearney, *Trade Unions and Politics*, p. 146.

51   Kearney, *Trade Unions and Politics*, pp. 152–64.

52   Kearney, *Trade Unions and Politics*, p. 108.

53   Kearney, *Trade Unions and Politics*, pp. 111–19.

54   Kearney, *Trade Unions and Politics*, pp. 94–5, 150, 161 etc.

55   Kearney, *Trade Unions and Politics*, p. 145.

56   Amarasinghe, op. cit., esp. pp. 224–6, 246–8.

57   Wilson, *Politics in Sri Lanka*, pp. 91–4.

58   Hollis B. Chenery et al., *Redistribution with Growth*, Oxford University Press, London 1974, 273–9 (section on Sri Lanka by Lal Jayawardene).

59   Chenery, op. cit.

60   Wilson, *Electoral Politics*, pp. 35, 92, 99, 115, 117–19.

61   Wilson, *Electoral Politics*, pp. 86, 109, 113, 118–19, and esp. 129–30: 'Some candidates may be relatives of Mrs Bandaranaike, but this could not be helped in a country where everyone was related to everyone else in some way or another. If the people wished to elect them to Parliament, what right has the Prime Minister to object?'

62   See e.g. Sara S. Berry, *Cocoa, Custom, and Socio-economic Change in Rural Western Nigeria*, Oxford 1975, pp. 207–8. Dunn & Robertson, *Dependence and Opportunity*, 66.

63   Wilson, *Electoral Politics*, p. 12; & *Politics in Sri Lanka*, pp. 39–41; & see, on the local level, Robinson, *Political Structure*, part IV.

64   *The Times*, 25 July 1975.

65   Wilson, *Politics in Sri Lanka*, pp. 76–87; *Electoral Politics*, pp. 170–1.

66   Jiggins, op. cit., pp. 107–8, 195.

67 Jiggins, op. cit., p. 260.
68 See Dunn & Robertson, *Dependence and Opportunity*, ch. 8. Dunn 'From Democracy to Representation' (chapter 6 above). And cf. Martin Staniland, *The Lions of Dagbon. Political Change in Northern Ghana*, Cambridge 1975 and Richard Crook, 'Colonial Rule and Political Culture in Modern Ashanti', *Journal of Commonwealth Political Studies*, XI, 1, 1973, 3–27.
69 Jiggins, op. cit., and see note *, p. 157.
70 Kearney, *Communalism and Language* gives a stimulating account up to the mid-1960s and Wilson, *Politics in Sri Lanka* brings it up to more recent times.
71 Paul Brass, *Language, Religion and Politics in North India*, Cambridge, Part 1 & passim.
72 Cf. generally Gombrich, *Precept and Practice*. Dr Gombrich's sensitive, subtle and ingenious book is in quite a different class from the rest of recent academic publication on either Ghana or Sri Lanka.
73 Wilson, *Electoral Politics*, p. 107.
74 Gombrich, *Social Compass*, 1973, loc. cit.
75 Smith (ed.), *South Asian Politics and Religion*, chs. 21 & 23.
76 Amarasinghe, op. cit., p. 295.
77 Wilson, *Electoral Politics*, pp. 135–6.
78 Wilson, *Electoral Politics*, pp. 134–5.
79 Dunn & Robertson, *Dependence and Opportunity*, p. 132.
80 See e.g. F.B. Welbourn, *Religion and Politics in Uganda 1952–62*, Nairobi 1965.
81 Dunn & Robertson, *Dependence and Opportunity*, pp. 132, 137.
82 Wilson, *Politics in Sri Lanka*, pp. 28–38.
83 Wilson, *Politics in Sri Lanka*, pp. 34–5.
84 *The Times*, 15 July 1975.
85 Kearney, *Trade Unions and Politics*, pp. 121–31.
86 Stephen Castles & Godula Kosack, *Immigrant Workers and Class Structure in Western Europe*, London 1973.
87 See Baron Holmes, op. cit., & E.Y. Twumasi, *Aspects of Politics in Ghana 1929–1939: A Study of the Relationships between Discontent and the Development of Nationalism*, D.Phil., Oxford 1971.
88 Gavin Williams, 'Political Consciousness among the Ibadan Poor' in Emanuel de Kadt & Gavin Williams (eds.), *Sociology and Development*, pb. London 1974, pp. 109–39 and Kenneth W.J. Post & George D. Jenkins, *The Price of Liberty*; *Personality and Politics in Colonial Nigeria*, Cambridge 1973. But cf. Sara S. Berry, op. cit., pp. 206–7 and, more generally, P.C. Lloyd, *Power and Independence: Urban Africans' Perception of Social Inequality*, London 1974.
89 Adomako-Sarfoh, op. cit., is interesting on the immediate impact.
90 Jiggins, op. cit., pp. 34, 62, 145–7. Woodward, op. cit., pp. 257–69.
91 See e.g. Robert Dahl, *A Preface to Democratic Theory*, Chicago 1963, pp. 113–18.
92 For a convenient brief discussion see J. Edwin Craig Jr, 'Ceylon', in W. Arthur Lewis (ed.), *Tropical Development 1880–1913. Studies in Economic Progress*, London 1970, ch. 9, and, at greater length, Snodgrass, *Ceylon*.
93 Robinson, *Political Structure*.
94 Robinson, *Political Structure*, pp. 56–7, 63, 183.
95 Wilson, *Politics in Sri Lanka*, 237.
96 Jiggins, op. cit., p. 34 etc.
97 Robinson, *Political Structure*.
98 Wilson, *Politics in Sri Lanka*, pp. 15–28. Kearney, *Communalism and Language*.
99 This point is made by Dennis Austin, 'Et in Arcadia Ego: Politics and Learning in Ghana', *Minerva*, XIII, 2, Summer 1975, 262.
100 Austin, *Politics in Ghana*.
101 Woodward, op. cit., 91 & 199.
102 J.A. Braimah & J.R. Goody, *Salaga: The Struggle for Power*, London 1967, ch. 22.
103 See Austin & Luckham (eds.), *Politicians and Soldiers*, London 1975.

104 Howard Wolpe, *Urban Politics in Nigeria. A Study of Port Harcourt*, Berkeley 1974, pp. 73—7, 157—76, 270.

105 Robin Luckham, *The Nigerian Military: A Sociological Analysis of Authority and Revolt*, Cambridge 1971.

106 Austin & Luckham (eds.), *Politicians and Soldiers*.

107 David Kimble, *A Political History of Ghana 1850—1928*, Oxford 1963, chs. 4—7. Francis Agbodeka, *African Politics and British Policy in the Gold Coast 1868—1900*, London 1971. And for the Ashanti perspective see the magisterial study by Ivor Wilks, *Asante in the Nineteenth Century. The Structure and Evolution of a Political Order*, Cambridge 1975.

108 Robinson, *Political Structure*, pp. 219, 233—4, 239, 241, 246—7, 250.

109 See e.g. Stephen Michael Greenwold, 'Kingship and Caste', *Archives Européennes de Sociologie*, XVI, 1, 1975, 49—75. E.R. Leach, 'Introduction: What Should We Mean by Caste?', in E.R. Leach (ed.), *Aspects of Caste in South India, Ceylon and North-West Pakistan*, pb., Cambridge 1971, pp. 1—10. Louis Dumont, *Homo Hierarchicus*, pb ed., London 1972.

110 John Duncan Powell, 'Peasant Society and Clientelist Politics', *American Political Science Review*, LXIV, 2, June 1970, 411—25. Teodor Shanin, 'Peasantry: Delineation of a Sociological Concept and a Field of Study', *Archives Européennes de Sociologie*, XII, 2, 1971, 289—300. Colin Leys, 'Politics in Kenya: The Development of Peasant Society', *British Journal of Political Science*, I, 1, 1971, 307—37. Ken Post, ' "Peasantization" and Rural Political Movements in Western Africa', *Archives Européennes de Sociologie*, XIII, 1972, 223—54. René Lemarchand, 'Political Clientelism and Ethnicity in Tropical Africa: Competing Solidarities in Nation-Building', *American Political Science Review*, LXVI, 1, March 1972, 68—90. James C. Scott, 'Patron—Client Ties and Political Change in Southeast Asia', *American Political Science Review*, LXVI, 1, March 1972, 91—113; & for an interesting example of clientelism imposing itself at least partially on a supposedly universalist political agency see Sidney G. Tarrow, *Peasant Communism in Southern Italy*, New Haven 1967.

111 See e.g. the chapters by Eric R. Wolf & Adrian C. Mayer in Michael Banton (ed.), *The Social Anthropology of Complex Societies*, pb., London 1968. Ralph W. Nicholas, 'Factions: A Comparative Analysis', in Michael Banton (ed.), *Political Systems and the Distribution of Power*, pb., London 1968, pp. 21—61. Marc J. Swartz (ed.), *Local-Level Politics*, London 1969. F.G. Bailey, *Stratagems and Spoils: A Social Anthropology of Politics*, Oxford 1969.

112 Theodore K. Rabb, 'The Expansion of Europe and the Spirit of Capitalism', *The Historical Journal*, XVII, 4, December 1974, 675—89.

113 The relation between the state and business opportunity in Ghana has not been at all systematically investigated (academically) — though see Victor T. Levine, *Political Corruption. The Ghana Case*, Stanford 1975. A very thorough and revealing account of the same relation in Kenya (Colin Leys, *Underdevelopment in Kenya; The Political Economy of Neo-Colonialism*, London 1975) provides a helpful model for initial reflection.

114 Thomas More, *Utopia*, Everyman ed., London 1910, p. 112 (spelling modernised).

115 Cf. de Tocqueville's evidence to a Select Committee of the British House of Commons in June 1835 (Alexis de Tocqueville, *Journeys to England and Ireland*, ed. J.P. Mayer, London 1958, p. 228): 'In election matters in France up to the present moment, the same ideas of honour and dishonour exist which are applied to all other human actions, and consequently the respectable persons who give their word keep it, and those who are not so, do not keep it; in the same way that some men steal and others have no desire to do so. I mean to say, that in election matters in France there have not yet arisen any notions of morality different from what apply to everything else.'

116 See e.g. chapter 6 above.

117 James C. Scott, *American Political Science Review*, 1972, and James C. Scott, 'The

Erosion of Patron—Client Ties and Social Change in Rural Southeast Asia', *Journal of Asian Studies*, XXXII, 1, November 1972, 5—37.

118 See chapter 6 above; Dunn & Robertson, *Dependence and Opportunity*; Staniland, *Lions of Dagbon*; Owusu, *Uses and Abuses of Political Power*. Comparable materials appear to be lacking for Sri Lanka.

119 Dumont, *Homo Hierarchicus*.

120 For an ethnographic study see Michael Banks, 'Caste in Jaffna', in E.R. Leach (ed.), *Aspects of Caste*, 61—77. The main authority on caste in the island of Ceylon as a whole is Bryce Ryan, *Caste in Modern Ceylon*, New Brunswick 1953. For local studies see Robinson, *Political Structure*, E.R. Leach, *Pul Eliya. A Village in Ceylon*, Cambridge 1961. Gananath Obeyesekere, *Land Tenure in Village Ceylon*, Cambridge 1967. Nur Yalman, *Under the Bo Tree*, Berkeley 1967.

121 See Gombrich, *Precept and Practice*, esp. pp. 294—317.

122 Jiggins, op. cit., Preface, p. 1. For the comparative richness of analysis which such recording makes possible, see Paul R. Brass, op. cit.

123 Cf. Jiggins, op. cit., pp. 33—4. But cf. also pp. 116—21. The Karava caste claim to be Kshatriyas but this claim is not accepted by members of other castes.

124 Lloyd I. & Suzanne H. Rudolph, *The Modernity of Tradition. Political Development in India*, pb., Chicago 1969. Reinhard Bendix, *Nation-Building and Citizenship*, New York 1964, ch. 7.

125 L.I. & S.H. Rudolph, op. cit.

126 André Béteille, *Caste, Class and Power. Changing Patterns of Stratification in a Tanjore Village*, pb., Berkeley 1971; and on a larger scale F.G. Bailey, *Tribe, Caste, and Nation*, Manchester 1960 and *Politics and Social Change. Orissa in 1959*, Berkeley 1963.

127 Robinson, *Political Structure*.

128 Jiggins, op. cit., ch. 4.

129 The *Wahumpura* and *Padu (Bathgama)*. Jiggins, op. cit., p. 144 and chs. 4 & 5 passim.

130 Jiggins, op. cit., ch. 5 passim.

131 Jiggins, op. cit., ch. 5 & esp. p. 197.

132 Jiggins, op. cit., pp. 107—8, 195.

133 Jiggins, op. cit., pp. 108, 195.

134 Contrast the intricate strategies for intra-communal caste movement discussed by Nur Yalman (in E.R. Leach (ed.), *Aspects of Caste*, pp. 78—112, 'Caste Principles in a Kandyan Community'.)

135 Jiggins, op. cit., pp. 218—20.

136 Jiggins, op. cit., pp. 101, 216, 218.

137 Jiggins, op. cit., pp. 101, 179, 218.

138 Max Gluckman, *Custom and Conflict in Africa*, pb., Oxford 1965, ch. II, 'The Frailty in Authority'.

139 Bruce J. Berman, 'Clientelism and Neocolonialism: Center—Periphery Relations and Political Development in African States', *Studies in Comparative International Development*, IX, 2, Summer 1974, 3—25.

140 James C. Scott, *Journal of Asian Studies*, 1972. Joel S. Migdal, *Peasants, Politics and Revolution. Pressures towards Political and Social Change in the Third World*, Princeton 1974. Jeffrey Race, 'Toward an Exchange Theory of Revolution', in John W. Lewis (ed.), *Peasant Rebellion and Communist Revolution in Asia*, Stanford 1974, pp. 169—204. Barrington Moore, *Social Origins of Dictatorship and Democracy*, Boston 1966. Eric R. Wolf, *Peasant Wars of the Twentieth Century*, New York 1969.

141 Dunn, *Transactions of the Historical Society of Ghana*, 1972, 123—4.

142 See Charles Tilly, 'Does Modernization Breed Revolution?', *Comparative Politics*, V, 2, April 1973, 425—47 and 'The Changing Place of Collective Violence', in Melvin Richter (ed.), *Essays in Theory and History*, Cambridge, Mass. 1970, pp. 139—64; and John Dunn, 'The Success and Failure of Modern Revolutions', chapter 9 below.

143 Inaugural Address of 1904. Cited by J. Gus Liebenow, 'Liberia', in Gwendolen M. Carter (ed.), *African One-Party States*, Cornell University Press, Ithaca, New York 1962, p. 333.

144 See Smith (ed.), *South Asian Politics and Religion*, pp. 487—8. Wilson, *Politics in Sri Lanka*, pp. 145, 160, 192, 272. Samuel P. Huntington, *Political Order in Changing Societies*, pb., New Haven 1969, pp. 451—2. Maurice Janowitz, *The Military in the Political Development of New Nations*, pb., Chicago 1964, pp. 70, 86—7.

145 Smith (ed.), *South Asian Politics and Religion*, ch. 23 & pp. 478—87.

146 S.W.F. Hegel, *Philosophy of Right*, addition to paragraph 324, in T.M. Knox (ed. & trans.), *Hegel's Philosophy of Right*, Oxford 1942, p. 295. For a helpful discussion of Hegel's conception of the place of war in human social existence see Shlomo Avineri, *Hegel's Theory of the Modern State*, Cambridge 1972, ch. 10.

147 Kearney, *Communalism and Language*, p. 114: 'In this country the problem of the Tamils is not a minority problem. The Sinhalese are the minority in Dravidastan. We are carrying on a struggle for our national existence against the Dravidastan majority.'

148 Quentin Skinner, 'Conquest and Consent: Thomas Hobbes and the Engagement Controversy', in G.E. Aylmer (ed.), *The Interregnum: The Quest for Settlement 1646—1660*, London 1972, pp. 79—98; and 'The Ideological Context of Hobbes's Political Thought', *The Historical Journal*, IX, 3, 1966, 286—317.

149 Peter Singer, *Democracy and Disobedience*, Oxford 1973, and cf. esp. pp. 137—8.

150 See W. Howard Wriggins & C.H.S. Jayewardene, 'Youth Protest in Sri Lanka (Ceylon)', in W. Howard Wriggins & James F. Guyot (eds.), *Population, Politics, and the Future of Southern Asia*, New York 1973, pp. 318—50.

151 Jiggins, op. cit., 112; & Wilson, *Politics in Sri Lanka*, p. 163. And see now the very interesting account in Robert N. Kearney and Janice Jiggins, 'The Ceylon Insurrection of 1971', *Journal of Commonwealth and Comparative Politics*, XIII, 1, March 1975, 40—64.

152 Robinson, *Political Structure*.

153 Fred Halliday, 'The Ceylonese Insurrection', in Robin Blackburn (ed.), *Explosion in a Subcontinent*, pb., Harmondsworth 1975, pp. 151—220.

154 Robert Nozick, *Anarchy, State, and Utopia*, Oxford 1974, p. 287.

155 See Ralph E. Giesey, *If Not, Not. The Oath of the Aragonese and the Legendary Laws of Sobrarbe*, Princeton 1968. There is no paradigm form for the oath. For the four primary versions see Giesey, op. cit., Appendix 1, p. 247.

8 Democracy unretrieved, or the political theory of Professor Macpherson

1 C.B. Macpherson, *The Political Theory of Possessive Individualism* (Oxford 1962), p. 1.

2 *The Political Theory of Possessive Individualism* (1962); *The Real World of Democracy* (Oxford 1966); *Democratic Theory: Essays in Retrieval* (Oxford 1973).

3 The earliest of the essays printed in *Democratic Theory* was first published in 1945.

4 *Possessive Individualism*, pp. 276—7. This theme appears to have been replaced in his subsequent writings by the prospective transcendence of scarcity.

5 See for example George Lichtheim, *The Concept of Ideology and Other Essays* (New York 1967), pp. 152—8, and the very appreciative review of the French translation of *Possessive Individualism* (Paris 1971) in *Les Études Philosophiques*, 1973, pp. 96—9. For more critical views see Sir Isaiah Berlin, 'Hobbes, Locke and Professor Macpherson', *The Political Quarterly*, XXXV (1964), 444—68, and Jacob Viner, ' "Possessive Individualism" as Original Sin', *Canadian Journal of Economics and Political Science*, XXIX (1963), 548—59 (and subsequent controversy with Macpherson, pp. 559—66).

6 For a more historical attempt to identify the relationship between Hobbes's values and the social relations of seventeenth-century England, see Keith Thomas, 'The Social Origins of Hobbes's Political Thought', in K.C. Brown, ed., *Hobbes Studies*

(Oxford 1965), pp. 185—236. For more historical accounts of the arguments re-constructed by Macpherson and more concrete explanations of why their authors should have advanced them, see (in the case of Hobbes) M.M. Goldsmith, *Hobbes's Science of Politics* (New York 1966); Quentin Skinner, 'The Ideological Context of Hobbes's Political Thought', *The Historical Journal*, IX (1966), 286—317, and 'Conquest and Consent: Thomas Hobbes and the Engagement Controversy', in G.E. Aylmer, ed., *The Interregnum: The Quest for Settlement 1646—1660* (London 1972), pp. 79—98; J.G.A. Pocock, *Politics, Language and Time* (London 1972), ch. 5: (in the case of the Levellers), Keith Thomas, 'The Levellers and the Franchise', in Aylmer, ed., *The Interregnum*, pp. 57—78: (in the case of Harrington), J.G.A. Pocock, *The Ancient Constitution and the Feudal Law* (Cambridge 1957), ch. VI; and *Politics, Language and Time*, ch. 4; J.G.A. Pocock, *The Machiavellian Moment*, Part III (Princeton 1975) and the extended introduction by Pocock to his edition of Harrington's *Collected Works* published by the Cambridge University Press: (in the case of Locke) see John Dunn, 'Justice and the Interpretation of Locke's Politi-cal Theory', *Political Studies*, XVI (1968), 68—87, and *The Political Thought of John Locke* (Cambridge 1969). For a careful account more sympathetic to Mac-pherson, see A. Ryan, 'Locke and the Dictatorship of the Bourgeoisie', *Political Studies*, XIII (1965), 219—30.

7 *Possessive Individualism*, pp. 35—46, 53—61. Cf. Hobbes, *De Cive*, ed. S. Lamprecht (New York 1949), pp. 22—3.

8 Cf. *Possessive Individualism*, esp. pp. 90—5.

9 *Real World*, ch. 1.

10 Even in the case of James Mill this characterisation is now in some dispute. See the controversy between William Thomas and Wendell Robert Carr in *The Historical Journal*, XII (1969), 249—84; XIV (1971), 553—80; XIV (1971), 735—50; XV (1972), 315—20.

11 *Democratic Theory*, ch. 1 and esp. ch. 3.

12 For a considerably more concrete and powerfully argued treatment of the lack of producer control over the means of production in both capitalist and state-socialist societies (and one which gives a more adequate account of the place of *ownership* in maintaining this) see Anthony Giddens, *The Class Structure of the Advanced Societies* (London 1973).

13 *Democratic Theory*, pp. 14—16, 21—2.

14 *Real World*, ch. 3.

15 *Real World*, pp. 24—5, 60 and esp. 65: 'They have rejected the market and have not lost but gained strength.'

16 *Democratic Theory*, chs. 4, 5, and 7.

17 *Possessive Individualism*, p. 158.

18 See e.g. Deborah D. Milenkovitch, *Plan and Market in Yugoslav Economic Thought* (New Haven 1971) and Jan Vanek, *The Economics of Workers' Management: a Yugoslav Case Study* (London 1972).

19 Cf. Michael Kidron, *Western Capitalism since the War* (London 1968); Andrew Glyn and Bob Sutcliffe, *British Capitalism, Workers and the Profits Squeeze* (Har-mondsworth 1972); David S. Yaffe, 'The Marxian Theory of Crisis, Capital and the State', *Economy and Society*, II (1973), 186—232; Bill Warren, 'Imperialism and Capitalist Industrialization', *New Left Review*, 81 (1973), 3—44.

20 Cf. *Democratic Theory*, pp. 16, 35—7 etc.

9 The success and failure of modern revolutions

1 See especially Polybius, *Histories*, vol. 3, book 4, trans. W.R. Paton (London 1954), pp. 268—403; K. Von Fritz, *The Theory of the Mixed Constitution in Antiquity: A Critical Analysis of Polybius's Political Ideas* (New York 1954), especially ch. 4; F.W. Walbank, *Polybius* Berkeley, California 1972), ch. 5; and Frank E. Manuel, *Shapes of Philosophical History* (Stanford, Calif. 1965), ch. 1. Plato's account of regime transformation in *Republic*, books 8 and 9, is a form of moral exegesis, not

a theory of concrete historical change. Aristotle's account of the mechanics of regime transformation in *Politics*, book 5, does provide a theoretical account of concrete historical change but it is not in any way a directional account.

2 The dangers of accepting strong characterisations of historical process in social analysis are well brought out in Robert A. Nisbet, *Social Change and History: Aspects of the Western Theory of Development* (London 1969).

3 See Filippo Buonarroti, *Conspiration pour l'égalité dite de Babeuf*, 2 vols. (Paris 1957). The first edition was published in 1828. For recent scholarship on Babeuf see Colloque international de Stockholm, *Babeuf et les problèmes du Babouvisme* (Paris 1963); Maurice Dommanget, *Sur Babeuf et la conjuration des égaux* (Paris 1970); M. Reinhard, ed., *Correspondance de Babeuf avec l'Académie d'Arras, 1785—1788* (Paris 1961); R.B. Rose, 'Tax Revolt and Popular Organization in Picardy 1789—91', *Past and Present* 43 (May 1969): 92—108; R.B. Rose, 'Babeuf, Dictatorship and Democracy', *Historical Studies* (Australia) XV, no. 58 (April 1972): 223—36; and K.D. Tönnesson, 'The Babouvists: From Utopian to Practical Socialism', *Past and Present* 22 (July 1962): 60—76. For the career of Buonarroti himself and his role in establishing the tradition, see Elizabeth L. Eisenstein, *The First Professional Revolutionist: Filippo Michele Buonarroti (1761—1837)* (Cambridge, Mass. 1959), and John M. Roberts, *The Mythology of the Secret Societies* (London 1972), pp. 222—37, 262—73, and 322—46.

4 George V. Taylor, 'Revolutionary and Non-revolutionary Content in the *Cahiers* of 1789: An Interim Report', *French Historical Studies* VII, no. 4 (Fall 1972): 479—502. For effective recent discussions of the causation of the revolution see George V. Taylor, 'Non-capitalist Wealth and the Origins of the French Revolution', *American Historical Review* 62, no. 2 (January 1967): 469—96, and Colin Lucas, 'Nobles, Bourgeois and the Origins of the French Revolution', *Past and Present* 60 (August 1973): 84—126.

5 See especially Judith Shklar, *Men and Citizens: A Study of Rousseau's Social Theory* (Cambridge 1969). A vivid résumé of the implications of utopian thought in France in the eighteenth century, notably insensitive to the gap between classical utopianism and revolutionary practice, is J.L. Talmon, *The Origins of Totalitarian Democracy* (pb. ed., London 1961).

6 Morelly, *Code de la nature ou le véritable esprit de ses lois*, ed. Gilbert Chinard (Paris 1950) (my translation).

7 For Müntzer see Norman Cohn, *The Pursuit of the Millennium* (pb. ed., London 1962), pp. 251—71 (and see ch. 12 for his Anabaptist successors); and for a major study of the theological and historical context of Müntzer's project see George Huntston Williams, *The Radical Reformation* (London 1962), especially chs. 3 and 4. For Savonarola see Donald Weinstein, *Savonarola and Florence: Prophecy and Patriotism in the Renaissance* (Princeton, N.J. 1970). For the Fifth Monarchists see B.E. Capp, *The Fifth Monarchy Men: A Study in Seventeenth Century English Millenarianism* (London 1972).

8 See Pauline Gregg, *Free-Born John: A Biography of John Lilburne* (London 1961); Joseph Frank, *The Levellers* (Cambridge, Mass. 1955); and H.N. Brailsford, *The Levellers and the English Revolution*, ed. Christopher Hill (London 1961).

9 John M. Roberts, *The Mythology* (chs. 6—10), gives an excellent idea of the extent of complicity in constructing these stereotypes from across the political spectrum. The career of Nechayev gives the most chilling historical picture of the privatised imagination which can result. See Michael Confino, *Violence dans la violence: le débat Bakounine—Nečaev* (Paris 1973); Michael Confino, *Daughter of a Revolutionary: Natalie Herzen and the Bakunin—Nechayev Circle* (London 1974); and John Dunn, 'The Private Problems of a Revolutionary', *The Listener* (B.B.C., London 12 June 1974), 775—6.

10 The importance of this point is well emphasised by Michael Freeman, 'Review Article: Theories of Revolution', *British Journal of Political Science* II (1972): 339—59, at p. 359.

11 A partly convergent line of thought, directed at rescuing the category of individual

moral action from an excessively appropriative philosophy of history, can be found in Leszek Kolakowski, 'Conscience and Social Progress', in his *Marxism and Beyond: On Historical Understanding and Individual Responsibility* (pb. ed., London 1971), especially pp. 147–50.

12 Alasdair Macintyre, 'Ideology, Social Science and Revolution', *Comparative Politics* V, no. 3 (April 1973): 321–42.

13 Edmund Burke, *Reflections on the Revolution in France* (London 1910), p. 83.

14 Erving Goffman, *Asylums: Essays on the Social Situation of Mental Patients and Other Inmates* (pb. ed., Garden City, N.Y. 1961); Michel Foucault, *Folie et Déraison: histoire de la folie à l'âge classique* (Paris 1961); R.D. Laing, *The Divided Self* (pb. ed., Harmondsworth 1965); etc. For a useful criticism of the application of psychiatric categories to revolutionary political action see Isaac Kramnick, 'Reflections on Revolution: Definition and Explanation in Recent Scholarship', *History and Theory* XI, (1972): 57–62.

15 Macintyre, 'Ideology, Social Science and Revolution', pp. 340–42.

16 Paul Sainte-Claire Deville, *La Commune de l'An 11: vie et mort d'une Assemblée révolutionnaire* (Paris 1946), pp. 305–9; Martyn Lyons, 'The 9 Thermidor: motives and effects', *European Studies Review* V, no. 2 (April 1975): 125–6.

17 For the objective force of the doubts in the case of Lenin see conveniently Roger Pethybridge, *The Social Prelude to Stalinism* (London 1974), chs 1–3. For Lenin's own anxieties on the matter see Moshe Lewin, *Lenin's Last Struggle* (pb. ed., London 1973).

18 Even providentialist divine right was seen in its heyday as exhibiting only the legitimacy of the new regime, not that of the usurpers who had inaugurated it. See, for example, the position of Sir Robert Filmer in John Dunn, *The Political Thought of John Locke: An Historical Account of the Argument of the Two Treatises of Government* (Cambridge 1969), ch. 6.

19 See, for example, Nicos Poulantzas, *Political Power and Social Classes*, trans. Timothy O'Hagan (London 1973).

20 See, for example, Vladimir Kusin: 'Reformed East European Socialism cannot as yet ensure its own sheer survival.' 'Socialism and Nationalism', in Leszek Kolakowski and Stuart Hampshire, eds., *The Socialist Idea: A Reappraisal* (London 1974), p. 146.

21 Compare Abram Bergson, 'Development under Two Systems: Comparative Productivity Growth since 1950', *World Politics* XXIII, no. 4 (July 1971): 579–617, and Bergson, *Planning and Productivity under Soviet Socialism* (New York 1968), with Alec Nove, 'Conclusion', in *An Economic History of the U.S.S.R.* (pb. ed., Harmondsworth 1972), and Maurice Dobb, *Soviet Economic Development since 1917*, 6th ed. (London 1966). A very helpful systematic attempt at comparison, now a little out of date, is Simon Kuznets, 'A Comparative Appraisal', in Abram Bergson and Simon Kuznets, eds., *Economic Trends in the Soviet Union* (Cambridge, Mass. 1963), pp. 333–82.

22 Cf. Nai-Ruenn Chen and Walter Galenson, *The Chinese Economy under Communism* (Edinburgh 1969); E.L. Wheelwright and Bruce McFarlane, *The Chinese Road to Socialism: Economics of the Cultural Revolution* (pb. ed., Harmondsworth 1973); Dwight H. Perkins, *Agricultural Development in China, 1368–1968* (Edinburgh 1968); Subramanian Swamy, 'Economic Growth in China and India, 1952–1970: A Comparative Appraisal', *Economic Development and Cultural Change* XXI, no. 4 (July 1973): 1–84 (especially pp. 82–3); and Gunnar Myrdal, *Asian Drama: An Inquiry into the Poverty of Nations* (pb. ed., New York 1968), vol. 1, ch. 7, and vol. 3, pp. 1831–4.

23 See A. Ross Johnson, *The Transformation of Communist Ideology: The Yugoslav Case 1945–1953* (Cambridge, Mass. 1972), and Milovan Djilas, *The Imperfect Society: Beyond the New Class* (London 1972), pp. 157–8.

24 Deborah D. Milenkovitch, *Plan and Market in Yugoslav Economic Thought* (New Haven 1971); Albert Meister, *Où va l'autogestion Yougoslave?* (Paris 1970); David S. Riddell, 'Social Self-government: the Background of Theory and Practice in

Yugoslav Socialism', *British Journal of Sociology*, XIX, no. 1 (March 1968): 47—75; Jiri T. Kolaja, *Workers' Councils: The Yugoslav Experience* (London 1965); Jan Vanek, *The Economics of Workers' Management: A Yugoslav Case Study* (London 1972); and Jaroslav Vanek, *The Participatory Economy: An Evolutionary Hypothesis and a Strategy for Development* (Ithaca, N.Y. 1971).

25 Franz Schurmann, *Ideology and Organization in Communist China*, 2nd ed. (Berkeley, California 1968); Mark Selden, *The Yenan Way in Revolutionary China* (Cambridge, Mass. 1971); Barry M. Richman, *Industrial Society in Communist China* (pb. ed., New York 1972); Stuart R. Schram, ed., *Authority, Participation and Cultural Change in China* (Cambridge 1973), especially the chapters by Gray, Bastid, Sigurdson, and Howe: and Rensselaer W. Lee III, 'The Politics of Technology in Communist China', in Chalmers Johnson, ed., *Ideology and Politics in Communist China* (Seattle 1973), pp. 301—25.

26 David Huw Beynon, *Working for Ford* (pb. ed., Harmondsworth 1973).

27 Maurice Meisner, 'Utopian Socialist Themes in Maoism', in John Wilson Lewis, ed., *Peasant Rebellion and Communist Revolution in Asia* (Stanford, Calif. 1974), pp. 207—52.

28 Cf. A. Walicki, *The Controversy over Capitalism: Studies in the Social Philosophy of the Russian Populists* (Oxford 1969).

29 Jon Sigurdson, 'Rural Industry and the Internal Transfer of Technology', in Schram, *Authority*, pp. 109—57; Jack Gray, 'The Two Roads: Alternative Strategies of Social Change and Economic Growth in China', in ibid., pp. 199—232; Gray, 'Mao Tse-tung's Strategy for the Collectivization of Chinese Agriculture: An Important Phase in the Development of Maoism', in Emmanuel de Kadt and Gavin Williams, eds., *Sociology and Development* (London 1974), pp. 39—65; Gray, 'The Chinese Model: Some Characteristics of Maoist Policies for Social Change and Economic Growth', in Alec Nove and D.M. Nuti, eds., *Socialist Economics* (pb. ed., Harmondsworth 1972), pp. 491—510; and Ronald Frankenberg and Joyce Leeson, 'The Sociology of Health Dilemmas in the Post-colonial World: Intermediate Technology and Medical Care in Zambia, Zaire and China', in de Kadt and Williams, *Sociology and Development*, pp. 255—78.

30 If one takes the revolutionary project as strictly as it is taken by Professor Kolakowski in his powerful essay 'The Myth of Human Self-Identity', there are certainly grave doubts about the logical coherence of revolutionary ambitions, in addition to more vulgar doubts about their empirical plausibility. See 'The Myth of Human Self-Identity: Unity of Civil and Political Society in Socialist Thought', in Kolakowski and Hampshire, *The Socialist Idea*, pp. 18—35.

31 John Dunn, *Modern Revolutions: An Introduction to the Analysis of a Political Phenomenon* (Cambridge 1972), ch. 2.

32 Regis Debray, *Révolution dans la révolution* (Paris 1967). This is not, of course, to deny the rationality of the Cuban revolution, but simply to emphasise its extreme improbability. See Dunn, *Modern Revolutions*, ch. 8.

33 See Lenin in 1916: 'Was there ever in history an example of a great revolution occurring by itself, not tied to war? Of course not.' Cited by Pethybridge, *Social Prelude*, p. 77. See also A.J. Ryder, *The German Revolution of 1918: A Study of German Socialism in War and Revolt* (Cambridge 1967); F.L. Carsten, *Revolution in Central Europe, 1918—19* (London 1972); Marc Ferro, 'The Russian Soldier in 1917: Undisciplined, Patriotic and Revolutionary', *Slavic Review* XXX, no. 3 (September 1971): 483—512; Dietrich Geyer, 'The Bolshevik Insurrection in Petrograd', in Richard Pipes, ed., *Revolutionary Russia* (Cambridge, Mass. 1968), pp. 164—79.

34 Dunn, *Modern Revolutions*, ch. 4, especially p. 101.

35 See Chalmers A. Johnson, *Peasant Nationalism and Communist Power: The Emergence of Revolutionary China 1937—1945* (Stanford, Calif. 1963); Donald G. Gillin, ' "Peasant Nationalism" in the History of Chinese Communism', *Journal of Asian Studies* XXIII, no. 2 (February 1964): 269—89; and Dunn, *Modern Revolutions*, ch. 3, especially pp. 90—4.

36 For a recent brief statement of Robinson and Gallagher's position see Ronald Robinson, 'Non-European Foundations of European Imperialism: Sketch for a Theory of Collaboration', in Roger Owen and Robert Sutcliffe, eds., *Studies in the Theory of Imperialism* (London 1972), pp. 118—42.

37 George Rudé, *The Crowd in the French Revolution* (Oxford 1959); Georges Lefebvre, 'Foules révolutionnaires', in Lefebvre, *Etudes sur la révolution française* (Paris 1954), pp. 271—87; Albert Soboul, *The Parisian Sans-Culottes and the French Revolution 1793—4* (Oxford 1964). But cf. Teddy J. Uldricks, 'The "Crowd" in the Russian Revolution: Towards Reassessing the Nature of Revolutionary Leadership', *Politics and Society* IV, no. 3 (1974): 397—413; and Marc Ferro, *The Russian Revolution of February 1917*, trans. J.L. Richards (London 1972), especially ch. 4 and Conclusion.

38 Improbable though the success of Castro's venture undoubtedly was, the consequences of his success were far from arbitrary. See Dunn, *Modern Revolutions*, ch. 8.

39 Dunn, *Modern Revolutions*, pp. 232 and 243.

40 Compare Chalmers Johnson's *Revolution and the Social System* (Stanford, Calif. 1964) and *Revolutionary Change* (London 1968) with his *Autopsy on People's War* (Berkeley, Calif. 1973), p. 108: 'I believe that it is time to take an entirely new tack in approaching this problem. We seem to suffer from too much reductionism and not enough attention to purposive action.' (Time for whom?)

41 Of particular importance, plainly, was its enormous impact on the political and historical imagination of Karl Marx. See Jean Bruhat, 'La Révolution française et la formation de la pensée de Marx', *Annales Historiques de la Révolution Française* XXXVIII, no. 184 (April—June 1966): 125—70, and George Lichtheim, *Marxism: An Historical and Critical Study* (London 1961), especially pp. 58 and 125.

42 For a fetching knockabout critique see Brian Barry, *Sociologists, Economists and Democracy* (London 1970), especially chs. 3 and 8. Is the United Kingdom still a stable polity? How long can the United States be guaranteed to remain one?

43 For a vigorous and imaginative exploration of the significance of this point see Edward Friedman, *Backward Toward Revolution: The Chinese Revolutionary Party* (Berkeley, California 1974).

44 This is the main argument of Dunn, *Modern Revolutions*, especially pp. 234—41.

45 Ted Robert Gurr, *Why Men Rebel* (Princeton, N.J. 1970), and John Urry, *Reference Groups and the Theory of Revolution* (London 1973). Urry makes an attempt to set his use of reference-group theory within an account of structural contradictions in society at large; but it is not a very successful attempt. See also James C. Davies, 'Towards a Theory of Revolution', *American Sociological Review* 27, no. 1 (February 1962): 5—13.

46 See especially the valuable article by Jeffrey Race, 'Toward an Exchange Theory of Revolution', in Lewis, *Peasant Rebellion*, pp. 169—204. See also Nathan Leites and Charles Wolf, Jr, *Rebellion and Authority: An Analytic Essay on Insurgent Conflicts* (Chicago 1970).

47 The prevalence of these agreeably relaxed criteria for explanatory success in historical writing was first emphasised by the philosopher William Dray in his *Laws and Explanation in History* (London 1957), especially ch. 5.

48 Charles Tilly, 'The Changing Place of Collective Violence', in Melvin Richter, ed., *Essays in Theory and History: An Approach to the Social Sciences* (Cambridge, Mass. 1970), pp. 139—64; and 'How Protest Modernized in France 1845—55', in Williams O. Aydelotte, Allan G. Bogue, and Robert William Fogel, eds., *The Dimensions of Quantitative Research in History* (London 1972), pp. 192—255. And see Jeanne Favret, 'Le Traditionalisme par excès de modernité', *Archives Européennes de Sociologie* VIII, no. 1 (1967): 71—93.

49 Charles Tilly, 'Does Modernization Breed Revolution?', *Comparative Politics* V, no. 2 (April 1973): 427—47, and 'Town and Country in Revolution', in Lewis, *Peasant Rebellion*, pp. 271—302, especially pp. 299—302.

50 In addition to previously cited treatments of the careers of Buonarroti and

Nechayev, see especially the careers of Blanqui, Bakunin, the development of the Russian revolutionary tradition up to Lenin, and even briefly of Marx himself. See, for example, Samuel Bernstein, *Blanqui* (Paris 1970); Arthur Lehning, 'Bakunin's Conceptions of Revolutionary Organization and their Role: A Study of his "Secret Societies" ', in Chimen Abramsky and Beryl J. Williams, eds., *Essays in Honour of E.H. Carr* (London 1974); Franco Venturi, *Roots of Revolution: A History of the Populist and Socialist Movements in Nineteenth Century Russia* (pb. ed., New York 1966); and 'Address of the Central Committee to the Communist League', in Karl Marx and Frederick Engels, *Selected Works*, vol. 1 (Moscow 1958), especially pp. 110—13.

51 See especially the excellent article by Race in Lewis, *Peasant Rebellion*, pp. 169—204, and the editor's cautious and thoughtful introduction to the same volume, especially pp. 18—22.

52 See Leon Trotsky, *The History of the Russian Revolution*, trans. Max Eastman (London 1934), ch. 1; Louis Althusser, *Pour Marx* (Paris 1966), especially pp. 92—116; Tom Kemp, *Theories of Imperialism* (London 1967); Roger Owen and Robert Sutcliffe, eds., *Studies in the Theory of Imperialism* (London 1972); and André Gunder Frank, *Latin America: Underdevelopment or Revolution* (New York 1969). Cf. George Lichtheim, *Imperialism* (London 1971); Benjamin J. Cohen, *The Question of Imperialism: The Political Economy of Dominance and Dependence* (London 1974); and V.G. Kiernan, *Marxism and Imperialism* (London 1974), especially ch. 1.

53 Hélène Carrère d'Encausse and Stuart R. Schram, *Marxism and Asia: An Introduction with Readings* (London 1969), pp. 134—70.

54 See the outstanding article by Theda Skocpol, 'A Critical Review of Barrington Moore's "Social Origins of Dictatorship and Democracy" ', *Politics and Society* IV, no. 1 (1973): 1—34.

55 But see Nicos Poulantzas, *Political Power and Social Classes*, trans. Timothy O'Hagan (London 1973) and for more intellectually attractive versions of this style of Marxist analysis see Perry Anderson, *Passages from Antiquity to Feudalism* (London 1975) and *Lineages of the Absolutist State* (London 1975).

56 R.N. Berki, 'On Marxian Thought and the Problem of International Relations', *World Politics* XXIV, no. 1 (October 1971): 80—105.

57 Macintyre, 'Ideology', p. 332.

58 See Peter R. Odell, *Oil and World Power: Background to the Oil Crisis*, 3rd ed., pb. (Harmondsworth 1974). To predict that such an event might well occur sooner or later, all that was necessary was elementary arithmetic and information which must have been available to tens of thousands of intelligent and responsible bureaucrats in dozens of different countries.

59 Tilly, in Lewis, *Peasant Rebellion*, p. 289.

60 Georges Lefebvre, *The Great Fear: Rural Panic in Revolutionary France*, trans. Joan White (London 1973); Georges Lefebvre, *The Coming of the French Revolution*, trans R.R. Palmer (pb. ed., New York 1957), especially chs. 6—10; and Norman Hampson, *A Social History of the French Revolution* (London 1963), ch. 3.

61 David H. Pinkney, *The French Revolution of 1830* (Princeton, N.J. 1972).

62 Richard Cobb, *Les Armées révolutionnaires: Instrument de la Terreur dans les départments Avril 1793—Floréal An 11*, 2 vols. (Paris 1961 and 1963), and Colin Lucas, *The Structure of the Terror: the Example of Javogues and the Loire* (London 1973).

63 For relationships between the Bolsheviks and the railway workers in 1917 see Roger Pethybridge, *The Spread of the Russian Revolution: Essays on 1917* (London 1972), ch. 1. For a brief account of the development of Bolshevik military efforts during the civil war see David Footman, *Civil War in Russia* (London 1961), especially ch. 3.

64 See Engels' 1895 Introduction to Karl Marx, *The Class Struggles in France 1848—1850*, in Marx and Engels, *Selected Works*, vol. 1 (Moscow ed.), pp. 130—4.

65 Bernard Brown, *Protest in France: Anatomy of a Revolt* (Morristown, N.J. 1974);

Daniel Singer, *Prelude to a Revolution: France in May 1968* (London 1970); Richard Johnson, *The French Communist Party versus the Students* (New Haven, Conn. 1972); Phillipe Bénéton and Jean Touchard, 'Les interprétations de la crise de Mai–Juin 1968', *Revue Française de Science Politique* XX, no. 3 (June 1970): 503–43.

66 See Michael Mann, *Consciousness and Action among the Western Working Class* (London 1973), and Anthony Giddens, *The Class Structure of the Advanced Societies* (London 1973); and cf. Sidney Tarrow, 'Sources of French Radicalism: Archaic Protest, Antibureaucratic Rebellion and Anticapitalist Revolt', mimeograph (paper presented at the first workshop on radicalism, Research Institute on International Change, Columbia University, 5 February 1975).

67 Urban guerrilla tactics do not yet appear to have produced the overthrow of any state power. But in Ulster they have already led to dramatic changes in the form of the regime. For the record of urban guerrilla enterprise see Robert Moss, *Urban Guerrillas* (London 1972); Martin Oppenheimer, *Urban Guerrillas* (pb. ed., Harmondsworth 1970); and Paul Wilkinson, *Political Terrorism* (London 1974).

68 Donald S. Zagoria, 'Asian Tenancy Systems and Communist Mobilization of the Peasantry', in Lewis, *Peasant Rebellion*, pp. 29–60.

69 Eric R. Wolf, *Peasant Wars of the Twentieth Century* (New York 1969); Hamza Alavi, 'Peasants and Revolution', in Ralph Miliband and John Saville, eds., *The Socialist Register 1965* (London 1965), pp. 244–77; Gerrit Huizer, *Peasant Rebellion in Latin America* (pb. ed., Harmondsworth 1973); Henry A. Landsberger, ed., *Rural Protest: Peasant Movements and Social Change* (London 1974); Joel S. Migdal, *Peasants, Politics and Revolution: Pressures towards Political and Social Change in the Third World* (Princeton, N.J. 1974); and see now Henry A. Landsberger, 'The Sources of Rural Radicalism', in Seweryn Bialer, ed., *Radicalism in the Contemporary Age*, vol. 1, *Sources of Contemporary Radicalism* (Boulder, Colo. 1977).

10 Political obligations and political possibilities

1 I take this conception from Bernard Williams, 'Internal and External Reasons', in Ross Harrison (ed.), *Rational Action*, Cambridge 1979, pp. 17–28, at p. 18. Susan James, Quentin Skinner and Jonathan Lear kindly read an earlier and very different draft of this essay and made extremely helpful comments on it. I am especially indebted to Bernard Williams for the patience and critical penetration of his discussion of the same draft.

2 See particularly Derek Parfit, 'Personal Identity', *Philosophical Review*, LXXX, 1, January 1971, 3–27; and 'Later Selves and Moral Principles', in Alan Montefiore (ed.), *Philosophy and Personal Relations*, London 1973, pp. 137–69.

3 Hence the importance of Parfit's line of argument. For a sharp criticism see Bernard Williams, 'Persons, Character and Morality', in Amelie O. Rorty (ed.), *The Identities of Persons*, pb. ed. Berkeley, Calif. 1976, pp. 197–216.

4 John McDowell, 'Are Moral Requirements Hypothetical Imperatives?', *Proceedings of the Aristotelian Society*, Supplementary Vol. LXII, 1978, 13–29; cf. Philippa Foot, 'Morality as a System of Hypothetical Imperatives', *Philosophical Review*, LXXXI, 3 July 1972, 305–16; and 'Reasons for Action and Desires', in Joseph Raz (ed.), *Practical Reasoning*, pb. ed. Oxford 1978, pp. 178–84; Gilbert Harman, 'Relativistic Ethics: Morality as Politics', *Midwest Studies in Philosophy*, III, 1978, 109–21.

5 For varying degrees of scepticism on this issue see David Wiggins, *Truth, Invention and the Meaning of Life*, Henriette Hertz Lecture, British Academy 1976; J.L. Mackie, *Ethics: Inventing Right and Wrong*, pb. ed. Harmondsworth 1977; Gilbert Harman, *The Nature of Morality*, pb. ed. New York 1977; R.M. Hare, 'Ethical Theory and Utilitarianism', in H.D. Lewis (ed.), *Contemporary British Philosophy: Personal Statements*, London 1976, pp. 113–31.

6 See e.g. Martin Hollis, *Models of Man: Philosophical Thoughts on Social Action*, pb.

ed. Cambridge 1977. For a rather different form of external reasons theory see Thomas Nagel, *The Possibility of Altruism*, Oxford 1970.

7 See e.g. note 2, p. 339.

8 See e.g. John Locke, *Two Treatises of Government*, ed. Peter Laslett, 2nd ed. Cambridge 1967, I, para 129; and Laslett's note p. 253n.

9 David Gauthier, 'The Social Contract as Ideology', *Philosophy and Public Affairs*, VI, 2, Winter 1977, 130—64. And cf. John Dunn, *The Political Thought of John Locke*, Cambridge 1969, pp. 265—7.

10 See e.g. Robert Paul Wolff, *In Defence of Anarchism*, pb. ed. New York 1970.

11 See e.g. Peter Singer, 'Famine, Affluence and Morality', in Peter Laslett & James Fishkin (eds.), *Philosophy, Politics and Society. Fifth Series*, Oxford 1979, p. 25n. 'I use "obligation" simply as the abstract noun derived from "ought", so that "I have an obligation to" means no more, and no less, than "I ought to".'

12 It will scarcely be surprising, for example, if one accepts broadly the account of the character of practical reason presented by David Wiggins, 'Deliberation and Practical Reason', in Raz (ed.), *Practical Reasoning*, pp. 144—52.

13 Robert Nozick, *Anarchy, State and Utopia*, Oxford 1974. For a particularly clear and decisive presentation of the fundamental viewpoint see the argument of pp. 90—5. (And cf. my review of Nozick's book, *Ratio*, XIX, 1, June 1977, 88—95.)

14 For a fine presentation of this trajectory see Quentin Skinner, *The Foundations of Modern Political Thought*, 2 vols., pb. ed. Cambridge 1979, esp. vol. 2, pp. 349—58.

15 Cf. Gianfranco Poggi, *The Development of the Modern State: A Sociological Introduction*, pb. ed. London 1978; Theda Skocpol, *States and Social Revolutions*, pb. ed. Cambridge 1979, esp. pp. 284—93.

16 Sheldon S. Wolin, *Politics and Vision*, London 1961, p. 434.

17 The importance of this issue in early modern political thought is stressed by Skinner, op. cit., vol. 1, pp. 108, 115—16, 217—19, 276, etc.

18 These are Hare's own terms: R.M. Hare, 'Political Obligation', in Ted Honderich (ed.), *Social Ends and Political Means*, London 1976, p. 1.

19 Hare, op. cit., p. 2.

20 R.M. Hare, 'The Lawful Government', in Peter Laslett & W.G. Runciman (eds.), *Philosophy, Politics and Society. Third Series*, Oxford 1967, pp. 157—72.

21 Hare, 'Political Obligation', p. 2.

22 Hare, 'Political Obligation', p. 6.

23 Hare, 'Political Obligation', p. 12.

24 Hare, 'Political Obligation', p. 4.

25 Hare, 'Political Obligation', p. 5.

26 Hare, 'Political Obligation', p. 4; cf. Lucien W. Pye, 'The Non-Western Political Process', *Journal of Politics*, XX, 3, August 1958, 468—86.

27 Hare, 'Political Obligation', pp. 6—7.

28 Thomas Nagel, 'Ruthlessness in Public Life', in Stuart Hampshire (ed.), *Public and Private Morality*, pb. ed. Cambridge 1978, pp. 87—8.

29 Hare, 'Political Obligation', p. 8; and cf., for example, the position sketched by Honderich in his *Three Essays on Political Violence*, Oxford 1976.

30 See, for instance, the offending examples collected by Carole Pateman, 'Political Obligation and Conceptual Analysis', in Laslett & Fishkin (eds.), *Philosophy, Politics and Society, 5th series*, pp. 227—56, esp. 227, 231.

31 Cf. Thomas Nagel, 'Moral Luck' in his *Mortal Questions*, pb. ed. Cambridge 1979, pp. 24—38.

32 For comparable levels of causal significance in decisions taken in world-historically more modest settings see John Dunn (ed.), *West African States: Failure and Promise*, pb. ed. Cambridge 1978, particularly the chapter by R.W. Johnson on Guinea, pp. 36—65 and the conclusion, pp. 214—16.

33 See e.g. Graham Allison, *Essence of Decision: Explaining the Cuban Missile Crisis*, pb. ed. Boston 1971, chs. 5 & 6. Cf. Nicos Poulantzas, tr. T. O'Hagan, *Political Power and Social Classes*, London 1973.

34 Cf. Bernard Williams' interesting discussion 'Politics and Moral Character', in Hampshire (ed.), *Public and Private Morality*, pp. 55—73.
35 Thomas Hobbes's *Leviathan* is one example of a political theory which derives strong conclusions from what is hoped to be a recipe of this kind.
36 See Bernard Williams, 'Consistency and Realism' in his *Problems of the Self*, Cambridge 1973, esp. pp. 201—5.
37 For a view of why this *can* be the case see Williams, *Problems of the Self*, pp. 166—206. For an analysis of the implications of an example in which it is presumed that it is so see Williams, 'A Critique of Utilitarianism' in J.J.C. Smart & B. Williams, *Utilitarianism: For and Against*, Cambridge 1973, pp. 98—100 et seq. (and see also Thomas Nagel, *Mortal Questions*, ch. 5). Most utilitarian theorists are hostile to the view that it *can* be so: see, for example, Honderich's criticism of a second example of Williams' in *Three Essays on Political Violence*, pp. 22—9.
38 See Parfit, 'Later Selves and Moral Principles', cited in note 2, p. 339.
39 See e.g. Adam Smith, *The Theory of Moral Sentiments*, ed. D.D. Raphael & A.L. Macfie, Oxford 1976, I, iii, 2, 3—5, pp. 52—4.
40 Dunn, *Political Thought of Locke*, ch. 6.
41 In some societies (for example amongst the Nuer in the precolonial period: E.E. Evans-Pritchard, 'The Nuer of the Southern Sudan', in M. Fortes & Evans—Pritchard (eds.), *African Political Systems*, London 1940, esp. p. 294) they would certainly be duties of mutual aid, rather than duties of individual subordination, irreproachably horizontal rather than vertical obligations. See Michael Walzer, *Obligations: Essays on Disobedience, War and Citizenship*, Cambridge, Mass. 1970, esp. p. 207.
42 Cf. Smith, *Theory of Moral Sentiments*, pp. 227—30: esp. VI, ii, 2, 2, p. 227: 'The state or sovereignty in which we have been born and educated, and under the protection of which we continue to live, is, in ordinary cases, the greatest society upon whose happiness or misery, our good or bad conduct can have much influence. It is accordingly, by nature, most strongly recommended to us' (and VI, ii, 2, 4).
43 Raz (ed.), *Practical Reasoning*, Introduction, p. 17. And see note 4, p. 339.
44 Smith, *Theory of Moral Sentiments*, VI, ii, 2, 17, esp. p. 234: 'in the great chessboard of human society, every single piece has a principle of motion of its own'.
45 See e.g. notes 2 & 3, p. 339.
46 For a helpful discussion see E.M. Curley, 'Descartes, Spinoza and the Ethics of Belief', in Eugene Freeman & Maurice Mandelbaum (eds.), *Spinoza: Essays in Interpretation*, pb. ed. La Salle, Illinois 1975, pp. 159—89.
47 See e.g. Honderich, *Three Essays on Political Violence*; Singer, 'Famine, Affluence and Morality', in Laslett & Fishkin (eds.), *Philosophy, Politics and Society. 5th Series*; Julian Glover, *Causing Death and Saving Lives*, pb. ed. Harmondsworth 1977; John Harris, 'The Marxist Conception of Violence', *Philosophy and Public Affairs*, III, 2, Winter 1974, 192—220.
48 Cf. Williams, *Problems of the Self*, chs. 11 & 12, esp. pp. 167, 169.
49 Williams, *Problems of the Self*, p. 203.
50 See J.O. Urmson, 'Saints and Heroes', in Joel Feinberg (ed.), *Moral Concepts*, pb. ed. Oxford 1969, pp. 60—73.
51 See note 4, p. 339.
52 Harman, 'Relativistic Ethics', *Midwest Studies in Philosophy*, III, 1978, 118 (and see 116).
53 Harman, 'Relativistic Ethics', 120 (and see 117).
54 Cf. for example Harman's interesting textbook, *The Nature of Morality: An Introduction to Ethics*, pb. ed. New York 1977.
55 Wolff, *In Defense of Anarchism*.
56 E.g. John Rawls, *A Theory of Justice*, pb. ed. London 1973.
57 E.g. Carole Pateman, *The Problem of Political Obligation*, London 1979.
58 See above note 17, p. 340.
59 Honderich, *Three Essays on Political Violence*.
60 Glover, *Causing Death and Saving Lives*, pp. 109—10, 116; Singer, 'Famine Affluence and Morality (Laslett & Fishkin (eds.), *Philosophy, Politics and Society. 5th Series*).

341

61   Harman, 'Relativistic Ethics', pp. 115—20; and cf. Harman, *The Nature of Morality*.

62   See above note 46, p. 341.

63   See especially Mancur Olson, *The Logic of Collective Action*, Cambridge, Mass., 1965.

64   This holds good for other societies besides wealthy capitalist democracies: (see e.g. John Dunn, 'But How Will They Eat?', *Transactions of the Historical Society of Ghana*, XIII, 1, June 1972, 113—24, esp. 123—4).

65   Cf. Gauthier, 'The Social Contract as Ideology'.

66   See S.I. Benn, 'Rationality and Political Behaviour', in Benn & Mortimore (eds.), *Rationality and the Social Sciences*, London 1976, pp. 260—2.

67   Dunn, 'Individuality and Clientage in the Formation of Locke's Social Imagination', in Reinhard Brandt (ed.), *Locke Symposium*, Berlin 1980. For the source of Locke's phrase see his letter (? to Thomas Westrowe), 20 October 1659. (*The Correspondence of John Locke*, ed. E.S. de Beer, Vol. I, Oxford 1976, 123.)

68   See e.g. Williams, 'Politics and Moral Character', in Hampshire (ed.), *Public and Private Morality*.

69   See Curley, 'Descartes, Spinoza and the Ethics of Belief', cited above note 46, p. 341.

70   See Curley, op. cit. This was perhaps the single major problem in Locke's ethical thinking (see Dunn, *Political Thought of Locke*, chs. 3, 4, 14, 17 and 18).

71   Cf. Alasdair Macintyre, 'Ideology, Social Science and Revolution', *Comparative Politics*, V, 3, April 1973, 321—42.

72   Jon Elster, *Logic and Society: Contradictions and Possible Worlds*, London 1978, pp. 48—64.

73   Elster, op. cit., p. 50.

74   Elster, op. cit., pp. 50—1, 57—9; and see above chapter 9.

75   Dunn, *Modern Revolutions*, pb. ed., Cambridge 1972, passim and esp. quotation from Guicciardini p. xiv; Skocpol, *States and Social Revolutions*, esp. pp. 14—18.

76   Elster, op. cit. p. 51; and see Macintyre, *Against the Self-Images of the Age*, London 1971, pp. 263—4.

77   Though one which might with advantage be reconstituted more sensitively along the lines suggested by Scanlon (T.M. Scanlon, 'Rights, Goals and Fairness', in Hampshire (ed.), *Public and Private Morality*, pp. 93—111, esp. 102—4)'.

78   See Williams in Williams and Smart, *Utilitarianism: For and Against*.

79   Nagel, 'Ruthlessness in Public Life', pp. 87—8 (note 28, p. 34).

80   See e.g. Barrington Moore Jr, *Injustice*, London 1978; Dunn (ed.), *West African States*, esp. pp. 214—16.

81   Michael Dummett, *Truth and Other Enigmas*, London 1978, ch. 10, 'Realism', pp. 145—65, esp. 152—3; C.D. Broad, *Scientific Thought*, London 1923, p. 72 (and see generally, ch. 2, pp. 53—84.)

82   For an interesting discussion of this point in relation to Hobbes see Charles D. Tarlton, 'The Creation and Maintenance of Government: A Neglected Dimension of Hobbes's *Leviathan*', *Political Studies*, XXVI, 2, September 1978, 307—27.

83   Cf. e.g. Stanley I. Benn, 'The Problematic Rationality of Political Participation', in Laslett & Fishkin (eds.), *Philosophy, Politics and Society. 5th Series*, pp. 291—312, at 307—12.

84   See e.g. Harman's 'fallacy of pacifism', 'Relativistic Ethics', p. 118. If ifs and ans were pots and pans there would be less need for tinkers.

85   See Dummett, *Truth and Other Enigmas*, ch. 21, pp. 358—74, 'The Reality of the Past', esp. pp. 369—70. And cf. John McDowell, 'On "The Reality of the Past" ', in Christopher Hookway & Phillip Pettit (eds.), *Action and Interpretation*, Cambridge 1978, pp. 134, 143—4.

86   Cf. the Utopia described by Robert Nozick, *Anarchy, State and Utopia*, ch. 10.

87   Such theorists as Glover's believers: *Causing Death and Saving Lives*, pp. 253—5.

88   Urmson, 'Saints and Heroes', p. 64.

89   Urmson, op. cit., p. 71.

90   Cf. Pateman, *The Problem of Political Obligation*.

91   See *Kant's Political Writings*, ed. Hans Reiss & tr. H.B. Nisbet, Cambridge 1971, pp.

143—6. But cf. Reiss's introduction, p. 31 and n, and his earlier article 'Kant and the Right of Rebellion', *Journal of the History of Ideas*, XVII, 2, April 1956, 179—92, esp. 189—91.

92 Hare, 'Ethical Theory and Utilitarianism', Lewis (ed.), *Contemporary British Philosophy*.
93 Hare, 'Political Obligation', Honderich (ed.), *Social Ends and Political Means*.
94 Harman, 'Relativistic Ethics', pp. 117—18.
95 This is stressed by Nagel, *Mortal Questions*, pp. 205—6.
96 See Williams, 'Persons, Character and Morality', Rorty (ed.), *The Identities of Persons*.
97 Nagel, *Mortal Questions*, pp. 204—6.
98 Nagel, *Mortal Questions*, p. 205.
99 Nagel, *Mortal Questions*, ch. 14 and esp. p. 205.
100 Nagel, *Mortal Questions*, ch. 9.
101 Nagel, *Mortal Questions*, p. 204.
102 See the articles by Frankfurt and Taylor in Rorty (ed.), *The Identities of Persons*.
103 See Williams, 'Internal and External Reasons', in Harrison (ed.), *Rational Action*.

Index

345